*P*rimary
*P*revention
*W*orks

Issues in Children's and Families' Lives

AN ANNUAL BOOK SERIES

Senior Series Editor

Thomas P. Gullotta, *Child and Family Agency of Southeastern Connecticut*

Editors

Gerald R. Adams, *University of Guelph, Ontario, Canada*

Bruce A. Ryan, *University of Guelph, Ontario, Canada*

Robert L. Hampton, *University of Maryland, College Park*

Roger P. Weissberg, *University of Illinois at Chicago, Illinois*

Drawing upon the resources of Child and Family Agency of Southeastern Connecticut, one of this nation's leading family service agencies, **Issues in Children's and Families' Lives** is designed to focus attention on the pressing social problems facing children and their families today. Each volume in this series will analyze, integrate, and critique the clinical and research literature on children and their families as it relates to a particular theme. Believing that integrated multidisciplinary approaches offer greater opportunities for program success, volume contributors will reflect the research and clinical knowledge base of the many different disciplines that are committed to enhancing the physical, social, and emotional health of children and their families. Intended for graduate and professional audiences, chapters will be written by scholars and practitioners who will encourage the reader to apply their practice skills and intellect to reducing the suffering of children and their families in the society in which those families live and work.

Volume 1: **Family Violence: Prevention and Treatment**
LEAD EDITOR: Robert L. Hampton
CONSULTANTS: Vincent Senatore, *Child and Family Agency, Connecticut*; Ann Quinn, *Connecticut Department of Children, Youth, and Family Services, Connecticut*

Volume 2: **The Family-School Connection**
EDITORS: Bruce A. Ryan and Gerald R. Adams

Volume 3: **Adolescent Dysfunctional Behavior**
EDITORS: Gary M. Blau and Thomas P. Gullotta

Volume 4: **Preventing Violence in America**
EDITORS: Robert L. Hampton, Pamela Jenkins, and Thomas P. Gullotta

Volume 5: **Primary Prevention Practices**
AUTHOR: Martin Bloom

Volume 6: **Primary Prevention Works**
EDITORS: George W. Albee and Thomas P. Gullotta

Primary Prevention Works

Editors
George W. Albee
Thomas P. Gullotta

Vol. 6 *Issues in Children's and Families' Lives*

SAGE Publications
International Educational and Professional Publisher
Thousand Oaks   London   New Delhi

For information address:

 SAGE Publications, Inc.
2455 Teller Road
Thousand Oaks, California 91320
E-mail: order@sagepub.com

SAGE Publications Ltd.
6 Bonhill Street
London EC2A 4PU
United Kingdom

SAGE Publications India Pvt. Ltd.
M-32 Market
Greater Kailash I
New Delhi 110 048 India

Printed in the United States of America

Library of Congress Cataloging-in-Publication Data
Main entry under title:

Primary prevention works/editors, George W. Albee and Thomas P. Gullotta.
    p. cm.—(Issues in children's and families' lives; v. 6)
   Includes bibliographical references and index.
   ISBN 0-7619-0467-0 (cloth: acid-free paper).—ISBN 0-7619-0468-9
(pbk: acid-free paper)
    1. Mental illness—United States—Prevention—Case studies. 2. Mental
health promotion—United States—Case studies. I. Albee, George W.
II. Gullotta, Thomas, 1948- . III. Series.
RA790.6.P745 1997
616.89'05—dc20   96-35643

97 98 99 00 01 02 03 10 9 8 7 6 5 4 3 2

Acquiring Editor:	C. Deborah Laughton
Editorial Assistant:	Eileen Carr
Production Editor:	Sherrise M. Purdum
Production Assistant:	Karen Wiley
Typesetter/Designer:	Marion Warren

This volume is dedicated to *Pierre the Pelican,* and his creator, Loyd Rowland, whose work continues to bring expectant mothers across this world practical information leading to healthier birth outcomes

* * *

In *Primary Prevention Works,* George Albee and Thomas Gullotta have assembled a stellar group of contributors. This state-of-the art book is essential reading for anyone with interests in the field of prevention. The coverage of topics is comprehensive, and many of the most significant prevention programs of the past two decades are presented. This book has the potential of providing us a new paradigm for how we conceptualize, implement, and evaluate prevention programs.

Leonard Jason, Ph.D.
Professor of Psychology
DePaul University

Contents

Foreword:
The Importance
of Prevention

ROSALYNN CARTER

> The Commission recognizes that mental health problems cannot be solved by providing treatment alone. Efforts to prevent problems before they occur are a necessary ingredient of a systematic approach to promoting mental health.
>
> —*The President's Commission on Mental Health (1978)*

As Honorary Chairperson of the President's Commission on Mental Health when we were in the White House, I was delighted to be able to help develop a report that clearly articulated the importance of preventive approaches to mental disorders. Today in America, one in four families grapples with the emotional, social, and financial burdens imposed by these illnesses. Although the emotional and social tolls cannot possibly be measured, the financial toll can—and it is astounding. Mental disorders cost our nation $72.7 billion each year in treatment, related support, and lost productivity. Given the overwhelming enormity of these costs, it is clear that a prudent approach to mental health must include prevention, treatment, and maintenance for persons with long-term care needs.

We need to invest in research that seeks to minimize risk factors and to enhance protective factors for mental health disorders and related behavioral health outcomes including the reduction of violence and substance abuse. At the same time, we must also create opportunities to bring effective prevention programs to communities across our nation.

During the Tenth Annual Rosalynn Carter Symposium on Mental Health Policy held at The Carter Center in the fall of 1994, participants recognized that our current investment in prevention research has produced a growing collection of programs that would make a profound difference in the lives of children and families if we could bring them to scale on a national level. The programs in this book have all received the National Mental Health Association's Lela Rowland Prevention Award. They are excellent examples of the kinds of programs that should be implemented in all our communities.

The National Mental Health Association (NMHA) established the Lela Rowland Prevention Award in 1978 to focus attention on prevention by recognizing effective programs and rewarding those who develop them. The award is named in honor of Lela Rowland, who worked closely with her late husband, R. Loyd Rowland, over a long career in mental health. Dr. Rowland was executive director of NMHA's Louisiana division and author of *Pierre the Pelican,* the widely known series of letters sent to first-time parents during pregnancy and the early months of infancy. The Award was funded through his efforts.

I commend this book to you and urge you not only to read about the excellent programs contained herein, but also to work to bring these and other high-quality prevention programs into your community. Share this information with your elected officials, business leaders, parent groups, and anyone who holds a stake in your community's well-being. With so many pressing problems confronting children and families in America, we must act now to begin to reduce the tragedy of needlessly wasted lives.

Introduction

This is a book about good health, about illness prevention, and about good parenting. This is a book about good decision making, about influencing a healthy infancy, early childhood, adolescence, and adulthood. This is a book about how we can each apply a common set of principles to reduce maladaptive behavior in ourselves, our children, and our society. Most of all, this is a book about doing—doing for ourselves, for our loved ones, and for others.

The origins of this volume can be traced to a discussion the two editors had with Michael Faenza of the National Mental Health Association (NMHA) in Washington, DC, in the fall of 1995. It was clear to us that significant changes were occurring in the decision-making process regarding the funding and delivery of human service programs in the United States. The role that the federal government had previously played in encouraging the growth and direction of services would likely be transferred to the states via the mechanism of block grant funding. True and very risky change was occurring. Depending on the ever swirling currents of political discussion, congressional and White House attitudes appeared to support block grants with minimal use restrictions being imposed on states. Phrases such as *economies of scale, greater efficiency,* and *waste reduction,* made it clear that funds to strengthen mental health services and other public health investments would be reduced in these new block grants.

We know that if minimal restrictions are placed on the use of these block grants, in some states funding intended for child care may be used to fill potholes in roads. Mental health dollars will find their way into state correctional budgets—the new institutional warehouses for many seriously emotionally disturbed individuals. Health care dollars will be diverted from public health into privately managed profit-making health maintenance organizations (HMOs). Indeed, in some states this is already occurring with health service funding packages that appear to be large social experiments being carried out with great risk to vulnerable citizens.

Although we deplore these impending actions and hope that citizens will organize so as not to allow this travesty to come to pass, we also recognize that adequately funded block grants would enable states with enlightened political leadership to encourage the health of its citizenry. We know also that in many states, because of the efforts of the NMHA and other national volunteer-led organizations, health promotion and illness prevention have gained a weak but tenacious foothold in legislative discussions. State and local affiliates of NMHA and other groups have worked collaboratively to educate their area policymakers to the savings in health care dollars and the decency associated with putting prevention into practice.

Thus, with this crisis in direction and funding of service delivery, there arose an opportunity that, if seized, could result in improved health for the U.S. citizenry. Recognizing that every opportunity brings with it yet other crises, we were faced with the reality that the opportunity to bring a richer and fuller life to many also offered itself as a time for every snake-oil salesperson to pitch goods to well-meaning but not necessarily well-informed local and state officials. With those realizations, and the insight that accompanies a cup of well-brewed coffee in a hotel lobby, the concept of this book was born.

This volume is divided into five sections. The first section provides a recent history of prevention in the United States (Chapter 1) and operationalizes Albee's incidence formula (Chapter 2). The next section is concerned with infants and toddlers. The three chapters in this section focus on successful programs that increase parent-child interaction and parenting ability. The third section focuses on preschool populations. The interventions described involve using parents as teachers (Chapter 6), quality child care programming (Chapter 7), and developing problem-solving abilities in early childhood (Chapter 8). The fourth section is concerned with school-aged youth and discusses interventions in school settings (Chapter 9), with children of divorce (Chapter 10), in developing social competency and improving life skills (Chapters 11, 12, and 13) and job readiness (Chapter 14). The fifth section focuses on preventive interventions in adulthood, especially on two issues of primary concern. The first is unemployment—an increasing fact of life in an ever changing economy (Chapter 15). The second is depression (Chapter 16). The epilogue (Chapter 17) issues a plea for collaboration among community mental health advocates and other groups who have found it difficult at times to come together on crucial public health issues.

We are very grateful to Loyd Rowland, an early founder of the prevention movement in the United States and a good friend, for his gracious gift to the NMHA by endowing the Lela Rowland Award. Over nearly two decades, the Lela Rowland Award has identified promising proven interventions that promote mental health and social competency. The 14 programs described in this volume represent the ever evolving sophistication in communicating health promoting skills. The programs described in this volume use three of prevention's four technologies: education, social support, and the enhancement of social competencies to promote a healthier citizenry.

As each of these programs demonstrates, it is not enough to provide treatment for individuals and families when the environment encourages maladaptation. The social conditions in which people needing help find themselves trapped will require social capital investments to correct generations of social neglect. Let's bring new commitment to the work of rebuilding our communities. The programs in this volume provide needed mortar for that process.

Finally, we must acknowledge the support of Sandy McElhaney, Director of Prevention at the National Mental Health Association, whose support and encouragement helped to make this volume possible. We also owe a debt of gratitude to the Lela Rowland Award recipients for the speed and attention each gave to preparing his or her chapter. This appreciation is also extended to C. Deborah Laughton at Sage for her diligence in bringing this project to speedy fruition. It is our hope that program developers, educators, and state and local elected officials will draw from this volume the knowledge necessary to develop these preventive services in their communities. For the graduate students and others in the helping services who study this volume, we hope that you will take its message forward and make its promise reality.

George W. Albee
Michael M. Faenza
Thomas P. Gullotta

The Principles of Prevention

CHAPTER 1

Primary Prevention's Evolution

GEORGE W. ALBEE

THOMAS P. GULLOTTA

A Historical Perspective

Remarkable changes in understanding and significant progress in interventions with people with mental and emotional disorders have occurred in the second half of the 20th century. What were the origins of these soon-to-be sweeping changes in mental health service delivery systems? As with most change, it was not some dramatic revelation but a routine Armed Forces screening procedure that detected unexpectedly high rates of mental (and physical) problems afflicting young potential American draftees. After the Second World War and later the Korean Conflict, providing treatment for veterans in government-funded Veterans Administration hospitals and clinics overtaxed the resources of available professional mental health service providers, contributing from the late 1940s to the 1960s to an active, tax-supported system of professional training programs in universities across the United States.

From the late 1940s to the 1960s, the horrors of poorly maintained, overcrowded, publicly funded mental hospitals and institutions for the retarded were exposed repeatedly by mass circulation magazines and in films like *The Snake Pit* and books like Deutsch's *The Shame of the States* (1948) and chapters like Albee's "Tear down the walls of hell" (1970). With public pressure growing, something had to be done—something major.

Increasingly, it has become clear that the "something major" must be a new direction, a new approach to the problem of mental and emotional disorders. The old approach—efforts at individual treatment—does nothing to reduce the rate, the incidence (new cases), in the population. Only by preventing new cases from occurring can we begin to catch up with the problem. To understand primary prevention, let's begin with the definition used by President Jimmy Carter's President's Commission on Mental Health (1978):

> Primary prevention in mental health is a network of strategies that differ qualitatively from the field's past dominant approaches. Those strategies are distinguished by several essential characteristics. This . . . section highlights primary prevention's essences using the direct contrast style of saying what it is and what it is not.
>
> (1) Most fundamentally, primary prevention is proactive in that it seeks to build adaptive strengths, coping resources, and health in people; not to reduce or contain already manifest deficit.
>
> (2) Primary prevention is concerned about total populations, and not about the provision of services on a case-by-case basis.
>
> (3) Primary prevention's main tools and models are those of education and social engineering, not therapy or rehabilitation, although some insights for its models and programs grow out of the wisdom derived from clinical experience.
>
> (4) Primary prevention assumes that equipping people with personal and environmental resources for coping is the best of all ways to ward off maladaptive problems, not trying to deal (however skillfully) with problems that have already germinated and flowered. (p. 218)

The President's Commission went on to a position that has become increasingly controversial in the intervening couple of decades: the view that stressful social conditions have a major influence on the nation's mental health by disrupting families and child care and by damaging social relations generally. In its preliminary report (President's Commission Mental Health, 1977), the commission told the president this:

> America's mental health problem is not limited to those individuals with disabling mental illness and identified psychiatric disorders. It also includes those people who suffer the effects of a variety of

societal ills that directly affect their everyday lives. Vast numbers of Americans experience the alienation and fear, the depression and anger associated with unrelenting poverty and the institutionalized discrimination that occurs on the basis of race, sex, class, age, and mental and physical handicaps. The Nation must realize the terrible emotional and mental damage that poverty and discrimination cause. . . .

At the Commission's public hearings, the social and economic conditions in which millions of minority persons live and which make them so vulnerable to psychological and emotional distress were vividly described by representatives of racial and ethnic minorities. These problems—malnutrition, inadequate housing, poor schools, unemployment, insufficient and inappropriate health and social services—are common to all minorities. However, each racial and ethnic minority group also has problems that are unique to it and that increase its vulnerability to mental and emotional distress.

Migrant and seasonal farmworkers and their families also live under conditions of terrible economic and social stress. Their emotional and mental problems are compounded by the almost total lack of mental health and other services available to them.

America's rural population is often susceptible to stresses associated with geographic isolation, the disruption of traditional ways of life, and poverty. The prevalence of severe emotional disorders in rural areas generally parallels that of urban areas, but people who live in rural areas have fewer mental health facilities and trained manpower to assist them. (pp. 2, 6)

These views represented a major change from those expressed two decades earlier by another federal commission. In the mid-1950s, President Eisenhower and the U.S. Congress had put together the Joint Commission on Mental Illness and Health (JCMIH) that was to be a major force in reorganizing the nation's priorities in the field of mental health. The final report of the JCMIH (1961) titled *Action for Mental Health* was delivered to the U.S. Congress and widely circulated to the states and other players in the field of mental health. This Commission, strongly supported by President Eisenhower and with the advice and assistance of a number of national professional and citizen's organizations concerned, was the first concentrated attempt to deal with the problems of the overwhelming number of persons with mental disorders and with the serious overcrowding of the public mental hospitals that could no longer accommodate the additional thousands lined up outside their doors. The Commission sponsored the publication of a dozen books produced by its task forces. The final report summarized these efforts.

Essentially the final report called for the training of a large number of additional therapists while protecting the tradition of medical responsibility and control. Against significant internal opposition, it proposed that nonmedical personnel (i.e., social workers, psychologists, psychiatric nurses) be allowed to engage in counseling and brief psychotherapy. The report also recommended significantly increased federal funding for the training of mental health personnel and for research into the causes of "mental illness." In only three or four places in the report was primary prevention mentioned at all. Those few references focused on programs for children and schools. Clearly the focus was on treatment and rehabilitation.

Senator John F. Kennedy read the report with care, and subsequently, as president, in 1963, he sent the first message ever to Congress by a president advocating federal funding for treatment and research into mental conditions. He spelled out the need for federally funded research into the causes and the prevention of mental retardation and mental disorder.

The final report of the Commission had advocated one clinic for every 50,000 population and a strict limitation on construction of new public mental hospitals. This worked out to be a proposed establishment of 4,000 clinics. Older mental hospitals were to be scaled down so that none would have more than 1,000 inmates. People who formerly were admitted to public hospitals now would be treated in new community-based mental health centers. The focus of care would be at home (homelessness was not part of the observed scene). Kennedy's appeal to Congress created considerable controversy because it was the first time an American president had advocated the use of federal funding for the "medical" treatment of mental conditions. (Veteran's hospitals and drug treatment hospitals were exceptions to this rule). The medical hierarchy in America saw this as another step toward socialized medicine and lobbied vigorously against the proposal. Leading members of Congress received personal telephone calls from their own physicians urging that federal funds not be expended for the hiring of salaried medical and other treatment personnel, even if funding (scaled down) of Kennedy's proposed 2,000 community mental health centers were to be approved. It was a strange situation in which mental health centers were to be built with federal funds, but no federal funds were to be available to staff them. It was not until Lyndon Johnson became president that limited funds were made available for the modest staffing of the centers.

The point to be underscored here is that the whole thrust of the Commission's "major new approach" focused exclusively on early outpatient treatment and on research, with virtually no mention in the final summary of efforts at primary prevention. Although one of the JCMIH volumes, titled *Mental Health Manpower Trends* (Albee, 1959), pointed out that the gap between the number of people needing help and the number of professionals and paraprofessionals available to provide the help was completely out of balance, the Commission's recommendations still focused on individual therapy, particularly the expansion of short-term treatment.

A Presidential Commission Urges Prevention

When Jimmy Carter became president in the mid-1970s, he appointed a new Commission on Mental Health. By this time, nearly everyone recognized that the only hope of catching up with the overwhelming need for new and innovative ways of dealing with the increasing demands for intervention with people with mental disorders was to find ways of cutting down on the number of people needing help. This led, logically, to an examination of primary prevention. One of the task panels that reported to the Carter Commission was a Task Panel on Prevention (1977). Although a couple of members on the Carter Commission opposed consideration of prevention efforts, Rosalynn Carter, Honorary Chair of the Commission, and Beverly Long, president of the National Mental Health Association, held out for a focused examination of prevention and for new federally funded prevention efforts. The Task Panel on Prevention had reviewed the available literature and had concluded that successful prevention approaches were indeed available and effective; therefore, among the final recommendations of the Carter Commission were (a) that an Office of Prevention be set up at the National Institute of Mental Health (NIMH) and (b) that primary prevention research be given major priority by NIMH. The Mental Health Systems Act, passed in the last year of the Carter administration, required the NIMH to institute these steps. Rather than comply immediately, however, the director of NIMH set up a "Study Group" to examine all over again the need and the strategy for prevention efforts. This stalled organized efforts at prevention until the end of the Carter presidency (see Albee, 1979). With the next administration, much of the Mental Health Systems Act was not renewed, major cuts in funding for mental health programs were made, and a new philosophy of research focusing on organic and biological causation was the order of the day.

In light of these reductions and because preventionists are, like their colleagues in the field of public health, nearly always grant dependent, the lack of funding in community mental health severely hampered prevention programs. Despite this, several states designated a person responsible for prevention efforts, and some states established offices of prevention (for example, California, Michigan, Georgia). Although mental health issues did not receive the attention they deserved, public concern with the rising use of alcohol and other substances led the two recent Republican administrations to invest resources into the prevention of drug addiction and alcoholism. With the creation of the Center for Substance Abuse Prevention (CSAP), important efforts were made toward building community partnerships across the United States to reduce alcohol and substance abuse. Local communities were able to receive evaluation and demonstration grants on a competitive basis to design comprehensive efforts to reduce alcohol and substance misuse among youth, pregnant women, and minority populations. This Federal interest (amounting to 280 million in FY 94/95) appears to be waning with various proposals under Congressional consideration that range from funding reductions of 66% to the total elimination of CSAP.

It is instructive to note that in the case of reduced CSAP funding, it is the beverage distributors, who deliver beer, wine, and other spirits, who lobbied Congress intensely on this issue. It appears that CSAP's antidrinking messages were too successful

(Kuntz, 1995). The alcohol industry's complaints against CSAP were the following:

> CSAP funded "community partnerships" have succeeded in "lowering legal blood alcohol content" for drunk-driving laws.
>
> One of CSAP's "major goals" is to "reduce alcohol consumption by 20%."
>
> [Negative CSAP Center statements such as] "We all pay a price for alcohol use and abuse—about $119 billion each year" in health costs and lower productivity. (Kuntz, 1995)

The repeated experience of preventionists in the stalled start of NIMH's efforts to promote emotional health and in the recent actions to cripple CSAP underscore for us a basic principle that all who would promote health must take to heart. That principle is that someone, somewhere, somehow profits from the misery, illness, and poor fortune of others. Although we may long for a world in which young people do not acquire a need for the nicotine contained in tobacco and although we may rejoice in lower rates of lung disease and associated cancers due to tobacco consumption, others view tobacco differently. For them, tobacco is a cash crop. For them, it is a product to manufacture, distribute, and sell. For them, it is a living.

Understanding that every profit entails a loss elsewhere helps us to place in context the actions of special interest groups to preserve access to their future markets. It helps us to understand guild actions to restrict the ability of others to practice their trade. It rationalizes the unnecessarily high rates of illness this country experiences. Understanding this does not mean accepting these realities. For preventionists, it means working to change these realities through education, social support, competency enhancement, and most important, community action.

A Time for Prevention

Primary prevention most certainly is "An idea whose time has come" (Klein & Goldston, 1977). In 1975 Kessler and Albee published a lengthy review article in the *Annual Review of Psychology* summarizing the available knowledge and theoretical approaches to primary prevention. In 1986 the National Mental Health Association's Commission on Prevention, chaired by Beverly Long, published *The Prevention of Mental/Emotional Disorders* and distributed its report to members of Congress.

This report assessed current knowledge about the prevention of psychological and emotional disorders, examined critically how this knowledge was being applied, and made recommendations for future prevention research and implementation. The NMHA Commission's final report (1987) was reprinted also in the *Journal of Primary Prevention.* It offered further evidence for the rationale and efficacy of preventive methods. In addition, the report included an extensive resource list for those interested in the current literature, both in book and periodical form, on primary prevention.

Learning From Public Health

The field of public health has long been concerned with the prevention of disease. Indeed, it is safe to say that public health measures are consistently more successful in keeping the population healthy than are the efforts of conventional medical intervention that use "repair" strategies. In its long history, public health has used primary prevention to reduce or eliminate many of the great plagues that have beset humankind over the centuries.

All public health strategies are relatively simple. The first step is to identify the noxious agent and attempt to remove it or neutralize it. The second strategy is to strengthen the resistance of the host to the noxious agent. The third strategy is to prevent transmission of the noxious agent to the host. Treating drinking water with chlorine, for example, kills noxious agents. Vaccinating children against polio and the common childhood diseases like measles, mumps, pertussis, and so forth has been so successful, at least in the industrial nations, that the high death toll of children characteristic of past centuries and of poverty-stricken nations today does not occur. Finally, preventing the transmission of the noxious agent to the host is clearly effective, whether it involves killing disease-bearing mosquitoes and thereby reducing the incidence of malaria in tropical lands or recommending the use of condoms to prevent transmission of the AIDS virus (see Albee & Ryan Finn, 1994).

In the early years of the 20th century, public health experts began to turn their attention to the problems of preventing mental disorders. If public health approaches were so successful at preventing organic diseases, could they not also be applied to the prevention of neuroses and psychoses? A leading figure at the time was Adolf Meyer, professor of psychiatry at Johns Hopkins University. He espoused the view that mental and emotional disorders were the result of lifelong social experiences. Prevention was a matter of ensuring more adequate child rearing under conditions that placed less stress on parents. Many public health and psychiatry faculty at Johns Hopkins University and its School of Public Hygiene joined with Clifford Beers, author of *A Mind That Found Itself* (1905), in forming The National Committee for Mental Hygiene (later the National Mental Health Association). Psychiatrists, however, had relatively little sophistication in statistics, and epidemiologists had relatively little understanding of psychiatry. Despite an uneasy alliance, it was this group of individuals that first attempted to enumerate the people with mental and emotional disorders in the population district studied by the university faculty. It was startling to discover that there was a higher rate of mental and emotional problems among poor people, those in mixed racial neighborhoods, and those who lived in sections where saloons and prostitution were common. The beginnings of efforts at the prevention of mental and emotional disorders were laid down with attempts at teaching poor mothers to be better parents in the hope that their children could avoid the temptations and dangers of their crime-ridden and poverty-stricken environments. It was also observed that there was a correlation between "slovenly housekeeping" and mental conditions. Gradually, children's mental health clinics were established in various parts of the country, and efforts were made to instill better parenting skills. In this way the child guidance movement spread. For a fascinating examination of how the child guidance movement strayed from its preventive, community-focused roots, we highly recommend *Helping Children: A Social History* (Levine & Levine, 1992). From a historical perspective, aspects of the Primary Mental Health Project by Hightower and Parents as Teachers by Winter and McDonald described in this book reflect elements of the work of the early child guidance clinics.

A very early contributor to efforts at primary prevention through improved parenting was Loyd Rowland of the Louisiana Mental

Health Association. He developed a series of informative pamphlets in the 1940s featuring "Pierre the Pelican." Mailed to all parents in the state following the birth of their first child, it continued with further informative pamphlets during the early months and years of the child's life. Later evaluations of parental behavior were positive, and the pamphlets were translated into several languages and widely distributed to parents in other countries. Rowland's work illustrates many of the basic principals of public health: (a) reach as many people as possible, those at risk included; (b) strengthen them by giving them social skills, better competencies, and support; (c) have a clear purpose (better parenting); and (d) evaluate the results (see Rowland, 1969).

Despite the ambivalence or opposition of the mental health establishment, prevention efforts have gained a beachhead in the field of mental health. In the NMHA's commission report is a review of many effective programs across the life span, and a Prevention Bookshelf is appended listing books dealing with the primary prevention of psychopathology.

Recent Efforts

Organized in 1975, the Vermont Conference on the Primary Prevention of Psychopathology has held an annual meeting on the campus of the University of Vermont with some specific focus on primary prevention. The resulting 19 volumes have been widely distributed. Beginning in 1991, the Child and Family Agency of Southeastern Connecticut, through its biennial Hartman Conference and its Gimbel Child and Family Scholars Program, has also focused attention on pressing issues appropriate for preventive interventions, such as family violence.

Emory Cowen (1982) edited a special issue of the *American Journal of Community Psychology* devoted to a baker's dozen of prevention programs that had been carefully evaluated. Under the sharp editorial eye of Cowen, all preventive work to be summarized was required to meet strict and restrictive criteria. One major criticism of primary prevention has often been that it lacks definitional clarity. The work presented in this Special Issue was thus required to meet a "taut" definition of primary prevention that included the building of competencies in unaffected individuals to avert maladjustment, the inclusion of a specific methodology, and a formal evaluation design.

Because prevention research is conducted within natural settings, critics often claim that it is impossible to establish one-to-one, cause-and-effect relationships, as is possible with many physical diseases. We do know, however, that certain situations or experiences can increase the risk that an individual will suffer from emotional and psychological problems. For example, feelings of powerlessness and helplessness often lead to maladaptive behavior patterns and reduce an individual's ability to respond effectively to environmental stressors. We know that early childhood is a formative period of life and that children can be placed at risk if denied proper nourishment, care, and developmental opportunities. Cowen's review includes programs to build competencies to deal with stress. This volume is filled with proven examples of programs that help children grow emotionally, intellectually, and physically.

In 1988 the American Psychological Association published *Fourteen Ounces of Prevention* (Price, Cowen, Lorion, & Ramos-McKay, 1988), demonstrating that prevention programs could be undertaken, become effective, and be carefully evaluated. Responding to growing public interest in prevention, the National Institute of Mental Health funded five prevention intervention research centers (PIRCS) that were asked to demonstrate, through research and application, successful approaches to the prevention of psychopathology.

The National Academy of Medicine has published a major report on primary prevention, *Reducing Risk for Mental Disorders* (Mrazek & Haggerty, 1994). This volume, encouraged and sanctioned by the Academy of Medicine, part of the National Academy of Science, is a powerful signal to the field. Finally, Martin Bloom (1996) in his volume, *Primary Prevention Practices,* integrates prevention theory, research, and proven practice to add his voice to a chorus of voices that say that *prevention works.*

In the context of all of the above, it is clear that despite continuing opposition, primary prevention is a concept that is here to stay. It is indeed the "Fourth Mental Health Revolution" (Albee, 1980). It has a technology (Albee & Gullotta, 1986; Gullotta, 1994), and it will not go away.

Logically, it is clear, as noted above, that even successful individual treatment never results in any significant reduction in incidence (the number of new cases). Only through the efforts at primary prevention have we seen significant decreases in, or the elimination of, the major plagues that have afflicted humankind over the centuries. This fact is clearly recognized, so it is interesting that very little notice has been taken of primary prevention efforts in textbooks or chapters concerned with psychopathology.[1] However, this situation is going to change. The evidence is clear that primary prevention of mental disorders works and that it is the only hope for reducing incidence. But it is hard to make a revolution—to change old paradigms, old ways, old models, old values, and old power bases.

Thomas Kuhn (1970) in his book *The Structure of Scientific Revolutions* describes how a new model is resisted by the current mainstream of opinion but gradually accumulates data that attract new younger scientists until only a few elderly holdouts remain.

A Clear Overview

A book by psychiatrists Foley and Sharfstein (1983) provides a fascinating factual account of the postwar struggle to develop community intervention alternatives to the 100-year domination of the state hospital system in the United States. It tells the story of the efforts of Washington's "Noble Conspirators," who struggled for more than 20 years after World War II to expand the amount of federal support for medical (including psychiatric) research, to get federal money for the care of people with mental disorders, and to obtain federal support for the training of mental health personnel and for research into the whole area of mental health.

The book names all of the characters in this struggle, including lobbyists like Mike Gormon, Mary Lasker, and Florence Mahoney, and especially the heroic psychiatric giant Robert Felix, the first director of the new NIMH, as well as federal medical administrator Boisfeuillet Jones. Felix and Gormon (the latter, head of a phantom group called the National Committee Against Mental Illness) felt an overpowering revulsion toward what was going on in the overcrowded state hospitals, and they set out to "break the back" of these institutions. Their congressional allies included Alabama Senator Lister Hill and New Jersey Representative John Fogerty.

Their efforts achieved limited success and have still not been fully realized. Large numbers of elderly state hospital inmates were transferred to equally oppressive nursing homes, and backward inmates were dumped into inhospitable communities to become the homeless who pitch their makeshift plastic tents over city steam vents at night and drift along the streets, cup in hand, during the day.

The state hospitals are no longer the repositories for long-term incarceration of people called "schizophrenic," but their budgets are still significant. We still spend most of our total mental health dollars in this country for disturbed people in hospitals and nursing homes (Kiesler & Sibulkin, 1987).

What the "Noble Conspirators" achieved was a greatly expanded number of professional mental health workers between 1955 and 1980, with the largest increase coming in psychology and social work. The story of the efforts to get Congress to reverse its historic reluctance to put federal funds into caring for the mentally ill is told with great clarity and interest. The development of the projected 2,000 community mental health centers has not been (and will not be) realized, despite the support of Presidents John F. Kennedy, Lyndon B. Johnson, and Jimmy Carter. Each period of increase in community mental health center development has been followed by efforts of other administrations to get the federal government out of these programs and to return the care of the mentally ill to state and local communities.

The complexities of this struggle are well covered by Foley and Sharfstein (1983). The authors are clear in describing the failure of society to provide for the continuing care of chronically disturbed people discharged from the state hospitals. The small number of understaffed community mental health centers are unable to take up the burden, and many of these handicapped, homeless people cannot secure welfare entitlements because of the regulation that no one is eligible for such benefits who lacks a home address. This is a peculiar Catch-22 situation: The bag ladies and the homeless men cannot afford permanent residences; thus, they are ineligible for the welfare payments that would allow them to obtain a permanent address! So there they sit—on door stoops in Georgetown, on the Mall, near civic centers in Indianapolis, Atlanta, and Los Angeles. So in these and other cities, they pitch their bag shelters and appeal for funds with styrofoam cups. So there in filth, disease, and squalor they stand or lie in social isolation as a testament to forever lost opportunities to make a productive life.

By the late 1970s, the community mental health centers were serving nearly 2 million people a year of the total of 6.5 million persons getting service from all mental health resources. One of the great mysteries is how our society plans to provide for the more than 44 million seriously disturbed individuals within our population who have been repeatedly identified as needing service. The phenomenal growth of correctional institutions and the profitable private nursing home industry hardly seems likely to solve the problem. Foley and Sharfstein (1983) do not propose an answer.

Different Approaches to Prevention

As approaches to the prevention of mental disorders proliferate, we can begin to see different strategies emerge. We will simply mention here some of the major dimensions. Detailed reviews are available elsewhere (Bloom, 1996; Gullotta, 1987, 1994).

1. *Voluntary Educational Programs.* The purpose of education is to inform. The assumption is that armed with factual information, individuals will most likely make the best decisions. For example, low fat diets are more health promoting than diets high in saturated fat. With this knowledge and the dietary information that now appears on many restaurant menus, informed choices can be made. Information can be used in anticipation of an event. The sayings, "To be forewarned is to be forearmed" and the Boy Scout motto, "Be Prepared" represent this concept. Preretirement planning and programs to reduce a child's fear of an inpatient surgical technique are examples of these truisms in action. Knowledge can be used to provide feedback to enable an individual to alter potentially harmful behaviors through techniques like biofeedback and meditation.

We should note that education is prevention's most widely used technology. Having said that, we should also say it is prevention's weakest technology. In our years editing volumes devoted to the promotion of health and in our experiences publishing *The Journal of Primary Prevention,* we have had the opportunity to review thousands of chapters and papers. From that experience and from our own efforts, we share with the reader the following observation: Education increases knowledge; occasionally, it changes attitudes; rarely does it alter behavior. To be effective, education must be combined with the next three technologies.

2. *Community Organization/Systems Change.* Society can and often does contribute to the dysfunctional behavior individuals demonstrate. Institutional practices can be destructive not only to the soul but to the body as well. And although American society supports the concepts of free will and individual choice, as a nation we are not so foolish as to permit individuals to yell "Fire!" in a crowded place or to exercise their property rights by building a hazardous waste site next to a public water supply or to harm others through deceptive advertising, physical assault, or embezzlement. We require the restraint of unbridled individual free will through a system of laws and regulations.

When the evidence suggests it and the public demands it, efforts have been taken on state and federal levels to reduce traumatic injuries due to vehicular accidents by requiring manufacturers to install safety belts and air bags and to improve the impact-resisting ability of vehicles. Interstate highway design has improved to remove passing left lane exit ramps and lethal lane dividers. In many enlightened communities, zoning laws have been developed to protect drinking water supplies and to require that smoke alarms be installed in multiple family dwellings. In some communities, local ordinances require that children use bicycle helmets. Long overdue, laws that prohibited a stranger from assaulting another individual have been extended to parents and spouses in the home. It is not legal to beat a child, a spouse, or significant other.

Because of the power of this preventive intervention to require affirmative action, prevent discrimination, and ensure a living wage, it is prevention's riskiest, most effective, and least used technology. Why? We noted earlier that every action is accompanied by a corresponding opposing reaction. Unless the action can overcome the reaction, whatever progress made in the area may be in jeopardy. For example, in some states, efforts to further improve environmental social conditions have resulted in not only the defeat of those proposals but a weakening of existing laws. Consider, also, the efforts of CSAP to reduce alcohol and substance misuse among young people, pregnant women, and minorities. These are three populations that are epidemiologically at significant risk. Society is genuinely concerned with the recent rise in substance misuse among youth. Ignore, if you can, the personal tragedy and focus instead on the high economic costs of caring for infants, then children, and still later adults damaged by fetal alcohol syndrome—the result of a woman ingesting excessive amounts of alcohol during her pregnancy. Recognize the connections that exist among minority youth, inner city gang behavior, the sale of drugs, and adolescent killings. Understand all of this, and then understand the words of David Rehr, a lobbyist for the National Beer Wholesalers Association, "We want to cut their funding, stop their lobbying and basically end the use of [CSAP] to bash the beer industry" (Kuntz, 1995).

3. *Social Support.* Ask random individuals who has the better chance of entering life and prospering, the poor child or the financially secure child, and most would favor the second over the first. Yet, despite enormous risk factors, many poor young people do survive. They grow up to lead productive lives. Why? Part of the answer can be found in four words: *simple sustained human friendship.* Whether parent to child, sister to brother, aunt to niece, or neighbor to neighbor, the act of genuine, honest, trusting, empathetic caring has great growth promoting power (Freedman, 1993). This preventive intervention also can be found in self-help groups, in neighborhoods where families join together to revitalize their area, and in churches and temples.

4. *Competency Promotion.* Prevention's final technology is well reflected in the pages of this book. It is an effort, by using elements of previously mentioned technologies, to promote the successful functioning of groups of people. We know that to be socially competent requires that an individual belong to a supportive group. We know that in addition to belonging, the individual must also have a valued role within that group. And we know that the individual must have frequent opportunities to make meaningful contributions to the general welfare of that group. Whether improving social skills, developing needed educational abilities, or entering the world of work, the programs receiving the honor of the Lela Rowland Award have as one focus improving self-esteem, internalizing locus-of-control, and changing self-concern to community concern.

A Final Word

Most people, if asked to rank order the social contributions of Albert Schweitzer, Mother Theresa, John Snow, and Ignatz Semmelweiss would put the first two names at the top and confess ignorance about the latter two. Yet in terms of contributions to humankind, such as the number of lives saved, human anguish prevented, and accomplishments for the betterment of people throughout the world, Snow and Semmelweiss tower over the other two.

It may seem subversive or mean-spirited to fail to praise Schweitzer and Theresa as great recent-day saints, but the canonization of Snow and Semmelweiss is probably more deserved.

As B.F. Skinner pointed out in one of his last public addresses, Schweitzer was trying to save humanity one person at a time. Similarly, Mother Theresa, with a heart full of compassion and kindness, is also trying to save the world one person at a time. It simply can't be done. By way of contrast, in the mid-19th century, John Snow figured out that cholera was a waterborne disease long before the noxious agent causing cholera had been identified. He observed that the pattern of cholera infection was related to where London's drinking water came from. In the most famous act in the history of public health, he removed the handle from the Broad Street pump and stopped a neighborhood cholera epidemic. Semmelweiss puzzled over the high rate of childbed fever and death in women who gave birth in the public wards of hospitals in Budapest. (In those days physicians didn't wash their hands but wiped them dry on the lapels of their frock coats, so the more experienced and therefore more sought-after physicians had stiffer and smellier coats.) Semmelweiss decided that somehow medical students and obstetrical trainees were carrying some poison from the dissecting rooms of the anatomy lab to the women giving birth. He ordered all of his medical trainees to wash their hands for 10 minutes before they delivered a baby. Suddenly and precipitously, the rate of childbed fever and death in his hospital wards dropped to almost nothing. Of course, the great experts of the day did not believe either Snow or Semmelweiss. But fortunately their research was eventually published and replicated and thus found to be accurate.

The point is that Snow's and Semmelweiss's work illustrates the truth of this dictum: "No mass disorder afflicting humankind has ever been eliminated or brought under control by attempts at treating the affected individual." These two public health saints have saved millions of lives while Schweitzer, full of compassion, was treating suffering individuals in his jungle hospital in Africa and while Mother Theresa is ministering to the poor and the hopeless in Calcutta. Individual treatment has no effect on incidence. Only prevention reduces it.

One cannot help but admire and respect those selfless people who reach out in humanitarian concern to support suffering individuals. But at the same time, if we respect evidence, efforts at primary prevention are even more humane and admirable if our criteria include the reduction of mass human suffering. A big handicap is the fact that in individual treatment we know whom we save, but in effective prevention we can point only to a change in rate.

The prevention of mental and emotional disorders must involve social change efforts at creating better parenting in a more equalitarian and just society. This is not to say that we should oppose research into health psychology, biology, physiology, genetics or other organic investigations. But we must strive to level the playing field, to create a just society for all, with resulting improvements in social support.

Recently we offered a couple of bright undergraduate students the opportunity to attend an annual conference on prevention, Improving Children's Lives: Global Perspectives on Prevention. After some agonizing they both decided that they would rather go to Alaska as volunteers to scrub oil off rocks on the beach. Somehow this symbolizes one of the critical intellectual conflicts in our society. Should we sit around and scrub oil off rocks after the oil spill or should we demand that safer tankers be required by international law? Treatment or prevention? Schweitzer and Mother Theresa or Snow and Semmelweiss?

Note

1. An exception to this statement is the adolescent text, *Adolescent Life Experiences,* by Adams, Gullotta, and Markstrom-Adams (1997).

References

Adams, G. R., Gullotta, T. P., & Markstrom-Adams, C. (1997). *Adolescent life experiences* (4th ed.). Pacific Grove, CA: Brooks/Cole.

Albee, G. W. (1959). *Mental health manpower trends.* New York: Basic Books.

Albee, G. W. (1970). Tear down the walls of hell. In B. Blatt (Ed.), *Exodus from pandemonium: Human abuse and a reformation of public policy.* Boston: Allyn & Bacon.

Albee, G. W. (1979). The prevention of prevention. *Physician East, 4,* 28-30.

Albee, G. W. (1980). A competency model must replace the defect model. In L. A. Bond & J. C. Rosen (Eds.), *Competence and coping during adulthood* (pp. 75-104). Hanover, NH: University Press of New England.

Albee, G. W., & Gullotta, T. P. (1986). Facts and fallacies about primary prevention. *Journal of Primary Prevention, 6*(4), 207-218.

Albee, G. W., & Ryan Finn, K. D. (1993). An overview of primary prevention. *Journal of Counseling and Development, 72*(2), 115-123.

Bloom, M. (1996). *Primary prevention practices.* Thousand Oaks, CA: Sage.

Commission on the Prevention of Mental/Emotional Disorders. (1987). National Mental Health Association report. *Journal of Primary Prevention, 7*(4), 175-241.

Cowen, E. (Ed.). (1982). Research in primary prevention in mental health [Special Issue]. *American Journal of Community Psychology, 10*(2).

Deutsch, A. (1948). *The shame of the states.* New York: Arno.

Foley, E. A., & Sharfstein, S. S. (1983). *Madness and government: Who cares for the mentally ill?* Washington, DC: American Psychiatric Press.

Freedman, M. (1993). *The kindness of strangers: Adult mentors, urban youth, and the new voluntarism.* San Francisco, CA: Jossey-Bass.

Gullotta, T. P. (1987). Prevention's technology. *Journal of Primary Prevention, 7*(4), 176-196.

Gullotta, T. P. (1994). The what, who, why, where, when, and how of primary prevention. *Journal of Primary Prevention, 15*(1), 5-14.

Joint Commission on Mental Illness and Health. (1961). *Action for mental health.* New York: Basic Books.

Kessler, M., & Albee, G. W. (1975). Primary prevention. *Annual Review of Psychology, 26,* 557-591.

Kiesler, C. A., & Sibulkin, A. E. (1987). *Mental hospitalization: Myths and facts about a national crisis.* Newbury Park, CA: Sage.

Klein, D. C., & Goldston, S. E. (1977). *Primary prevention: An idea whose time has come.* Washington, DC: Government Printing Office.

Kuhn, T. S. (1970). *The structure of scientific revolutions* (2nd ed.). Chicago: University of Chicago Press.

Kuntz, P. (1995, August 14). Alcohol beverage industry lobbies for bill to gut substance abuse agency seen as threat. *Wall Street Journal,* p. A12.

Levine, M., & Levine, A. (1992). *Helping children: A social history.* New York: Oxford University Press.

Mrazek, P. J., & Haggerty, R. J. (1994). *Reducing risk for mental disorders: Frontiers for preventive intervention research.* Washington, DC: National Academy Press.

President's Commission on Mental Health. (1977). *Report to the President.* Washington, DC: Government Printing Office.

President's Commission on Mental Health. (1978). *Report to the President.* Washington, DC: Government Printing Office.

Price, R., Cowen, E., Lorion, R., & Ramos-McKay, J. (Eds.). (1988). *Fourteen ounces of prevention: A casebook for practitioners.* Washington, DC: American Psychological Association.

Rowland, L. (1969). Let's try prevention. In W. Ryan (Ed.), *Distress in the city: Essays on the design and administration of urban mental health services* (with an introduction by Erich Lindemann). Cleveland, OH: Press of Case Western Reserve University.

Task Panel on Prevention, President's Commission on Mental Health (1978). *Report to the commission* (Vol. 4). Washington, DC: Government Printing Office.

• *CHAPTER 2* •

Operationalizing Albee's Incidence Formula

THOMAS P. GULLOTTA

Between the absolutes of birth and death, human behavior occurs in a countless variety of forms. Some behaviors are considered functional, whereas others are considered dysfunctional. In the world of Western medicine where all health problems have specific causes and sets of symptoms, illness has biogenic roots. Operating from this premise, many within the medical community in the late 19th century searched for germs in a futile attempt to find an explanation for dysfunctional behavior. This exploration was replaced in the 20th century by a search for viruses, chemical imbalances, and presently, for genes, which many psychiatrists argue are responsible for dysfunctional behavior. The problem is that the majority of emotional problems are not diseases that can be traced to some microorganism, chemical imbalance, or other single cause. As the former Surgeon General of the United States C. Everet Koop (1995) recently observed, "Diseases are of two types: those we develop inadvertently and those we bring upon ourselves by failure to practice preventive measures. Preventable illness makes up approximately 70% of the burden of illness and associated costs" (p. 760).

The purpose of this chapter is to examine stress theory and its contribution to prevention. In particular, we will examine Albee's (1980, 1985) *incidence formula* and how that formula serves as a foundation for primary prevention's alternative health care paradigm. It is this alternative health paradigm that Lela Rowland

Award recipients used to design their interventions to promote the health of populations epidemiologically at risk.

Prevention and
Selye's Stress Theory

In recent years, interest has grown in exploring ways in which the incidence of emotional disturbances could be reduced and emotional health increased. Both of these efforts have been subsumed under the title of prevention. Over three decades ago, Caplan (1964), borrowing terminology from the public health field, suggested that prevention activities could exist on any one of three levels: primary, secondary, or tertiary. His model lacked clarity. It conceptualized the term *prevention* and suggested means of effecting prevention's goal of reducing the incidence of emotional illness and promoting emotional health. As numerous critics were quick to observe, this model permits almost any intervention to be categorized as prevention. As a result of this justified consensus, Caplan's model has been substantially refined (Klein & Goldston, 1977). Activities that were formerly labeled as tertiary prevention are now considered rehabilitation activities. Activities that were considered secondary prevention are now referred to as early treatment activities. Primary prevention emerges, then, as synonymous with prevention. It is understood to involve actions that either *anticipate a disorder* or *foster optimal health* (Goldston, 1977, p. 20).

Furthermore, prevention focuses on groups of people not yet showing any signs of disturbance and is thus proactive rather than reactive. Prevention is comprised of planned, comprehensive, ongoing interventions that can be observed, recorded, and evaluated for effectiveness. And finally, preventionists pay careful attention to the ethical questions involving work with groups under conditions where informed consent is not always possible (Albee & Gullotta, 1986; Cowen, 1982; Gullotta, 1987, 1994; Klein & Goldston, 1977).

From this definitional position, different theoretical approaches to explaining disturbed human behavior were examined. Those models, for instance Lamb and Zusman (1979), that claimed that "major [emotional] illness is probably in large part genetically determined"(p. 1349) were still popular. Instead, preventionists chose to view the forces contributing to either emotional illness or health as multicausal. Yes, nature matters, but so too does the environment shape and influence behavior. As Albee (1980) has argued, emotional problems are not diseases that can be traced solely to some microorganism or thread of DNA. "Rather we are concerned with problems in living, problems often created by blows of fate, by the damaging forces of a racist, sexist, agist society where preparation for competent adaptation is minimal" (p. 77). The theoretical formulation best able to accommodate the views of preventionists is stress theory.

The development of stress theory must be credited to Cannon (1939) and, in particular, to Selye (1982). Selye's (1936) initial work on the metabolic response of rats to stress gave rise to the concept of the general adaptation syndrome. Selye (1982) contends that the human organism responds in a "stereotyped pattern" regardless of the stressor (that is, the external event that affects the host). In this model, stress can be understood to mean any change in life demanding it. Depending on our interpretation of the stressor, some events may be understood to be harmless or beneficial (that is eustress).

Selye (1982) suggested that regardless of the nature of the stressor, it activates the general adaptation syndrome to varying degrees. The human body reacts, he contended, in a predictable sequence of alarm, resistance, and, if adaptation does not occur, ultimately exhaustion. In the state of *alarm,* the body determines the magnitude of the stressor and whether it is beneficial, neutral, or harmful and responds accordingly. Because no organism can remain in a state of alarm for an extended period of time (hours, days, perhaps weeks), either death or the next stage, called *resistance,* is entered. In this stage, the body engages the stressor. If the stressor is perceived as distressful, it is fought. If the stressor is neutral or beneficial, it is passively tolerated. It is in the stage of resistance that the body displays its *adaptive* energy. No organism can remain in a constant struggle with a stressor. It must ultimately either accept or defeat the stressor, or it will enter into the stage of *exhaustion* in which physical illness, emotional disturbance, and even death result.

Selye (1982) compared the general adaptation syndrome to life in that

These three stages are reminiscent of childhood, with its characteristic low resistance and excessive response to any kind of stimulus, adulthood, during which the body had adapted to most commonly encountered agents and resistance is increased, and senility, characterized by loss of adaptability and eventual exhaustion, ending with death. (p. 10)

He further argued that the adaptive energy found in the stage of resistance "might be compared to an inherited bank account from which we can make withdrawals but to which we apparently cannot make deposits." He suggested that every activity "causes wear and tear, [leaving] some irreversible chemical scars, which accumulate to constitute the signs of aging. Thus, adaptability should be used wisely and sparingly rather than squandered" (pp. 10-11).

The preventionist can translate these statements into efforts that will reduce, eliminate, or modify withdrawals from the bank account of resistance (Hollister, 1977). So-called stress inoculation (Meichenbaum, 1977) or anticipatory guidance (Gullotta, 1987) programs, directed toward promoting emotional health, are not in conceptual conflict with the notion of a fixed bank account of adaptive resources. It is true that some preventionists believe these efforts to be the means by which the bank account of resistance may be strengthened by deposits, but one may also view them as efforts that prepare the organism in such a way as to reduce the withdrawal of adaptive resources. This is possible because anticipatory guidance enables the soon-to-be affected population to adjust the meaning it should attach to a particular life event. What is "meaning"? Meaning is purpose. It is value. It is understanding and acceptance.

We know from the early work of Reuben Hill (1949) the importance that individual meaning has for determining and interpreting a life event. For example, the importance of work to the emotional and physical well-being of humankind has long been understood. The loss of employment is a devastating life event for many. In the current period of economic upheaval, in which even traditionally employment secure industries like banking and insurance are reeling under deregulation and the poor investment decisions made a decade earlier, hundreds of thousands of layoffs have occurred. This has been matched in turn by similar layoffs in the telecommunications and computer industries. Working for Ma Bell, IBM,

Boeing or the local hometown bank no longer offers the job security it once did. How should an individual interpret a layoff in these circumstances? In many families, there is a rise in alcohol and drug use; children feel the heavy hand of their unemployed parent; and the spousal relationship sours as emotional and physical hurts accumulate. As Caplan and his associates describe in Chapter 15 of this volume, here is an excellent opportunity to apply stress inoculation and other interventions to reduce the harmful consequences of unemployment.

For intervention purposes, the issue now becomes one of determining which factors contribute to an accelerated rate of withdrawal of adaptive energy and which slow, stem, or alter this withdrawal process. Such a model can be used to reduce the incidence of dysfunctional behavior and promote health.

Albee's Incidence Formula

George Albee's (1985) most recent version of a formula for the incidence of emotional illness in society is expressed in the following equation:

$$\text{Incidence} = \frac{\text{Organic factors \& stress exploitation}}{\text{Coping skills \& self-esteem \& support groups}}$$

This formula is an elaboration of an earlier equation (Albee, 1980) in which

$$\text{Incidence} = \frac{\text{Organic causes and stresses}}{\substack{\text{Competence, coping skills, self-esteem \&} \\ \text{social support}}}$$

An examination of this formula suggests that actions that increase the size of the numerator will increase the incidence of dysfunctional behavior in society, and activities that reduce, modify, or eliminate these factors will diminish the incidence of dysfunction. Efforts that reduce the size of the denominator will correspondingly increase the incidence, whereas efforts that increase the size of the denominator will reduce incidence. In the following paragraphs, each of the elements of this equation will be examined.[1]

The Numerators

Organic Factors

The issue of the influence of genetic factors on emotional health and their contribution to such dysfunctions as schizophrenia, the major affective disorders, and alcoholism continue to be heatedly debated (see Marlowe & Weinberg, 1983, for an excellent example of divergent views on this subject). It may well be that genetic factors influence some specific dysfunctions, but work in this area has been disappointingly inconclusive, and even the more thorough twin studies suggestive of genetic factors in schizophrenia have not escaped severe criticism (Abrams & Taylor, 1983; Lidz & Blatt, 1983). This has led Plomin (1990) to observe that "heritabilities for behavior [in the best of studies] seldom exceed 50%"(p. 187), providing enormous opportunities for living situations to affect the ultimate outcome.

Still, not all organic factors remain hidden in the mysteries of DNA. Preventionists recognize that a number of conditions exist (Tay-Sachs disease, phenylketonuria, galactosemia, tuberous sclerosis, and Huntington's disease, for example) whose origin is genetic. In the sense Albee uses it, *organic* refers to environmental factors that have an impact on the organism. For example, we know that the ingestion of lead, exposure to mercury, infection by such pathogenic microorganisms as treponema pallidum and neisseria gonorrhea or the HIV retrovirus causes brain damage or madness or both. We know that pregnant women who smoke, use certain drugs, or consume excessive amounts of alcohol expose the fetus to such risks as prematurity, low birth weight, and fetal alcohol syndrome. We know that denied an adequate diet, an expectant mother is more likely to deliver a low birth weight infant who, if also denied an adequate diet, is at considerable risk of falling at least 250 grams below the normal 1400 grams in brain weight by age 6 (Hodgkinson, 1979). We also know that environmental interventions can make a difference.

People can be helped to not poison themselves with alcohol and harmful drugs during pregnancy (or at other times for that matter). Through its regulatory mechanisms, society can reduce the existing dangers of noxious poisons like lead in paint by removing them from products and by establishing the means by which existing lead contaminated products can be made safe. People can be helped to avoid infections during the fetal period (rubella and toxoplasmosis) or in early childhood (pertussis, measles, meningitis, and tuberculosis) that can cause severe mental retardation as well as perceptual and cognitive defects. People can be educated to seek preventive health care services.

In the cases of the genetic disorders phenylketonuria and galactosemia, both of which can cause mental retardation, special dietary plans can prevent the disorder. Sound nutritional diets can assist children and reduce their overall risk of impaired mental development. Through programs such as Women, Infants, Children (WIC); food stamps; and school meal programs (breakfast and lunch, especially breakfast), society can improve the health of infants and young children.

Clearly, there are a number of areas in which action can be taken to reduce the exposure of endangered groups to deleterious agents in our environment. Such efforts need not await the resolution of the nature versus nurture controversy.

Stress

It is evident from its position in the numerator that Albee understands stress to be harmful (that is, distress) rather than neutral or beneficial (that is, eustress). This remark, although easily stated, is more difficult to define. For example, stimulus-oriented theories like the Holmes and Rahae (1967) Life Events Scale have been found to be too simple. The linear connection they believe exists between specific life events and ill health are rather more tenuous. In recent years, work has been directed toward identifying the factors that, together with a specific life event or a series of events, contribute to ill health (see for example, Bloom, 1985; Burr, 1982; Elliott & Eisdorfer, 1982; Goldberger & Breznitz, 1982; Hill, 1949; McCubbin & Patterson, 1982). Thus the question is, What are the conditions that interact with one or more life events to increase an individual's risk of illness?

Several of these conditions have been identified. The first is the meaning an individual or individuals attach to the event (Hill, 1949; Lazarus, 1966). For example, the birth of a child is heralded as a joyous occasion (eustress) unless that child is unwanted or born with a serious birth defect (distress). The death of a spouse brings lamenting and a loss of self (distress) unless that spouse was despised by his or her mate.

A second factor involves the suddenness of the event(s) (Burr, 1982). Research has clearly established a relationship between distress and unexpectedness. Both animals and humans, for instance, will select more painful and longer aversive stimuli if they are forewarned rather than unexpected aversive stimuli, even if these are less painful and of shorter duration (Elliott & Eisdorfer, 1982).

An important aspect of unexpectedness is the point in the life span at which an event is encountered. "Off-time" events are typically more distressful. For example, ultimately all of us will die. However, parents expect to die before their offspring and very few (if any) parents expect to experience the heartbreaking loss of an infant due to sudden infant death syndrome or the loss of a son or daughter in an automobile accident or a drive-by killing.

Another element that needs consideration is the length of time a stressor exists (Burr, 1982). Like a low-grade, chronic infection, some events like poverty, racism, sexism, or a handicapping condition can slowly and insidiously sap an individual's adaptive energy. Such a situation in combination with the "pile up" or addition of other life events that are perceived to be distressful can exacerbate a situation and thus contribute to or cause illness (Elliott & Eisdorfer, 1982; McCubbin & Patterson, 1982).

Finally, the environmental condition of overcrowding (increased social density) contributes to events being perceived as distressful. For example, numerous animal studies have found that crowding produces sustained high blood pressure (hypertension) (Elliott & Eisdorfer,1982; Vance, 1982).

The preceding factors are not all inclusive. Rather, they are a first step toward defining those circumstances in which a life event will be perceived as distressful.

Exploitation

Albee has written extensively on his belief that the powerlessness that results from exploitation is a primary factor contributing to the higher incidence of psychopathology among women and minority groups (Albee, 1985, 1995; Albee & Gullotta, 1986; Joffe

& Albee, 1981; Kessler & Albee, 1977). In their exhaustive review of the literature on primary prevention, Kessler and Albee (1977) stated that

> Everywhere we looked, every social research study we examined, suggested that major sources of human stress and distress generally involve some form of excessive power . . . It is enough to suggest the hypothesis that a dramatic reduction and control of power might improve the mental health of people. (pp. 380-381)

We believe powerlessness as contributing to, if not in itself, responsible for, learned helplessness—that is, behavior that results from negative experiences over which one has no control. Seligman's (1974, 1975) classic studies in this area stand as a testimony to Albee's contention that feeling helpless because one has no power, no control over one's life, contributes significantly to emotional illness.

Seligman (1975), for example, describes one experiment in which a dog is placed in a harness and administered a painful shock. The animal cannot escape the shock nor can it do anything to avoid it. Later this animal is placed in a box that is divided into two compartments. Each is easily accessible to the animal. The experiment now calls for the animal to be shocked again. To escape the shock, the animal need only move to the other compartment. Whereas other unconditioned dogs quickly learn to escape the aversive situation, two thirds of the experimental dogs simply give up, lie down, and cry.

Having control or power over one's own life not only promotes health (Kobasa, 1979) but also increases involvement in community life. Karasek (cited in Elliott & Eisdorfer, 1982, pp. 134-135) has collected data that suggest that the greater the sense of control employees have in their work environment, the greater the degree of involvement those employees have in the life of their communities. Employees with greater feelings of control showed higher levels of community participation than employees with feelings of less control over their work environment. Thus, it does not surprise us, nor should it surprise others, that those without power—those most commonly exploited, namely, women, minorities, and migrant farmworkers—are found in disproportionate numbers filling the rosters of the emotionally disturbed.

The Denominators

Coping Skills

What provides one with the resources to handle distressful events in a manner that will not be seen by others as dysfunctional? We would suggest that several factors are involved. The first is the person's position in society (Burr, 1982). As has already been suggested, status contributes to competence, and competence facilitates coping. Closely associated with this factor are the bonds one has to society (Burr, 1982). Those who are not identified with society are either ignored or ostracized by society. Recognition and identification are related to the contribution an individual is able to make to society: The less the worth attached to the contribution, the less value is attached to the individual. Thus, competency can be understood to mean belonging to a society, being valued by that society, and having the opportunity to make a meaningful contribution to that society (Gullotta, Adams, & Montemayor, 1990).

Coping involves the ability to muster the resources necessary in the stage of resistance to either defeat or tolerate some stressor (Pearlin & Schooler, 1978). It involves problem solving under conditions in which it is not necessarily clear what actions are appropriate (Janis, 1982). This ability to change or adapt is enhanced, Vance (1982) believes, in people who are open to new experiences and who are able to use their cognitive skills to place distressful events in perspective. In short, it is being able to view the world as manageable and, when a situation cannot be conquered, being able to accept it and continue living. Those best able to engage in this practice are individuals who have coped successfully in the past (Burr, 1982). Although one cannot easily reorder society, Albee and other preventionists believe that many of the attributes that help one survive in it can be developed. For example, a growing literature establishes the fact that children can be helped in learning social problem solving skills to avoid such dysfunctional behaviors as substance misuse and aggressive behaviors (see, for example, Mrazek & Haggerty, 1994).

Self-Esteem

In many ways, when one is talking about self-esteem, one is referring to self-identity. Whether self-esteem is a form of self-love, self-acceptance, or a sense of competence is unimportant to this discussion; what does matter is that low self-esteem is predictive of interpersonal problems.

Self-esteem grows or is stunted in response to one's environment. Essential to a child's sense of self is the family. The success parents have in instilling a strong sense of self is affected by their position in society. When one's race, religion, sex, or ethnic background is held in contempt, it is very difficult to create a sense of pride in oneself or one's children.

The clinical and research literature is rich in observations that low self-esteem is a contributing (if not a major) factor in many different types of dysfunctional behavior (Adams, Gullotta, & Markstrom-Adams, 1997). Nor should it be surprising that socially competent people show a vigorous attitude toward life, possess a strong positive sense of self, and display an internal locus of control (Gullotta, 1987). Thus, self-esteem can aid in insulating an individual from the stressors that contribute to ill health. Stripped of this protective clothing, a human being stands exposed to the elements. In a protective, warm, nurturing environment, little risk ensues, but as the climate deteriorates, risk of ill health increases.

Support Groups

The final factor in Albee's equation has been described by one author as natural caregiving (Gullotta, 1987, 1994). It involves three elements, each providing the nurturing essential to health. The first is *indigenous caregiving,* and represents the responsibility each of us has for our own health, the health of our family members, and our greater responsibility for the health of other humans. In short, it is a genuine benevolent interest for others. The literature is rich with examples of the influence over time that a single individual can have in the life of another for good. That individual needs to be invested in the other person, be able to discern the good in that person, and communicate positive regard for that person. Together these behaviors constitute what could be called good parenting, a loving relationship, or a warm and trusting friendship. Regrettably, they are too often absent in the lives of those who live alone on the streets, whose parents take out their anger on them, or who migrate harvesting the fruits and vegetables we find on our tables.

Next is *trained indigenous caregiving*. For example, most of us will never seek help from mental health professionals even in times of trouble. Instead, in times of difficulty, when friends and family cannot provide help or are missing, most of us will turn to the clergy, teachers, and others for advice and guidance. These are the people whose lessons and examples we have incorporated into our lives.

The final element is the *mutual self-help group*. Here individuals experiencing a similar form of distress join together to help each other and be helped in return. Programs like Widow to Widow illustrate the power each of us can have for good in the lives of others (Silverman, 1972). Having experienced the same life event, the care giver and care receiver exchange support, concrete advice, and tears as both struggle to make some sense out of an event that makes no sense.

Individuals without one of these forms of social support are islands unto themselves. Dohrenwend, Krasnoff, Askensy, and Dohrenwend (1982) postulate a "pathogenic triad; that is, 1. a fateful life event, 2. an event likely to exhaust the individual physically, [and] 3. [the] loss of social support," leading to ill health (p. 339). Research suggests that people with trusting and supportive relationships are less likely to suffer adverse health outcomes following some life event (Cassell, 1976; Cobb, 1976). Evidence suggests that people who have social supports live longer (Berkman & Syne, 1979) and exhibit more positive mental health (Mitchell, Billings, & Moos, 1982). Thus, the promotion of social support strengthens an individual's ability to encounter distress and to either conquer or accept it.

Summary

This chapter has examined the interrelationship of stress theory and the prevention of behaviors that may be considered dysfunctional. Albee's incidence formula provides a model for understanding the complicated interaction of factors that foster health or sickness. But more important, it suggests the means by which each of us can encourage the growth of health and discourage the suffering associated with illness. And it is this individual ownership of one's health that underscores the emerging alternative health paradigm and primary prevention.

Note

1. Maurice Elias (1987) has reworked Albee's equation and developed a systems-level prevention equation. This paper can be found in the *American Journal of Community Psychology, 15*(5), 539-553.

References

Abrams, R., & Taylor, M. A. (1983). The genetics of schizophrenia: A reassessment using modern criteria. *American Journal of Psychiatry, 140*, 171-175.

Adams, G. R., Gullotta, T. P., & Markstrom-Adams, C. (1997). *Adolescent life experiences.* Pacific Grove, CA: Brooks/Cole.

Albee, G. W. (1980). A competency model must replace the defect model. In L. A. Bond & J. C. Rosen (Eds.), *Competence and coping during adulthood.* Hanover, NH: University Press of New England.

Albee, G. W. (1985). The argument for primary prevention. *Journal of Primary Prevention, 5*, 213-219.

Albee, G. W. (1995). Ann and me. *Journal of Primary Prevention, 15*, 331-350.

Albee, G. W., & Gullotta, T. P. (1986). Facts and fallacies about primary prevention. *Journal of Primary Prevention, 6*, 207-218.

Berkman, L. F., & Syne, S. L. (1979). Social networks, host resistance, and mortality: A nine year follow-up study of Alameda residents. *American Journal of Epidemiology, 109*, 186-204.

Bloom, B. L. (1985). *Stressful life event theory and research: Implications for primary prevention* (National Institute of Mental Health Publication No. ADM 85-1385). Washington, DC: U.S. Department of Health and Human Services.

Burr, W. (1982). Families under stress. In H. I. McCubbin, A. E. Cauble, & J. M. Patterson (Eds.), *Family stress, coping, and social support.* Springfield, IL: Charles C Thomas.

Cannon, W. B. (1939). *The wisdom of the body.* New York: Norton.

Caplan, G. (1964). *Principles of preventive psychiatry.* New York: Basic Books.

Caplan, G. (1974). *Support systems and community mental health.* New York: Behavioral Publications.

Cassell, J. (1976). The contribution of the social environment to host resistance. *American Journal of Epidemiology, 104*, 107-123.

Cobb, S. (1976). Social support as a moderator of life stress. *Psychosomatic Medicine, 38*, 300-314.

Cowen, E. L. (1982). Primary prevention research: Barriers, needs, and opportunities. *Journal of Primary Prevention, 2*, 131-137.

Dohrenwend, B. S., Krasnoff, L., Askensy, A. R., & Dohrenwend, B. P. (1982). The psychiatric epidemiology research interview life events scale. In L. Goldberger & S. Breznitz (Eds.), *Handbook of stress*. New York: Free Press.

Elias, M. (1987). Establishing enduring prevention programs: Advancing the legacy of Swampscott. *American Journal of Community Psychology, 15*(5), 539-553.

Elliott, G. R., & Eisdorfer, C. (Eds.). (1982). *Stress and human health*. New York: Springer.

Goldberger, L., & Breznitz, S. (Eds.). (1982). *Handbook of stress*. New York: Free Press.

Goldston, S. E. (1977). Defining primary prevention. In G. W. Albee & J. M. Joffe (Eds.), *Primary prevention of psychopathology: Vol. 1. The issues*. Hanover, NH: University Press of New England.

Gullotta, T. P. (1987). Prevention's technology. *Journal of Primary Prevention, 7,* 176-196.

Gullotta, T. P. (1994). The what, who, why, where, when, and how of primary prevention. *Journal of Primary Prevention, 15,* 5-14.

Gullotta, T. P., Adams, G. R., & Montemayor, R. (1990). *Developing social competency in adolescence*. Newbury Park, CA: Sage.

Hill, R. (1949). *Families under stress*. New York: Harper & Row.

Hodgkinson, H. (1979). What's right with education? *Phi Delta Kappan, 61,* 159-162.

Hollister, W. G. (1977). Basic strategies in designing primary prevention programs. In D. C. Klein & S. E. Goldston (Eds.), *Primary prevention: An idea whose time has come*. Washington, DC: Government Printing Office.

Holmes, T. H., & Rahae, R. H. (1967). The social readjustment rating scale. *Journal of Psychosomatic Research, 11,* 213-318.

Janis, I. K. (1982). Decision making under stress. In L. Goldberger & S. Breznitz (Eds.), *Handbook of stress*. New York: Free Press.

Joffe, J. M., & Albee, G. W. (1981). Powerlessness and psychopathology. In J. M. Joffe & G. W. Albee (Eds.), *Prevention through political action and social change*. Hanover, NH: University Press of New England.

Kessler, M., & Albee, G. W. (1977). An overview of the literature of primary prevention. In G. W. Albee & J. M. Joffe (Eds.), *Primary prevention of psychopathology: Vol. 1. The issues*. Hanover, NY: University Press of New England.

Klein, D. C., & Goldston, S. E. (1977). *Primary prevention: An idea whose time has come*. Washington, DC: Government Printing Office.

Kobasa, S. C. (1979). Stressful life events, personality, and health: An inquiry into hardiness. *Journal of Personality and Social Psychology, 37,* 1-11.

Koop, C. E. (1995). A personal role in health care reform. *American Journal of Public Health, 85*(6), 759-760.

Lamb, R., & Zusman, J. (1979). Drs. Lamb and Zusman reply. *American Journal of Psychiatry, 136,* 1349.

Lazarus, R. S. (1966). *Psychological stress and the coping process*. New York: McGraw-Hill.

Lidz, T., & Blatt, S. (1983). Critique of the Danish American studies of the biological and adoptive relatives of adoptees who have become schizophrenic. *American Journal of Psychiatry, 140,* 426-435.

Marlowe, H. A., & Weinberg, R. B. (1983). *Primary prevention: Fact or fallacy?* Tampa, FL: University of South Florida Press.

McCubbin, H. I., & Patterson, J. M. (1982). Family adaptation to crises. In H. I. McCubbin, A. E. Cauble, & J. M. Patterson (Eds.), *Family stress, coping, and social support.* Springfield, IL: Charles C Thomas.

Meichenbaum, D. (1977). *Cognitive-behavior modification: An integrative approach.* New York: Plenum.

Mitchell, R. R., Billings, A. G., & Moos, R. H. (1982). Social support and well being: Implications for prevention programs. *Journal of Primary Prevention, 3,* 77-98.

Mrazek, P. J., & Haggerty, R. J. (1994). *Reducing risks for mental disorders: Frontiers for preventive intervention research.* Washington, DC: National Academy Press.

Pearlin, L. I., & Schooler, C. (1978). The structure of coping. *Journal of Health and Social Behavior, 19,* 2-21.

Pearlin, L. I. (1982). The social contexts of stress. In L. Goldberger & S. Breznitz (Eds.), *Handbook of stress.* New York: Free Press.

Plomin, R. (1990). The role of inheritance in behavior. *Science, 248,* 183-188.

Seligman, M. E. P. (1974). Submissive death: Giving up on life. *Psychology Today,* pp. 80-85.

Seligman, M. E. P. (1975). *Helplessness: On depression, development, and death.* San Francisco, CA: Freeman.

Selye, H. A. (1936). A syndrome produced by diverse nocuous agents. *Nature, 138,* 32.

Selye, H. A. (1982). History and present status of the stress concept. In L. Goldberger & S. Breznitz (Eds.), *Handbook of stress.* New York: Free Press.

Silverman, P. R. (1972). Widowhood and preventive intervention. *The Family Coordinator, 21,* 95-102.

Vance, E. T. (1982). Social disability and stress. In L. Goldberger & S. Breznitz (Eds.), *Handbook of stress.* New York: Free Press.

T W O

Infant and Toddler Programs

CHAPTER 3

The Prenatal/Early Infancy Project: Fifteen Years Later

DAVID OLDS

Many of the most pervasive, intractable, and costly problems faced by young children and parents in our society today are a consequence of adverse maternal health-related behaviors such as cigarette smoking, drinking, and drug use during pregnancy, dysfunctional infant caregiving, and stressful environmental conditions that interfere with parental and family functioning. These problems include infant mortality, preterm delivery, and low birth weight; child abuse and neglect; childhood injuries; youth violence; closely spaced pregnancy; and thwarted economic self-sufficiency on the part of parents. Standard indicators of child health and well-being indicate that many children in our society are suffering.

- Nine infants out of every thousand in the United States die before their first birthday. As a result of high rates of low birth weight (< 2,500 grams) our infant mortality rate is worse than 19 other nations, despite dramatic reductions in infant mortality in the last two decades due to improvements in newborn intensive care (Children's Defense Fund, 1992; National Center for Health Statistics, 1991). Low birth weight babies who survive are 50% more likely to use special education services once they enter school than are normal birth weight controls (Chaikind & Corman, 1991).
- Over 2.5 million children were reported as being abused or neglected in 1990, and one in three of the victims of physical abuse

41

were infants less than 1 year of age. Between 1,200 and 1,500 children die each year as a result of parent or caregiver maltreatment (Daro & McCurdy, 1990). Not only is maltreatment morally unacceptable, but the social consequences are so devastating that the U.S. Advisory Panel on Child Abuse and Neglect has called child maltreatment a national emergency (U.S. Advisory Board on Child Abuse and Neglect, 1990).

• Childhood injuries are the leading cause of death among children aged 1 through 14 (National Center for Health Statistics, 1991).

• High rates of violence among adolescents, both as victims and as perpetrators, threaten the safety and well-being of our neighborhoods. Among young people aged 15 to 24, homicide is a leading cause of death, and for African Americans in general, it is number one (National Center for Health Statistics, 1991).

Although these problems cut across all segments of U.S. society, they are more common among children born to poor, teenage, and single parents and among women who have rapid, successive pregnancies (Furstenberg, Brooks-Gunn, & Morgan, 1987). A significant portion of these problems can be traced to parental behavior—in particular to women's health-related behaviors during pregnancy and to the qualities of care that parents provide to their children. Low-income, single, adolescent mothers can have good pregnancy outcomes and children who do well, but their capacity to care for themselves and for their children is often compromised by histories of maltreatment in their own childhoods, psychological immaturity or depression, stressful living conditions, and inadequate social support. These conditions contribute to the greater likelihood that socially disadvantaged parents will abuse cigarettes and other drugs during pregnancy and will fail to provide adequate care for their children, often with devastating results.

Women who smoke cigarettes and use other substances during pregnancy, for example, are at considerable risk for bearing low birth weight newborns, and their children are at heightened risk for neurodevelopmental impairment (Kramer, 1987; Olds, Henderson, & Tatelbaum, 1994a; Weitzman, Gortmaker, & Sobol, 1992). Even subtle damage to the fetal brain can undermine a child's intellectual functioning and capacity for emotional and behavioral regulation.

Parents' capacities to read and respond to their infants' communicative signals form the basis for children's sense of security and trust in the world and their belief in their capacity to influence that world (Ainsworth, 1979). Breaches of that trust have long-term consequences, especially when caregiving dysfunction is combined with neurodevelopmental impairment on the part of the child.

A recently reported longitudinal study of a large sample of Danish children and their families found that children who experienced the combination of birth complications and parental rejection in the first year of life were at substantially increased risk for violent criminality at age 18 in comparison to children who experienced only birth complications or parental rejection alone. Although only 4.5% of the sample experienced both birth complications and parental rejection, that group accounted for 18% of all violent crimes among the 18-year-olds. Parental rejection or birth trauma by themselves did not increase the risk for violence (Raine, Brennan, & Mednick, 1994). When risk factors accumulate, the risk for adverse outcomes increases, often in synergistically vicious ways.

Although the problems listed have been resistive to government intervention over the past 30 years, scientific evidence is accumulating that it is possible to improve the outcomes of pregnancy, to improve parents' abilities to care for their children, and to reduce welfare dependence with programs of prenatal and early childhood home visitation—but it is not easy. Our optimism stands in contrast to earlier research on home visitation (Combs-Orme, Reis, & Ward, 1985). The earlier research was difficult to interpret because the programs studied were often not designed to address the needs of parents in sensible and powerful ways, and the research itself frequently lacked scientific rigor (Olds & Kitzman, 1990, 1993).

In the following sections, we review a program of prenatal and early childhood home visitation that was tested with a randomized trial design and that has been shown to improve the outcomes of pregnancy, the qualities of care that parents provide to their children, and families' economic self-sufficiency when it was provided to low-income European American families in and around Elmira, New York. An economic evaluation of the program, from the standpoint of government spending, has shown that its cost, when focused on low-income families, was recovered with dividends by the time the children were 4 years of age. More recently, we have replicated the program of research in Memphis, Tennessee (where it was tested with African American families living in an urban area) and Denver, Colorado (where nurses and paraprofessionals are compared to determine their unique contributions as home visitors). The results from these trials are not yet available. In the course of conducting the program in new settings, the program content and methods have been refined over time. We will start by describing the program model, giving particular emphasis to its theoretical foundations.

Program Model

The home visitation program was designed to improve three aspects of maternal and child functioning: (a) the outcomes of pregnancy, (b) qualities of parental caregiving (including reducing associated child health and developmental problems), and (c) maternal life course development (helping women return to school, find work, and plan future pregnancies). In the Elmira program, the nurses completed an average of 9 (3 SD) visits during pregnancy and 23 (15 SD) visits from birth through the second year of the child's life. The content and methods of the program, while adhering to a common core and set of theoretical foundations, have evolved over time. This evolution is described below and articulated in greater depth elsewhere (Olds, Kitzman, Cole, & Robinson, in press).

The program has been grounded in theories of human ecology (Bronfenbrenner, 1979, 1992), self-efficacy (Bandura, 1977), and human attachment (Bowlby, 1969). The earliest formulations of the program gave greatest emphasis to human ecology, but as the program has evolved, it has been grounded more explicitly in theories of self-efficacy and human attachment.

Human Ecology Theory

The original formulation of this program was derived in large part from Bronfenbrenner's theory of *human ecology* (Bronfenbrenner, 1979), which emphasizes the importance of social contexts as influences on human development. Parents' care of their infants, from this perspective, is influenced by characteristics of their families, social networks, neighborhoods, communities, and cultures, as well as by interrelations among these structures. Bronfenbrenner's original theoretical framework has been elaborated more recently (with greater attention to individual influences) in his person-process-context model of research on human development (Bronfenbrenner, 1992).

Figure 3.1 displays how this model applies to the current program of research. The *person* elements of the model are reflected in the boxes that refer to "parent" and "child," and have to do with behavioral and psychological characteristics of each. In the formulation of the theoretical foundations of the program, parents, and especially mothers, are considered both developing persons and the primary focus of the preventive intervention. Particular attention is focused on parents' progressive mastery of their roles as parents and as adults responsible for their own health and economic self-sufficiency. This program emphasizes parent development because parents' behavior constitutes the most powerful and potentially alterable influence on the developing child, particularly given parents' control over their children's prenatal environment, their face-to-face interaction with their children postnatally, and their influence on the family's home environment.

The concept of *process* articulated here, and denoted by the arrows in the figure, encompasses parents' interaction with their environment as well as the intrapsychic changes that characterize their mastery of their roles as parents and providers. Three aspects of process emphasized here relate to individuals' functioning: (a) program processes (e.g., the ways in which the visitors work with parents to strengthen parents' competencies), (b) processes that take place within parents (i.e., the influence of their psychological resources—developmental histories, mental health, and coping styles—on behavioral adaptation), and (c) parents' interaction with their children, other family members, friends, and health and human service providers. For the sake of simplicity, the discussion of these *processes* has been integrated below into the *person (parent)* part of the model.

The focus on parents elaborated here is not intended to minimize the role that contextual factors such as economic conditions, cultural patterns, racism, and sexism play in shaping the opportunities that parents are afforded (Olds, 1980). Most of those features of the environment, however, are outside of the influence of preven-

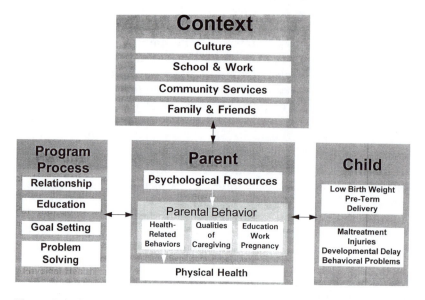

Figure 3.1. Person-Process-Context Model of Program Influences on Pregnancy Outcomes, Child Health and Development, and Maternal Life Course

tive interventions provided through health and human service systems. Certain contexts, nevertheless, are affected by parents' adaptive competencies. It is these features of the environment that the current program attempts to affect, primarily by enhancing parents' social skills. This is why in Figure 3.1 the effect of the program on context is mediated by parents' behavior. The aspects of context that we are most concerned about have to do with informal and formal sources of support for the family, characteristics of communities that can support or undermine the functioning of the program and families, the impact of going to school or participating in work on family life, as well as cultural conditions that need to be taken into consideration in the design and conduct of the program.

One of the central hypotheses of Bronfenbrenner's (1979) human ecology theory is that the capacity of the parent-child relationship to function effectively as a context for development depends on the existence and nature of other relationships that the parent may have. The parent-child relationship is enhanced as a context for development to the extent that each of these other relationships involves mutual positive feelings and that the other parties are supportive of the developmental activities carried on in the parent-child relationship. Conversely, the developmental potential of the parent-child relationship is impaired to the extent that each of the other relationships in which the parent is involved consists of mutual antagonism or interference with the developmental activities carried on in the parent-child relationship (p. 77).

Program Implications

Human ecology theory has played an important role in identifying which families would be enrolled in the study and when. We chose to work with women who had no previous live births and thus were undergoing a major role change that Bronfenbrenner calls an *ecological transition.* We began the program during pregnancy and the early years of the child's life because during pregnancy women have not yet formally assumed the parental role. In providing support to young people prior to and while they were learning about being parents, we reasoned that the visitors would enhance their influence on parents' enduring orientation to their roles as parents and providers. The skills and resources that parents develop around the care of the first child would also carry over to later children. And to the extent that the program was successful in helping parents plan for their futures (including planning subsequent pregnancies), parents would have fewer unintended children. This would ease some of the challenges of caring for the first child.

Human ecology theory also focused the home visitors' attention on the systematic evaluation and enhancement of the material and social environment of the family. As indicated in Figure 3.1, the visitors assess and promote informal social support (individuals within the family and friend network who can serve as reliable sources of material and emotional support for the mother in her efforts to care for her children) and the families' use of formal community services.

Human ecologists would hypothesize that women's capacity to improve their health-related behaviors is influenced by their levels of informal support for change. Women's efforts to reduce cigarette smoking during pregnancy, for example, are affected by the extent to which individuals close to them believe that smoking is bad for pregnant women and their fetuses and the extent to which they actively support women's efforts to quit. Consequently, the visitors encourage mothers during pregnancy to invite other family members and friends to the visits in an effort to enhance friends' and family members' support of the mothers' efforts to improve their health-related behaviors and to prepare for labor, delivery, and early care of the child.

The involvement of other family members, friends, and mothers' partners is especially important in helping women practice contraception, finish their educations, and find work. In discussions of family planning and contraception, the visitors make every effort to conduct some of those visits when mothers' partners are present. In addition, returning to school after delivery or finding work usually requires finding appropriate care for the child. In low-income families this usually means that the mother must find someone in the household or network of friends who might be able to provide reliable and safe care for the baby. The nurses help mothers identify safe and nurturant care within their network of family members and friends and, if none can be found, help them find appropriate subsidized center-based care. To the extent that the visitors have been successful in helping women to complete their educations and participate in the work force, they have altered the ecology of the family by placing additional demands on other family members and friends. Moreover, in spending more time in educational or work settings, women are integrated into social contexts where there are greater pressures to conform to societal expectations. These activities change the ecology of the family in fundamental ways.

Human ecology theory also focuses the visitors' attention on the identification of family stressors and needed health and human services. The visitors assess families' needs and then systematically help them make use of other needed services in an attempt to reduce the situational stressors that many low-income families encounter. Families are helped to obtain services such as Medicaid, Aid to Families with Dependent Children (AFDC), subsidized housing, help with family counseling, nutritional supplementation, substance abuse counseling, and assistance with finding clothing and furniture.

An important part of the program involves the visitors helping women interact effectively with the office-based nursing staff and physicians who provide their primary care. In this way, the visitors can clarify and reinforce recommendations made by the office staff and thus help ensure greater compliance with physician and nurse recommendations. During pregnancy, the visitors remind women about such things as maintaining regular antepartum visits, finishing prescribed medications, and strict bed rest for the early signs of hypertensive disorders.

After the baby is born, the visitors continue to inform mothers and other family members about the availability of formal community services and provide mothers with the skills to use those services more effectively. As they did during pregnancy, the visitors communicate with the children's physicians and their office staff to reinforce the medical staff's recommendations in the home and to enable the medical staff to provide more informed and sensitive care in the office. Parents are taught to observe their children's indicators of health and illness, to use thermometers, and to call the physician's office with appropriate signs of their children's illnesses. The expectation is that this approach will increase the appropriate use and decrease the inappropriate use of emergency departments.

As the program model was transferred from Elmira, New York (where it served a primarily European American population) to Memphis and Denver, it was reviewed from the standpoint of its congruence with the cultural beliefs of the African American and Mexican American families that it increasingly served. This work was facilitated by the creation of community advisory committees that reviewed the protocols. The reassuring message in both Memphis and Denver was that the protocols were essentially culturally competent. This sanctioning of the program was based in part on its inclusion of other family members and friends in the program and on its creation of racially and ethnically diverse teams of visitors and supervisors.

Limitations of Human Ecology Theory

Compared to other developmental theories, Bronfenbrenner's framework provides a more extended and elaborated conception of the environment. The original formulation of the theory, however, tended to treat the immediate settings in which children and families find themselves as shaped by cultural and structural characteristics of the society, with little consideration given to the role that adults (parents in particular) can play in selecting and shaping the settings in which they find themselves.

Consequently, self-efficacy and attachment theories were integrated into the model to provide a broader conception of the parent-setting relationship. The integration of these theories allows for a conceptualization of development that encompasses truly reciprocal relationships in which settings, children, and other adults influence parental behavior and in which parents simultaneously select and shape their settings and interpersonal relationships.

Self-Efficacy Theory

Self-efficacy theory provides a useful framework for promoting women's health-related behavior during pregnancy, their care of their children, and their own personal development. According to Bandura (1977), differences in motivation, behavior, and persistence in efforts to change a wide range of social behaviors are a function of individuals' beliefs about the connection between their efforts and their desired results. According to this view, cognitive processes play a central role in the acquisition and retention of new behavior patterns. In self-efficacy theory, Bandura (1977) distinguishes *efficacy* expectations from *outcome* expectations. Outcome expectations are individuals' estimates that a given behavior will lead to a given outcome. Efficacy expectations are individuals' beliefs that they can successfully carry out the behavior required to produce the outcome. It is efficacy expectations that affect both the initiation and persistence of coping behavior. Individuals' perceptions of self-efficacy can influence their choice of activities and settings and can determine how much effort they will put forth in the face of obstacles.

Program Implications

Although self-efficacy theory played a role in the design of the Elmira program through an emphasis on helping women set small, achievable objectives for themselves that would strengthen their confidence in their capacity for behavioral change, it was not emphasized explicitly as a theoretical foundation in Elmira to the same degree as it was in Memphis and Denver. The increased focus on self-efficacy in the later trials grew out of our observation that several of the most important program effects in Elmira (in particular, the reduction in child maltreatment and emergency department encounters for injuries) were concentrated among women who at registration had little sense of control over their life circumstances (Olds, Henderson, Tatelbaum, & Chamberlin, 1986). We hypothesized that the promotion of self-efficacy played a central role in enabling at-risk women to reduce their prenatal cigarette smoking, rates of subsequent pregnancy, and rates of unemployment (Olds et al., 1986, 1988), given that the nurses used these methods in helping women manage these aspects of their lives. We reasoned that the nurses' emphasis on helping women gain control over specific life circumstances such as these promoted women's generalized self-efficacy.

As a result of these observations, in the Memphis and Denver trials, the visitors were trained explicitly in self-efficacy theory and its applications, and the program protocols were written in a way that distinguishes efficacy expectations from outcome expectations. For instance, women may acknowledge that smoking is harmful for themselves and their babies (an outcome expectation), but not believe that they will be able to quit (an efficacy expectation). Distinguishing these two aspects of the problem helps in the specification of smoking reduction efforts and other individualized interventions.

Much of the educational content of the program was focused on helping women understand what is known (or thought about) the influence of particular behaviors on the health and growth of the fetus, on women's own health, and on the subsequent health and development of the child. The educational program represents an effort to bring women's outcome expectations into alignment with the best evidence available.

Improvements in individuals' behavior depends on their confidence in their ability to change. According to Bandura, helping services like those carried out in the current program achieve their primary effect by creating and strengthening the individual's expectation of personal efficacy. Self-efficacy theory has a number of direct implications for the methods that the home visitors use to promote mothers' healthy behavior, optimal caregiving, family planning, and economic self-sufficiency.

First, because the power of efficacy information is greater if it is based on the individual's personal accomplishments than if it derives from vicarious experiences or verbal persuasion (Bandura, 1977), the home visitors emphasize methods of enhancing self-efficacy that rely on women's actually carrying out parts of the desired behavior. Verbal persuasion methods are used, of course, but whenever possible, they serve as guides and reinforcers for behaviors that the women already have enacted. Women who already display some adequate prenatal health behaviors are encouraged for what they are doing well. Similarly, the visitors reinforce caregiving behaviors that are close to the goals of the program—such as the sensitive identification of and response to the child's cries, or removal of safety hazards in the home environment. This identification of family strengths helps build mothers' and other family members' confidence in their roles as parents and provides incentives for their acquiring new caregiving skills.

Second, the visitors employ methods of behavioral and problem analysis that emphasize the establishment of realistic goals and behavioral objectives in which the chances for successful performance are increased. The same principles apply whether the individual is trying to quit drinking, correct her diet, or improve her relationship with her boyfriend. Because perceptions of self-efficacy predict coping and self-regulatory behavior, the home visitors periodically ask women about their beliefs concerning their abilities to manage all types of problems related to the overall goals of the program or to the concerns of the women themselves. This information is used to help the home visitors focus their efforts on creating opportunities for women to accomplish small, achievable objectives related to particular goals. As a result of these observations, visitors in the Memphis program developed a series of questionnaires used clinically to assess women's and other family members' health-related beliefs (outcome and efficacy expectations) and behaviors, their care of their children, and their life course. These assessments now provide visitors with a basis on which to begin their educational work with mothers and other family members.

Our articulation of self-efficacy in the program protocols has evolved over each of the three trials. In the Memphis trial we augmented the emphasis on setting small, realistic objectives with a program of goal setting and problem solving (Haley, 1991; Wasik, Bryant, Ramey, & Sparling, 1992). The theory of self-efficacy was built into the training program more formally, and we began teaching the problem-solving method (defining the problem, generating sets of possible solutions, trying certain solutions, and evaluating the results) as a general approach to coping (Haley, 1991; Wasik et al., 1992). In addition, assessments of efficacy and outcome expectations with respect to critical behaviors were added to the formal test of program effects. In the Denver trial, the program model has been further refined with solution-focused methods that emphasize the competence of family members and that are focused on parents' successes (O'Brien & Baca, in press).

Limitations of Self-Efficacy Theory

Although self-efficacy theory provides powerful insights into human motivation and behavior, it is limited in several respects.

The first limitation is that it is primarily a cognitive-behavioral theory. It attends to the emotional life of the mother and other family members only through the impact of behavior on women's beliefs or expectations, which in turn affect emotions. Many people have experienced multiple adversities in the form of overly harsh parenting, rejection, or neglect that often contribute to a sense of worthlessness, depression, and cynicism about relationships. Self-efficacy gives inadequate attention to methods of helping parents cope with these features of their personal history or the impact of those early experiences on their care of their children. We have augmented the theoretical underpinnings of the program regarding these social and emotional issues with attachment theory (discussed below).

The second limitation is that self-efficacy theory attends to environmental influences in a cursory way. People can give up because they do not believe that they can do what is required, but they also can give up because they expect that their efforts will meet with punitiveness, resistance, or unresponsiveness. Although Bandura acknowledges that adversity and intractable environmental conditions are important factors in the development of individuals' sense of futility (Bandura, 1982), the structure of those environmental forces is not the subject of his theory. In other words, individuals' feelings of helplessness and futility are not simply intrapsychic phenomena but are connected to environmental contexts that provide limited opportunities and that fail to nurture growth and well-being. The structure of those environmental influences is the primary subject of human ecology theory discussed above.

Finally, although Bandura (1982) discusses self-efficacy in terms of groups, communities, and nations, the focus of the theory tends to be on the individual. In this sense, the theory may be less relevant for cultural groups that place greater emphasis on group accomplishments (or survival)—such as kin networks, families, and communities.

Attachment Theory

Historically, the program described here owes much to Bowlby's theory of attachment (Bowlby, 1969). *Attachment theory* posits that human beings (and other primates) have evolved a repertoire of behaviors that promote interaction between caregivers and their infants (such as crying, clinging, smiling, signaling) and that these behaviors tend to keep specific caregivers in proximity to defenseless youngsters, thus promoting their survival, especially in emergencies. Humans (as well as many other species) are biologically predisposed to seek proximity to specific caregivers under times of stress, illness, or fatigue in order to promote survival. This organization of behavior directed toward the caregiver is *attachment*.

In recent years, a growing body of evidence indicates that caregivers' levels of responsiveness to their children can be traced to caregivers' own child-rearing histories and attachment-related experiences (Main, Kaplan, & Cassidy, 1985). Caregivers' attachment-related experiences are thought to be encoded in "internal working models" of self and others that create styles of emotional communication and relationships that either buffer the individual in times of stress or that lead to maladaptive patterns of affect regulation and create feelings of worthlessness (Carlson & Sroufe, 1995). Differences in internal working models, according to attachment theorists, have enormous implications for mothers' capacities for developing sensitive and responsive relationships, especially with their own children.

Program Implications

Attachment theory has affected the design of the home visitation programs in three fundamental ways. The first has to do with its emphasis on the visitors' developing an empathic relationship with the mother (and other family members where possible). The second has to do with the emphasis of the program on helping mothers and other caregivers review their own child-rearing histories. And the third has to do with its explicit promotion of sensitive, responsive, and engaged caregiving in the early years of the child's life.

A fundamental element of the program has been the visitors' developing close, therapeutic alliances with the mother and other family members beginning during pregnancy. The establishment of such a relationship, consisting of empathy and respect, was expected to help modify each woman's internal working models of herself and her relationships (most important, her developing relationship with her child).

It is important for the visitors to know about women's child-rearing histories and their internal working models of relationships because without intervention, destructive models are likely to undermine the quality of care that parents provide to their own children. By assessing women's beliefs and attitudes toward their children's behavior during pregnancy, the visitors were able to help women and other caregivers develop accurate conceptions about the infant's motivations and methods of communicating.

Program protocols have been designed to present systematically how infants communicate, giving special attention to nonverbal cues, crying behavior, and colic, and how parents can meet their infants' and toddlers' emotional needs. An emphasis on mothers and other caregivers correctly reading and responding to the infant's cues begins during pregnancy and continues through the end of the program.

To promote sensitive and responsive caregiving, increasingly comprehensive parent-infant curricula were incorporated into the program in each of the three trials. For example, in the Elmira program, all of the nurses were trained in the Brazelton newborn examination (Brazelton, 1973). The nurses in the Elmira program, however, felt that the primarily didactic nature of the parent-child curriculum failed to provide them with the kind of guidance they needed to promote emotionally responsive caregiving. We realized that we had too few activities incorporated into the program to promote parents' sense of success in interacting with their children. In the Memphis program, the number of standardized materials employed to promote sensitive and responsive caregiving was expanded to include activities such as Barnard's Keys to Caregiving program, her NCAST feeding scale (Barnard, 1979), and an adaptation of Sparling's Partners for Learning program (Sparling & Lewis, 1984). In the Denver program, a curriculum has been incorporated to explicitly promote parents' emotional availability and joy in interacting with their children. Known as the Partners in Parents Education (PIPE), the program was designed originally for adolescents in classroom settings (Dolezal, Butterfield, & Grimshaw, 1994) but has been adapted for home visitors in the Denver trial. Like Partners for Learning, it uses recommended activities for caregivers and children. One of the key differences is its focus on shared positive emotions as the goal of the activity. Although to date we have only preliminary feedback from staff supporting the value of this component of the program, as we have reflected on the development and shortcomings of the home visitation program to date, we are increasingly convinced that the emphasis on the emotional features of the relationship is fundamental.

Limitations of Attachment Theory

Although attachment theory provides a rich set of insights into the origins of dysfunctional caregiving and possible preventive interventions focused on parent-visitor and parent-child relationships, it gives scant attention to the role of individual differences in infants as independent influences on parental behavior and it provides inadequate attention to issues of parental motivation for change in caregiving. Moreover, it minimizes the importance of the current social and material environments in which the family is functioning as influences on parents' capacities to care for their children. For more systematic treatments of these issues, we turned to self-efficacy and human ecology theories (discussed above).

Given that the results of the program based on the Memphis and Denver trials have not yet been published, we now turn to a discussion of the effects of the program employing data from the Elmira trial.

Elmira Study

Starting in 1977, we carried out a study of the program described above in and around Elmira, New York (Olds, Henderson, & Kitzman, 1994; Olds et al., 1986, 1988; Olds, Henderson, & Tatelbaum, 1994a, 1994b). We enrolled 400 women before the 30th week of pregnancy, 85% of whom were either low-income, unmarried, or teenaged. None had a previous live birth. Of the sample, 89% were Caucasian. The findings reported below apply to the Caucasians. We randomly assigned the participating women to receive either home visits by nurses (from pregnancy through the child's second year of life) or home visits plus transportation for health care and screening for health problems or to transportation and screening alone. Details of the research design can be found in our original empirical reports (Olds et al., 1986, 1988)

Prenatal Findings

We found that during pregnancy nurse-visited women improved the quality of their diets and those identified as smokers at the beginning of pregnancy smoked 25% fewer cigarettes by the end of pregnancy than did their counterparts in the comparison group. By the end of pregnancy, nurse-visited women had fewer kidney infections, experienced greater informal social support, and made better use of formal community services. Among women who smoked, those who were nurse-visited had 75% fewer preterm deliveries, and among very young adolescents (aged 14-16) those who were nurse-visited had babies who were nearly 400 grams heavier than those of their counterparts assigned to the comparison group (Olds et al., 1986).

Infancy and Early Childhood Findings

Child Maltreatment, Injuries, and Qualities of Caregiving

During the first two years after delivery, according to state records, 19% of the poor, unmarried teens in the comparison group abused or neglected their children as opposed to 4% of the poor, unmarried teens visited by a nurse. This result was corroborated by independent observations of maternal-child interaction and conditions in the home and reviews of medical records. It is important to note that the impact of the program on child maltreatment was further moderated by women's sense of control (or mastery) over their life circumstances when they registered in the program during pregnancy (Figure 3.2). For poor, unmarried teenagers in the comparison group, the rates of child maltreatment were substantially higher for those with little sense of control. The program moderated this risk.

We see in Figure 3.3 the same pattern of results for emergency department (ED) encounters during the second year of the children's lives for the sample as a whole (Olds et al., 1986). This same pattern was reflected in ED encounters for injuries. The concentration of effects in the second year of the child's life makes sense, given the dramatic increase in injuries at that time, when children become more mobile and the rates of injuries increase.

In addition, between their 24th and 48th month of life, the children of nurse-visited women were 40% less likely to visit a physician for an injury or ingestion than were their comparison group counterparts. Although there were no differences in the rates of state-verified cases of child maltreatment during the 2-year period after the end of the program (Olds, Henderson, & Kitzman, 1994), secondary analyses of the comparison and nurse-visited children identified through state records as having been maltreated indicated that those who had been in the nurse-visited group were at substantially lower risk for harm than were their maltreated counterparts in the comparison group. They paid 87% fewer visits to the physician for injuries and ingestions during the 2-year period after the program ended; they lived in homes with

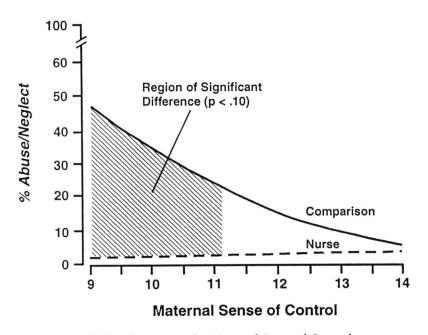

Figure 3.2. Child Maltreatment, by Maternal Sense of Control
SOURCE: From "Preventing Child Abuse and Neglect: A Randomized Trial of Nurse Home Visitation," by D. L. Olds, C. R. Henderson, Jr., R. Chamberlin, & R. Tatelbaum, 1986, *Pediatrics, 78*, p. 75. Copyright 1986 by the American Academy of Pediatrics. Reprinted with permission.

fewer safety hazards; and their homes were more conducive to their intellectual and emotional development (Olds, Henderson, Kitzman, & Cole, 1995). These differences between "maltreated" children in the nurse-visited group and those in the comparison group were so large that they are not likely to be due to the beneficial effects of the program on parents' qualities of caregiving but, rather, are likely to be due to the more complete detection of low severity maltreatment in the nurse-visited families (Olds et al., 1995). The rate of actual maltreatment is likely to be higher in the comparison group than was reflected in the state central registries, because milder forms of maltreatment were less likely to be detected in the comparison group families.

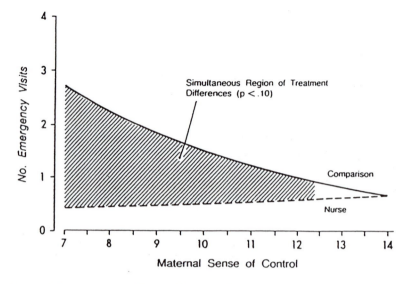

Figure 3.3. Emergency Room Contacts, by Maternal Sense of Control
SOURCE: From "Preventing Child Abuse and Neglect: A Randomized Trial of Nurse Home Visitation," by D. L. Olds, C. R. Henderson, Jr., R. Chamberlin, & R. Tatelbaum, 1986, *Pediatrics, 78,* p. 75. Copyright 1986 by the American Academy of Pediatrics. Reprinted with permission.

Maternal Cigarette Smoking During Pregnancy
and Children's Intellectual Functioning

Children born to women visited during pregnancy and who smoked 10 or more cigarettes when they registered in the program had IQ scores at 3 and 4 years old that were 4 to 5 points higher than their counterparts in the comparison group (Olds, Henderson, & Tatelbaum, 1994b). This is due, in part, to a decline in intellectual functioning over the first 4 years of life among children born to comparison group women who smoked 10 or more cigarettes during pregnancy, which we think is due to neurodevelopmental impairment resulting from prenatal exposure to the adverse effects of cigarettes (Olds, Henderson, & Tatelbaum, 1994a). The protective effect of the program was most likely due to the nurse-visited women's reduction in cigarette smoking and improvement in quality of diet during pregnancy (Olds, Henderson, & Tatelbaum, 1994b).

Maternal Life Course

During the 4-year period after delivery of the first child, among low-income, unmarried women in the program, the rate of subsequent pregnancy was reduced by 42%, and the number of months that nurse-visited women participated in the workforce was increased by 83%. Moreover, much of the impact of the program on workforce participation among the adolescent portion of the sample did not occur until the 2-year period after the program ended, when the teens were old enough to obtain jobs (Olds et al., 1988).

Cost Analysis Through Age 4

We examined the impact of the program on families' use (and corresponding cost) of other government services (Olds, Henderson, Phelps, Kitzman, & Hanks, 1993). In 1980 dollars, the program cost $3,173 for 2.5 years of intervention. We conceived of government savings as the difference in government spending for these other services between the group that received home visitation and the comparison group. Savings also were expressed in 1980 dollars and were adjusted using a 3% discount rate. By the time the children were 4 years old, low-income families who received a nurse during pregnancy and through the second year of the child's life cost the government $3,313 less than did their counterparts in the comparison group. When focused on low-income families, the investment in the service was recovered with a discounted dividend of about $180 per family within two years after the program ended.

New Research Endeavors

As a result of these promising findings, we set in motion three additional studies. The first consisted of a 15-year follow-up of the Elmira sample to determine the extent to which the trajectories set in motion early in the life cycle would propel nurse-visited families toward more adaptive functioning later in life. With funds from the National Institute of Mental Health, we are currently completing an evaluation of the children's adaptive functioning in school, at home, and society, as well as the mothers' rates of long-term welfare dependence, substance abuse, child maltreatment, and additional childbearing. We have hypothesized that the program will reduce the rates of children's disruptive behavior, given the impact of the program on (a) neurodevelopmental impairment of the child due to the reduction in cigarette smoking and improvement in diet during pregnancy (Olds, Henderson, & Tatelbaum, 1994a, 1994b), (b) abuse and neglect of the child at earlier phases (Olds et al., 1986; Olds, Henderson, & Kitzman, 1994; Olds et al., 1995), and (c) rates of subsequent children, welfare dependence, and economic self-sufficiency measured in the first 4 years after delivery of the first child (Olds et al., 1988; Olds et al., 1993).

The second study consisted of an urban replication of the Elmira trial conducted in Memphis, Tennessee. The Memphis trial was designed to find out whether the promising effects of the Elmira program could be replicated with a large sample of low-income African American families living in a major urban area when the program was carried out through an existing health department. The program recruited 1,138 women who were less than 29 weeks pregnant from the obstetrical clinic at the Regional Medical Center in Memphis, Tennessee. Of these women, 92% were African American, 97% were unmarried, 65% were 18 or younger at registration, 85% came from households with incomes at or below the federal poverty guidelines, and 22% smoked cigarettes at registration. These women were randomized to receive either (a) home visitation plus transportation for prenatal care and developmental screening for their children at 6, 12, and 24 months of age or (b) transportation for prenatal care and developmental screening alone. We are currently conducting a 5-year follow-up of the families in the Memphis trial to determine the long-term effects in that community. At the time that this chapter was written, the findings from the Memphis trial had not been published, although it is safe to say that many of the most important findings from the Elmira trial were replicated and, in some cases, extended and refined (Olds, 1995).

The third study was undertaken in Denver with support from the Colorado Trust. The Denver trial is designed to determine the extent to which the positive results produced by nurse home visitors can be reproduced with paraprofessional home visitors. This study was motivated by the observation that although many home visitation programs are staffed by visitors who often reside in the communities they serve and who have no professional training in health or human services, there is no good scientific evidence of the efficacy of this approach (Olds & Kitzman, 1990, 1993). The Denver trial has enrolled 736 pregnant women. Of these, 45% are Mexican American, 35% European American, 16% African American, and 4% Asian or American Indian. All either receive Medicaid or have no private health insurance, 84% are unmarried, and 30% smoked cigarettes at registration during pregnancy. They have been randomly assigned to one of three treatment conditions: (a) paraprofessional home visitation, (b) nurse home visitation, or (c) comparison services. Families in all three groups are provided sensory and developmental services for the children at 6, 15, and 24 months of age. Suspected problems are referred for further clinical evaluations and treatment. The nurse and paraprofessional visitors in each program follow essentially the same program protocol that was developed in Elmira and refined in Memphis.

Programmatic Dissemination Efforts

As data accumulate that this program of prenatal and early childhood home visitation can improve the outcomes of pregnancy and the quality of parental caregiving (and children's corresponding health and development), as well as mothers' own personal development, we have begun to lay the groundwork for disseminating the program in new settings. Legitimate questions can be raised, however, about the extent to which results from randomized trials can be used to predict results from programs that are scaled up on the basis of such experiments. Replicated programs often fail to adequately resemble the models on which they were based. Consequently, effectiveness may, and frequently does, fall short of expectations. Compromising the model in the process of replicating or institutionalizing it is apt to compromise its performance (Blakely et al., 1987). In light of these experiences and observations, we have begun a series of new research-related activities to strengthen the applicability of our findings for policy and program planners.

Studies of Program Dissemination

In the winter of 1994-1995, we were approached by leaders in the U.S. Department of Justice about disseminating our program to some of its "Operation Weed and Seed" sites. Operation Weed and Seed is a multiagency strategy that attempts to "weed out" violent crime, gang, and drug activity in targeted high-crime neighborhoods and then "seed" the area by restoring these neighborhoods through social and economic revitalization.

Our program was selected for dissemination in selected Weed and Seed sites because of its scientific foundations, its effects on child maltreatment and welfare dependence, and its potential for reducing the rates of delinquency, crime, and violence among children as they mature (Olds, Pettitt, et al., in press). We accepted the invitation from the staff of Operation Weed and Seed because it will give us an opportunity to study the dissemination process and thus learn how to help new communities develop a successful replication. A grant to provide training and technical assistance to Weed and Seed sites was awarded in the winter of 1995-1996.

In the Weed and Seed initiative, we are not conducting additional randomized trials but we are instead conducting process studies. These inquiries will enable us to explore those factors at the levels of communities, organizations, staffs, and populations served that influence how effectively the program is carried out in accordance with the original program model. Given that many programs lose their vitality once they are institutionalized, we hope to learn something about what it will take to maintain that vitality, including the influence of our own role as developers of the model and coordinators of the dissemination.

Conclusions

Evidence from our series of trials now indicates that it is possible to improve the outcomes of pregnancy and early child rearing and to reduce the risks for welfare dependence, conduct disorder, and violence with this program of prenatal and early childhood home visitation. Although the program described here is expensive, evidence indicates that the long-term costs to government of failing to provide these services exceed the initial investment in the service.

One of our next challenges is to understand how to scale up this program so that it might be carried out in many more settings while preserving the vitality and essential elements of the original model.

References

Ainsworth, M. D. S. (1979). Attachment as related to mother-infant interaction. In J. S. Rosenblatt, R. A. Hinde, C. Beer, & M. Busnel (Eds.), *Advances in the study of behavior* (Vol. 9). New York: Academic Press.

Bandura, A. (1977). Self-efficacy: Toward a unifying theory of behavioral change. *Psychological Review, 84*, 191-215.

Bandura, A. (1982). Self-efficacy mechanism in human agency. *American Journal of Psychology, 37*, 122-147.

Barnard, K. E. (1979). *Nursing child assessment satellite teaching manual.* Seattle: University of Washington.

Blakely, C. H., Mayer, J. P., Gottschalk, R. G., Schmitt, N., Davidson, W. S., Roitman, D. B., & Emshoff, J. G. (1987). The fidelity-adaptation debate: Implications for the implementation of Public Sector Social Program. *American Journal of Community Psychology, 15*, 253-268.

Bowlby, J. (1969). *Attachment and loss: Vol. 1. Attachment.* New York: Basic Books.

Brazelton, T. B. (1973). Neonatal Behavioral Assessment Scale. *Clinics in Developmental Medicine, 50*, Philadelphia, PA: Lippincott.

Bronfenbrenner, U. (1979). *The ecology of human development: Experiments by nature and design.* Cambridge, MA: Harvard University Press.

Bronfenbrenner, U. (1992). *The process-person-context model in developmental research principles, applications, and implications.* Unpublished manuscript, Cornell University, Ithaca, NY.

Carlson, E. A., & Sroufe, L. A. (1995). Contribution of attachment theory to developmental psychopathology. In D. Cicchetti & D. J. Cohen (Eds.), *Developmental psychopathology: Vol. 1. Theory and method.* New York: John Wiley.

Chaikind, S., & Corman, H. (1991). The impact of low birthweight on special education costs. *Journal of Health Economics, 10*, 291-311.

Children's Defense Fund. (1992). *The state of America's children.* Washington, DC: Author.

Combs-Orme, T., Reis, J., & Ward, L. D. (1985). Effectiveness of home visits by public health nurses in maternal and child health: An empirical review. *Public Health Reports, 100*, 490-499.

Daro, D., & McCurdy, K. (1990). *Current trends in abuse reporting and fatalities: The results of the 1990 annual fifty-state survey.* Chicago: National Committee for the Prevention of Child Abuse.

Dolezal, S., Butterfield, P. M., & Grimshaw, J. (1994). *Listen, listen, listen: A curriculum for partners in parenting education.* Denver, CO: Read Your Baby.

Furstenberg, F. F., Brooks-Gunn, J., & Morgan, S. P. (1987). *Adolescent mothers in later life.* New York: Cambridge University Press.

Haley, J. (1991). *Problem-solving therapy* (2nd ed.). San Francisco, CA: Jossey-Bass.

Kramer, M. S. (1987). Intrauterine growth and gestational duration determinants. *Pediatrics, 80,* 502-511.

Main, M., Kaplan, N., & Cassidy, J. (1985). Security in infancy, childhood, and adulthood: A move to the level of representation. In I. Bretherton & E. Waters (Eds.), *Growing points of attachment theory and research. Monographs of the Society for Research in Child Development, 50*(1-2, Serial No. 209), 66-104.

National Center for Health Statistics. (1991). Advance report of final mortality statistics 1991. *Vital statistics of the United States* (Vol. 1). Washington, DC: U.S. Department of Health and Human Services.

O'Brien, R. A., & Baca, R. P. (in press). Application of solution focused interventions to nurse home visitation for pregnant women and parents of young children. *Journal of Community Psychology.*

Olds, D. (1980). Improving formal services for mothers and children. In J. Garbarino and S. G. Stocking (Eds.), *Protecting children from abuse and neglect.* San Francisco: Jossey-Bass.

Olds, D. (1991). The prenatal/early infancy project: An ecological approach to prevention. In J. Belsky (Ed.), *In the beginning: Readings in infancy.* New York: Columbia University Press.

Olds, D. (1995, May). *Effect of home visitation by nurses on caregiving and maternal life-course.* Paper presented at the 35th annual meeting of the Ambulatory Pediatric Association, San Diego, CA.

Olds, D. L., Henderson, C. R., & Kitzman, H. (1994). Does prenatal and infancy nurse home visitation have enduring effects on qualities of parental caregiving and child health and 25 to 50 months of life? *Pediatrics, 93,* 89-98.

Olds, D., Henderson, C. R., Kitzman, H., & Cole, R. (1995). Effects of prenatal and infancy nurse home visitation on surveillance of child maltreatment. *Pediatrics, 95,* 365-372.

Olds, D. L., Henderson, C. R., Phelps, C., Kitzman, H., & Hanks, C. (1993). Effect of prenatal and infancy nurse home visitation on government spending. *Medical Care, 3,* 1-20.

Olds, D. L., Henderson, C. R., & Tatelbaum, R. (1994a). Intellectual impairment in children of women who smoke cigarettes during pregnancy. *Pediatrics, 93,* 221-227.

Olds, D. L., Henderson, C. R., & Tatelbaum, R. (1994b). Prevention of intellectual impairment in children of women who smoke cigarettes during pregnancy. *Pediatrics, 93,* 228-233.

Olds, D. L., Henderson, C. R., Tatelbaum, R., & Chamberlin, R. (1986). Preventing child abuse and neglect: A randomized trial of nurse home visitation. *Pediatrics, 78,* 65-78.

Olds, D. L., Henderson, C. R., Tatelbaum, R., & Chamberlin, R. (1988). Improving the life-course development of socially disadvantaged mothers: A randomized trial of nurse home visitation. *Pediatrics, 77,* 16-28.

Olds, D. L., & Kitzman, H. (1990). Can home visitation improve the health of women and children at environmental risk? *Pediatrics, 86,* 108-116.

Olds, D. L., & Kitzman, H. (1993). Review of research on home visiting. *The Future of Children, 3*(4), 51-92

Olds, D. L., Kitzman, H., Cole, R. C., & Robinson, J. (in press). Theoretical and empirical foundations of a program of home visitation for pregnant women and parents of young children. *Journal of Community Psychology.*

Olds, D. L., Pettitt, L. M., Robinson, J., Eckenrode, J., Kitzman, H., Cole, R. C., & Powers, J. (in press). Reducing risks for antisocial behavior with a program of prenatal and early childhood home visitation. *Journal of Community Psychology.*

Raine, A., Brennan, P., & Mednick, S. A. (1994). Birth complications combined with early maternal rejection at age 1 year predispose to violent crime at age 18 years. *Archives of General Psychiatry, 51,* 984-988.

Sparling, J., & Lewis, I. (1984). *Learning games for the first three years: A guide to parent-child play.* New York: Berkley.

U.S. Advisory Board on Child Abuse and Neglect. (1990). *Child abuse and neglect: Critical first steps in response to a national emergency.* Washington, DC: Government Printing Office.

Wasik, B. H., Bryant, D. M., Ramey, C. T., & Sparling, J. J. (1992). Mediating variables: Maternal problem solving. In R. T. Gross, D. Spiker, & C. Hayes (Eds.), *The infant health and development program.* Palo Alto, CA: Stanford University Press.

Weitzman, M., Gortmaker, S., & Sobol, A. (1992). Maternal smoking and behavior problems of children. *Pediatrics, 90,* 342-349.

CHAPTER 4

Early Intervention for High-Risk Families: Reflecting on a 20-Year-Old Model

GRACE-ANN CARUSO WHITNEY

In this chapter, I will discuss the practical importance and theoretical significance of early intervention. I will use the term *early intervention* to include a variety of supportive services to young families including home visits, infant stimulation and child care instruction, resource information, and tangible aid to families determined by using broadly defining criteria of need to be at risk. In particular, I will describe in detail the Optimum Growth Project, an early intervention program that operated from 1977 through 1986, serving young families in southern Palm Beach County, Florida. Optimum Growth was funded by the State of Florida Mental Health Program Office and was designed as a 6-year research and demonstration project to provide prenatal care and infant stimulation instruction, community resource information, and general family support to low income and teen mothers through regular home visitation until the target child reached age 6. I will describe the program's history and methodology and its evaluated impact on the lives of participants as well as on the broader community. I will describe how, through the efforts of a skilled, dedicated, and adventurous team of colleagues, a substantial cohort of children and families in the project community experienced fewer incidents of reported maltreatment, foster placement, and immediate recurrent births as well as better school performance and greater personal growth.

The results of the Optimum Growth Project, as well as other programs using this model, are important to consider. In a practical sense, these results are significant for policymakers and human services providers because they illustrate how the provision of services while children and families are still young can prevent the need for more costly services later on. In other words, they demonstrate that prevention in early childhood works! Individual growth and family health and stability are promoted, thus saving millions of dollars in medical care, special education, and treatment. Especially when resources are scarce, the development of policies and programs that are efficient and effective has very practical benefits because they have the potential to decrease overall tax spending on social programs and prevent the loss of valuable tax revenue from the gainful employment of parents in the short term and of their children in the long term.

Early intervention services have important humanitarian benefits as well. When preventive efforts enhance the quality of life for children and families, unnecessary challenge and despair are avoided and greater human potential is achieved. Children develop physically, mentally, and socioemotionally in environments that promote and support their growth. Adolescents and young adults develop as parents and contributing members of neighborhoods, schools, and communities, receiving the support necessary for personal growth as they support the development of their families. Program participants, professionals, and taxpayers all reap the rewards of success.

Conceptual Framework

Theoretically, we now understand more clearly the importance of early intervention and both the short-term and long-range benefits to children and families when provided with a variety of preventive services. Advances in theoretical conceptualizations such as the ecological perspective (Bronfenbrenner, 1977, 1995) and the transactional model (Sameroff, 1993) have expanded our grasp of the breadth of factors associated with the development of each child and remind us that the interactions among individual and environmental factors are complex and ongoing. Furthermore, organization of the myriad factors influencing development within a framework of risk conditions and protective factors has led to a clearer picture of clusters of risks associated with particular developmental outcomes and has begun to suggest variations in the processes by which they influence the developmental course (Garbarino & Abramowitz, 1992; Rutter, Champion, Quinton, Maughan, & Pickles, 1995; Zeanah, 1993). These findings lead to more informed preventive efforts. Likewise, studies of protective factors, such as preventive interventions themselves, provide empirical support for particular strategies—for example, that extended home visitation can prevent physical abuse and neglect among families with single parents, teen parents, and poverty (MacMillan, MacMillan, & Offord, 1992, cited in Mrazek, 1993). This outcome was certainly suggested in earlier work with Optimum Growth. Thus, theoretical and empirical advances now provide more elaborated support for the importance of early intervention with young families.

Previous Pertinent Research

In the early 1970s, when Optimum Growth was originally conceived, efforts were being pioneered to promote healthy growth by preventing the impact of debilitating effects even from birth. Meier (1973) had pointed to the prevalence of mental retardation in rural and urban poor populations. Any interventions, it was suggested, needed to be early; interventions begun at 3 or 4 years were really remedial in nature and not preventive (Meier, 1973; Weikert, 1967). Researchers continued to expand on the work of Bowlby (1953) concerning the importance of the quality of the mother-infant dyad in the development of the infant and how early lack of stimulation or disturbances of mothering could produce long-lasting detrimental effects. Lichtenberg and Norton (1970) emphasized that intervening with the parent who is the central agent in the life of the child was of key importance in affecting the child. Although Head Start was demonstrating significant contributions in detecting delays and disabilities and in enhancing school readiness for children ages 3 to 5, several studies had begun to show that gains may not persist, that lack of earlier intervention could result in irreversible deficits, that continuing care over an extended period would be most beneficial, and that parent involvement was essential in intervention efforts.

The late Ira Gordon was influential at the start of the program as well (Gordon, 1970, 1974). Gordon and his colleagues at the University of Florida served as consultants in the early years of the program. Gordon's own work focused on exploring the impact of mothering on intellectual development as he worked to conceptualize the "social roots of competence." Gordon developed the curriculum of infant stimulation tasks that was at the heart of the Optimum Growth model.

Thus, the Optimum Growth model was conceived. The goal of the program was to intervene into the environment of children from birth to 6 years to alter conditions believed to cause or correlate highly with mental, emotional, and physical delays and disabilities. Specific program objectives included enhancing mental and motor development of target children through infant stimulation instruction, preventing immediate recurrent births and child abuse and neglect, and promoting mothers' returning to school or work. In addition to having an impact on families and children, the program sought to influence project staff who were indigenous to the community being served by encouraging their career development and to influence the broader community by providing baseline data for planning of services to children and families, by identifying needed services, and by aiding the development of these services.

Description of the Initiative

Methods

Participants

Women in their third trimester of pregnancy who were receiving prenatal care at a local public health clinic between 1975 and 1978 served as participants in the program. Staff contacted potential participants at their homes to explain the program and invite participation. Women resided in the three adjacent cities comprising the catchment area of the public health clinic and were assigned to treatment and comparison groups based on their city of residence. Those residing in the city in which the program office was located were assigned to the treatment group. The three cities were judged to be sufficiently similar for comparison, and when participants in treatment and comparison groups were compared on a variety of demographic variables, they were found to be statistically similar in ethnicity, marital status, and relative frequency of mothers under age 16 at the time of the target child's birth. However, mothers in the comparison group were somewhat younger overall. A detailed discussion of sample selection and characteristics can be found in Caruso (1989). Demographic data for treatment and comparison groups appear in Table 4.1.

The program employed staff who were indigenous to the target community. All possessed high school degrees and either postsecondary education or prior work experience in the field of early childhood. The sponsoring agency provided extensive preservice and in-service training to all staff.

Materials

At the heart of the program was the infant stimulation curriculum made up of developmentally sequential tasks and exercises for children birth through 3 years. A single sheet of paper contained an illustration, rationale, and instructions for individual tasks presented by staff at each visit. Prenatal tasks and activities for older children were added to the curriculum by Optimum Growth staff. Several examples from the curriculum appear in Table 4.2.

The mental and motor scales of the Bayley Scales of Infant Development (Bayley, 1969) were used to assess developmental progress. This tool is standardized and widely used for assessing general development up to 30 months. At follow-up, when children were 6 years old, the local public school system's Kindergarten Checklist, which reflects task mastery at the middle and end of the kindergarten year, was used as a developmental measure. The checklist consists of 69 tasks grouped into four skill areas of motor skills, visual skills, auditory skills, and environmental awareness.

An in-house survey, the Initial Home Visit Report, was used to gather descriptive data at enrollment, and a modified version of the survey, the Follow-up Home Visit Report, was used to obtain updated information at age 6. During the first 3 years of the

Table 4.1 Preliminary Results: Demographic Characteristics
of Participants

	Treatment Group (n = 171)	Comparison Group (n = 91)
Ethnic group		
Black	147 (86%)	73 (80%)
White	11 (6%)	6 (7%)
Hispanic	12 (7%)	11 (12%)
Other	1 (1%)	1 (1%)
Age at time of target child's birth		
Under 16	20 (12%)	6 (7%)
16-19 years	63 (37%)	50 (55%)
Over 19	88 (51%)	35 (38%)
Marital status		
Married	44 (26%)	22 (24%)
Unmarried	127 (74%)	69 (76%)

SOURCE: Burden and Krehbiel (1978).

program, an additional survey employing a multiple choice format, the Home Visit Report, was completed after each home visit to record staff observations of mother-infant interaction during the visit. In addition, staff shared information on various topics of interest by distributing local agency brochures and commercial pamphlets.

Procedures

Treatment and comparison group participants were contacted in their homes and offered program services. Participants in both groups completed the Initial Home Visit Report and agreed to periodic developmental assessment of the target child at 12, 18, and 24 months of age. Participants understood they would be contacted again when the target child completed kindergarten to obtain permission to access school records and to complete the Follow-up Home Visit Report. In addition, treatment group participants agreed to receive regular home visits during which they would

Table 4.2 A Selection of Prenatal and Infant Stimulation Tasks

Prenatal	Hygiene during pregnancy
	Development of fetus
	Making toys for infants
0-3 months	Holding the baby for better looking at things
	Holding the baby in a comforting way
	Calming by touching
3-6 months	Looking and touching
	Helping the baby to see talking
	Helping the baby to hold his or her head up
6-12 months	Talking to a mirror image
	Sitting with toys
	Pointing to and naming objects
12-18 months	Reading with simple rhymes
	Using crayons
	Getting familiar objects
18-24 months	Finding my house
	Feeding the doll
	Two-word phrases

receive infant stimulation instruction and information on child care and community resources.

An assigned mental health worker, who maintained a supportive relationship with the family over time, made regular visits to the participant's home. These visits were 30 to 45 minutes long and were made according to a set schedule as follows: weekly during pregnancy and until the target child's first birthday; biweekly until the child was 2; and on an as-needed basis, usually monthly, up to 3 years old, at which time contacts continued as needed but, usually, twice a year. Visits could be made more often, temporarily, if a particular need arose.

Staff presented a task from the infant stimulation curriculum during each visit. Staff would model the task, ask the parent to practice the task, and discuss the task during the home visit. Parents were then asked to repeat the task until the next home visit. In addition, during the visit, staff would tune in to any concerns the parent raised that might affect the functioning of the home and provide general support and a referral if required. Often a non-judgmental listener was all that was needed, but staff were knowledgeable regarding community agency services should referrals need to be made. Discipline was frequently an issue raised by parents.

As target children got older and frequency of visits waned, parents could choose to continue more frequent contact by participating in various group activities that were jointly planned by parents and staff. Children's groups would meet biweekly in a parent's home to provide group experiences for 3- and 4-year-olds. These children's groups were typically neighborhood based and involved no more than five children. Parent groups, which served as informal support networks and which any participant could attend, were held weekly at the program office. These groups focused on various topics of interest to parents. Typically, however, both group attendance and scheduling were sporadic.

Studies of Effectiveness

Preliminary Results: 1980

Preliminary findings were tabulated by Burden and Krehbiel (1978) and reported in the program application for the 1980 Lela Rowland Prevention Award. This preliminary analysis involved comparing treatment and comparison groups on five variables, including scores on the Bayley Scales of Infant Development, reports of child maltreatment resulting in removal from the home, number of recurrent births prior to target child reaching 18 months, number of mothers returning to school, and number of mothers returning to work. Results are presented in Table 4.3.

A statistical comparison of data was not calculated, and because original data were unavailable later, further analysis was not attempted. However, results are in the direction expected and are suggestive of positive impact.

In the report of preliminary findings, a regression analysis showed no significant difference between the two children's groups on the Bayley scores that were related to the variables of income of

Table 4.3 Preliminary Comparison of Groups (in percentages)

	Treatment Group	Comparison Group
	(n = 171)	(n = 91)
Bayley scores below 100	2.11	18.68
Child abuse and neglect	.53	7.70
Recurrent birth within 18 months	2.11	12.09
Mothers returning to school	13.68	9.90
Mothers returning to work	42.63	31.87

SOURCE: Burden and Krehbiel (1978).

mothers, educational level of mothers, and birth order of the child. Some major differences were found between groups on the Bayley scores of those children in the treatment group having mothers 19 years old and under (Burden & Krehbiel, 1978).

The pre- and postcomparison of the eight items on the Home Visit Report for the group receiving treatment showed a gain on all but two items for all parents having target children at least 9 months old. The two items that did not show gains were related to the mother's ability to interact spontaneously with the child. It was thought that the low priority given to physical and verbal play between adult and infant by the target population influenced the emergence of this behavior.

Preliminary results also included an evaluation of impact on the broader community. With respect to impact on indigenous staff, four of the original staff pursued further education through college courses in education and early childhood. The rising number of referrals for program services in the community served as evidence of the positive regard for Optimum Growth among service agencies. After research group assignments ceased in 1978, the program continued to enroll families solely on a service need basis. The number of referrals steadily rose.

Trends such as this and preliminary results demonstrating the low incidence of reported child abuse and neglect in the treatment group served to support the receipt of a 3-year grant from the National Center on Child Abuse and Neglect in 1978 to expand Optimum Growth services to underserved areas of a housing project and to migrant farmworker camps. Optimum Growth was recognized by the National Council of Community Mental Health Centers to receive the Minority Program Award in 1979. Staff had begun to provide consultation and education to parenting programs and community agencies within and outside of the state.

Final Results: 1986

By 1980, the Optimum Growth Project had evolved into a comprehensive family support program serving a wide variety of families with at least one child under 6 referred for or seeking services. The program served the entire catchment area of the mental health center, maintaining an active caseload of over 300 families and enrolling about 150 new families each year. In contrast to earlier years, families now entering the program had more extensive needs and thus often required coordination of efforts with child protective services, medical clinics, special education programs, spouse abuse services, mental health resources, and others. Services were provided using a family case management model built around the core concept of developmentally appropriate stimulation for children. The original infant stimulation curriculum remained an important component of services, and parts of it were translated into Spanish and Haitian Creole. Although Optimum Growth changed substantially from the original research design for families enrolled after 1978, families in the original treatment and comparison groups continued to receive services according to the original design, receiving visits according to the established schedule and being contacted at follow-up for collection of data as required.

Data on families in the research component were reviewed, and three cohorts of project children were established: those completing kindergarten in the Spring of 1981, 1982, and 1983. Of the 262 families included in the preliminary evaluation, 205 families had children who, according to their dates of birth, were of age to complete kindergarten during these years. Of the 205 families (125 in the treatment group and 80 in the comparison group) 110 were successfully contacted (66 in the treatment group and 44 in the comparison group). Thus, 53% of the treatment group and 55% of the comparison group were contacted for follow-up. Demographic characteristics of families included in the final evaluation appear in Table 4.4.

The two groups were found to be statistically similar with respect to ethnicity, age at birth of target child, marital status, and sex of target child. For the final evaluation, the treatment and comparison groups were compared on the following variables: number of target children promoted to grade 1 at the completion of the kindergarten year, mean total scores on the Kindergarten Checklist, number reported for child maltreatment, number of mothers receiving further education or training after the birth of the target child, and number of mothers employed outside the home at follow-up. The results of the final evaluation appear in Table 4.5.

As were findings at the time of the preliminary comparison, results of the final evaluation are in the direction expected, suggesting positive impact. Children in the treatment group were more likely to be promoted to grade 1 and had a higher group mean score on the Kindergarten Checklist, a measure of skill mastery. None of the families in the treatment group had been reported for child abuse or neglect, compared to just over 14% of families in the comparison group. This difference was found to be statistically significant using the chi-square statistic and substituting a frequency of 1 in the empty treatment group cell ($\chi^2 = 6.33, p < .02$). Five families in the comparison group had been reported for child maltreatment, and three children had been removed and placed outside the home. More mothers in the treatment group than in the comparison group had received further education since the target child's birth and were employed outside the home at follow-up. Although all group differences were calculated using the chi-square statistic, the group difference on reported child maltreatment was the only variable to reach statistical significance.

A multiple regression analysis using the child's Kindergarten Checklist score as the dependent variable and group (treatment versus comparison), gender of child, child's preschool participation, age of mother at target child's birth, and mother's educational attainment as independent variables resulted in mother's education being the only significant predictor. When treatment and comparison groups were compared using a separate variance t test no difference was found for mother's education as measured by last grade completed. Simple correlations computed for checklist scores

Table 4.4 Follow-up: Demographic Characteristics of Participants (in percentages)

	Treatment Group (n = 66)	Comparison Group (n = 44)
Ethnic group		
Black	93.3	92.7
White	0.0	2.4
Hispanic	1.6	4.9
Other	3.1	0.0
Mother's age at target child's birth		
Under 16	17.2	9.8
16-19 years	32.8	29.2
Over 19	50.0	61.0
Mother's marital status		
Married	33.0	30.0
Unmarried	67.0	70.0
Target child's sex		
Male	48.4	61.0
Female	51.6	39.0

and mother's education did differ: for the treatment group $r = .36$ ($p < .01$) and for the comparison group $r = .10$ (n.s.).

That the prevention of child abuse and neglect was a clear and persistent impact of the program is illustrated by both preliminary and final evaluation results. Children in the treatment group were less likely to be reported as victims of child maltreatment. Although no significance test was made at the time of the preliminary evaluation, data indicate a dramatic difference between groups at that time (.53% for the treatment group and 7.70% for the comparison group), and findings at follow-up when the target children were 6 years old were found to be statistically significant. These data suggest that for low-income and teen parents served by the program, home-based early intervention involving regular infant stimulation, child care instruction, and general family support was an effective child abuse prevention strategy. Recent literature

Table 4.5 Follow-up: Results at Age 6 (in percentages)

	Treatment Group (n = 66)	Comparison Group (n = 44)
Promoted to Grade 1	78.1	73.2
	(n = 66)	(n = 44)
Kindergarten checklist means	81.6	77.5
	(SD = 18.0)	(SD = 18.5)
	(n = 64)	(n = 41)
Absence of maltreatment	100.0	85.7
	(n = 63)	(n = 35)
Additional education of mothers	43.1	39.5
	(n = 58)	(n = 38)
Gainful employment of mothers	58.6	48.7
	(n = 58)	(n = 37)

reports similar results (Behrman, 1993). Further efforts should be made to follow samples to determine whether this impact persists through middle childhood and adolescence.

Although treatment group children were more likely to be promoted to first grade and to score higher on the Kindergarten Checklist, a measure of skill mastery, final results relating to child performance were not dramatic nor were group differences on the variables statistically significant. However, at the time of the preliminary evaluation, even though a comparison of group means on the Bayley Scales was not reported in terms of statistical significance, the difference between treatment and comparison groups on child performance was notable. Regular Optimum Growth Project services ended when the target children turned 3, and intervention effects may have "washed out" by the time children entered school. Perhaps more frequent parent contact aimed at intellectual stimulation and adaptive skill development after age 3 and continuing until children entered school would have enhanced children's school performance. It is now more widely accepted that intervention specifically focused on the area of risk (Meisels, Dichtelmiller, & Liaw, 1993) should continue for as long as risk persists

(Sameroff, 1993). Although a number of project families did better overall by the time children entered school, many continued to live in impoverished conditions and at risk for school failure.

Finally, and related to overall family gains, slightly more mothers in the treatment group than in the comparison group had obtained further education and training and were employed outside the home at follow-up. Results were in the direction expected, but this difference was not dramatic nor was it statistically significant. Relationships between groups on these variables seemed to be similar at both preliminary and final evaluation. Although no dramatic long-term impact was found for project mothers regarding education and employment, it was found that treatment group mothers who had furthered their education had children who had higher Kindergarten Checklist scores and were therefore less likely to be retained. Although this association may have occurred by chance, it may also suggest a different response among project families to the intervention. In fact, more recent early intervention research has demonstrated variations in client response (Olds & Kitzman, 1993). This is another area for continued study in contemporary prevention efforts.

In addition to examining effects on children and families, the program aimed to make an impact on program staff and the broader community. In this regard, of the eight mental health technicians originally employed by the program, two received additional education and training in child development and opened much needed neighborhood child care centers in the target community; two obtained teaching degrees and began teaching in the target community in public elementary schools; and two remained in the mental health field in programs serving different populations. In later years, staff generally possessed at least bachelor's degrees and more than half were bilingual.

At the community level, the Optimum Growth Project aimed to identify needed services and aid in their evolution. Thus, project staff and participants engaged in efforts to promote change. Project participants joined parent advisory groups for Head Start centers, public housing projects, and an innovative migrant camp for families. Participants became involved in efforts to make their neighborhoods more safe and family oriented and planned activities for both children and teens. Some participants became involved through attendance at public meetings at which they provided testimony on issues affecting their lives and the welfare of their families.

Staff provided leadership on planning committees and boards of directors to promote the development of needed programs and services. New programs established through the efforts of staff included a crisis nursery program providing emergency shelter for children ages birth to 7 years, a day care program for infants and toddlers located in a public housing project, and a parent center at a local community college that offered a broad range of parent education courses and support groups. New services initiated through the advocacy of staff included transportation and translation services as adjuncts to medical and special education programs and day care services for special needs children within existing child care centers.

Another objective of Optimum Growth at the community level was the provision of baseline data for the planning of services for children and families. The program provided baseline data for the development of child abuse and neglect prevention and treatment programs, a family assistance program for Cuban and Haitian entrants, homemaker and family management services for high risk families, and Chapter I funding for handicapped children. Within Optimum Growth itself, utilization and impact findings from program evaluation activities conducted each year helped to modify project services to meet changing community needs and to remain responsive as new challenges emerged.

The Optimum Growth Project also influenced communities far from its local neighborhoods. Optimum Growth was recognized as a prevention model by Florida, North Carolina, and Ohio and by the National Center on Child Abuse and Neglect. As a result, staff participated on many occasions in mutual sharing with colleagues at conferences and professional meetings. Staff provided consultation toward the development of similar programs to agencies throughout the United States. Four years after the Optimum Growth Project ceased to operate, its model was disseminated by the Florida State Legislature as it again worked to stimulate "new" prevention efforts statewide. Funded by the Ounce of Prevention Fund, a new generation of the model was established in the original target community. In 1991, materials from Optimum Growth were used to train caregivers in a Romanian orphanage. The legacy of Optimum Growth has reached on in many ways.

Cost-Benefit Data

The final evaluation of the impact of the Optimum Growth Project on participating children and families suggested several results that may be discussed in terms of savings to taxpayers. A formal cost-benefit analysis was not done as part of preliminary and final evaluations, but for purposes of present discussion, today's figures can be used to gain some sense of benefits achieved.

One of the variables in the final evaluation was the number of children successfully completing kindergarten and promoted to first grade. The final evaluation showed that fewer children in the treatment group than in the comparison group were retained at the end of the kindergarten year. In 1995 dollars, the cost to taxpayers of one year of education is $4,544 (A. Blood, Budget Department, School Board of Palm Beach County, personal communication, January 26, 1996). By converting results reported in percentages, one might say that 5 fewer children per 100 were retained, thus saving $22,720 per school year for every 100 students.

Another finding in the final evaluation was that fewer children in the treatment group than in the comparison group were reported to be victims of maltreatment and removed from their homes. It is estimated that in FY1995-1996, one year of protective supervision in response to a report of maltreatment costs $13,200 per child and $28,800 per family, based on a 2.24 person family size (Donna Newsome, Florida Department of Health and Rehabilitative Services, Palm Beach County, personal communication, February 6, 1995.) In addition, in FY1995-1996, the cost per year of foster home placement ranged from $3,684 for Level 1 care to $4,128 for Level 3 care per child under 12 years. For therapeutic foster care, the yearly cost was $7,260 per child, and group residential care was $16,740 per child per year (Becky Walker and Donna Newsome, Florida Department of Health and Rehabilitative Services, Palm Beach County, personal communication, February 6, 1996.) The level of out-of-home care is fixed by the needs of the child at the time of placement. By converting evaluation results reported as percentages, 14 children per 100 were reported as victims of maltreatment and 9 per 100 were removed from their homes and placed in out-of-home care as compared to none in the treatment group. Thus, the cost of a year of protective supervision might be calculated at $66,000 for five children who were reported but remained at home, or $144,000 for five families. Depending on the level of care required by the children who were removed from their homes, using today's figures with converted estimates of need, cost to taxpayers for out-of-home care might range from $33,156 per year if all nine children were placed in Level 1 foster care to $150,660 for all nine children if group residential placements were needed, although it is more likely that needs would require some combination of levels of service. Over all, average length of stay in out-of-home care is approximately 2.5 years until adoption is arranged.

These figures must be used with caution because they are taken out of temporal context. Also, figures are unavailable to determine the cost of operating the Optimum Growth Project because costs for services to research families were included in budgets for the expanded program and would be impossible to resurrect after so much time has passed. These figures can be informative, however, as the kind of indicators that might be used today to assess tax dollars saved. Other data to examine, but unavailable for this discussion, include cost per year of counseling and other treatment services that often accompany protective supervision, foster home, and group residential care when maltreatment has occurred. Figures on tax dollars earned in future years as the result of mothers returning to school and work would also be useful. Furthermore, extending cost-benefit analysis to include the more humanitarian benefits of prevention will surely enhance the overall discussion.

Closing Summary

The Optimum Growth Project was certainly a pioneering effort of its originators both because of its model and because its creators chose to measure what the model might do. In hindsight, the evaluation and even the model seem primitive in comparison to what we now have available regarding serving high-risk families and promoting optimal development in early life. Whole volumes are now available on home visiting as a preventive strategy and its use with a wide range of families in need (e.g., Behrman, 1993). Programs have become more specialized as they have become more varied in the services they offer to meet individual needs, be they in medical, social welfare, education, or mental health settings, and it is more clearly understood that to have an impact on both children and parents, programs must have substantial child- and family-focused components (Meisels, Dichtelmiller, & Liaw, 1993) and that gains are more likely to persist when supports continue for as long as risks remain. Optimum Growth opened doors for children, parents, and professionals working together to discover how early development might be enhanced. It is important that this search continue.

References

Bayley, N. (1969). *Bayley Scales of Infant Development.* New York: Psychological Corporation.

Behrman, R. E. (Ed.). (1993, Winter). *Home visiting: The future of children.* Los Angeles: David and Lucile Packard Foundation.

Bowlby, J. (1953). *Child care and the growth of love.* New York: Penguin.

Bronfenbrenner, U. (1977). Toward an experimental ecology of human development. *American Psychologist, 32,* 513-531.

Bronfenbrenner, U. (1995). Developmental ecology through space and time: A future perspective. In P. Moen, G. Elder, Jr., & K. Luscher (Eds.), *Examining lives in context: Perspectives on the ecology of human development* (pp. 619-647). Washington, DC: American Psychological Association.

Burden, T. M., & Krehbiel, S. (1978, August). *Optimum Growth Project: A primary prevention program in a community mental health center.* Paper presented at the meeting of the American Psychiatric Association, Atlanta, GA.

Caruso, G. L. (1989). Optimum Growth Project: Support for families with young children. *Prevention in Human Services, 16,* 123-139.

Garbarino, J., & Abramowitz, R. H. (1992). Sociocultural risk and opportunity. In J. Garbarino (Ed.), *Children and families in the social environment* (pp. 35-70). New York: Aldine De Gruyter.

Gordon, I. J. (1970). *Baby learning through baby play.* New York: St. Martin's.

Gordon, I. J. (1974). *An investigation into the social roots of competence* (Final report to the National Institute of Mental Health). Gainesville, FL: University of Florida.

Lichtenberg, P., & Norton, D. G. (1970). *Cognitive and mental development in the first five years of life* (NIMH Public Health Service Publication No. 2057. Washington, DC: National Institute of Mental Health.

Meier, J. (1973). *Screening and assessment of young children at developmental risk.* Washington, DC: Department of Health, Education and Welfare.

Meisels, S. J., Dichtelmiller, M., & Liaw, F. (1993). A multidimensional analysis of early childhood intervention programs. In C. H. Zeanah, Jr. (Ed.), *Handbook of infant mental health* (pp. 361-385). New York: Guilford.

Mrazek, P. J. (1993). Maltreatment and infant development. In C. H. Zeanah, Jr. (Ed.). *Handbook of infant mental health* (pp. 159-170). New York: Guilford.

Olds, D. L., & Kitzman, H. (1995). Review of research on home visiting for pregnant women and parents of young children. In R. E. Behrman (Ed.), *Home visiting, the future of children* (pp. 55-92). Los Angeles: David and Lucile Packard Foundation.

Rutter, M., Champion, L., Quinton, D., Maughan, B., & Pickles, A. (1995). Understanding individual differences in environmental-risk exposure. In P. Moen, G. H. Elder, Jr., & K. Luscher (Eds.), *Examining lives in context: Perspectives on the ecology of human development* (pp. 61-93). Washington, DC: American Psychological Association.

Sameroff, A. J. (1993). Models of development and developmental risk. In C. H. Zeanah, Jr. (Ed.), *Handbook of infant mental health* (pp. 1-13). New York: Guilford.

Weikert, D. P. (1967). Preschool programs: Preliminary findings. *Journal of Special Education, 1,* 163-182.

Zeanah, C. H., Jr. (Ed.). (1993). *Handbook of infant mental health.* New York: Guilford.

• CHAPTER 5 •

Infant-Family Resource Program

ELSIE R. BROUSSARD

The magnitude of psychosocial disorder and the resultant disruption to family life and cost to industry has been well documented (Anderson, Williams, McGee & Silva, 1987; Leighton et al., 1963; Maier, Lichtermann, Klinger, Heun, & Hallmayer 1992; Regier et al., 1988; Zimmerman & Coryell, 1989). About 5 million Americans experience severe mental disorders in a 1-year period. The estimated cost of treatment is 20 billion annually, with an additional 7 billion in nursing home costs (Health Care Reform, 1993). It is incumbent on us to seek ways to reduce the magnitude of the problems.

AUTHOR'S NOTE: The author wishes to express her appreciation to the following individuals who were involved in various aspects of the interventions: Evelyn Atreya, Marilyn Bushey, Katherine Cone, Cleon Cornes, Deborah Dickey, Karen Fullerton, Margaret Gillick, Ruth Gumerman, Linda Haller, Fredricka Latshaw, Margaret McFarland, Mary Meldrum, Geraldine Rensko, Judith Rubin, Alba Ruckert, Lawrence Staab, Claudia Titelman, Linda White, Robin Woods, and Lucy Zabarenko.

Funding for the program has come from a variety of sources. These include state, local and national levels of government, private donations, the University of Pittsburgh, and the following foundations: Buhl, Staunton-Farm, Claude Benedum, Howard Heinz, Vira Heinz, Pittsburgh, Pittsburgh Child Guidance Center, De-Luxe Check Printers, Amelia Miles, Pittsburgh National Bank Trust, and Stylette Plastics. Without their assistance our work would not have been possible.

Reprints may be obtained from Elsie R. Broussard, Department of Health Services Administration, Graduate School of Public Health, 209 Parran Hall, University of Pittsburgh, Pittsburgh, PA 15261.

The primary goal of the Infant-Family Resource Program (IFRP) is to facilitate optimal development of infants and their families and reduce the incidence of psychosocial disorder (through a multi-faceted approach of basic research, preventive-intervention services to infants and families, and education and consultation for health professionals). The long-range goals are dedicated to enhancing the quality of life in the home and workplace.

Conceptual Framework

When we think of the many things that happen to infants and their families during the long developmental process, *all* infants are at risk. Any number of intervening life variables can interfere with progressive development at any point along the way. Although not all problems go back to earliest infancy, the most severe do seem to. There is general consensus among professionals that the foundations for the ability to love (the bonds of attachment) and for the ability to learn (cognitive development) are rooted in the first 18 months of life. Thus, we increasingly move in the direction of trying to prevent the development of psychosocial disorder or to minimize its impact through very early identification of those at risk and early intervention.

Childhood is usually portrayed as a happy time—bouncing babies, dimpled cheeks, and the best years of life. Children are expected to reflect for those around them the pleasure of childhood, reflecting to themselves, as they look into the mirror, the joy in the experience of their existence. Yet as we know, not all children experience childhood as happy. Some faces do not reflect joy but, rather, portray what we call "The Sadness of No Smile."

The quality of childhood is learned through the quality of the environment—through human relationships, especially those of infant and mother. Through interaction, mothers function as mirrors for their children, reflecting to their babies from earliest infancy their perception of themselves and of the world around them. Some mothers and babies laugh and smile together, reflecting to each other mutual positive feelings. Other mothers and babies do not experience such positive reflecting. The awareness of these observable differences in mother-infant pairs was the basis of the development of the Broussard Neonatal Perception Inventories (Broussard, 1964).

Within my clinical pediatric work, I served families from a wide variety of socioeconomic levels as well as racially diverse populations. This work suggested that the mother's perception of the neonate was often determined by factors that seemed to come from within her, rather than solely from the actual physical condition of the infant or from other factors such as economics or racial background.

The mother's perception of her newborn seemed to be a crucial factor relating to the subsequent development of the infant. Some mothers made a smooth transition from pregnancy to motherhood and had pride and pleasure in raising their infants, and their infants thrived. Others lacked pride in their infants and had little pleasure in motherhood although we as physicians had judged the infants' biologic endowments to be normal and saw them as appealing. Physician and mother looked at the same infant and saw different things—as though the beauty lay in the eye of the beholder.

With the cooperation and assistance of many, the Pittsburgh firstborn studies evolved as I attempted to answer my puzzlement about maternal perception: How do mothers perceive their babies? What influences their perception? Is their perception related to the infant's subsequent development? If so, can it be modified? Thus, I began studies to identify high-risk newborns and subsequently to provide early preventive intervention programs designed to modify the maternal perception and facilitate the infant's development.

Background Information

Although detailed reports of the study population and methodology have previously been reported in the literature (Broussard, 1970, 1971, 1976, 1979, 1983, 1984, 1986), some summary background information is indicated.

In 1963, I began a prospective longitudinal study of 318 normal, full-term, firstborn infants, born in five Pittsburgh hospitals during a specified 2.5-month period. All were single births. Selecting this population ensured that infants were within the range of normal endowment, so that the infant was biologically equipped to elicit response from the mother and not handicapped in his or her ability to respond to maternal care.

Using the mother's concept of the average baby as an anchor for comparison of her own infant's behavior, I designed the *Neonatal Perception Inventories* (NPI). The NPI represents a measurement of the mother's perception of her neonate, and the score represents the discrepancy between the mother's perception of the "average" infant and her own infant. The NPI may be viewed as a projective measure. The mother is presented with a set of ambiguous stimuli on which she projects her concept of her own baby and that of the average. It provides a measure of the adaptive potential of the mother-infant system.

These inventories were administered to the mothers on the first or second postpartum day and again when the infants were 1 month old. The 61% of the infants who were rated better than average by their mothers at 1 month old were considered at Low Risk for the subsequent development of emotional disorder. The 39% of the infants not rated as better than average by their mothers were considered at High Risk. The NPI was found to have both construct and criterion validity.

Establishing Predictive Validity

To test the hypothesis that the maternal perception of her 1-month-old infant as measured by the NPI was predictive of later psychosocial developmental outcome, follow-up studies were done at 4.5, 10 to 11, 15, and 19 years. At each of these ages, the firstborns were clinically evaluated during a single office interview by a psychiatrist who had no knowledge of the predictive risk rating on the NPI. At each age, a statistically significant association was present between the NPI rating at 1 month and the later psychosocial developmental rating. A greater proportion of High Risk newborns later developed psychosocial disorders than Low Risk newborns. (At 4.5 years, $p < .0002$, $N = 120$; at 10/11 years, $p < .017$, $N = 104$; at 15 years, $p < .007$, $N = 81$; and at 19 years, $p < .0021$, $N = 99$.) Attrition is always a factor in longitudinal research. Following the 1 month postpartum home visit, we had no contact with these subjects until children were 4.5 years old. A total of 164 different firstborns came in for one or more evaluations of their psychosocial development. The number of subjects seen for office evaluation at each time varied. Parents often willingly participated with home interviews, yet were not able to bring the child into the office.

No attempt at intervention was made with the 1963 cohort. This was a study of the natural history and developmental outcome of the firstborns. These findings provided the direction for the next phase, and we then began a preventive intervention program.

Preventive Intervention Program for Infants at High Risk Based on a Negative Maternal Perception

In 1973, we began our preventive intervention efforts (Broussard, 1981). I selected another cohort of 281 primiparae delivering healthy, normal, full-term firstborns in one Pittsburgh hospital during a specified 2.5-month period. All were single births. The NPI was administered during the immediate postpartum hospital stay and again at 1 month.

Based on the NPI at 1 month, 205 infants (73%) were categorized into a low-risk group and 76 (27%) into a high-risk group. We noted a decrease in percentage of high-risk infants, 39% versus 27%, over the 10-year period. This may reflect the increased use of family planning methods; that is, that fewer of the *consciously* unwanted babies were born. The change could not be accounted for by differences in social position because there was no significant difference between the cohorts on the Hollingshead Index of Social Position.

The 76 infants in the high-risk group were randomly divided into an experimental group of 39 to whom intervention was offered and a comparison group of 37 to whom no intervention was offered. Following the 1-month postpartum home visit, I telephoned each mother whom we had randomly selected and asked if she wished to participate in the firstborn program being offered for first-time parents. The program was described as an opportunity for parents to talk with other parents and staff about their concerns regarding child rearing. Travel expenses were reimbursed.

It is important to emphasize that our preventive-intervention program was not designed for infants already designated as patients in need of help by the parents or referred by an agency. *This unique feature of providing intervention to infants not designated as patients* has influenced much of our method of procedure. First, we recognized that the NPI was a screening instrument and as such was but the first step—a way to select a population of infants for more careful assessment—to see if, indeed, further intervention was warranted.

It is not feasible to tell parents of a healthy, full-term firstborn that their infant is considered at high risk for subsequent emotional difficulty. To do so might have the potential for establishing a self-fulfilling prophecy—that is, the mother's already negative perception of her newborn would be compounded by such a prediction. In addition, this would fail to take into account that there are a multiplicity of life variables that have an impact on development that may modify the effect of the negative maternal perception, such as the presence of other family members, various support systems, or some unique capacity within the infant.

Of the 39 mothers in the experimental group, 17 white mothers elected to participate in the intervention program. Intervention contacts consisted of an initial individual interview with one or both parents, participation in mother-infant group meetings, and home-based intervention. Two groups, each composed of seven or eight mothers and their infants, met every other week for 1.5 hours. These began when the infants were 2 to 4 months old and continued until they were 3.5 years old. The group leaders were Broussard (ERB) and Cornes (CC).

The group structure was designed to meet the changing needs of the mother-infant pairs and to encourage optimal growth and development. We did not have a formal agenda for each meeting. The mothers set the pace and introduced the topics they wished to discuss. We did not follow an authoritarian, didactic, educational approach. Instead, we encouraged the mothers to become experts in recognizing and responding to their children's needs. We regarded their ability to exercise initiative as a means of strengthening their impaired self-images and promoting group interaction and cohesiveness. We titrated our giving so as not to accentuate their dependency, and we supported the progressive tendencies of the mothers.

Initial Phase

During the initial phase of "getting to know you," we actively observed, were empathically available, and exercised cautious restraint. Although we often felt an identification with a helpless, ungratified infant, we avoided responding to the urgency of trying to modify the mother's behavior too quickly by giving advice. In our judgment, to move too quickly and give advice had the potential to reinforce the mother's negative self-image and negative perception of her infant.

A description of the first meeting of one of the groups illustrates the concept *cautious restraint*. Mrs. Z arrived 20 minutes late, breathless. She carried 2.5-month-old Jeannette in a very unusual way. She carried her face down with one hand between the legs under the crotch and the other under the shoulders. The mother's arms were extended so that Jeannette was held quite distant from her body. This position limited visual and tactile contact between mother and child.

We were immediately aware that Mrs. Z was sensitive about her mode of carrying Jeannette. She told us that a stranger commented about it as she entered the building, adding that Jeannette was comfortable only in this unusual position. A number of options were open as we struggled with our own feelings of identification with the unhappy infant. Simultaneously, we observed the mother's troubled face. So, although it was tempting to suggest a different way of holding, we did not.

Dr. Margaret McFarland observed each meeting from behind a one-way vision mirror and served as a consultant. She commented that Mrs. Z carried Jeannette in a way similar to the way parents handled children in body casts. Later, we learned that as an infant, Mrs. Z herself had been in a body cast following an automobile accident. One hypothesis was that Mrs. Z carried Jeannette in the way she herself had been carried as an infant. Although Jeannette had no deformity, her mother treated her as though she did.

We consider the ability to exercise *cautious restraint* and to suspend action to be very important during the initial period of engagement—the "getting to know you" phase. This is not easy. Professionals often are so accustomed to being the experts—giving advice, teaching, and providing the answers to questions that this ability to restrain is something to be learned.

Many mothers, like Mrs. Z, had difficulty in tolerating the closeness required in mothering. They put distance between themselves and their infants beyond that which we considered optimal. We were concerned that these infants would not have an experience of mothering that was relatively predictable, comfortable, and facilitating during this early period of development. The mothers often had trouble reading the infants' cues, and the infants were having little success in beginning to acquire a sense of having some impact on their environment.

During the initial phases of engagement, we continually assessed the quality of the bonds of attachment between mother and infant. We focused our efforts on meeting the mothers' dependent needs by offering support that they could accept. *Our primary goal during the initial phase of engagement was to foster the development of the bonds of attachment between mother and infant. These bonds were at jeopardy in many of the pairs.*

Although growth-supportive attention was being given to the children, we continued to move toward a fundamental goal, that of altering each mother's perception of herself and her perception of her child. We responded with appreciation and acceptance of the mothers and spontaneous enjoyment and admiration of the infants. Thus, the mothers had opportunities to observe our appreciation of their accomplishments and those of their children.

We emphasized giving to the mother—so as not to be seen as interested only in children. When we offered to hold the baby, it came in the context of "would you like me to hold Jeannette, so you can take off your coat (or sit to drink your coffee)?" Although the emphasis was on relieving mother, this approach made possible our holding Jeannette in ways comfortable to us—ways that facilitated eye contact as well as closer body contact. Mrs. Z observed us intently and gradually modified her carrying mode.

Our interventions were guided by our observations of the way information is transferred between mother and child. While observing the communication process between mother and infant and infant and mother, we may note that the perceptual flow between them is impaired—diminished or perhaps distorted in some way. Such an observation will be a stimulus to the intervenor to try to enter into the system to amplify or correct the distortion of the perceptual flow back and forth between this mother and this baby. We do this demonstratively by our behavioral interventions.

We frequently sat on the floor near the babies, who were often on mats. The mothers began to move from their chairs down to the floor to be closer to their infants. We saw a shift from their marked anxiety and depression, and the atmosphere in the group room often was one of a "party." They began to refer to topics discussed in a previous meeting. Mothers began to bring toys for their infants to play with. More positive mother-child interaction emerged, with mothers becoming more available to their infants.

We did many things that seemed casual. Coffee and donuts were available. We served these to the mothers—giving recognition of their needs and permission for them to meet their needs. We took photographs using a Polaroid® camera during the meetings. These were put into albums and became a focal point of interest. Mothers often looked through the albums, laughing in memory at their past shared experiences.

The Middle Phase

During the second 6 months, when the children became more mobile, we added age-appropriate children's toys and furniture. The mothers seemed surprised and pleased. These external changes became both a real and symbolic example of the staff's interest in encouraging growth and development.

We avoided behavior that could be viewed as competitive with mother and stressed the child's preference for the mother. The mothers of infants at high risk often lose their infants from their perceptual field, unaware of impending danger and unaware of the infants' cues to them. When engaged with another individual, they seem unable to disengage from that relationship and focus on their own infants. When incidents occurred requiring rapid adult action to comfort or protect the infant, if a mother did not intervene, one of the group leaders would act to meet the immediate need and then bring the child to the mother for comfort.

The mothers tested us in many ways to see if we would accept those aspects of themselves and their infants that they found disturbing. For example, one day 11-month-old Jeannette fell and began to cry. As I picked her up to hand her to her mother for comforting, she vomited on us. Mrs. Z was very upset and wanted to leave immediately for fear the soiled clothing would be objectionable to us. With reassurance (and the loan of some clothing) she remained for the rest of that meeting. She continued to participate regularly until termination when Jeannette was 3.5 years old.

Participation in the program provided for the infant's earlier contact with other adults and children in a more optimal environment for socialization than otherwise would have been available. Very early the children developed attachments to each other, to the other mothers, and to the group leaders. We supported the importance of play, and the mothers came to regard their children's play as having value. Play for the children became another means of moving along in their development at a more optimal rate than otherwise might have been possible. This, of course, was facilitated through the direct supportive empathy of the workers available to the children and through assistance to the mothers in facilitating their play.

The mother-infant group was not a traditional psychotherapy group, although it did perform some of the therapeutic functions suggested by Yalom (1975), for example, instillation of hope, development of socializing techniques, universality, imitative behavior, and group cohesiveness. However, we did not impose other typical conditions of psychotherapy group, such as a contract to attend all meetings, a periodic restatement of the goals and purposes of the group, and agreement to avoid interaction with other members outside the group. Over time, the group evolved as a support system of peers. Friendships developed between subjects; there were telephone contacts, shared transportation to meetings, and visits to each other's homes.

Within the room, the mothers began to congregate at one end, giving the toddlers most of the space to explore and play. We began plans to implement discrete mother and toddler groups. This was intended to enhance the mother's opportunity for more intense discussion without interruption by the children and to give the junior toddlers an opportunity to practice brief separations from their mothers supported by the presence of empathic staff. The transition was accomplished gradually over the next several months.

When the children were 19 months old, a child development specialist (Claudia Titelman) began to assist the two group leaders in the mother-infant group. She was able to learn the coping styles of the individual children and their respective developmental needs. Her relationship with the children evolved gradually in the mothers' presence and allowed them to observe this new person soon to be entrusted with the children's care. They could observe how she structured, yet facilitated, play for the children, simultaneously providing safety.

At age 2, the children evidenced an increasing ability to cope with brief absences from their mothers, so we initiated discrete groups. After a brief period of joint activity in the familiar room, the leaders (ERB & CC) and the mothers left to meet in an adjacent room near, yet apart from, the children. The children remained in the familiar room under the supervision of Claudia Titelman and Fredricka Latshaw. The mothers were free to move back and forth as needed. The discrete groups lasted for one hour, and then the mothers and leaders rejoined the children.

The curriculum within the children's group evolved around aiding them in mastery of the developmental tasks faced by all children, as well as specific life tasks presented by the environment (such as the birth of a sibling, divorce, or moving to a new home). Following each group, the staff convened as a whole to share observations and plan for interventions. Titelman (1983) described and delineated specific intervention techniques used in attempting to support the children's mastery of the developmental issues during the rapprochement subphase, encompassing the age range 19 to 30 months. She developed the Rapprochement Assessment Profile, which corresponds to Mahler's developmental theory of Separation-Individuation, Early Rapprochement, Rapprochement Crisis, and Consolidation of Individual Solutions to the Task of Rapprochement (Mahler, Pine, & Bergman, 1975).

Within the discrete mothers' group, the mothers spoke about feeling lonely and inadequate and often disparaged themselves. They reported having more difficulty setting limits and cited examples of regression in their children's behavior. The mothers' own conflicts and anxiety about separation became a focus of discussion. Within the mothers' group, the transferences toward the group leaders became more visible. They expressed considerable anger toward the group leaders for not recognizing that "the children are not ready for this yet." For the most part, this seemed to reflect the mothers' difficulties with separation. We encouraged the mothers' interest in understanding their feelings and reactions toward the children. Gradually, the mothers expressed more positive feelings about the discrete groups. There was evidence of much more

warmth and enthusiasm at the time of reunion with the children
and more understanding of the interrelationships between their
own moods and feelings and those of their children.

Termination Phase

In the third year, the material in the discussion began to flow
from the children's activities—to the mothers' feelings—to
relationships with important people—to memories about their
early lives. For most women, that seemed to be a useful trend. The
birth of several second children modified the course of the group
during the third year. There was much discussion about displacement, sibling rivalry, and competitive wishes. Clinically we saw
growth and positive changes in the mothers. They were less
depressed, more confident, and many had modified their behavior
considerably toward their children in positive ways.

The mothers began to talk about returning to work, sending their
children to nursery school, and other activities of their own that
were separate from those of their children. When we introduced
the idea of terminating the group, the mothers responded with
anxiety and voiced anger toward the leaders for not understanding
their needs. We pointed out that they were beginning to move into
new and broader activities in the community that would replace the
group. They perceived this as rejection and reacted with regression,
describing themselves as inadequate and lacking in competence. We
continued to work through the termination process for about 6
months, trying to help them to see that separations can be good and
need not necessarily be repetitions of painful separations in their
pasts. They did seem to achieve a more realistic view of the leaders
and group process, as well as of themselves and their children. After
termination, one group met several times in their homes.

Evaluation

In addition to our clinical observations, we conducted a formal
developmental evaluation of the children at ages 1 and 2.5 years
using an evaluator who did not know the group membership of the
children or their NPI risk rating. The sequence of the evaluation
procedure was structured as follows: (a) a period of free play for
the mother and infant, (b) administration of the Bayley test with

the mother present, (c) observing the child's reaction to the mother leaving the room with the examiner present, (d) observing the mother-child reunion. The 1-hour evaluation protocol was videotaped via a one-way vision mirror. Each child was then rated according to the Broussard Optimal Lines (1979), a series of single-item graphic scales representing specific items of development.

At 1 year, there was not a statistically significant difference in the functioning between the intervention group and the comparison group to whom no intervention was offered. However, when the intervention continued, and the children were again evaluated at age 2.5 years, there were statistically significant differences between the intervention group and those children in the comparison group who had not had the intervention services. At age 2.5, the Optimal Lines included measures such as coping ability, frustration tolerance, affective balance, investment in language, ability to sustain interest, quality of symbolic play, and attachment to mother. The adaptation of the high-risk intervention group was more optimal than the high risk, no intervention group and more closely approximated the adaptation of the children originally considered at low risk (Broussard, 1979). However, it must be noted that within the groups there were varying degrees of successful outcome. There were two instances in which we recommended therapy following termination of the group.

Others have also noted results suggesting that the impact of intervention is associated with the child's later development, but not at age 1. Greenspan (personal communication, April 24, 1981) reported similar results with a population of high-risk infants. Likewise Beckwith (personal communication, 1988) reported a positive impact of intervention on the cognitive functioning of a cohort of premature infants at age 2 that was not evident at age 1.

Our model of group intervention was designed to do the following:

1. Leave the child's relationship with the mother intact within the family context while (a) supplementing for the child what the mother cannot be at the moment; and (b) supplementing for the mother the lacks in her past and present relationships

2. Foster the development of trust in the leaders—a prerequisite to being able to learn from the leaders

3. Permit modeling of caring-for behavior that the mother may be able to adopt after she has learned to trust

4. Provide an opportunity for helping the mother with her depression and low self-esteem through (a) support of the mother's efforts in her capacity of mother, (b) encouragement to find solutions within herself and within the group, and (c) empathy with her struggles and praise for her successes

5. Provide, through the relationship with the group leaders, a new image of potential relationships with other adults. When the mother feels valued and respected, she can then begin to modify her self-perception and her perception of her child

6. Support the child's progressive development

Many of the mothers of infants at high risk related that they had grown up in households that had varying degrees of marital discord. In addition, many had chosen spouses they viewed as nonsupportive and often reported their marital relationships to be nongratifying.

The group leaders were a male and a female who were not competitive, hostile, or seductive with one another. This provided the group members with a model of male/female relationships that was often quite discrepant with their prior experiences. In addition, the group leaders were not competitive, hostile, or seductive with the group members. This provided the mothers with the opportunity to experience gratifying relationships with caring, supportive adults. This experience facilitated the mothers' ability to identify with the caregiving leaders and modify their caregiving of their own children.

Mothers of infants at high risk do not seem to perceive a potential within their children for healthy developmental advance, nor within themselves for "competent mothering." When the mother has not experienced good mothering and a pleasurable infancy herself, she may be hampered in her ability to provide good mothering for her child. In essence, she is handicapped in trying to talk a language for which she has never had the textbook. When the deficits are great, preventive intervention is more difficult; and we must search in the mother's history for the shadows of satisfaction on which to build.

Preventive intervention is not easy, and there is no single, simplistic approach. It is essential to seek ways to clarify and refine our techniques and to determine how to select intervention modalities appropriate to the unique needs of specific infants and their families. In an attempt to do so, we elected to work with adolescent parents and infants.

Preventive-Intervention Program
for Adolescent Parents and Infants

During an informal telephone survey of 29 human service providers in Allegheny County in 1982, sufficient medical services were reported to be available for parents 17 years old and younger. Few reported services designed specifically for adolescents. In general, the providers had difficulty engaging teenagers except during pregnancy, delivery, and the immediate postdelivery hospital stay, and only a very few teenage parents were reported to obtain child-rearing guidance through the infant's first year.

Infants of adolescent mothers are generally considered at high risk for maladaptive development due to factors associated with pregnancy at an early age. They may also be considered at risk because of environmental factors related to low socioeconomic status, maternal emotional immaturity, and the stress of being reared by a single parent. In addition, adolescent mothers are confronted with the psychological developmental tasks of making the transition from adolescence to adult status, the stress of child rearing, continuing their education, and negotiating a personal future. Thus, there is a need for intervention to facilitate the mother's developmental progress through adolescence as well as to aid her in her parenting. For the infants, primary prevention is essential to facilitate development during the crucial stages of infancy. Therefore, we initiated an outreach program to provide preventive-intervention services to adolescent mothers and their infants. This was designed to facilitate the optimal development of the infants and to aid the adolescents in continuing their own developmental thrust into adulthood.

This cohort consisted of 241 adolescent mothers (113 white and 128 black). They were not over 17 at time of conception and delivered full-term, healthy, firstborn singleton infants at Magee-Women's Hospital.

The intervention services consisted of supplementary guidance to the infants and their families in the form of infant-parent/family group meetings. We conducted three groups, each consisting of 10 to 12 infant-parent systems. (Quite by chance, one group consisted of all black mothers, one was all white, and one was a mixture of black and white.) Each met for 1.5 hours on a biweekly basis and continued for 3 years. Travel expenses were reimbursed.

The existence of a group where adolescent mothers and their infants could talk about their concerns was itself an intervention; the constancy of such a group constituted another, perhaps even more powerful intervention. These mothers let it be known how little constancy they had experienced in their lives. Was there any reason to trust that this experience would be different?

During the process of intervention, we actively observed the functioning of the mother-infant pair and intervened with each individual dyad according to our understanding of its developmental needs. This understanding influenced our timing as well as the nature of the interventions. Again, we used knowledge of human development and of the parenting process to guide our responsiveness to changing parent and infant needs. We modified our approach somewhat to take into account the fact that these mothers were adolescents. Specifically, we dealt with issues stemming from the mothers' simultaneous experiences of parenthood and adolescence.

The mothers made it clear that they resented people telling them what to do. As one mother said to the others, "Have you gotten the 'you're so young bit?'" When the others replied that they had, she continued, "They're always telling you what to do; they think you think the baby is a Barbie doll. They made their mistakes raising their kids; let me fall on my face a few times." This perception of others as "meddlers" influenced our intervention techniques. We respected the mothers' sovereignty as parents; we did not lecture or judge and shame. We maintained our right to interact with them and their infants in ways that demonstrated our feelings, our empathy, our commitment, and our respect. We showed that we valued them and their babies. These principles guided our efforts to provide a supportive atmosphere in which the adolescents could come to trust us and to learn ways of modifying their behavior.

The process of engaging and sustaining adolescents' participation in an ongoing process is difficult. Throughout the project, we were acutely aware that these people had not volunteered; they had been invited. They were not patients but the targets of an outreach program. They were not obliged to reveal anything. Although we were always interested in anything that touched upon their lives and their babies, the teenagers were never pressured. Thus, the content and timing of the mothers' statements were matters of great importance, for it meant that the data were volunteered. We knew that the messages might be disguised or encoded, but our experience and training enabled us to perceive or estimate meanings without having to disturb the (perhaps essential) disguise. Observing and listening is an *active* process, requiring that our senses be highly tuned for any indication of additional information with which the participants might be ready to entrust to us. As the relationships between adolescents, babies, and leaders strengthened and deepened, we were more able to probe and clarify issues.

We have often been asked, "But what do you do?" (Broussard & Cornes, 1981). The earlier descriptions of our previous work came from us. There were both a priori decisions based on our past clinical experience guiding our techniques and techniques that emerged during the conduct of the groups.

External Appraisal of Intervention Techniques

In an attempt to define in greater detail those aspects of the intervention processes used with the adolescent parents and how these may relate to the infants' more favorable developmental outcomes, we recruited an experienced clinician researcher, unfamiliar with the project (Clinician I), to study the videotapes of the group meetings. Another clinician, familiar with the project (Clinician II), also studied a sample of tapes to establish interrater reliability. By subjecting our work to review by an external evaluator, we anticipated the possibility of validating or refuting our perceptions of what we were doing. This process also offered the potential for learning more than we already knew. After viewing each of the videotapes, the clinician dictated protocols documenting observations of each mother-infant pair, the group, and the leaders' interventions. Each protocol contained the following components: (a) one or more themes describing the general feeling and impression of the sessions, (b) patterns exemplifying these themes, and (c) specific behaviors documenting the patterns. Because there were a number of sources about an intricate and complicated set of phenomena, the clinicians were encouraged to use themselves as clinical instruments, that is, to be holistically rather than reductionistically oriented. The clinician's appraisal was not based on a priori beliefs of what the leaders *should* say, what the leaders might *want* to say, or what the leaders *believed* they were saying but on what emerged from the clinician's observations of the material studied.

Following her observations of the first 14 sessions of a group in which all the participants were black, Clinician I prepared a report based on her observations and on her previously dictated protocols. Details of her report have been published in The National Mental Health Association: Eighty Years of Involvement in the Field of Prevention (Broussard, 1989). A portion of this report follows and gives a picture of some of the challenges we faced during the initial phases:

* * *

The leaders responded to the participants' suspicions about the leaders' offers in a variety of ways; for example, before each session, a staff member telephoned the mothers and invited them to come to attend the scheduled meeting. This practice emphasized the existence and constancy of the group. It also reiterated that the adolescents truly were wanted, that the leaders were interested in them and their babies.

And as it became an expected, dependable reminder, the telephoning was also a potent if subtle response to questions about the leaders' sincerity. The phone call also served as an organizing force for the mothers' chaotic lives.

Group Features

It appeared from these data that the group structure was built gradually but unceasingly of many kinds of material. The group's customs, its availability, and its boundaries began to emerge as did the participants' perceptions of them.

Group Customs

The time limits of the meetings were kept as regular as possible. Often mothers came early, and there was always a staff member to greet them, help with the babies' clothes, and chat. However, the beginning of a group session was signaled by the entrance of the leaders, Broussard (ERB) and Cornes (CC). Though the initial staff member might linger a bit, bringing the leaders up to date on recent developments, she soon left. Similarly, attempts were made to end the session at the specified time. The value of these kinds of temporal structures to any psychological work has been described by many authors. Time limits help to define the extent of the task and the claim of the participants on the leaders. Like all boundaries, they often inspire irritation, despair, and defiance, but these are affects with which the leaders could deal.

Group Availability

The group as a resource, as a door never closed, was a palpable interventional asset. As early as the second session, it was plain that the leaders always fussed over arrivals, knitting the fabric of the group on those crucial occasions. This was an invariant accompaniment to the building of the group. No participant ever came or departed without being made to feel recognized and special. When participants returned after missed sessions, special welcomes and inquiries were always extended.

Group Boundaries

The boundaries of the group were relatively flexible, and adjustments were made in response to issues that arose as the work progressed. For example, whispered buzzing by the parents evoked a leader to say, "I can't hear you. Will you share the joke with the rest of us?" The message was "We don't hide things here. We're interested in everything and don't like to be shut out."

The leaders tried to penetrate subgroups without disrupting them, to be able to hear and be available. When individual participants became isolates, the leaders sought to bring them into the group. Sometimes their position as outsiders seemed the result of peer power currents, sometimes it was because mothers or babies were depressed, sometimes because they were embarrassed, but on many occasions, it was for reasons that were unclear or unknown. Whatever the etiology, the leaders strove to return them to the group, to dispel their aloneness. Participants were always informed about a leader's absence (illness or vacation), demonstrating their right to be informed.

The freedom to bring friends and family was a feature of the setting much used by the adolescents. However, as members increasingly brought relatives and friends, never announcing their intentions in advance, some limit on the group size was necessary. This was a delicate matter, because acceptance and openness were part of the group's interventional strengths. Yet it was a matter to be dealt with. One way was not to provide travel money for guests. Upon discovery that other groups existed, several of the mothers began to attend weekly. The leaders chose to restrict their attendance to their assigned group meeting every other week.

Impact of the Interventions

Expecting to see changes in the behavior of adolescent mother-infant pairs after 14 sessions falls somewhere in the unpleasant territory between ill-advised and absurd. The program was designed to operate over time, with at least two implicit assumptions. First, it was assumed that if changes could be effected, they would follow only after trust in the setting and the leaders developed. Second, it was assumed that the patterns on which parenting is based are well in place even by adolescence. In the strictest sense, it is impossible to claim that changes that can be documented were the result of participation in the groups. It is always possible that such changes would have occurred without any intervention. If the intervention program did help, we do not and may never know the rate at which it did so. With these sober considerations in mind, however, we can nevertheless record impressionistic gestalts, the forerunners of hypotheses.

The neediness of these mothers was compelling. They seemed entangled in pathological and pathogenic processes of the kind seen in patients with chronic, dangerous, and incurable disease, such as brittle diabetes and cardiac decompensation. For such patients, keeping the condition stable, in a sort of safety sling, is an achievement. Most medical personnel are content, if not euphoric, when they can prevent deterioration, maintain the most reasonable comfort and quality of life, and stave off malignant and threatening crises.

None of the facts that follow can legitimately be claimed to be results solely of the intervention. One might posit that these participants were in so much danger that alteration might be dismissed as main effects; that is, due entirely to the impact of offering something in the way of help. However, even in these first 14 sessions, there was movement in a positive direction. At least three varieties of change can be identified: group patterns, participant patterns, and evidence that the adolescents emulated the leaders.

Group Patterns

Several patterns related to behavior within the group emerged. The pattern of bringing nonparent guests began in the seventh session, and thereafter no session occurred without nongroup guests accompanying one or more of the mothers.

"Departure-hunger," the tendency of participants to resume or escalate eating as soon as the end of the session was at hand, was first documented in Sessions 2 and 3. In some participants, it continued well beyond the initial meetings. In later sessions, many adolescents made a point of leaving at their own rate, giving signals that they resented the time limits of the meetings and would resist them as they dared, not only by delaying departures but by choosing their arrival time.

Participant Patterns

Each mother changed and grew as we watched. The style, direction, and speed of development were strands in the larger patterns of the group, and it seemed reasonable to guess that the process was reciprocal—that is, that participation in the group contributed to the ways in which the adolescents unfolded. The latter process was more difficult to assess. An example of one change in patterns follows.

Tricia and her son Ricky, the most assiduous group participants, were present at the first session and at 11 of the first 14 sessions. David, Ricky's 15-year-old father, attended 6 of these sessions. Tricia bore the heaviest psychological burdens among the mothers in this group, or at least the most obvious ones.

The first impression of this adolescent appeared in the theme statement dictated after viewing each session: "High quantities of rage and need evenly balanced," and it was as valid in Session 14 as in Session 1. In Session 2, "She was often rocking with baby; it was hard to tell who was being comforted the most. She also jiggled her foot, cracked gum—almost anything, it seemed, to soothe herself. Her finger was in her mouth frequently." This behavior was still present in Session 5.

Tricia's hungriness was described in the protocol for Session 2: "Tricia was very much a child, taking in everything via her eyes. She looked hungrily and eagerly, like a youngster, at the camera and the leaders." The hungry look was still very much present in Session 3.

In Session 10 one pattern was "I'm starving for everything, but I *almost* know that this is the place where nurturing is dependable." Tricia took some food from every container on the tray and mur-

mured 'Thanks' to ERB." Because few of the adolescents acknowledged the food provided them, Tricia's "Thanks" was not a minor
matter.

Anger was so pandemic a feature of Tricia's feelings that it was
transsessional, an incessant accompaniment to all that occurred. In
Session 1, "The anger of the two parents was barely contained. The
faces of the two adolescents were full of hate and fear." In Session 3,
"There was still a vast expanse of opaque facial expression, a smidgen
of the smoldering anger from previous sessions." And in Session 5 "a
strong current of sullen anger" was the major theme statement.

The counterpoint and subsidiary megathemes to anger and need
were Tricia's other constant psychological companions—shame and
despair. Her shame was immediately manifest in her appearance.
Most of the mothers took pride in appearing at group meetings in
more formal outfits than they would wear at home or even at school.
But in Session 10, the observer noted: "Tricia doesn't dress up like
the other mothers. Her hair was hastily bundled, and her kinetics
shouted, 'I'm worthless and too angry and defeated to try to compete
with the others.' " As early as Session 2, she came across as "a gawky
teenager." Her sitting posture, legs apart, body leaning forward,
seeming to want to curl up, was evidence for this. She is still not quite
sure how to manage her own body, at least in this situation where the
evidence of its sexuality is in the forefront. She wasn't uncomfortable
to come to a special and rather strange, formal occasion with a curler
in her hair. In Session 5, "Her attire emphasized the adolescent
gangliness of her build." And in Session 8, "Her dress was even more
indifferent than usual."

If Tricia's appearance bespoke eloquently her shame and embarrassment, her efforts to hide herself were even more poignant. As late
as Session 7, she continued to put her hand in front of her eyes in the
same manner she had used in Session 1: "Tricia held her hand over
her eyes several times. It was almost as though she were a criminal
suspect hiding her face to preserve her anonymity." In Session 2, the
theme for Tricia was "The aw-shucks mother. Several times she put
her hand over her eyes apparently to 'hide' from the camera. This
primitive measure said in part at least, 'I don't want to be seen; if I
can't see, then I won't be visible.' She burst out with embarrassed
laughter. This was an explosive relief of tension, but produced no real
easing of it. The laughter died, snuffed out in a second, leaving behind
the same taut feeling."

Yet through the malignant fog of hopelessness and rage,
Tricia made progress, moving toward something she valued even
in this first block of sessions. In the first session, one of the pat-

terns was "If there was any reason for being present, it was little R. Both parents fed and played with him. There was a hint of thawing (late in the session). When Tricia did smile, it was an eager, bashful, hungry smile." By Session 5, a pattern emerged: "Despite all the difficulties, Tricia was not completely refractory or unresponsive when the leaders were patient and persistent. She could actually thank CC for picking up her son's pacifier from the floor."

In Session 7, although Tricia was ashamed and abashed, she was working with it. She smiled briefly at ERB on a number of occasions and was comfortable enough to "go and get herself a table for her can of soda." The observer wondered, "Was she too sad to let ERB do it for her, or was she feeling enough at home to do it just as ERB would?"

In Session 12, Tricia's main theme was "I've brought both the jewel-baby and my despair." By then she seemed to know that the leaders were fond of her and her son. CC spent some time playing with Ricky, and "during the interlude between them, she looked on almost regally. She sat up a bit straighter and smiled briefly. One of Tricia's responses was to play with Ricky in an animated way for some time."

By Session 14, "Tricia and her son were a silent, strongly bonded unit. In this session, she bounced him, jiggled him, played pat-a-cake, kissed him, tossed him in the air. Ricky batted at her chair, and she rocked him." This went on amid the eddying excited chatter and elevated decibel level of other activities in the playroom, and it gives some clue about the strength of the tie between mother and son.

Despair was almost as unrelenting for this mother as anger. Session 7's theme statement was "Tricia's anger and sadness were overwhelming in the first part of the session, partially dissipated toward the very end. The photo album offered by ERB as consolation was accepted grudgingly. She smiled in spite of herself as she looked at the pictures, but she lapsed quickly back into glumness."

Session 8 was the first time Tricia came without David. The theme for her in this session was "Can things get worse? What shall I do with this baby burden and my life? She was so depressed that her sense of caste was gone, a signal about how low her self-esteem had sunk. She had brought a paper bag again to contain the baby's supplies, and it was even smaller than the one she brought to the last session." Tricia's shabby baggage seemed highly significant. All mothers except Tricia seemed to take special pride in the containers they used to tote the materials (bottles, diapers, toys) needed to travel with an infant.

Emulation of the Leaders

If we consider (a) that the group was observed during a brief period, (b) that the resistance and doubts the adolescents had about the enterprise were substantial, and (c) that even the most ready group takes time to gear up for work, it was surprising that any instances of emulation occurred. But despite all the countervailing forces, the neediness of the participants and the sincerity and competence of the leaders fused to make it possible for some identificatory templates to take hold. Observations of the adolescents relating to their babies in the same style as the leaders strongly suggested that the intervention was producing change.

As early as Session 2, "Tricia emulated ERB's behavior by holding a plastic ring quite still at an appropriate distance and position for Ricky's visual field. Her kinetic stillness, quite unlike Tricia's usual style of using her body, was plainly borrowed from ERB." In Session 7, "Tricia took Ricky from his father and, very much in the style of the leaders, talked with the baby and kissed him, put him on the floor and gave him a rattle." Although his parents' behavior suggested that they retained considerable ambivalence about Ricky, there was also ample evidence that both were involved in his daily care and took some pleasure in parenting. By the end of these 14 sessions, little Ricky was given an impressionistic nickname for his dawning personality. This observer dubbed him "The Sparkler."

By Session 10, Ricky had hatched into a group participant. "The baby was the countertheme to his mother's despair. He approached the session with lively optimism that never dimmed, and he never missed a trick. He was crawling rapidly and expertly, and twice made his way straight to CC, who picked him up. Ricky could look at the adults, spin a rattle that he grasped, and crawl, all simultaneously."

In Session 12, the observer declared, "Ricky is rapidly becoming a personality, a force in the group. His hair had been done up in even more elaborate cornrows than at the last observation, but the sparkle came from within. He was at home in the group, a tiny Alexander who could hardly wait to explore and conquer. He approached other babies on the floor, made his way to Tricia's lap, and was played with. At one point, Ricky sat on the blanket, cheerfully crunching a cookie and taking in everything about him with his eyes. He looked directly at the camera and smiled. A number of subtle expressions panned across his face."

By this time, "Ricky and CC were definitely an item. Ricky, as he had room in his busy schedule, found CC. They did pick-up-and-put-down, sit-on-my-knee, but this time something was added. He explored CC's face with his hand, and CC returned the exploration, gently supporting the baby all the while."

* * *

The preceding edited excerpts from Clinician I's protocols of the first 14 group meetings provide some examples of the magnitude of difficulties faced during the initial phase of our work with engaging the adolescents and their infants. The external clinician's critical appraisal of our work was useful in several ways. First, it provided an independent documentation of the techniques of intervention. It is important to note that, in general, she identified the same techniques that we had previously thought we were using and substantiated the validity of our earlier impressions. Second, she noted the substantial resistance of the adolescent mothers to the intervention processes. Third, she emphasized the magnitude of the problems faced by those who chose to do this type of preventive intervention.

Structured Evaluation

At approximately one year postdelivery, we conducted home visit interviews with 91 mothers. We found that those who took part in the intervention services fared better than those who did not in regard to educational status and repeat pregnancy. Of mothers in the Intervention Group, 10% had dropped out of high school, compared with 26.66% of those who did not receive services. In addition, 25% of those in the Intervention Group were involved in post-high-school education, compared with 8.33% of those who did not receive services. Among the Intervention Group, 9.52% of the mothers reported a repeat pregnancy compared with 16.66% of those who did not receive services.

Office-Based Infant Evaluation

To monitor the developmental progress of the infants, we conducted a formal assessment of 36 infants ranging in age from 12 to 18 months during an individual office visit.

For the purposes of data analysis of the 1-year office evaluation of the infants, the following groups were defined: an *Intervention Group* (N = 16—subjects who had attended 14 to 25 meetings prior to the office evaluation) an *Intervention-Refused Group* (N = 9—those who were invited to participate in meetings but did not do so), and a *Comparison Group* (N = 11—those who were never invited to participate in meetings).

There were 14 males (10 black and 4 white) and 22 females (15 black, 7 white). Group comparisons are tempered by the unequal distribution of race and sex and by small numbers.

Evaluation Procedure

The sequence of the evaluation procedure was identical with the one used to evaluate the 1973 population and included (a) a period of free play for mother and infant; (b) administration of the Bayley Scales of Development with mother present; (c) observing the child's reaction to his or her mother leaving the room with the examiner present; and (d) observation of the mother-child reunion.

The single-item graphic scales (Optimal Lines) were grouped into five clinical clusters: (a) Appropriate and Specific Attachment to Mother, (b) Separation Indicators, (c) Aggression, (d) Implementation of Contacts with the Non-Human Environment, and (e) Affective Balance. Cluster index scores were obtained for each subject.

There were no statistically significant differences between the groups on the Cluster Scores. These findings are consistent with the evaluation results of our previous preventive-intervention work with the 1973 cohort. The impact of intervention of one year's duration was not evident at age 1 year. However, when the intervention continued and the children were again evaluated at age 2.5, they were functioning more optimally than those children who had not had the intervention services (Broussard, 1979).

We continued the intervention with the adolescent parents and their infants until the infants were 2 to 3 years of age; however, lack of funds precluded our repeating a formal developmental evaluation of the children at termination. It is likely that the infants, having continued to receive intervention services, would have shown more optimal development than those infants in the Intervention Refused and Comparison groups—with the results being similar to the findings with the 1973 cohort.

A two-way analysis of variance using the BNDP Program was performed for race and sex. There was no interaction between race and sex on any of the variables. However, there were statistically significant differences for race and sex on a number of variables. In general, for the total population of 36 infants, whites scored more optimally than blacks and females more optimally than males.

Comments

During our work with these families, we were impressed with the magnitude of deprivations they faced. Most lived in family groups where the generations were often cramped, sometimes even tele-scoped. This could mean that, like their own mothers, the adoles-cent mothers had little psychological space in which to experience adolescence. Little opportunity—privacy, parental inclination, physical resources—existed to enable them to work through the dramas adolescence usually entails. In addition, there was probably little chance of their consolidating maturational gains that might have been attained, let alone advancing to new developmental levels.

Participation in the project offered the adolescent mothers an opportunity to consider the possibility of an identity that included education and work with dignity and remuneration. It also offered them and their infants a place (both physical and psychological) where they were respected and valued. Hence, there was the potential for disrupting patterns that had been maladaptive for these families. For the most part, the adolescents we were able to engage in the project became quite invested in participating in the group and recognized our investment in them. As difficult as this work may be, it is essential to continue our efforts if we wish to have an impact on these cycles of despair. Despite the infant's normal biological endowment as judged by professional assessors, the woman whose early experience has not supported the develop-ment of a healthy self-esteem within herself seems to view the infant produced by herself to be defective as she feels defective. The mirroring of the mother's negative perception of what she has created and her inability to gratify the child's needs seem to foster the development of another generation with emotional difficulty. Early preventive intervention with mothers and infants is a must if we hope to modify the generational transmission of emotional disorder.

Summary Discussion

The techniques we followed can be used for prevention of a wide variety of psychosocial disorders—for example, attachment disorders, child abuse and neglect, behavior disorders. This chapter has briefly described programs designed for two specific high-risk populations. In a utopian world, the needs of all infants would be met. But in the real world, because resources are limited, it is essential that we identify those at higher risk and focus on these target groups.

Preventive intervention requires personnel who have a sound understanding of child development and of parenthood. Our recognition of the importance of training a cadre of skilled workers led us to develop several training programs at the local, state, and national levels, such as Maternal and Infant Health Promotion: A Continuing Education Program for Pennsylvania's Community Health Nurses (1982); and the Child Abuse and Neglect Interdisciplinary Training Program at the University of Pittsburgh.

References

Anderson, J. C., Williams, S., McGee, R., & Silva, P. A. (1987). *DSM-III* disorders in preadolescent children: Prevalence in a large sample from the general population. *Archives of General Psychiatry, 44*(1), 69-76.

Broussard, E. R. (1964). *A study to determine the effectiveness of television as a medium for counseling groups of primiparous women during the immediate postpartum period.* Unpublished doctoral dissertation, University of Pittsburgh.

Broussard, E. R. (1976). Neonatal prediction and outcome at 10/11 years. *Child Psychiatry and Human Development, 7*(2), 85-93.

Broussard, E. R. (1979). Assessment of the adaptive potential of the mother-infant system: The Neonatal Perception Inventories. *Seminars in Perinatology, 3*(1), 91-100.

Broussard, E. R. (1983). Primary prevention of psychosocial disorders: Assessment of outcome. In L. A. Bond & J. M. Joffee (Eds.), *Primary prevention of psychopathology: 6. Facilitating infant and early childhood development* (pp. 180-196). Hanover, NH: University Press of New England.

Broussard, E. R. (1984). The Pittsburgh firstborns at age 19. In R. Tyson, J. Call, & E. Galenson (Eds.), *Frontiers of infant psychiatry* (Vol. 2). New York: Basic Books.

Broussard, E. R. (1986). Prospective longitudinal study of firstborn neonates. In L. Erlenmeyer-Kimling & N. E. Miller (Eds.), *Life span research on the prediction of psychopathology.* Hillside, NJ: Lawrence Erlbaum.

Broussard, E. R. (1989). The infant-family resource program: Facilitating optimal development. In R. E. Hess & J. DeLeon (Eds.), *The National Mental Health Association: Eighty years of involvement in the field of prevention* (pp. 179-224). Binghamton, NY: Haworth.

Broussard, E. R., & Cornes, C. C. (1981). Identification of mother-infant systems in distress: What can we do? *Journal of Preventive Psychiatry, 1*(1), 119-132.

Broussard, E. R., & Hartner, M. S. S. (1970). Maternal perception of the neonate as related to development. *Child Psychiatry and Human Development, 1*(1), 16-25.

Broussard, E. R., & Hartner, M. S. S. (1971). Further considerations regarding maternal perception of the firstborn. In J. Hellmuth (Ed.), *Exceptional infant: 2. Studies in abnormalities* (pp. 432-449). New York: Brunner/Mazel.

Health care reform for Americans with severe mental illnesses: Report of the National Advisory Mental Health Council (1993). *American Journal of Psychiatry, 150*(10), 1447-1465.

Leighton, D. C., Harding, J. S., Macklin, D. B., Hughes, C. C., & Leighton, A. L. (1963). Psychiatric findings of the Stirling County Study. *American Journal of Psychiatry, 119*(5), 1021-1026.

Mahler, M. S., Pine, F., & Bergman, A. (1975). *The psychological birth of the human infant.* New York: Basic Books.

Maier, D., Lichtermann, T., Klinger, T., Heun, R., & Hallmayer, J. (1992). Prevalences of personality disorders (DSM-III-R) in the community. *Journal of Personality Disorders, 6*(1), 187-196.

Maternal and infant health promotion: A continuing education program for Pennsylvania's community health nurses. (1982). (Available from the Division of Maternal/Child Health, Commonwealth of Pennsylvania, Department of Health)

Regier, D. A., Boyd, J. H., Burke, J. D., Jr., Rae, D. S., Meyers, J. K., Kramer, M., Robins, L. N., George, L. K., Karno, M., & Locke, B. Z. (1988). One-month prevalence of mental disorders in the United States: Based on five epidemiologic catchment area sites. *Archives of General Psychiatry, 45*(11), 977-986.

Titelman, C. J. (1983). *A model for assessment and intervention to prevent emotional-developmental dysfunction in the rapprochement age child (19-30 months): An application of Mahler's theory of separation-individuation.* Unpublished doctoral dissertation, University of Pittsburgh.

Yalom, I. (1975). *Theory and practice of group psychotherapy.* New York: Basic Books.

Zimmerman, M., & Coryell, W. (1989). DSM-III personality disorder diagnoses in a nonpatient sample: Demographic correlates and co-morbidity. *Archives of General Psychiatry, 46*(8), 682-689.

THREE

Preschool Programs

CHAPTER 6

Parents as Teachers: Investing in Good Beginnings for Children

MILDRED M. WINTER

DANICA S. MCDONALD

> In every child who is born, under no matter what circumstances and of no matter what parents, the potential of the human race is born again, and in him, too, once more, and each of us, our terrific responsibility toward human life.
>
> —James Agee, *Let Us Now Praise Famous Men*

Our children are our potential and our future, not our problem. Investing in the very beginning of life diminishes the probability of investing later in social costs such as remedial education, juvenile detainment, welfare (or its alternative) dependency, child abuse, and neglect. "If we don't invest in the early rearing of our children, we're going to be paying the bills for the rest of our lifetimes," says University of Wisconsin psychologist Christopher Coe. "The bills will be for mental disorders and physical diseases, and for putting many of these kids in jail" (cited in Kotulak, 1993, p. 32).

Parents as Teachers brings together families, schools, and communities in a three-way partnership to reduce the number of children in need of special or remedial education on entering school and increase the chances all children deserve for healthy, successful futures. It has grown from a pilot project in a handful of Missouri public schools to an extensive network reaching nearly half a million families in 47 states and 6 countries. Parents as Teachers was one of the first statewide family support and education initiatives emphasizing the child's earliest years and one of the first large-scale home visiting programs. The Parents as Teachers program has captured the attention of educators, health and social service professionals, business leaders, policymakers, and—most important—parents, because it works. As an early intervention effort, Parents as Teachers has demonstrated its success in preventing and ameliorating many of the problems that contribute to underachievement and school failure. It offers a practical way to create an environment of opportunity and growth for all children. Experience has shown that participation in the Parents as Teachers program can result in confident, competent parents and happy, well-rounded, academically able children.

Conceptual Framework

The underlying philosophy of the Parents as Teachers program is perhaps best embodied in words attributed to Plato: "The beginning is half of the whole." Making a quantum leap to the second half of the 20th century, substantive federal and private investments in the 1960s and 1970s in research on human development and in early intervention programs produced findings that confirmed the wisdom of Plato's statement and shaped the conceptual framework of Parents as Teachers.

To cite a few examples of such findings, Benjamin Bloom's review of longitudinal data on human development led him to conclude that 50% of intelligence as measured at age 17 is developed by age 4 and that the greatest change in such a characteristic can be effected during the period of its most rapid growth (Bloom, 1964). The Harvard Preschool Project, directed by Burton White, set out to track the emergence of major abilities and child-rearing practices that influence children during the first three years, concluding that one can predict at age 3, with few exceptions, how a child will look at age 6 in all areas of development (White, Kaban, Attanuci, & Shapiro, 1978). Urie Bronfenbrenner's study of early intervention programs initiated in the 1960s as part of our nation's social reform efforts concluded that working with the family rather than bypassing parents is critical to helping children get off to the best possible start and to sustaining gains after the program ends (Bronfenbrenner, 1979).

The Parents as Teachers program is based on two simple truths—that babies are born learners and that parents play a critical role from the beginning in determining what their child will become. The program is designed to enhance child development and school achievement by reaching out to families beginning even before the child's birth. Acknowledging that all parents deserve support in laying a strong foundation for their child's success, Parents as Teachers was designed for the voluntary participation of all families.

The program's ten major goals are to:

- empower parents to give their children the best possible start in life;
- help each child reach his or her full potential;
- increase parents' feelings of competence and confidence;
- increase parents' knowledge of child development and appropriate ways to stimulate children's curiosity, language, social, and motor development;
- give children a solid foundation for school success;
- improve parent-child interactions and strengthen family relationships;
- turn everyday settings into learning opportunities;
- deepen a sense of family success;
- prevent and reduce child abuse; and
- develop true home-school-community partnerships.

Parents as Teachers is based on the following assumptions:

- Children are born to learn. We don't have to entice them into learning—they are ready, willing, and able.
- Children learn the most from the people they love—their parents. Whether by accident or design, parents are teaching their child through every action they take and every word they say.
- Parents are the experts on their own children by virtue of their special knowledge and insight that comes from everyday living with them. They should be acknowledged as the real decision makers about their child's rearing.

- Parents as Teachers parent educators are generalists with research-based information on child development who work in partnership with parents to develop strategies that parents may choose to try in their family. They can demystify the schools' expectations and add to parents' understanding of how and why learning occurs.

- A variety of family forms can promote the development of healthy children and healthy adults. Because this program is designed for everyone, there is no stigma attached to participation. Families who are considered to be at high risk are likely to be attracted to Parents as Teachers because they know it is for everybody.

- Ethnic and cultural differences are to be valued. An understanding and appreciation of the history and traditions of the families in a community are essential for a parent educator who seeks to serve them.

- All families have strengths, and all parents want to be good parents. These beliefs are fundamental. Parents do not enroll in this program to be "fixed," but rather to learn to build on their strengths and draw on outside help in giving their child the best possible beginning.

Pertinent Research

Few would argue that all formal education is influenced by the learning experiences of the first years of life. Studies in the 1950s and early 1960s from the fields of developmental psychology, education, and medicine agreed on the importance of the early years for the development of language, intelligence, and emotional well-being.

In his Pulitzer Prize-winning series of articles, *Unlocking the Mind,* Ronald Kotulak (1993) details strides taken toward understanding how the human brain develops. As Kotulak explains, profound discoveries have overturned the previous notion that the brain is a static machine, developing at a steady pace according to a set of predetermined rules. Scientists now know that the brain must receive certain kinds of stimulation to develop such powers as vision, language, smell, muscle control, and reasoning and that it relies on the outside world to send it such stimuli. Genes provide the blueprint, and the environment provides the instructions for final construction (Kotulak, 1993). The wiring along this blueprint is made up of synapses, the connections rapidly forming between brain cells as they compete to find a job to perform and are stimulated by the outside world. The major bursts of synaptic activity happen in four phases—in fetal development, in newborns, between ages 4 to 10, and thereafter—but these bursts have essentially already started to fizzle out as early as the end of the first year of life. These findings have led scientists to the "use them or lose them" theory of synapses, believing that because the human brain is still being formed and organized after birth, certain kinds of learning must occur at certain stages of development. Meeting these "time windows" with the appropriate stimulation is critical to ensuring that children get the start they deserve and continue their lives equipped with the tools to be successful.

Kotulak (1993) quotes Harvard child psychiatrist Felton Earls, who says, "All infants require milk before they can eat solids. Is there an equivalent state of affairs for the brain? The answer is clearly an affirmative one. It requires stimulation: touch, holding, sound and vision." In the brain's hungriest moments, in the very beginning of life, infants rely on the humans taking care of them for their brain food. There are real consequences of missing the windows of development: if an infant brain does not receive visual experience by the age of 2, the child will never be able to see; if a child does not hear words by age 10, she will lose the gift of language forever (Kotulak, 1993).

In his article "Building a Better Brain for Baby," George Johnson (1994) states, "The implication, apt to incite anxiety among even the most attendant families, is that neglectful parents are guilty not only of a sin of omission—not providing enough mental stimulation—but a sin of commission as well: fating their children to confront the world with underdeveloped brains" (p. 6). By the time children enter preschool, the architecture of the brain has essentially been constructed. The brain will never again match the incredible pace of learning that occurs in the first few years (Clinton, 1996). There are clear indications that parents play a key role during these years in determining how their children will fare in school and in life—a more important role than the formal education system, which encounters the child after his foundation for learning and living has been laid.

The strong evidence presented by neuroscience on early brain development should be driving the nation's policy making, should be prompting reform, so that tomorrow's children aren't forced to rely on a safety net of later interventions that may not be there to catch them. As First Lady Hillary Rodham Clinton (1996) puts it, "If we . . . decide not to help families develop their children's brains, then at least let us admit we are acting not on the evidence but on a different agenda. And let us acknowledge that we are not using all the tools at our disposal to better the lives of our children" (p. 61).

Description of the Initiative

Laying the Groundwork

Despite its reputation as the "show-me state," in 1984 Missouri became the first state in the nation to mandate that every school district provide parent education and support services from birth to kindergarten entry for all families wishing to participate. A series of events orchestrated by the Missouri Department of Elementary and Secondary Education beginning in 1972 led to the passage of the Early Childhood Development Act by the Missouri General Assembly in 1984, resulting in statewide implementation of the Parents as Teachers program a year later.

In 1972, the State Board of Education adopted a position paper on early childhood education, defining the role and responsibility of the public education system during the years when home is the child's school. A campaign was mounted through conferences and forums to educate state and local decision makers from all sectors, as well as the public at large, on the critical need for children to have optimal beginnings, on the damaging effects of poor parenting, and on the cost-effectiveness of parent-child early education. A blue ribbon committee of influential Missouri citizens, appointed by the Commissioner of Education, took a leadership role in generating interest and support. Governor Christopher S. Bond, who became a first-time father at age 41, became a strong advocate and succeeded in getting bipartisan support for the pending enabling legislation.

Lessons learned from the investment of federal dollars in public school Title I preschool programs for disadvantaged children had shown that intervening at age 3 was already late for many. As a result, the decision was made in 1981 to test out the feasibility of influencing children's education from the onset of learning by partnering with their parents. The pilot Parents as Teachers project was launched that year as a cooperative effort of the Department of Elementary and Secondary Education, four diverse school districts selected on the basis of competitive proposals, and the Danforth Foundation, which funded the consultant services of Burton White. A total of 380 families, who were expecting their first children between December 1981 and September 1982, were enrolled. The families, who were representative of each school district's population, were provided services from the third trimester of pregnancy until the child turned 3. The 1985 results of the independent evaluation of the project's benefits to participating children and parents, as assessed at children's third birthdays (Pfannenstiel & Seltzer, 1985), led to funding for statewide implementation in 1985 and to widespread interest and inquiry about this program that was born in Missouri.

How the Program Works

Service Delivery

Families, schools, and communities share a common goal: to have all children develop to their fullest potential—to be all that they can be. With "beginning at the beginning" as its hallmark, Parents as Teachers was intended as a first step in achieving that goal. This home-school-community partnership supports and assists parents in their role as children's first and most influential teachers, building on family strengths. Now as in the pilot project phase, Parents as Teachers offers the following to all families:

- regularly scheduled personal visits by certified parent educators, who provide timely information on the child's development and who model ways parents can make the most of everyday learning opportunities;
- group meetings where parents share, compare, commiserate, and congratulate;
- monitoring of children's progress by both parent and professional educators to detect and treat any emerging problems as early as possible; and
- linkage with needed services that are beyond the scope of the program.

The intensity of the program varies according to the needs of the family; those who are facing the greatest challenges can receive additional personal visits and help in accessing other support services.

Instructional Home Visits

The personal visit, generally held in the home, is the heart of the Parents as Teachers program. It offers families the special advantage of one-to-one relationships that promote child and adult growth and development. It increases the potential for improving the ecology of family life because of the remarkable insight gained from working in the home on a sustaining basis. The visitor thereby acquires a sense of unmet health, economic, education and social service needs that impinge on parenting (Winter, 1995).

Home visits signal the program's willingness to accommodate family schedules, even when mothers work outside the home, and to operate on the family's turf. This sets the tone for a less formal, more relaxed relationship between the visiting professional and parents. It helps to equalize the balance of power between parent and visitor, which is especially important with families whose prior experiences with school and other agencies have not been positive. Parents who feel isolated and burdened with the demands of parenting respond to visitors who evidence genuine interest and empathy. It is not uncommon for participants to come to regard the parent educator more as a friend or a member of the family than as an outside expert.

Another benefit of home visiting is the opportunity for parents to have their questions and concerns about parenting answered in the privacy of their home. Parents of all social and economic strata want to do a good job, but limited positive experience or knowledge about child rearing can get in the way. They struggle to understand their children's behavior and are anxious to find out if what they observe and experience with their children is normal. Parents are often reluctant in a group setting to ask questions that might suggest ignorance on their part. Receiving assurance from the home visitor that this is normal behavior and hearing praise for the child's accomplishments give parents a sense of relief and pleasure and bolster their self-confidence.

Finally, children benefit. They are dependent on the key adults in their lives to foster a sense of security, trust, and self-esteem. Children's feelings of self-worth are enhanced when they see that their parents or other primary caregivers are valued and respected by others, particularly by someone whom they come to regard as teacher. Another obvious benefit for children is the opportunity that home visiting affords for all of the caring adults to knowledgeably share observations and insights that help guide the child's development.

Home visits in the Parents as Teachers program are generally one hour in length and are scheduled monthly for most families to allow time for parents to act on the information gained. If family needs warrant, visits may be offered biweekly or weekly. Parent materials, written at two different reading levels, reinforce and expand on the information discussed during the visit.

Group Meetings

Group meetings serve three major purposes: first, to provide a vehicle for additional input from the staff as well as from outside speakers; second, to create opportunities for families to share successes and common concerns about their children's behavior and development; and third, to help parents build support networks. Parent-child activities are provided during many group meetings to reinforce the importance of family interaction. Group meetings may be combined with social events, such as potluck suppers. They are offered at least monthly and are held in the school or community facility during the evening or on Saturdays as well as during weekdays to allow fathers and mothers who work outside the home to participate. Special meetings designed only for dads and other father figures help them to define and enjoy their role.

Drop-in and play times are offered by many programs to provide families the opportunity to use the center's facilities with their children, to visit with other parents, and to talk informally with the parent educator. Fathers as well as mothers, and sometimes grandparents, bring the child to play and interact with other children of a similar age. A parent educator is present during these sessions of about an hour in length, perhaps working or planning, but available for questions and conversation. She or he may take advantage of opportunities that arise for teaching child development informally around certain child behaviors as they occur.

Monitoring Child Development

A final means of input of information for families and staff is the developmental assessment component of the Parents as Teachers program. The purposes are twofold: first, to reassure parents if the child is developing on target; and second, to identify problems early to assist parents with appropriate interventions. Developmental screening is conducted annually, beginning at age 1. In addition, parents are helped to observe and monitor the child's development on an ongoing basis. Parent and parent educator observations, coupled with periodic screening, serve to safeguard against undetected delays or learning difficulties during the first years of life.

Linkage with Other Services

The Parents as Teachers program was not designed to be all things to all families. The community council is an integral part of the Parents as Teachers program, assisting with planning and implementation, building community support, and recruiting and referring families. Members of the council help to identify resources in the community, including diagnostic services, programs for children with special needs, learning resources for children and parents, health and social service programs, and so forth. Families are helped to link with programs and services they need that are beyond the scope of Parents as Teachers.

Organizational Structure

The most successful Parents as Teachers programs take the program's home-school-community philosophy to heart and use the skills of members from each sector. Local programs are strongly encouraged, though not required, to follow an organizational structure provided in the *Parents as Teachers Program Planning and Implementation Guide* provided as part of the initial Parents as Teachers training.

A school district or agency administrator may serve as overall *program supervisor* along with his or her other administrative tasks. The *parent educator,* in addition to planning for and making personal visits, participates in recruitment activities, screening activities, and group meetings with parents. She or he also keeps records on home visits, reports to the program coordinator on screening results that seem to warrant referral, and supervises children in the center at scheduled times. In programs employing more than one parent educator, it is advisable for one to serve as program coordinator. She or he is a working member of the educational staff as well as the supervisor of the other staff members. A *clerk-typist* is usually essential as well. In addition, programs may find *volunteers,* such as senior citizens and high school child development students, to be very useful in complementing services of regular staff members.

Competencies and Qualities of an
Effective Parent Educator

The parent educators are the jewels in the crown of the Parents as Teachers program. Most are parents themselves; all have backgrounds in teaching or early childhood development and have received special preservice training to deliver Parents as Teachers services. They are credentialed on an annual basis by the Parents as Teachers National Center, Inc., contingent on the administrating agency's approval of their service to families and their completion of the required hours of in-service training. Responsibility for the selection and supervision of service personnel rests with the local administrating agency.

Home visiting is demanding work that is best carried out by mature individuals whose life experiences enhance their capacity to help others. Their responsibilities range from discouraging a rural mother from using a dried pig's ear as a teething ring, to making a special nighttime visit to a mother who seems to be "on the brink," to arranging for a hearing test for a child whose language development is delayed. Home visitors need to be outgoing, comfortable with strangers, unflappable in new situations, well organized, nonjudgmental, and tactful. In identifying individuals who will work best as parent educators, the families to be served must be considered—their backgrounds, their attitudes about children, the cultural values that influence them as parents. Whom would they welcome into their home? Whom would they respect and to whom would they listen?

Home visitors are required to be both child development specialists and family specialists. Candidates need in-depth knowledge of early childhood development and should have had supervised experience working with young children and parents. They should also have strong working knowledge of how adults learn, since their role is to help parents become the best possible teachers and nurturers of their children and to enhance their sense of efficacy as parents. They may come from the fields of education, health care, or social work. Former classroom teachers must be able to make the transition from managing a group of children in a classroom to working with adults and children in someone else's living room.

Programs often choose local community members as key staff contacts with parents. This approach offers the advantages of providing training and employment for community residents, drawing on knowledge of the community gained from living there, and avoiding disparities in culture, language, and values between families and staff. It is not critical that home visitors be of the same ethnicity or culture as the families they serve, but they must understand and respect the values and beliefs of various cultures so that they can respond sensitively.

The quality of the human connection between home visitor and families is probably the best predictor of service effectiveness. "Warm and caring" probably tops the list of characteristics programs look for in choosing home visitors. Other interpersonal qualities that are essential for home visiting include a nonjudgmental, healthy attitude toward families and the ability to set boundaries (e.g., not to become so involved in family stress as to lose the focus of the home visit). The ability to maintain an appropriate sense of humor in the face of stress is not to be overlooked.

Active listening is key to establishing a trusting relationship because it communicates, "I hear what you are feeling, I value your abilities, I am interested and concerned, I am not judging or evaluating." One needs to be comfortable with silence, to ask open-ended questions, to avoid filling in or stepping in, to be sensitive to verbal and nonverbal communication from the family.

It is critical that the home visitor's body language and voice tone convey warmth, respect, and genuine interest.

Because a major purpose of home visiting is to tailor information on child development and child-rearing practices to family needs and interests, home visitors must be able to convey this information in language that is clearly understood, positive in nature, and not condescending. Information and issues addressed, as well as parent-child activities suggested, should be geared to the interests and concerns of father figures as well as of mothers, to nurture male involvement in children's development and learning. Male caregivers have their own special way of interacting with young children that should be acknowledged and encouraged. Every effort should be made to schedule visits when father figures and other significant caregivers can be present.

Observation is one of the most important skills needed by the home visitor and one that must also be fostered in parents. Understanding the organization of the home and the resources available to the family, as well as the interaction among family members, gives the home visitor a base on which to draw in building on family strengths. It is the means by which the visitor identifies parental expectations as well as behavior and development of children in relation to expected norms. Objective, positive observation is essential for documenting the proceedings of a home visit for accountability purposes and for planning the next visit.

Last, but certainly not least, is the ability to empower parents—facilitating or maintaining the family's ability to define its own goals and make its own decisions. Empowerment implies that many competencies are already present or are possible and that new competencies can be learned. This calls for a helping relationship that works continually toward promoting parents' independence in coping and problem solving.

Adaptations: A Program for All Parents

From the outset, Parents as Teachers has faced the challenges of adapting the curriculum to fit special populations, reaching at-risk groups, and providing quality services within budgetary restrictions. The program, which was originally designed for families with children aged birth to 3, was extended upward to age 5 in response to demand. One of the most important lessons learned from the Missouri experience is that model programs must be crafted and molded to fit the particular demands of local culture and politics.

The widespread interest in Parents as Teachers can be attributed to its many benefits. Health care providers see it as improving children's physical well-being. Mental health, social services, and corrections view it as preventing and reducing abuse and neglect. Churches endorse it as strengthening family life. The corporate world sees its potential for reducing stress and improving quality of life for employees. Schools, of course, realize the benefits of reducing the need for special and remedial education and of forming a positive relationship with families early on.

Because Parents as Teachers is not high in cost and not dependent on a particular setting or agency sponsorship, it can be widely replicated or adapted. Parents as Teachers is offered by public and private organizations as a stand-alone program or as part of a more comprehensive delivery of services as the following examples illustrate.

Parents as Teachers
for Teen Parents

The tenet central to the mission of Parents as Teachers that *all* parents deserve to be supported in their critical role as first teachers includes those who are most vulnerable—adolescent parents. With a teen birthrate that is among the highest in the industrialized world, our society is seriously affected emotionally, socially, and financially by teen pregnancy and parenting.

Parents as Teachers for Teen Parents is usually connected with a local secondary school, a connection which allows for optimum accessibility of the program by pregnant and parenting teens. School counselors and nurses advise expectant teens of Parents as Teachers, assuring a smooth and discreet transition into the program.

The curriculum includes adolescent as well as child development information, and issues unique to teenage parents are addressed with honest sensitivity. Techniques and strategies for group meetings with peers, often held during the school day, and personal visits are modified to meet the developmental needs of the adolescent.

Research indicates that a father's involvement in his child's life is highly significant to the developing child. Many teen fathers do not play an active role in raising their babies, if they play any role at all. Parents as Teachers for Teen Parents encourages young fathers to stay involved with their children by providing father support groups in the secondary schools, where they learn about child development. As one St. Louis teen father put it, "The program has helped me to grow up. I had to learn how to cope with a lot of things—my daughter, her mother, and her grandmother. That's really hard. The program helps me know what my rights are, as well as my responsibilities" (Parents as Teachers National Center, 1994, p. 23).

During the home visit, the parent educator makes every effort to draw in all members of the household who share in the caregiving of the child with the goals of developing consistency, providing the child a more stable home environment, building the teen mother's capabilities, and approaching conflicts through dialogue. The multigenerational approach to the teen home visit provides the parent educator with additional information about the teen's situation within the family. This enables the parent educator to help the teen develop coping strategies. At the same time, the teen's family is acknowledged, strengthened, and empowered in its crucial role of providing emotional and practical support for the teen and her baby. Including other family members in home visits allows for many voices to be heard, giving a clearer picture of how caregiving duties are divided, decisions are made, and conflicts are handled. The parent educator is available to discuss each person's questions, concerns, and frustrations relating to the teen and her baby.

The potential for one person to make a difference in a teenager's life should not be underestimated. In the words of Marian Wright Edelman (1995), "hope is one of the best contraceptives to teenage pregnancy" (p. 122). Although national statistics indicate that 50% to 80% of pregnant females drop out of high school, experience has shown that a high percentage of Parents as Teachers parents not only graduate from high school but go on with future vocational or education plans.

Parents as Teachers in the
Child Care Center

More than half of our nation's mothers return to the workforce within a year of the baby's birth, and many of their infants and toddlers spend 35 or more hours per week in substandard care (Carnegie, 1994). This makes the search for high quality child care a very real stressor for young families. The Parents as Teachers model was adapted for child care settings to address this growing need. Parents as Teachers in the Child Care Center is a home-center partnership designed to enhance the quality of infant-toddler care and to improve the communication and relationship between the two sets of very important people in a child's life—parents and other caregivers.

Parents as Teachers in the Child Care Center has been implemented in diverse child care settings including corporate, community college, hospital, university, United Way-funded, and private for-profit and not-for-profit centers. The initial personal visit with families is conducted in the home to give child care workers opportunity to see the family environment. Subsequent visits are scheduled at the child care center and allow parents to observe their child interacting with peers, to pick up timely child development information, to partake in planned activities with their child, and to compare observations with those of the caregiver. Regularly scheduled group meetings are offered for parents in the infant and toddler rooms, allowing families of children who are at the same developmental level to form intimate support groups. The program also provides minivisits between the parent and caregiver with a daily exchange of information about the child. All services are scheduled at times that accommodate working parents' schedules.

In 1994, the Public Policy Research Centers, University of Missouri—St. Louis, conducted a developmental assessment of Parents as Teachers in the Child Care Center at six diverse Midwestern sites for the purpose of enhancing training and program design. Primary benefits of the model were found to include increased communication and comfort level between parents and caregivers, changed attitudes on the part of caregivers toward parents and their role, higher level of professionalism and morale of caregivers involved, and increased knowledge of child development on the part of parents of lower socioeconomic and educational levels. The most significant result of this home-center partnership is perhaps one that is not so easily documented—children see the most important people in their lives working together for their benefit (Public Policy Research Centers, 1995).

Parents as Teachers for Native Americans

The average family income in Torreon, New Mexico, is between $3,000 and $5,000 per year. Families depend on Aid to Families with Dependendent Children (AFDC), food stamps, and Women, Infants, and Children (WIC) programs. Local leaders in Torreon estimate that less than 20% of the population has completed high school. Of the children entering kindergarten, 90% speak only Navajo. This community has limited facilities and on-site social services. There is one small general store in town but no gas station. Indian Health Service operates clinics that offer preventive health care, but clinic hours are limited, and emergency health care is problematic. It is unlikely that one program could meet all these needs, but fortunately, Torreon is one of the 23 sites that are home to a program making a difference in the lives of Native Americans.

Searching for solutions, the U.S. Bureau of Indian Affairs created the Family and Child Education program (FACE), the overall purpose of which is to address the problems of underachievement in school and the literacy needs of the family. FACE serves families with children from birth to age 8, based on three national models— Parents as Teachers, Parent and Child Education, and High/Scope— which have been combined to meet the needs of Native American families. Parents as Teachers provides the earliest piece of the program, the home-based component beginning at birth.

Parents as Teachers for Native Americans builds on the strengths these parents possess and is based on their real needs and real-life experiences. Parents become the change agents for themselves and their families. This system gives ownership to the tribes and the communities; in fact, the parent educators are themselves Native American, members of the tribes they serve. The educators are committed to ensuring that the beliefs, customs, values, and language of their respective tribes are validated, respected, recognized, and appreciated. Sites make their activities culturally appropriate by supporting Native American child rearing practices and weaving Native American language and tradition into the home and group activities. Parents as Teachers program coordinators and parent educators are faced daily with the goal and challenge of working in a close, cooperative manner with parents, tribal elders, and others in the community. The Parents as Teachers curriculum is flexible enough so that parent educators can implement it in a way suitable to the individual Native American communities.

The FACE program, begun in 1990 in six Native American communities, has expanded to 23 reservations in 10 states. A case study commissioned by the U.S. Department of Education to examine the effects of the program reports that active participants from all FACE sites believe that they have improved their parenting skills and consider this the most beneficial program result. Other important changes include an increase in parents' self-worth and confidence, as well as an increased awareness of the importance of education for both parents and children. As for the children, the study shows improved developmental progress and enhanced self-confidence and independence (Schultz, Lopez, & Hochberg 1995).

Parents as Teachers Specialized for Even Start and Head Start

Collaboration with other agencies and programs that serve young families has been integral to Parents as Teachers from the outset, because no single program can respond to all the family problems that impact on the young child's healthy development. Parents as Teachers has provided leadership in the formation and growth of effective partnerships through training, technical assistance, and cooperative implementation. In tenuous political environments, it is imperative that partnerships among agencies and organizations be developed to maximize access to new funding streams and to advocate on behalf of all children and families.

Requests for Parents as Teachers training from Even Start and Head Start programs have steadily increased, and institutes have been designed to specifically meet their needs. Along with the natural fit between Parents as Teachers and these two programs, several factors have contributed to this demand: the downward expansion of Head Start to include service for children from birth to age 3; a recommendation from the Senate Appropriations Committee to the U.S. Department of Education that ways be developed for Parents as Teachers to play a larger role in Even Start; and the inclusion of Parents as Teachers in the Even Start language of the 1994 Reauthorization of the Elementary and Secondary Education Act.

Parents as Teachers shares common goals with Head Start and Even Start, including promoting the healthy development of children, empowering and involving parents, building on family strengths, enhancing family literacy, and establishing links to other community sources of support for families. Parents as Teachers is continually working to nurture these connections by adapting training and curriculum materials to meet the needs of Head Start and Even Start personnel.

Parents as Teachers in Housing Projects

Many of the residents of Hollybrook Homes have little more than subsistence income. Most have not finished high school; many are unemployed. The National Benevolent Association of the Christian Church (Disciples of Christ), funder of the Hollybrook Homes Housing Complex, has implemented a program to help resident families make their way to a better life for themselves and their children. Creating Healthy Activities to Nurture Children through Education (CHANCE) was created based on the belief that no matter what a parent's struggle may be, children still need adequate care and attention during their early years, which in large measure may determine their future. Parents as Teachers is the essential first component of CHANCE. Along with the standard components of home visits and group meetings, mothers residing at Hollybrook come to the Parents as Teachers office for consultation and enrollment, screening, and borrowing books and educational toys from the lending library. Program impact can be measured by what is happening on a daily basis in these homes. Under the guidance of the parent educator, these mothers are reading to their children, teaching them shapes, colors and names, talking with them, listening to their reactions, and encouraging them. The children of Hollybrook Homes are getting the attention they need to develop successfully, and this new focus is making life more meaningful and enjoyable for the parents.

Housing projects are also used by school districts and other agencies as centers of operation for Parents as Teachers.

Proven Effectiveness

True success is measured in terms of changed lives, hence the challenge to continually evaluate the work of Parents as Teachers. Program evaluation has been integral in the evolution of the Parents as Teachers program since it originated, despite financial resource limitations. The studies vary extensively in their sample sizes, type of outcome indicators, and use of comparison groups. Some have investigated Parents as Teachers as a stand-alone program, whereas others have looked at it as part of a more comprehensive initiative. Several studies have been more qualitative, attempting to understand the evolution of Parents as Teachers or the way in which home visits are delivered. All known evaluation reports regarding Parents as Teachers are collected by the Parents as Teachers National Center, Inc., and reviewed by staff and a small group of research consultants. The first independent evaluation of Parents as Teachers was funded by the Missouri Department of Elementary and Secondary Education. Subsequent studies of the Missouri program have been funded by the Department with assistance from the Ford (Pfannenstiel, 1989; Pfannenstiel, Lambson, & Yarnell, 1991), A. L. Mailman (Pfannenstiel et al., 1991), and Smith Richardson Foundations (Smith & Wells, 1990). Studies of the program in other states have been supported by local school districts and private foundations. What follows is a select review of past and current Parents as Teachers evaluations.

The release by the *New York Times* in 1985 of an independent evaluation by Research & Training Associates of results of the Parents as Teachers pilot project generated interest in the program across the United States and around the world. This evaluation showed that at age 3, children of participating families were significantly advanced over the comparison group in language, social development, problem solving, and other intellectual abilities. Project parents credited the program with increasing their confidence and competence in child rearing and knowledge of child development (Pfannenstiel & Seltzer, 1985).

A follow-up study of pilot project and comparison groups showed that Parents as Teachers participant children scored significantly higher on standardized measures of reading and math achievement at the end of first grade. In all behavioral areas assessed by their teachers, Parents as Teachers children were rated more highly than the comparison group children. A significantly higher proportion of Parents as Teachers parents took an active role in their child's schooling (Pfannenstiel, 1989).

Statewide expansion of Parents as Teachers extended the program to include all rather than only first-time parents. A Second Wave evaluation, completed in 1991, focused on 395 randomly selected children and their parents enrolled in programs in 37 diverse school districts including urban, suburban, and rural settings. The Second Wave study indicated that the school districts involved were providing a level of service comparable to the pilot project. Children participating in Parents as Teachers were found to perform significantly higher than national norms on measures of intellectual and language abilities, despite the fact that the sample was over-represented on all traditional characteristics of risk compared to state and local populations. Parents' knowledge of child development and parenting practices increased for all types of families in the program (Pfannenstiel et al., 1991).

A follow-up study of the Second Wave sample was initiated in 1993 to assess the longer-term impacts of program participation. This study focused on the early school experiences and performance of the Parents as Teachers children and on their parents' involvement in their children's schools and activities to support learning in the home. Parents as Teachers children scored high on measures of complex and challenging tasks. Overall, the levels of achievement children demonstrated at the completion of the Parents as Teachers program were maintained in the first (or second in some cases) grade. This held true despite the broad diversity in children's experiences with preschool, child care, kindergarten and primary grades. The Parents as Teachers parents demonstrated high levels of school involvement, which they frequently initiated (Pfannenstiel, 1996).

Studies of the impact of Parents as Teachers have also been conducted by local Missouri school districts, such as the ones noted here from rural Missouri, Joplin, and Parkway School District. Results of a 1993 study of 516 students entering kindergarten in

22 rural school districts in southwest Missouri show that children who participated in the program at least one year scored significantly higher on the Kindergarten Inventory of Developmental Skills (KIDS), a commonly accepted measure of school readiness, than children who did not participate. Parents as Teachers children scored significantly higher in number concepts, auditory skills, pencil and paper skills, language skills, and visual skills. Of the sample, 224 came from families experiencing financial stress (Wheeler, 1994).

Kindergarten screening results from the Joplin (Missouri) School District indicate that Parents as Teachers children who entered kindergarten in the fall of 1994 clearly outscored children whose parents did not participate. Using the Early Screening Profile from American Guidance Services with 601 new kindergartners, children who had not been in Parents as Teachers had an average score of 55%, whereas those in the program scored 68%. The difference is even greater for those who entered Parents as Teachers as infants; their average score was 73% (Norton, 1994).

Finally, third graders who had participated in Parents as Teachers in the Parkway School District in St. Louis County, Missouri, scored significantly higher on standardized measures of achievement than their nonparticipating counterparts. According to the 1994 study, third graders who had received Parents as Teachers services had a national percentile rank of 81, whereas the nonparticipating students had a rank of 63 on the Stanford Achievement Test, with a significant difference in scores on all subtests. Parents as Teachers graduates were less likely to receive remedial reading assistance or to be held back a grade in school (Coates, 1994).

The rapid expansion of the Parents as Teachers program to other states has resulted in a number of studies of the program's implementation and effectiveness outside Missouri. One such evaluation, Increasing Children's Readiness for School by a Parental Education Program, conducted in the Binghamton, New York School District states, "Results indicate that PAT is a valuable investment for communities, with dividends at least four times the original investment." Their pilot study focused on a small sample of poor, high-needs children to determine if Parents as Teachers augments the effects of Head Start and Title I prekindergarten; the full study focused on all kindergartners in Binghamton. Testing in prekindergarten and again in kindergarten showed that the Parents as Teachers children had significantly higher cognitive, language, social, and motor skills than nonparticipants. According to the report, "twice as many Parents as Teachers grads are predicted to be ready to learn how to read when they enter school, avoiding special placement or retention in kindergarten."

The study also suggests "that participation in the PAT program is associated with lowered rates of welfare dependence and child abuse." By the children's first birthdays, welfare dependence within the Parents as Teachers group had dropped by 10%, but dependence nearly doubled for the comparison group. The drop indicates "a greater tendency for these parents to seek control over their lives, due to improved self-confidence as parents and interest in their children's future" (Drazen & Haust, 1994).

On the other side of the country, SRI International researchers have been investigating the implementation and effectiveness of several Parents as Teachers programs to discover if Parents as Teachers can help parents in at-risk situations offset the threats to their children by teaching effective parenting approaches that support healthy child development. The Salinas Valley Parents as Teachers Evaluation assessed more than 500 children and their parents from a community that has a large Latino population, high poverty, and high mobility associated with employment of migrant workers in the agriculture industry. The children were randomly assigned to either a Parents as Teachers or a comparison group. Preliminary reports from the Salinas study show consistently positive impacts for parents and children participating in the Parents as Teachers program. Parent and child outcomes were measured through a battery of instruments and procedures administered at or near the children's first birthdays. On the HOME (Home Observation for Measurement of the Environment) rating scale, Parents as Teachers parents consistently scored higher on measures of parenting behavior. These parents also outscored control group parents on the KIDI (Knowledge of Infant Development Inventory) regardless of mother's ethnic background and age (Wagner, 1992).

The continuing growth of Parents as Teachers warrants a long-term evaluation strategy for the program. A multiyear proposal for Advancing the Parents as Teachers Program Through a Comprehensive Evaluation Strategy has been submitted to several potential funders. Phase I of this multisite study, which will focus on families with low income, has been funded by the Carnegie Corporation, with preparatory activities underwritten by the Danforth and Ewing Marion Kauffman Foundations. The study, which is a collaborative effort with SRI International, proposes to follow Parents as Teachers participants through to kindergarten to examine the extent to which early intervention from birth to age 3 adds value to the benefits of Head Start and other programs in preparing high-needs children for school success. Evaluation findings will be translated into practice by the Parents as Teachers National Center through its training and program development and will serve to inform the field of early childhood education as well.

In today's political climate, widely replicated programs such as Parents as Teachers have to be willing to subject themselves to the scrutiny of academic researchers and professional evaluators to survive. Policy makers and funders want to know "what works." Documentation of the program's effectiveness was a requirement of the Innovations in State and Local Government Award received in 1987 from the Ford Foundation and Kennedy School of Government, Harvard University. This held true also for Parents as Teachers' acceptance into the U.S. Department of Education's National Diffusion Network. But it is truly the words and real experiences of families that linger long after the evaluation data have been analyzed. The benefits of Parents as Teachers can be seen through such examples as a school district reducing its dropout rate for expectant and parenting adolescents to zero; a group of Ozark Mountain parents asking the school to teach them correct English so they can better teach their children; inner-city homeless families living in shelters attending appropriately to their children's developmental needs despite the many stresses they are experiencing; toddlers of mentally retarded mothers developing on target because parent educators gear the program to those parents' level of understanding; and a parent in Rhode Island crediting her PAT parent educator with observations that led to early detection of a brain tumor in her young son.

Cost-Effectiveness

Because preventive and early intervention services receive a small fraction of our nation's resources, cost-effectiveness is a major concern. "Two-generation programs that address the needs of parents and children have the potential to produce large benefits in the short term as well as in the long term, and therefore appear to be an important focus for economic evaluation" (Barnett, 1993, p. 106). It is difficult, however, to assign dollar values to the life-enhancing outcomes programs strive to produce.

Part of the appeal of the Parents as Teachers program is its low cost—the major expense being the salary and travel of parent educators. At most sites, the program does not require extensive facilities or a large investment in materials. Parents are encouraged to take advantage of learning opportunities that occur in everyday living, using materials that are commonly found in the home. School districts and other sponsoring agencies commonly make in-kind contributions, such as an office and group meeting space, clerical assistance, and program supervision.

Eighty-nine percent of the Parents as Teachers programs that submitted annual program reports to the Parents as Teachers National Center in 1995 indicated an expenditure of less than $1000 per family. Cost varies, of course, according to the number of personal visits provided, amount of travel required, parent educator salaries, administrative cost, and the amount of in-kind contributions. As to cost savings, a school district in Bryan, Texas submitted relevant information on the 15 children who exited the Parents as Teachers program in 1993 at age 4. During the course of the program, the number of children exhibiting delays was reduced from seven to two. The district estimated its savings for the five children who did not require special services at school entry to be $39,440 per year (Parents as Teachers National Center, 1994).

It was the realization that savings in human potential and tax dollars can result from this early prevention program that led Missouri to appropriate state funds to implement Parents as Teachers in every school district in 1985. Funding has increased each year since then, with the goal of enabling all families with age-eligible children to participate by the year 2000.

Conclusion

Parents as Teachers is not intrusive or imposing, nor does it presume to be the cure-all for all populations. Rather, it is designed to be adapted to accommodate the people it serves. The program respects the diversity of parents and families while uniting them around a universal goal—raising healthy and successful children.

There is an increasing awareness of the importance of this goal at all levels—family, community, state, and federal. The burgeoning growth of Parents as Teachers attests to this fact. It has been recognized by the U.S. Congress as an effective family education and support program in the Goals 2000: Educate America Act, the 1993 Family Preservation and Support Services Act, and the 1994 Reauthorization of the Elementary and Secondary Education Act.

"In our search for excellence [in education] . . . we have ignored the fundamental fact that to improve the nation's schools, a solid foundation must be laid. We have failed to recognize that the family may be a more imperiled institution than the school and that many of education's failures relate to problems that precede schooling, even birth itself . . . One point is clear: in our search for excellence . . . children must come first" (Boyer, 1991, p. 3).

And truly putting children first means investing in good beginnings for them all.

References

Barnett, W. S. (1993, Winter). Economic evaluation of home visiting programs. *The Future of Children, pp. 93-112.*

Bloom, B. (1964). *Stability and change in human characteristics.* New York: John Wiley.

Boyer, E. L. (1991). *Ready to learn: A mandate for the nation.* Princeton, NJ: Carnegie Foundation for the Advancement of Teaching.

Bronfenbrenner, U. (1979). *Is early intervention effective?* Lexington, MA: Lexington Books.

Carnegie Corporation of New York. (1994). *Starting points: Meeting the needs of our youngest children.* New York: Author.

Clinton, H. R. (1996). *It takes a village and other lessons children teach us.* New York: Simon & Schuster.

Coates, D. (1994, June 30). *Early childhood evaluation.* A report to the Parkway Board of Education, Parkway, MO.

Drazen, S., & Haust, M. (1994). *Increasing children's readiness for school by a parental education program.* Binghamton, NY: Community Resource Center.

Edelman, M. W. (1995). *Guide my feet: Prayers and meditations on loving and working for children.* Boston: Beacon.

Johnson, George (1994, April 17). Building a better brain for baby. *New York Times,* E1, E6.

Kotulak, R. (1993, December 14). Why some kids turn violent: Abuse and neglect can reset brain's chemistry. In *Unlocking the mind*. Series in the *Chicago Tribune*.

Norton, S. (1994). *Early childhood evaluation*. Joplin, MO: Joplin School District.

Parents as Teachers National Center, Inc. (1994, November). *Ready to learn: Community partnerships for young children*. (Available from the Parents as Teachers National Center, 10176 Corporate Square Drive, St. Louis, MO 63132)

Pfannenstiel, J. (1989). *New Parents as Teachers project follow-up study*. Overland Park, KS: Research & Training Associates.

Pfannenstiel, J. (1996). *Follow-up to the second wave study of the Parents as Teachers program*. Overland Park, KS: Research & Training Associates.

Pfannenstiel, J., Lambson, T., & Yarnell, V. (1991). *Second wave study of the Parents as Teachers program*. Overland Park, KS: Research & Training Associates.

Pfannenstiel, J., & Seltzer, D. (1985). *Evaluation report: New Parents as Teachers project*. Overland Park, KS: Research & Training Associates.

Public Policy Research Centers. (1995). *Parents as Teachers in child care centers: A developmental assessment for training and technical assistance*. St. Louis, MO: Author.

Public Policy Research Centers. (1995). Parents as Teachers National Center, Inc. Annual Report (1994). (Available from the Parents as Teachers National Center, 10176 Corporate Square Drive, St. Louis, MO 63132)

Schultz, T., Lopez, E., & Hochberg, M. (1995, June 30). *Early childhood reform in seven communities: Front-line practice, agency management and public policy* (Vol. 2). Washington DC: U.S. Department of Education.

Smith, L., & Wells, W. (1990). *Difficult to reach, maintain and help urban families in PAT: Issues, dilemmas, strategies, and resolutions in parented education*. St. Louis, MO: Washington University.

Wagner, M. (1992). *Home the first classroom: A pilot evaluation of the Northern California Parents as Teachers project*. Menlo Park, CA: SRI International.

Wheeler, H. (1994). *A study of the Missouri Parents as Teachers program and its effects on the readiness skills of children entering kindergarten in Southwest Missouri Public Schools*. Unpublished doctoral dissertation, University of Mississippi.

White, B., Kaban, B., Attanuci, J., & Shapiro, B. (1978). *Experience and environment: Major influences on the development of the young child* (Vol. 2). Englewood Cliffs, NJ: Prentice Hall.

Winter, M. (1995). *Home visiting: Forging the home-school connection*. Washington, DC: U.S. Department of Education.

• CHAPTER 7 •

High/Scope Perry Preschool Program

DAVID P. WEIKART

LAWRENCE J. SCHWEINHART

T he public spirit that led to the civil rights movement and other major social changes of the late 1950s and early 1960s—school integration, voting rights, open housing, and ultimately the War on Poverty—also inspired people working in many smaller yet significant projects. For example, in 1960, because they were concerned about the persistently poor high school performance of their students from low-income neighborhoods, a group of public school principals and special services staff in Ypsilanti, Michigan, led by David P. Weikart, developed a plan for intervention. Thus, at a time when many were searching for action solutions to intractable problems, the study that was to be known as the High/Scope Perry Preschool Project was born. The project's underlying assumption was that reaching youngsters well before adolescence, at the preschool level, might establish a foundation that could lead to more successful futures for them. Though the project's initiators did not initially intend to follow the study subjects beyond their school years, because of the preschool program's encouraging impact, the study was eventually extended to include follow-up of the children through young adulthood, with interviews at ages 19 and 27.

After 2 years of planning, the work of the project began in 1962; and it has operated since that time under the direction of David P. Weikart, principal investigator. Since 1970, it has been conducted under the auspices of the High/Scope Educational Research Foun-

146

dation, which was established in that year by Weikart to continue the study and to carry out related research and curriculum development. The High/Scope Perry Preschool study focuses on the lives of 123 at-risk, African American children who were selected from 3- and 4-year-olds in a low-income neighborhood of Ypsilanti. The 123 children entered the study in five waves between 1962 and 1965. Assigned on a random basis, half of them participated in a high-quality preschool education program, and the other half remained in their normal setting, without any special intervention program. The study was planned as a carefully designed research project, because to bring children of preschool age into any school program, unless there was an extraordinary family need for service, was considered a questionable practice at the time (Weikart, 1967; Weikart, Deloria, Lawser, & Wiegerink, 1970).

Periodic follow-up of the 123 study participants over more than 30 years has now demonstrated unequivocally that high-quality early childhood education can significantly alter the life chances of children. It can improve their capacity, as adults, for positive family development and positive community participation, both economic and social. Furthermore, the cost of providing such services for young children represents an effective use of public dollars, with a return (in constant dollars) that greatly exceeds the investment (Schweinhart, Barnes, & Weikart, with Barnett & Epstein, 1993).

The High/Scope Perry Preschool Project specifically has found many differences in the life experiences of the two groups of study participants—the "preschool" and "no-preschool" groups. Those who participated in the preschool program, when compared over more than two decades with their peers who had no preschool, have persistently reported higher academic achievement. As young adults, the preschool group have achieved higher incomes as well as such positive social outcomes as fewer out-of-wedlock births and higher rates of home and car ownership. They have also reported significantly fewer arrests for criminal behavior and less welfare participation. The benefit-cost study that investigated these findings reported a $7.16 savings for each dollar invested in the preschool program. Such strong results have convinced many policymakers and business people that preschool education can be an appropriate social investment for public dollars (Weikart, 1995).

But not all preschool programs are effective. Only high-quality early childhood programs are likely to produce the results described

here. Effective, high-quality programs are built around active involvement of children and provide them with a sense of control by
giving them a choice in both what and how they learn. Programs
that direct young children in specific academic learning, that lead
children to use materials in limited and prescribed ways, that
organize reward strategies to interest children in teacher-desired
outcomes, and that employ other procedures that do not permit the
full development of independent decision making by the child are
either ineffective or have reduced impact (Schweinhart & Weikart,
1996). The task of the early childhood education field is to deliver
validated high-quality programs to effectively serve children, their
families, and the community, thereby justifying the large-scale
public investment that this requires.

The Project's Conceptual Framework

When the High/Scope Perry Preschool Project and other preschool studies began in the 1960s, they were based on the idea that
preschool programs could make a difference in the development of
human intelligence—that during the early years, the ability to do
well in school could be improved. Weikart (1967) derived the Perry
study rationale from animal studies on environmental enrichment
(Krech, Rosenzweig, & Bennett, 1960; Scott, 1962); from Bloom's
(1964) observation that "50 percent of [variance in intellectual]
development takes place between conception and age 4" (p. 88);
and from the emerging work of Piaget on the development of the
thinking process in young children (Hunt, 1961; Piaget & Inhelder,
1969). The Perry study's conceptual framework was also favored
by the social context of the late 1950s and early 1960s, including
the social mandate to provide equal educational and employment
opportunities to all Americans.

In the years since 1962, theory in child development has advanced on many fronts. Most important has been the development
of theory on the temporal unfolding of the relationship between a
person's heredity and environment. No longer is the question
simply whether a personal trait such as intelligence is inherited or
the product of experience. Rather, a trait is best viewed as a
dynamic relationship between genetic material and environmental
opportunities (e.g., Sameroff & Chandler, 1975). Effects of genetic

inheritance and effects of experience are inseparably intermixed and indistinguishable; all that can be observed and measured is a person's performance in the setting. Human development may be modeled as a series of interactions or transactions between performance and setting.

Evidence for Preschool Program Effects

An examination of the literature reveals that evidence for the effectiveness of high-quality preschool programs for children living in poverty comes from both sets of studies and individual studies.

The *sets of studies* include reviews (e.g., Berrueta-Clement, Schweinhart, Barnett, Epstein, & Weikart, 1984; Haskins, 1989; Ramey, Bryant, & Suarez, 1985); meta-analyses (McKey et al., 1985); and even collaboratively conducted research (Lazar, Darlington, Murray, Royce, & Snipper, 1982).

The Head Start Synthesis Project meta-analysis of all available studies of Head Start's effects (McKey et al., 1985) identified 50 studies that found evidence of immediate improvements in children's intellectual performance, socioemotional performance, and health that lasted several years. It also found that these Head Start programs provided and linked families with health, social, and educational services and influenced various institutions to provide such services. Ramey et al. (1985) identified another 11 experimental studies in which the mean intelligence test scores of children who participated in preschool programs were as high as or higher than the mean intelligence test scores of children in the studies' control groups. Lazar et al. (1982) analyzed data from the constituent studies of a collaborative effort called the Consortium for Longitudinal Studies. On the basis of earlier findings of constituent studies and a common follow-up assessment in the late 1970s, they reported findings of positive program effects on intelligence test scores at school entry, on special education placement, and on grade retention.

The *individual studies* that are relevant to the subject of preschool effectiveness include Garber (1988); Gray, Ramsey, and Klaus (1982); Lally, Mangione, and Honig (1988); Levenstein, O'Hara, and Madden (1983); Monroe and McDonald (1981); Palmer (1983);and Ramey, Bryant, Campbell, Sparling, and Wasik

(1988). Large-scale individual studies include Fuerst and Fuerst (1993), and Irvine (1982). All the programs examined in these individual longitudinal studies served young children living in poverty and at special risk of school failure. Children entered the programs at some time between birth and age 5 and remained in them at least for a single school year, and at most through nearly their entire early childhood, from birth to school entry. In some of these studies, assessment has not yet progressed beyond early childhood; whereas in others, follow-up has continued up to age 21. Most of the studies include the possibility of future follow-up with study participants at later ages. All of these studies were able to follow up on at least 70% of the original study participants.

Each of these individual studies that collected data on early childhood intellectual performance found its program group to have a significantly higher mean intellectual performance score than its no-program group ($p < .05$, two-tailed), at least during the program and shortly thereafter. Some of the studies reported that significantly fewer program-group than no-program-group members were ever placed in special education classes. The magnitude of the special education percentages in each study was a function of the initial degree of risk of school failure for the participants in that study. Some studies reported that significantly fewer program group than no-program group members were ever retained in a grade. Some studies found the program group to have a significantly higher rate of high school graduation than the no-program group.

Fade-out of Preschool Program Effects?

Although some have claimed that most effects of good preschool programs for children in poverty fade away (e.g., McKey et al., 1985), there is virtually no evidence of fade-out of the effect on children's special education placement, high school graduation, or delinquency; and fade-out evidence is mixed for effects on children's socioemotional behavior and school achievement. Clear evidence of fade-out has been found only for gains in children's intelligence-test scores. In the 1960s, the hypothesis was that even though early educational programs were found to raise young children's test scores, subsequent educational programs would not affect them. Instead, it may be argued, a difference in intelligence-test scores reflects a difference in educational settings. When children who *have* attended preschool programs and children who *have not* attended preschool programs come together into the same, standard elementary school classrooms, their intelligence test scores also come together.

The Preschool Program

For the High/Scope Perry Preschool Project, teachers conducted a program based at the Perry Elementary School in Ypsilanti. The program was comprised of a daily 2.5-hour classroom session for children on weekday mornings and a weekly 1.5-hour home visit to each mother and child on weekday afternoons. The 30-week school year began in mid-October and ended in May. Of the 58 children in the program group, the 13 in Wave Zero participated in the program for one school year at age 4, and the 45 in Waves One through Four participated in the program for two school years at ages 3 and 4. Each pair of successive waves—Zero and One, One and Two, Two and Three, and Three and Four—attended the program together one school year, one wave being age 4 and the other being age 3. In 1966-67, the final year of the program, 11 3-year-olds, who were not included in the longitudinal sample, attended the program with the 12 4-year-olds in Wave Four. Thus, the four teachers in the program served 20 to 25 children each school year, resulting in a child-teacher ratio of 5.00-6.25 per teacher. This ratio was set to accommodate the demands, not of the classroom sessions, but of the weekly home visits.

The teachers visited the homes of each child in their classes (a) to involve the mother in the educational process and enable her to provide her child with educational support and (b) to implement the curriculum with each child in the child's home (Weikart, Rogers, Adcock, & McClelland, 1971). The teacher also helped the mother remain involved in the home visit by helping her deal with any problems that arose during the visit. Teachers took about a half hour to prepare for the home visit, planning how to extend what the child was doing in the classroom. Initially, both teachers and mothers, coming from different backgrounds, had to overcome a certain hesitation about participating in home visits. But after the first few visits, teachers and mothers usually were able to establish the rapport that was essential to the success of home visits. Project staff also convened group meetings of mothers and of fathers.

The High/Scope Perry Preschool program cost $1,510 per child per school year in 1960s dollars (Schweinhart, Barnes, & Weikart 1993), which is the equivalent of $7,252 in 1992 dollars. This cost included *all* program costs, even school-district administration and building overhead costs. The high cost was principally due to having four public school teachers who were paid 10% above the district's standard pay scale—1 teacher for every 5.7 children (overall project average). It is reasonable to assume that the quality of the program could have been maintained if the number of children per staff member had been increased to 10. The High/Scope Preschool Curriculum Comparison Study (Schweinhart & Weikart, 1996) found that preschool programs could be highly effective with 8 children per staff member; and the National Day Care Study (Ruopp, Travers, Glantz, & Coelen, 1979) provided evidence that program effectiveness does not decline substantially until the number of children per staff member exceeds 10. Increasing even to 8 children per staff member, but making no other changes, would have reduced the program cost to $5,187 per child in 1992 dollars.

Development of the High/Scope Curriculum

The preschool program developed for the High/Scope Perry Preschool Project involved a systematic approach to classroom and home-visit activities that was based on principles of active learning. Originally called the Cognitively Oriented Curriculum to distinguish it from approaches that did not include a systematic emphasis on cognitive development (Weikart et al., 1971), the approach was later named the High/Scope Curriculum (Hohmann & Weikart, 1995; see also Hohmann, Banet, & Weikart, 1979; Weikart & Schweinhart, 1993).

The High/Scope Perry Preschool Program developed in 1962 was one of the first programs designed to help children overcome the negative effects of poverty on schooling. (The Head Start programs, which began in 1965, had a similar aim.) Staffed by both psychologists and teachers, the preschool program established a creative tension between the psychologist's demand for explicit rationale and the preschool teacher's more intuitive approach to dealing with children. Thus, the High/Scope Curriculum evolved from give-and-take among people who had definite ideas about how to do things but were open to new ideas and could integrate them into their thinking and practice.

As the High/Scope Perry Preschool program entered its second year, the staff encountered and embraced the child development ideas of Jean Piaget. Piaget offered a conceptual structure around which a preschool curriculum model could be built, an explicit rationale for preschool activities. Piaget offered the idea of the child as active learner, an idea that not only had intuitive appeal but also had strong roots in early childhood tradition going back at least to Friedrich Froebel in the first half of the 19th century. Starting from this base, the High/Scope Curriculum developed several major components.

Active Learning by the Child

Adults who use the High/Scope Curriculum must be fully committed to providing settings in which children learn actively and construct their own knowledge. The child's knowledge comes from personal interaction with ideas, direct experience with physical objects, and application of logical thinking to these experiences. The adult's role is to supply the context for these experiences, to help the child think about them logically, and, through observation, to understand the progress the child is making. In a sense, children are expected to learn by the scientific method of observation and inference at a level of sophistication consonant with their development.

Role of the Teacher

Teachers play an important, unique role in the High/Scope Curriculum. Just as the children are active learners, so too are the teachers. By daily team evaluation and planning using the High/Scope key experiences as a framework, teachers study their experiences with children and with classroom activities and strive to achieve new insights into each child's unique tapestry of skills and interests. Members of the teaching team challenge themselves by continually observing one another's performance and interacting in mutually supportive ways.

Another important aspect of the teacher's role concerns interaction with the child. Although broad developmental milestones are employed to monitor youngsters' progress, the teacher does not teach a defined subject matter. Instead, the teacher listens closely to what children plan and then actively questions and works with them to extend their activities to challenging levels, as appropriate. The teacher's questioning style emphasizes seeking information from the youngster—information that will help the adult to participate in the child's activity. "Test" questions, such as those about color, number, or size, are rarely used. Instead, the teacher asks, "What happened?" "How did you make that?" "Can you show me?" "Can you help another child?" and so on. This questioning style permits free conversation between adult and child and models language for child-to-child interaction. This approach permits the teacher and the child to interact as partners—as mutual thinkers and doers rather than as active teacher and passive pupil, which are the traditional school roles. All are sharing and learning as they work.

The teacher does not do a number of things that are standard in many classroom and day care programs. The teacher does not introduce projects for the children to undertake (Katz & Chard, 1993). Neither does the teacher use planned curriculum activities, such as workbooks or study guides, to train children in the alphabet or simple arithmetic skills (Bereiter & Engelmann, 1966). (See Epstein, Schweinhart, & McAdoo, 1996, for a careful review of a range of major early childhood approaches.) The High/Scope Curriculum is based on the recognition that a group of 3- and 4-year-olds seldom would be able or wish to do the same thing at the same time and in the same manner without strong adult decision making, direction, and imposition of authority. Young children learn at different rates and from having a variety of experiences. Thus, the adults in a High/Scope program do not make the children pay attention, wait, perform tasks of little interest, and, most important, act on someone else's decisions. Rather, they develop and equip a stimulating environment; maintain a consistent daily routine; introduce ideas and activities, as appropriate, to extend child-developed plans or enable skill development; and interact naturally with children.

A Daily Routine to Support Active Learning

To create a setting in which children can learn actively, a consistent daily classroom routine is maintained that varies only when children have fair warning that things will be different the next day. Field trips are not sprung as surprises, nor are special visits or events planned for the classroom on the spur of the moment. This adherence to routine gives children the consistency they need to develop a sense of responsibility and at the same time enjoy opportunities for independence.

The High/Scope Curriculum's daily routine is made up of a *plan-do-review* sequence and several additional elements. The plan-do-review sequence gives children opportunities to express intentions about their activities while keeping the teacher intimately involved in the whole process. The elements of the daily routine are described in the following paragraphs.

Planning Time. It is not unusual for young children to make choices and to make decisions about implementing their choices. But in most preschool programs, children seldom think about these decisions in a systematic way or reflect on the possibilities and consequences of their choices. In the High/Scope approach, planning time gives children a structured, consistent chance to express their ideas to adults and to see themselves as individuals who can act on decisions. They experience the power of independence and the joy of working with an attentive adult as well as with peers. Children's planning helps them to be conscious of their intentions, and this supports the development of purpose and confidence.

The teacher talks with children about the plans they have made before the children carry them out. This helps children to clarify their ideas and think about how to proceed. Talking with children about their plans provides an opportunity for the teacher to encourage and respond to each child's ideas, to suggest ways to strengthen the plans so they will be successful, and to understand and gauge each child's level of development and thinking style. Both children and adults receive benefits: children feel reinforced and ready to start their work; and adults have ideas of what opportunities for extension might arise, what difficulties children might have, and where problem solving may be needed. In such a classroom, all are playing appropriate and important roles.

Work Time. The next part of the plan-do-review sequence—work time—is generally the longest single time period in the daily routine. Teachers new to the High/Scope Curriculum sometimes find work time confusing because they are not sure of their role. Adults do not lead work-time activities—children execute their own plans of work—but neither do adults just sit back and watch. The adult's role during work time is to observe children to see how they gather information, interact with peers, and solve problems—and then to enter into the children's activities to encourage, extend, and set up problem-solving situations.

Cleanup Time. Cleanup time is naturally integrated into the plan-do-review sequence in the obvious place, after the "doing." During this time, children return materials and equipment to their labeled places and store their incomplete projects. This process restores order to the classroom and provides opportunities for the children to learn and use many basic cognitive skills. Of special importance is the way the learning environment is organized to facilitate children's use of materials. All materials in the classroom that are for children's use are within their reach and on open shelves. Clear labeling—usually consisting of easy-to-understand representations of the various objects on each shelf—is essential. With this organizational plan, children can realistically return all work materials to their appropriate places. Knowing where everything they need and use is located also gives children a sense of control, ownership, and even mastery.

Recall Time. Recall time, the final phase of the plan-do-review sequence, is the time when children represent their work time experience in a variety of developmentally appropriate ways. They might recall the names of the children they involved in their plan, draw a picture of the building they made, or describe the problems they encountered. Recall strategies include drawing pictures, making models, physically demonstrating how a plan was carried out, or verbally recalling the events of work time. Recall time brings closure to children's planning and work time activities; it provides them opportunities to express insights on what they have experienced. The teacher supports children's linkage of the actual work to the original plan. This review permits children to reflect on what they did and how it was done. Putting their ideas and experiences into words also facilitates children's language development.

Small-Group Time. The general format of small-group time is familiar to most preschool teachers. The teacher presents a short activity in which children participate for a given period of time. These activities may have to do with children's cultural backgrounds, field trips the group has taken, the seasons of the year, or age-appropriate aspects of music, movement, or art. In the High/Scope Curriculum, the teacher introduces the activity, but children are encouraged to contribute ideas and solve in their own way any problems presented by the activity. Activities follow no prescribed sequence but respond to the children's needs, abilities, interests, and cognitive goals. Children work with materials in their own way and at their own rate. The activity that actually results may be different from what the teacher originally intended. Once each child has had the opportunity for individual choice and problem solving, the teacher extends the child's ideas and actions by asking open-ended questions and by supporting additional problem-solving situations. In planning and implementing small-group time, active involvement by all children is important. An active small-group time gives children the chance to make choices, to explore materials and objects, and to talk and work with adults and other children.

Large-Group Time. At large-group time, the whole group meets together with an adult for 10 to 15 minutes to play games, sing songs, do finger plays, perform basic movement activities, play musical instruments, or reenact a special event. This time provides an opportunity for each child to experience a sense of community, to share and demonstrate ideas, and to take part in group problem solving. Although the adult may bring the group together and initiate the activity, children act as leaders as well and are encouraged to make as many individual choices as possible.

Key Experiences in Child Development

Child progress in the High/Scope Curriculum is understood in terms of a set of key experiences. Whereas the plan-do-review sequence within a consistent daily routine is the focus of the

High/Scope Curriculum for the child, the key experiences are the focus for the teacher. Key experiences help the teacher to support and extend the child-initiated activities in developmentally appropriate ways, so that opportunities for growth are constantly available to the child. They provide a way of thinking about curriculum that frees the teacher from using activity workbooks, from organizing and directing group projects, or from consulting scope-and-sequence charts. They provide the framework for observing and assessing each child's developmental progress.

The key experiences describe the growth of rational thought in children the world over, regardless of nation or culture. They are also very simple and pragmatic. Preschool key experiences have been identified in these areas:

High/Scope Key Experience Categories for Preschool Children

- Creative representation
- Language and literacy
- Initiative and social relations
- Movement
- Music

- Classification
- Seriation
- Number
- Space
- Time

Each of these categories is divided into specific types of experiences. For example, the key experiences in Creative Representation are the following:

Experiences in Creative Representation

- Recognizing objects by sight, sound, touch, taste, and smell
- Imitating actions and sounds
- Relating models, pictures, and photographs to real places and things
- Pretending and role playing
- Making models out of clay, blocks, and other materials
- Drawing and painting

Classroom learning activities are not compartmentalized, and therefore any given activity may involve several types of key experiences. This list of key experiences gives the teacher a tool to use in thinking about the program and observing youngsters. In addition, the key experience approach provides a way to give the curriculum structure while maintaining an openness to new types of experiences. The key experiences are also a device that enables the High/Scope Curriculum to continue to evolve as a forceful tool in promoting children's growth and development.

Parent Involvement

From the outset of development of the High/Scope Curriculum, parent participation has been one of its hallmarks. The key to effective parent involvement is the two-way flow of information. Although the school and its staff have knowledge and training to provide to the family, the staff are also informed by the parents about the child, the family's culture, and their language and goals. The belief that parents and staff are each experts in their own domains is essential to the success of the program and to its use in various settings.

High/Scope Curriculum Training

Effective training in the High/Scope Curriculum has several key elements. Training is on-site and curriculum-focused. It is adapted to the actual work setting of the teacher, physically and socially; adapted to the group of children involved (e.g., disabled, bilingual); and related to the culture of the children, involving parents in some systematic way. Training sessions are scheduled about once a month because teachers need time to integrate the training experience, to put it into practice, to share it, to think about it, to see the gaps in their own thinking and in the program being presented, and to make adaptations to their own setting. Consistent delivery to the individual teacher is maintained by observations and feedback (Epstein, 1993).

Nearly 1,300 early childhood leaders in the United States and other countries have successfully completed High/Scope's 7-week Training of Trainers program, and they are now training teachers in the High/Scope Curriculum. An estimated 29% of all Head Start staff, for example, have received some High/Scope Curriculum training from these trainers (Larner & Schweinhart, 1991).

Research Support for the High/Scope Curriculum

By virtue of its careful experimental design and long-term duration, the evaluation of the High/Scope Perry Preschool program is
one of the most thorough examinations of program effects ever
undertaken. The basic evaluation question is whether the
High/Scope Perry Preschool program affected the lives of participating children. As explained earlier, the study focused on 123
African Americans born in poverty and at high risk of failing in
school. In the early 1960s, at ages 3 and 4, these children were
randomly divided into a program group (who received a high-
quality, active learning preschool program) and a no-program
group (who received no preschool program). The two groups have
been carefully studied over the years. At age 27, 95% of the original
study participants were interviewed, and additional data were
gathered from their school, social services, and public records.
Post-preschool differences between the groups represent preschool
program effects (see Figure 7.1).

The following findings about preschool program effects were
statistically significant (with a two-tailed probability of less than .05):

Social responsibility: By age 27, only one-fifth as many program
group members as no-program group members were arrested five
or more times (7% vs. 35%), and only one-third as many were ever
arrested for drug dealing (7% vs. 25%).

Earnings and economic status: At age 27, four times as many
program group members as no-program group members earned
$2,000 or more per month (29% vs. 7%). Almost three times as
many program group members as no-program group members
owned their own homes (36% vs. 13%), and over twice as many
owned second cars (30% vs. 13%). Three-fourths as many program
group members as no-program group members received welfare
assistance or other social services at some time as adults (59% vs.
80%).

Educational performance: One-third again as many program
group members as no-program group members graduated from
regular or adult high school or received General Education
Development certification (71% vs. 54%). Earlier in the study, the
program group had significantly higher average achievement scores
(at age 14) and literacy scores (at age 19) than the no-program
group.

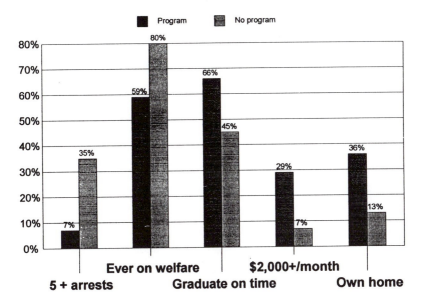

Figure 7.1. Major Findings at Age 27
SOURCE: From *Significant Benefits* (p. 190) by L. J. Schweinhart et al., 1993, Ypsilanti, MI: High/Scope Press. Copyright 1993 by High/Scope Educational Research Foundation. Adapted with permission.

Commitment to marriage: Although the same percentages of program males and no-program males were married (26%), the program males were married nearly twice as long as the no-program males (an average of 6.2 years vs. 3.3 years). Five times as many program females as no-program females were married at the age-27 interview (40% vs. 8%). Program females had only about two-thirds as many out-of-wedlock births as did no-program females (57% of births vs. 83% of births).

Return on investment: A benefit-cost analysis was conducted by estimating the monetary value of the program and its effects, in constant 1992 dollars discounted annually at 3% (see Figure 7.2). Dividing the $88,433 in benefits per participant by the $12,356 in cost per participant results in a benefit-cost ratio of $7.16 returned to the public for every dollar invested in the High/Scope Perry Preschool program, substantially exceeding earlier estimates. The program was an extremely good economic investment, better than

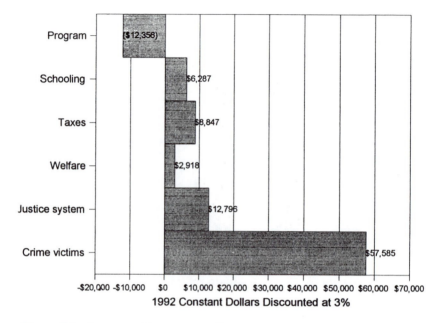

Figure 7.2. Return to Taxpayers on Per-Participant Investment
SOURCE: From *Significant Benefits* (p. 168) by L. J. Schweinhart et al., 1993, Ypsilanti, MI:
High/Scope Press. Copyright 1993 by High/Scope Educational Research Foundation. Adapted
with permission.

most other public and private uses of society's resources. By increasing the number of children per adult from 5 to 8, the program's cost per child per year could be reduced to $5,500, with
virtually no loss in quality or benefits.

Implications

The High/Scope Perry Preschool study and similar studies suggest
that early childhood programs have significant, lasting benefits:

- *They empower children* by enabling them to initiate and carry out their
  own learning activities and make independent decisions.
- *They empower parents* by involving them in ongoing relationships as
  full partners with teachers in supporting their children's development.

- *They empower teachers* by providing them with systematic in-service curriculum training, supportive curriculum supervision, and observational tools to assess children's development.

Combined with similar findings from other studies, these data have wide-ranging implications. They indicate that high-quality preschool programs for children living in poverty can have a positive long-term effect on their lives. Their early educational success leads to later school success, higher employment rates, and fewer social problems such as crime and welfare dependence. Early childhood education can help individuals realize their innate potential. But the findings show more than good outcomes for individuals. They also indicate that the general public can expect substantial improvement in the quality of community life. An effective program can help reduce street crime and bring welfare dependency to a more manageable level. Furthermore, an important improvement can be made in the available workforce because of better educational attainment and improved job-holding ability.

Conclusions

High-quality early childhood education enables disadvantaged children, on average, to achieve greater success in school and community. Although making no claim that high-quality early childhood education is a *total* cure for poverty, the High/Scope Perry Preschool study does repudiate the view that the War on Poverty was a colossal policy blunder with no redeeming successes (Herrnstein & Murray, 1994). Given the power of the preschool approach outlined here, it is clear that it is one means to aid in the development of a more productive and just society.

It is important to note that the High/Scope Perry Preschool Project has shown that a *high-quality* preschool program works. There is no evidence that an average or mediocre program would accomplish the same powerful results. The Project's preschool program was constructed so that children developed a sense of control over themselves and their environment. This objective can be reached only when a program permits children to state intentions, generate action, and engage in verbal reflection. A program in which child-initiated learning occurs in a developmentally appropriate setting clearly leads to the types of outcomes found in the High/Scope Perry Preschool Project. The public should demand that early childhood programs have these characteristics that have been proven to lead to lasting results. Anything less is a waste of both human and financial resources.

When the early research on preschool programs first began, it was thought that at-risk children could not benefit because they did not have the "ability" or the "cultural background" to learn. But early childhood education for disadvantaged children has developed extensively over the last 30 years. Research shows that we now have models that work. Our obligation is to apply that knowledge to benefit children as well as their families and society at large.

References

Bereiter, C., & Engelmann, S. (1966). *Teaching disadvantaged children in preschool.* Englewood Cliffs, NJ: Prentice Hall.

Berrueta-Clement, J. R., Schweinhart, L. J., Barnett, W. S., Epstein, A. S., & Weikart, D. P. (1984). *Changed lives: The effects of the Perry preschool program on youths through age 19* (Monographs of the High/Scope Educational Research Foundation, 8). Ypsilanti, MI: High/Scope Press.

Bloom, B. S. (1964). *Stability and change in human characteristics.* New York: John Wiley.

Epstein, A. S. (1993). *Training for quality: Improving early childhood programs through systematic in-service training* (Monographs of the High/Scope Educational Research Foundation, 9). Ypsilanti, MI: High/Scope Press.

Epstein, A. S., Schweinhart, L. J., & McAdoo, L. (1996). *Models of early childhood education.* Ypsilanti, MI: High/Scope Press.

Fuerst, J. S., & Fuerst, D. (1993). *Chicago experience with early childhood programs: The special case of the child-parent center programs.* Manuscript submitted for publication.

Garber, H. L. (1988). *The Milwaukee project: Preventing mental retardation in children at risk.* Washington, DC: American Association on Mental Retardation.

Gray, S. W., Ramsey, B. K., & Klaus, R. A. (1982). *From 3 to 20: The early training project.* Baltimore: University Park Press.

Haskins, R. (1989). Beyond metaphor: The efficacy of early childhood education. *American Psychologist, 44,* 274-282.

Herrnstein, R. J., & Murray, C. (1994). *The bell curve: Intelligence and class structure in American life.* New York: Simon & Schuster, Inc.

Hohmann, M., Banet, B., & Weikart, D. P. (1979). *Young children in action: A manual for preschool educators.* Ypsilanti, MI: High/Scope Press.

Hohmann, M., & Weikart, D. P. (1995). *Educating young children: Active learning practices for preschool and child care programs.* Ypsilanti, MI: High/Scope Press.

Hunt, J. M. (1961). *Intelligence and experience.* New York: Ronald Press.

Irvine, D. J. (1982). *Evaluation of the New York state experimental prekindergarten program.* Paper presented at the annual meeting of the American Educational Research Association, New York.

Katz, L. G., & Chard, S. C. (1993). The project approach. In J. L. Roopnarine & J. E. Johnson (Eds.), *Approaches to early childhood education* (2nd ed., pp. 209-222). New York: Macmillan.

Krech, D., Rosenzweig, M. R., & Bennett, E. L. (1960). Effects of environmental complexity and training on brain chemistry. *Journal of Comparative Physiological Psychology, 53,* 509-519.

Lally, J. R., Mangione, P. L., & Honig, A. S. (1988). The Syracuse University Family Development Research Program: Long-range impact of an early intervention with low-income children and their families. In D. R. Powell (Ed.), *Parent education as early childhood intervention: Emerging directions in theory, research, and practice* (pp. 79-104). Norwood, NJ: Ablex.

Larner, M. B., & Schweinhart, L. J. (1991, Winter). Focusing in on the teacher trainer: The High/Scope Registry survey. *High/Scope ReSource, 1*(10), 1, 10-16.

Lazar, I., Darlington, R., Murray, H., Royce, J., & Snipper, A. (1982). Lasting effects of early education: A report from the Consortium for Longitudinal Studies. *Monographs of the Society for Research in Child Development, 47* (2-3, Serial No. 195).

Levenstein, P., O'Hara, J., & Madden, J. (1983). The Mother-Child Program of the Verbal Interaction Project. In Consortium for Longitudinal Studies, *As the twig is bent . . . Lasting effects of the preschool programs* (pp. 237-263). Hillsdale, NJ: Lawrence Erlbaum.

McKey, R. H., Condelli, L., Ganson, H., Barrett, B. J., McConkey, C., & Plantz, M. C. (1985). *The impact of Head Start on children, families, and communities* (Final report of the Head Start Evaluation, Synthesis, and Utilization project). Washington, DC: CSR.

Monroe, E., & McDonald, M. S. (1981). *Follow-up study of the 1966 Head Start program, Rome City Schools, Rome, Georgia.* Unpublished paper.

Palmer, F. H. (1983). The Harlem study: Effects by type of training, age of training, and social class. In Consortium for Longitudinal Studies, *As the twig is bent . . . Lasting effects of preschool programs* (pp. 201-236). Hillsdale, NJ: Lawrence Erlbaum.

Piaget, J., & Inhelder, B. (1969). *The psychology of the child.* New York: Basic Books.

Ramey, C. T., Bryant, D. M., Campbell, F. A., Sparling, J. J., & Wasik, B. H. (1988). In R. H. Price, E. L. Cowen, R. P. Lorion, & J. Ramos-McKay (Eds.), *Fourteen ounces of prevention: A casebook for practitioners* (pp. 32-43). Washington, DC: American Psychological Association.

Ramey, C. T., Bryant, D. M., & Suarez, T. M. (1985). Preschool compensatory education and modifiability of intelligence: A critical review. In D. Detterman (Ed.), *Current topics in intelligence* (pp. 247-296). Norwood, NJ: Ablex.

Ruopp, R., Travers, J., Glantz, F., & Coelen, C. (1979). *Children at the center: Summary findings and their implications* (Final report of the National Day Care Study, Vol. 1). Cambridge, MA: Abt Associates.

Sameroff, A., & Chandler, M. (1975). Reproductive risk and the continuum of caretaking casualty. In F. Horowitz (Ed.), *Review of child development research* (Vol. 4, pp. 187-244). Chicago: University of Chicago Press.

Schweinhart, L. J., & Weikart, D. P. (1996). *Lasting differences: The High/Scope preschool curriculum comparison study through age 23* (Monographs of the High/Scope Educational Research Foundation, 12). Ypsilanti, MI: High/Scope Press.

Schweinhart, L. J., Barnes, H. V., & Weikart, D. P. with Barnett, W. S. & Epstein, A. S. (1993). *Significant benefits: The High/Scope Perry preschool study through age 27* (Monographs of the High/Scope Educational Research Foundation, 10). Ypsilanti, MI: High/Scope Press.

Scott, J. P. (1962). Critical periods in behavioral development. *Science, 138,* 949-957.

Weikart, D. P. (1967). Preschool programs: Preliminary findings. *Journal of Special Education 1,* 163-181.

Weikart, D. P. (1995, Summer). High/Scope in action: The milestones, 25 years. *High/Scope ReSource, 14*(3), 13-14, 19.

Weikart, D. P., & Schweinhart, L. J. (1993). The High/Scope Curriculum in early childhood care and education. In J. L. Roopnarine & J. E. Johnson (Eds.), *Approaches to early childhood education* (2nd ed., pp. 195-208). New York: Macmillan.

Weikart, D. P., Deloria, D., Lawser, S., & Wiegerink, R. (1970). *Longitudinal results of the Ypsilanti Perry Preschool Project* (Monographs of the High/Scope Educational Research Foundation, 1). Ypsilanti, MI: High/Scope Press.

Weikart, D. P., Rogers, L., Adcock, D., & McClelland, D. (1971). *The cognitively oriented curriculum: A framework for preschool teachers.* Urbana, IL: University of Illinois.

CHAPTER 8

Interpersonal Cognitive Problem Solving: Primary Prevention of Early High-Risk Behaviors in the Preschool and Primary Years

MYRNA B. SHURE

Over 25 years of research has shown that children can, or can learn to, successfully resolve everyday problems as early as age 4. Systematic evaluation over the same period has also shown that youngsters, across income levels and in several ethnic groups, who most improve in trained problem solving skills, also most reduce behaviors such as impulsivity, inhibition, poor peer relations, and other behaviors that research has now shown predict later, more serious problems such as violence, substance abuse, teen pregnancy, and some forms of psychopathology (Parker & Asher, 1987). Problem-solving-trained youngsters that do not show behavior problems in preschool are less likely than comparable controls to begin showing them as they move through the early grades, a finding that supports the primary prevention implications of this cognitive approach.

Perhaps the benefits of prevention efforts in general, and the impact of the problem solving approach in particular, can be best summarized by Gary VanderBos, Administrative Officer of the Mental Health Policy of the American Psychological Association, who, in a letter to the chairman of the Subcommittee on Health and Scientific Research (dated June 21, 1979) stated, "By failing to be responsive to the emotional/behavioral problems of children and youth, later problems and costs of dealing with the mental health problems of an older population are compounded" (p. 9). In light of increased violence and psychological dysfunction among our nation's youth, this comment, made in 1979, may be even more critical today.

Conceptual Framework

The approach described in this chapter provides, I believe, one viable response to the growing need to prevent early high-risk behaviors in young children. The research and subsequent interventions are based on the theoretical position as set forth by Spivack (in Spivack & Shure, 1974; 1982; Spivack, Platt, & Shure, 1976). Briefly, the quality of social relationships and capacity to cope with interpersonal problems are central to any theory of social adjustment or psychopathology. How well one can solve one's interpersonal problems depends on a complex mix of emotional and cognitive factors. However, to fully appreciate the efficiency with which a person navigates through a problem, it is necessary to understand how well that person recognizes and thinks through the interpersonal situation.

There seems to be a group of interpersonal cognitive problem solving (ICPS) skills that help to guide the quality of social adjustment—skills that are not the same as reasoning through impersonal, abstract problems as measured by IQ. With the focus on *how* one thinks, and not on *what* one thinks, the goal is not to generate any particular belief system, but rather a way to think and to use one's beliefs and values in decision making when problems do arise. If a person does not use ICPS skills in interpersonal situations, this may be because (a) that person did not learn this way of thinking sufficiently well to begin with, (b) effective ICPS thought has been learned but is not being exercised on a particular occasion due to interfering emotions and consequent non-ICPS thinking (e.g., irrational or defensive thinking) or (c) once-learned ICPS processes have deteriorated (e.g., with advanced age or neurological damage). Any therapeutic or educational program that enhances the operation of ICPS skills or removes barriers to their exercise will enhance the social adjustment of those involved or decrease chances of deterioration in social adjustment.

Educators and clinicians have assumed that one could think straight if only he or she could relieve emotional tension. We have tested the reverse, that if one could think straight, it would be possible to relieve emotional tension. If behavior is guided—at least to a significant extent—by thinking processes, and if we would find that there is a significant relationship between identified ICPS skills and behavior, we would develop interventions to test the hypothesis that behavior could be guided by enhancing those thinking skills rather than by focusing directly on the behavior itself.

Early Research

The first step was to identify specific ICPS skills that would conceptually relate to maladaptive behaviors. Spivack and Levine (1963) found that residentially placed, emotionally disturbed adolescent boys, characterized as impulsive, were, regardless of IQ, less able to plan sequenced steps toward an interpersonal goal, to recognize potential obstacles that could interfere with reaching that goal, and to appreciate that problem solving takes time, than were their more normal age-mates in public schools. This skill, called *means-ends thinking,* was subsequently examined by Shure and Spivack (1972), who confirmed those differences among younger children aged 9 to 12. Even within a more homogeneous group of fifth graders in the same public school classroom, not only were more impulsive youngsters poor means-ends thinkers relative to their less impulsive classmates, but so too were the more socially withdrawn. Means-ends thinking, and another skill, the ability or tendency to weigh the pros and cons—*consequential thinking*—also distinguished the better adjusted from their more poorly adjusted peers, not only in middle childhood and adolescence, but in adults as well (Spivack, Platt, & Shure, 1976).

Still younger children were unable to engage in means-ends thinking and the weighing of pros and cons. In youngsters as young as 4 and 5, it was the ability to think of separate alternative solutions to interpersonal problems (e.g., one child has a toy another wants), and separate alternative consequences (e.g., if one grabs that toy) that distinguished those who were impatient; over-emotional in the face of frustration; aggressive; overly withdrawn, or unable to make friends; and unaware or unconcerned about the feelings of others in distress from those who did not display these behaviors. Importantly, the relationship between competence in ICPS thinking skills and behavior was, as in the older groups, not explained by IQ (Shure, Spivack, & Jaeger, 1971; Spivack & Shure, 1974).

Given the association between these and other identified ICPS skills (causal thinking, sensitivity to problems as interpersonal, understanding the motives behind another's behavior), we designed an intervention to test the hypothesis that behavior can be guided by enhancing these identified ICPS skills. With the assumption that the earlier we could affect behavior the better, and our research findings that low-income youngsters were poorer problem solvers than their middle-income peers and that poverty is a greater index for mental health disturbance, our first pilot study was with inner-city, primarily African American, 4-year-olds attending federally funded day care. With encouraging results—finding that the six youngsters taught to think of alternative solutions to problems and consequences to acts did show behaviors of less impulsivity—we began a more systematic effort to develop a full-scale intervention to more adequately test whether behavior could be guided through interpersonal problem solving thinking.

The Interventions

The first intervention (Shure, Spivack, & Gordon, 1972) was designed to teach inner-city 4-year-olds to think of alternative solutions and consequences to hypothetical problems that pre-schoolers could relate to, such as one child not sharing a toy or not helping to clean up, one child hitting another or grabbing a toy, and so on. Soon I began to notice that when I asked the children for a "different" way to solve a hypothetical problem, some would repeat the same solution over and over. Some of the children did not understand my question. They did not know the meaning of the word *different*.

That experience, and the model set forth by Roeper and Sigel (1967) that in teaching cognitive skills—in their case, Piaget's conservation—it is more productive to begin with skills prereq-uisite to the final skill to be learned, than to begin with the final skill itself. I began with a series of lessons, in game form, that would help children focus on a set of word pairs that would set the stage for later problem-solving thinking. Word pairs included *is/is not, and/or, same/different, might/maybe,* and *why/because* as well as the phrase *if—then.* By associating these words with fun, youngsters could later think, "I can do this *or* I can do that." *If* my idea is *not* a good one, *then* I can think of something *different* to do. My idea *is* or is *not* a good one *because* of what *might* happen next.

Because research was showing that ability to understand and appreciate another's feelings and view of a problem were important in a child's development (Shantz, 1975), and we were finding that many low-income preschoolers could not identify "feeling" words, words such as *happy, sad, angry,* and *afraid* were included. Sensitivity to others' preferences are also important in later decision making. For example, a child who wants to trade a toy for a desired object must also appreciate the other's preferences, for example, "I like dolls, but he does *not.* But he does like trucks."

With other activities inserted to maintain interest, the third stage of the intervention included the final problem-solving skills to be learned, *alternative solution* and *consequential thinking.* In the above example, the child would be encouraged to think of more alternatives should the other child not accept the trade. With hypothetical problems such as, "One child won't help another clean up the toys," questions, such as, "What's one way the boy could get the girl to help him clean up the toys?" were followed by "The idea of this game is to think of lots of *different* ways. Who has idea number 2?" etc. With no adult value judgments placed on any of their ideas, the next set of lesson-games helped the youngsters think of consequences by asking, "What *might* happen next if . . ?"

Having developed an intervention that was ready to take to teachers, I trained four day care teachers to teach their whole class (15 children) the problem-solving curriculum. I chose to train the whole class, as opposed to isolating only behaviorally aberrant youngsters, because children being isolated would feel stigmatized, and because similarly, children not being chosen would feel left out of the fun with puppets, pictures, role-playing, and so on. Equally important, we would eventually examine through follow-up research whether trained children not showing behavior problems in preschool would be less likely than nontrained youngsters to begin showing behavior problems in later grades—a test of prevention, as well as treatment effects.

During the problem-solving phase of the first teacher-trained project, showing pictures of hypothetical children, I was very pleased and proud to observe a group of children competently responding to questions such as, "What is the problem?" "How does (A) feel?" "What happened next when (B) [hit] (A)?" "Can (B) think of a *different* way to [get (A) to help him clean up]?" However, 5 minutes after the lesson ended, one child pushed another, and the teacher shouted, "How many times do I have to tell you we don't push in school!" and promptly sent the perpetrator to time-out. I said to myself, "Wait, something's missing. Why can't this teacher use the same line of questioning to a real problem that she just did to the hypothetical one?" And that is how what I came to call *ICPS dialoguing* was born.

Over the past 25 years, I have developed, tested, and revised several curricula for classroom teachers of three different age groups as our research continued: for preschool, for kindergarten and the primary grades, and for the intermediate elementary grades (Shure, 1992a, 1992b, 1992c). Originally called Interpersonal Cognitive Problem Solving (ICPS), all the curricula are now called *I Can Problem Solve* (also ICPS). For parents of 4-year-olds, I developed an ICPS curriculum for use at home, found in *Problem Solving Techniques in Childrearing* (Shure & Spivack, 1978), and for 4- to 7-year-olds in *Raising a Thinking Child* (Shure, 1994, 1996a, 1996b) and in *Raising a Thinking Child Workbook* (Shure, 1996c). All of the curricula teach a *process* of thinking, rather than a content. The goal is to help children develop empathy, ability to cope with frustration, and problem-solving skills—all ingredients of social and emotional competence that can be enhanced and nurtured from a very early age.

I will illustrate examples from the curriculum guides for use by teachers of young children and show how the ICPS concepts can be applied in the home. It is important to note that the curricula designed for teachers for use in the classroom can also be reinforced by counselors, school psychologists, social workers, school nurses, and other student support personnel for consistency in approach and for additional help for youngsters who may need it.

Teacher Program: Preschool

Although our research that provided the basis for the development of the preschool curriculum was conducted with 4-year-olds, experience has shown that children as young as 2-years-old can play the word pair games and that many 3-year-olds can participate in the games that teach how people feel. However, the final lesson-games that teach alternative solution and consequential thinking are most suitable for age 4 and older.

Prerequisite Word Pairs. To help children later evaluate whether their idea *is* or is *not* a good one, children are told: "Robert *is* a boy. He is *not* a _____." After "girl" is usually chanted, the children are encouraged to have fun and be silly, and think of lots of things Robert is *not*. Children enjoy thinking of things like "giraffe," "balloon," "floor," etc. Later, to help children think of a variety of solutions, and that, for example, "hitting" is kind of the *same* as "kicking"—they can both hurt someone—and then think of something *different* to do, children first begin with body motions with which they are familiar. For example, after rolling their arms, sometimes the children are asked to think of something *different* to do, and sometimes they are asked to do the *same* thing. To help children appreciate that different people can feel different ways about the *same* thing, and have different preferences, one game includes one child naming a food, a TV show, a sport that he or she likes, and then asking another child, "Do you like_____ too?" To the same end, the word pair *might-maybe* is introduced so children can learn to think, "*Maybe* he likes dolls, and *maybe* he does *not*."

Feelings. If people's feelings are considered in problem solving, one must first be able to identify and verbalize them. Using *if-then* logic, children are taught to label and identify emotions: "*If* he is crying, *then* he is sad." Earlier concepts further aid children to identify emotions by recognizing who *is* and *is not* smiling (happy) and crying (sad) and that happy and sad are *different* feelings. Use of if-then logic progresses to beginning to think of one's own feelings: "*If* I do this, *then* I *might* feel sad," and of others' feelings: "He *might* feel mad." And introducing the concept "There's more than one way," children learn to think about the idea that if one way does *not* make someone happy, it is possible to try a *different* way. One lesson-game from the preschool manual called *Let's Pretend* illustrates the focus on people's feelings (see Figure 8.1) after they have already learned to identify them, and how to find out how another feels (from Shure, 1992a, pp. 89-90).

Teacher Script

"Now let's pretend."

Instruct one child to grab an object from another child.

"Remember, this is just a game."

(To Child 1, whose object was just grabbed)

"How do you feel about that?"

(To Child 2)

"Now, give it back to (him/her)."

(To Child 1)

"How do you feel now?"

Repeat with a couple more children.

"Now let's pretend that (Child 3) lost (his/her) dog. (Child 3), can you look *sad?*" (*If necessary, help the child with the proper expression.*)

(To the group)

"How does (Child 3) feel?"

"Yes, _____. (*If needed, sad.*)

"How would (Child 3) feel if (his/her) dog came home again?" (*If needed, happy.*)

"Now let's pretend (Child 4) found (Child 3's) dog but wouldn't give it back."

"How might (Child 3) feel?"

"Let's find out. How can we find out?" (*Encourage child to ask*)

"Let's pretend next that it's really cold outside and (Child 5) doesn't have any mittens."

"If (he/she) took yours (*point to Child 6*), how would you feel?"

"(Child 7), what would make you angry?"

Although we learned that some children become more upset than usual while discussing their emotions, such discomfort is only temporary. Once children can think through their emotions, most can cope with them better than before. If a child does become upset

Figure 8.1.
SOURCE: Shure (1992).

during these lessons, children are encouraged to think of ways to help make them feel happy again. Most children will soon smile and rejoin the games.

Causality. To help children understand the effect of one's behavior on another and of another's behavior on oneself, the concept of causality is presented. Using the words *why* and *because,* games focus on why a child may feel the way she does: "She's mad *because* I took her toy." The why-because connectives will also be associated with later consequential thinking, such as, "She hit me *because* I took her toy."

Fairness. Preschoolers, as found by Shure (1968), are able to understand when two children have equal rights (e.g., to a school toy) and when one party has extra rights (e.g., one child looked hard for a toy and found it). Concepts of fairness provide thought about the rights of others in decision making. Children are encouraged to think about what *is* and is *not* fair. The word pair *some/all* was included to help children recognize, for example, that it *not fair* for one child to have *all* the turns and another not to have any. At any given moment, what is fair for one child may *not* be fair for another. Inherent in these lessons is the idea that in being fair, one must sometimes wait.

Problem-Solving Skills: Alternative Solution Thinking. Using pictures, puppets, and role-playing techniques, children are shown pictures of hypothetical children and asked to think of as many ways to solve the stated problem as they can. Following is one such lesson (from Shure, 1992a, pp. 157-158):

Teacher Script

"Let's pretend these girls (see Figure 8.2) were playing with these toys *(point to picture)* and it's time to put them away. There is a problem here. A problem is when something is wrong—something is the matter."

"Let's pretend this girl *(point to the girl walking away)* is going to leave and won't help this girl *(point to the other girl)* put the toys away."

"Now remember, both girls were playing with the toys."

"Was this girl *(point to the first girl)* playing?"

"Was this girl *(point to the second girl)* playing?"

"Who should help put the toys away?"

"Is it *fair* for this girl *(point to girl standing by toys)* to put *all* of the toys away and for this girl *(point to the girl walking away) not* to help?"

"Is it *fair* for both girls to help clean up?"

"*Why* is it *fair* for both girls to help clean up? Because
_____."

"Yes, it is *fair* for both girls to help clean up *because* they were both playing."

"So the problem is that this girl "(point to the girl walking away)" will not help clean up, put the toys away."

"Now, what can this girl "(point to the girl standing by toys) do or say so the other girl will help her put the toys away?"

"I'm going to write *all* your ideas on the chalkboard. Let's fill up the whole board."

(Sample response)

"Ask her."

(Teacher): "That's *one* way. Now the idea of this game is to think of lots of *different* ways to solve the problem."

"Who's got Way Number 2?"

(Continue in this manner.)

Figure 8.2.
SOURCE: Shure (1992).

The teacher writes all the different, relevant solutions given on the board. Although the children cannot read, writing down their ideas is an excellent motivating technique, and they will notice if what they say is not recorded—"You didn't write *my* idea." Ideas are reinforced, not for content: "That's a *good* idea," but rather for the process of thinking: "Good, that's a *different* idea," or "Good thinking!" Focusing on the content reinforces a particular solution, and may inhibit the children from thinking of further options.

Children who offer solutions that are variations on a previously given theme, e.g., "Tell her she won't invite her to her house," and "She won't invite her to her birthday party" are told, "Those are kind of the *same* because they both won't invite her somewhere. Can you think of something *different* from not inviting her somewhere?" This kind of probing helps children think of different categories of solution, a skill found to be associated with social adjustment and interpersonal competence.

Problem-Solving Skills: Consequential Thinking. After children become accustomed to thinking of lots of ways to solve a problem, they are asked to decide whether their ideas are or are not good ones *because* of what *might* happen next—including how they and others might feel. Again, with pictures, puppets, or role-playing techniques, children offer one solution to a problem, and are then asked, "What *might* happen next *if* (e.g., one child hits another, grabs a toy, etc.)" (negative solutions) as well as, "ask him, be his friend, etc." (positive solutions). In this section, children are encouraged to think of lots of different consequences to the same solution.

Problem-Solving Skills: Solution/Consequence Pairing. In this section, children are asked to give one solution and to immediately pair one possible consequence, followed by another solution/consequence pair. By doing this, children will ultimately be able to choose from among a number of solutions based on their most likely consequences.

In addition to lesson-games relating to *hypothetical* children and adults, the earlier-mentioned "dialoguing" process was applied to real problems that arise to help children associate how they think with what they do and how they behave. If, for example, one child is hitting another, the teacher might ask,

> "What's the matter? What's wrong?"
> "What happened next when you hit him?"
> "How do you think he feels when you hit him?"
> "How did *you* feel when that happened?

"Can you think of a different way to (e.g., get a turn with the toy) so he won't feel (mad), you won't feel (mad) and he (won't fight)?"

By engaging children in the process of solving the problem, they are listening because they are participating, and they are more likely to carry out their own idea than one demanded, suggested, or even explained by an adult.

Teacher Program:
Kindergarten/Primary Grades

The format for the kindergarten and primary grades is the same as that for preschool (Shure, 1992b) with concepts upgraded in sophistication for youngsters through Grade 2 or Grade 3, depending on the level of the class. In special education classes, even fourth-grade youngsters can benefit from the early prerequisite skills lessons, found not to be too simple for many of them.

One new concept in the kindergarten/primary manual is thinking about doing "two things at the *same* time." In game form, the teacher might say, "I can roll my arms and stamp my foot at the *same* time. I can*not* talk and sing at the same time." Children enjoy thinking of things they can and cannot do at the same time. Then, for example, when a child actually interrupts a teacher talking with someone else, the teacher can ask, "Can I talk with you and with _____ at the *same* time?" Children who are not listening to the teacher, or to another child can be asked, "Can you (e.g., talk to your neighbor) and listen to me at the *same* time?" These questions, combined with the fun associated with playing the game may be all that needs to be said.

The word pair *before/after* and the feeling words *proud* and *frustrated* are added, with some children learning them more easily beginning in the first grade. After introducing several examples of sequencing in preparation for further consequential thinking, children can be asked, "What happened *before* (e.g., you hit him)?" and then, "What happened *after* that?" These questions, associated with the lesson-games, are much less threatening than the more accusatory, "Why did you hit him?" which often leads to children saying, "I don't know," shrugging their shoulders in silence, or lying. Distinguishing *proud* from *happy* makes children feel very

competent when asked, "How did you feel when you solved that
problem by yourself?" And words such as *worried* and *relieved* help
children appreciate that when they are in conflict with another, they
might feel *worried before* the problem is solved, and *relieved after*
it is solved.

In addition to applying the prerequisite and problem solving
skills learned in hypothetical situations to real life ("ICPS Dialoguing"), interpersonal concepts for all age groups are also incorporated into the standard curriculum. For example, preschoolers
are asked, "What might happen if you never brush your teeth?" and
"How would you feel if that happened?" whereas third graders may
be asked, "What might have happened if George Washington's men
had never showed up at the Delaware?" and "How might he have
felt about that?"

Parent Program

Early Parent Research

Our early correlational studies showed that mothers of inner-city
African American 4-year-olds who explained and reasoned with
their children ("induction") had better adjusted children than those
who demanded, commanded, punished, or even made suggestions
without explanation. But in two separate studies, this was true only
if the child was a girl (Spivack & Shure, 1975, Shure & Spivack,
1978). Because boys were not poorer problem solvers than girls and
ICPS-competent boys were as well adjusted as ICPS-competent
girls, we did not, and still do not, know why mother's use of
induction has less impact on boys than on girls, not only among
low-income, mostly father-absent youngsters, but in middle-class,
intact homes as well (Howie, 1977). The question became whether
teaching parents of boys and girls to engage in ICPS dialoguing, a
technique one step beyond that of induction, would improve the
problem-solving ability and the social adjustment of those preschoolers whose thinking skills and behavior could improve.

Parent Training

The parent intervention began with African American parents of
4-year-olds attending federally funded day care, children who did

not receive the training at school (Shure & Spivack, 1978). The concepts were the same as those for the school curriculum for preschool, except that they were applied to settings in the home. For example, parents would ask questions using the ICPS word pairs at the dinner table, such as holding up a fork, then a spoon, and asking, "Are these the *same* thing *or* something *different*?" "I am eating a hamburger. I am *not* eating a _____." After playing these and other games that teach the prerequisite and problem solving skills described for the teacher manuals, they would be applied to problem situations that arise in the home, such as, "Is playing with water in the living room (jumping on the furniture, running inside, drawing on the wall) a good idea?" "What might happen if you do that?" "How might I (you) feel if that happens?" "Can you think of a different place to play (jump, run, draw, etc.)?" Children who teased or otherwise tormented their younger brothers or sisters were asked questions such as, "Can you think of a *different* way to tell your brother how you feel?"

When the parent program was expanded for use with children up to age 7 (Shure, 1994, 1996a, 1996b, 1996c), the earlier-described "two things at the same time" game was associated with real life situations at home, such as when a child interrupts mom on the telephone—"Can I talk to you and to my friend *at the same time*?" One 6-year-old boy remembered playing with the word *different* and replied, "No, and I can think of something different to do." As true of the programs designed for use in schools, parents were taught how to "dialogue" with their children, engaging them in the process of solving the problem by asking, rather than by demanding, suggesting, or even explaining.

Effectiveness of the interventions

When Trained by Teachers. ICPS-trained nursery and kindergarten children improved in cognitive ability to think of alternative solutions to real life interpersonal problems more than comparable controls (e.g., wanting a toy another child has), and also in ability to anticipate potential consequences to acts (e.g., grabbing that toy). Within a range of 80 to 120+, these cognitive gains were not explained by either initial IQ nor change in IQ.

One year of training (nursery or kindergarten) was sufficient for significant ICPS gains and also for behavioral improvements in decreased impulsivity, decreased inhibition, and increase in concern for others in distress, cooperation, sharing, and in positive peer relations. If training did not occur in nursery, kindergarten was not too late, although ICPS youngsters may begin kindergarten from a better behavioral vantage point. A significant link was found between ICPS skill gains, especially alternative solution thinking and behavior gains, supporting Spivack's earlier-mentioned theory that ICPS ability is a significant mediator of overt behaviors.

At 1- and 2-year follow-up, gains were maintained. Importantly, trained youngsters who had not previously shown behavior problems were less likely than controls to begin showing them during the follow-up periods, suggesting a preventive, as well as a treatment component to ICPS intervention (Spivack & Shure, 1974; Shure & Spivack, 1979, 1980, 1982).

In addition to controlled research by ourselves and others (see Denham & Almeida [1987] for a review), three known service evaluations were conducted by school systems who have used ICPS with kindergarten and first graders. In Dade County, Florida, ICPS training included children of diverse ethnic and income levels about equally distributed between low- to middle-income Hispanic and African American youngsters and predominantly white middle-income youngsters. All groups showed gains in measured alternative solution skills and significant decreases in teacher-rated acting out and inhibited behaviors, as well as gains in peer acceptance, concern for others, and initiative (Aberson, 1987). The mental health associations of Illinois (Callahan, 1992), and of Memphis, Tennessee (Weddle & Williams, 1993), have found similar outcomes based on pilot studies; and as a result, the school systems in Memphis and Chicago are now expanding the implementation of ICPS in kindergartens and first grades.

When Trained by Mothers. Compared to nontrained controls, low-income African American 4-year-olds trained by their mothers improved in solution and consequential thinking skills. Mothers who improved in their own problem-solving thinking skills and used the ICPS approach when handling problems with their children had children who most improved in the trained ICPS skills and subsequent behavioral adjustment. The improved behavior of children trained at home generalized to the school, suggesting that the benefits of acquiring ICPS mediating skills are not situation specific.

When Trained by Teachers or by Teachers and Mothers. Our most recent research, a 5-year longitudinal study (Shure, 1993) began with training African American low-income youngsters in kindergarten. Once again, compared to comparable controls, ICPS skills and behaviors improved in youngsters whether they were trained by their teachers in kindergarten only, in kindergarten and first grade, or by their teachers in kindergarten and their mothers in first grade. Without further training, these gains lasted through Grade 2. Although these gains were lost in Grade 3, initial gains made by youngsters trained twice by their teachers (in both kindergarten and first grade) re-emerged at the end of Grade 4, 3 years after completion of the last training. At that time, they were showing the least negative, and most positive behaviors.

Children of parents who best learned how to use problem-solving communication ("ICPS dialoguing") when real problems came up showed more behavioral improvement than those of parents who did not learn, or chose not to use dialoguing, highlighting the importance of associating the concepts of the lesson-games to real life. Although these findings are very encouraging, given that intervention was stopped at the end of Grade 1, they also suggest the possibility that for school interventions, even greater benefits might have occurred had the program been continued throughout—not only for the children, but also for the teachers in the higher grades, who would have learned problem-solving techniques of handling behavior problems when they arose. Further research can answer that and other questions regarding the optimal and most cost-effective amounts and timing of training in schools.

Cost-Benefit Data

Although no formal cost/benefit data are available, the ICPS manuals and workbooks for both teachers and parents are very inexpensive, and only materials already found in the classroom or in the home are needed. One Chicago school principal reports fewer suspensions as documented to Grade 4 among children trained in kindergarten (Levin, 1992), and most ICPS teachers have reported less lost time in classroom management.

ICPS Beyond the Primary Years

Although our initial research and interventions focused on the training of younger children, as did our most recent 5-year longitudinal study, we were also interested in the impact of ICPS training if started at a later age. To that end, an intervention was designed to include the ICPS skill of means-ends thinking found in our above-described correlational research with 9- to 12-year-olds (Shure & Spivack, 1972), as well as age-appropriate tests of those skills trained in younger children.

With materials appropriate for the fourth to sixth grades (Shure, 1992c), children discuss their own and others' feelings, causal connections, alternative solutions to problems, and consequences to acts, as well as two additional skills that our research has found to be developmentally appropriate and related to high-risk behaviors at that age (reviewed in Spivack, Platt, & Shure, 1976). One skill, called *dynamic orientation,* is an understanding of the motives of others, which is important in making decisions about how to react. Just as there is more than one way to solve a problem, and more than one consequence to an act, there is more than one possible reason people do what they do. For example, a child who doesn't wave at his friend might not wave because he doesn't like him, or because he is preoccupied, or because he doesn't see him. This skill helps children avoid coming to quick and faulty conclusions and possibly engaging in behavior that would be inappropriate at the time (e.g., hitting back under the assumption that the child was hit on purpose).

Means-ends thinking was taught to fourth- to sixth-graders by first explaining, with examples, how steps (means) are sequenced, that things might get in the way of reaching the stated goal (obstacles), that it may take time to reach a goal, and that there are good times and not good times to do something. After a story root is given—e.g., Andrew let his friend David borrow his new bike a couple of days ago, but David hasn't given it back—the class is asked to create a story, using the model of the popular game, "Continuation." The teacher writes the unfolding story on the board, circling means, obstacles, and elements of time. Guiding questions include

> What's the first thing Andrew thinks about? Step 1?
>
> What's Step 2? What might he do next?
>
> Is there anything that could block that step? An obstacle?
>
> What can he do to get around that obstacle?
>
> When is a *good time* to take that step?
>
> What about a *not-good time?*
>
> How long might it take for Andrew to reach his goal?
>
> What's the very next thing that happens in this story? (Shure, 1992c, p. 350)

Questions such as these can also be used when real problems come up to help children plan what they will do, what to do if their plan is not successful, and to be patient in trying to reach their goal.

In older children (Shure & Healey, 1993), low-income African American fifth graders, one exposure to ICPS training enhanced ICPS skills and positive prosocial behaviors, but it required a second exposure (in Grade 6) to reduce negative impulsive and inhibited behaviors. No such cognitive or behavior gains occurred in a placebo control group (trained in impersonal cognitive skills such as Piagetian conservation) in either the fifth or sixth grade. In fact, the controls actually increased their negative behaviors from Grade 5 to Grade 6. These findings suggest that ICPS training is a viable prevention model for this age group as well.

Among both the younger children and the older ones, standardized achievement test scores and reading levels also improved. Although direct incorporation of ICPS with academic skills had not yet been incorporated into the training manuals, perhaps ICPS-mediated behavioral gains allowed the children to concentrate better on the task-oriented demands of the classroom, and subsequently to do better in school.

Although ICPS training may help to reverse a natural tendency for the appearance of increased behavior problems as youngsters move through the elementary grades (Spivack & Swift, 1977), full behavioral impact for latency-aged, low-income youngsters may take longer than the briefer exposure required for younger preschool and kindergarten-aged youngsters.

Summary

Our own research and evaluations and those of others support the position that as early as age 4, and regardless of IQ, youngsters who behave differently, think differently. Children who display impulsive, aggressive behaviors think more about "now" without consideration for their own or others' feelings, for the consequences of their acts, or for different ways to solve a problem. These youngsters often have difficulty making friends and are unaware of, or unconcerned about, others in distress. We know that as early as preschool, genuine concern for others in distress does exist and can be trained. Furthermore, lack of this kind of genuine feeling early in life, along with other ICPS skill deficiencies and their accompanying behavioral impulsivity, can predict later violence (a form of hurting others), substance abuse (a form of hurting oneself), and other forms of psychological dysfunction. Withdrawn children are also poor problem solvers (Shure, Spivack, & Jaeger, 1971) and are at risk for later, more internalizing problems such as depression or, in extreme cases, even suicide (Rubin, 1985). It is critical that withdrawn children not fall through the cracks and go unnoticed because their behavior is less visible.

Although one might wonder how we know that we prevented something if that something never occurred, after a quarter of a century of carefully documented research by independent investigators who consistently find that those exposed to the interventions are less likely than comparable, nontrained controls to display dysfunctional behaviors, it seems clear that now is the time to place prevention at the top of our priorities. Rather than spending our money on treatment of mental health dysfunction *after* it occurs, or more jails *after* someone gets hurt, wouldn't it be better to spend our resources in efforts to significantly reduce the need for them in the first place?

References

Aberson, B. (1987). *I Can Problem Solve (ICPS): A cognitive training program for kindergarten children.* Report to the Bureau of Education, Dade County, FL: Dade County Public Schools.

Callahan, C. (1992). *1991-1992 evaluation report for the Mental Health Schools Project.* Chicago, IL: Mental Health Association of Illinois.

Denham, S. A., & Almeida, M. C. (1987). Children's social problem-solving skills, behavioral adjustment, and interventions: A meta-analysis evaluating theory and practice. *Journal of Applied Developmental Psychology, 8*(4), 391-409.

Howie, R. D. (1977). The relationship between interpersonal problem solving ability of 4-year-olds and parental values and attitudes. Unpublished manuscript. Millersville, PA: Millersville State College.

Levin, W. H. (1992, October). A professional development seminar, presented to the Mental Health Association in DuPage County, sponsored by the DuPage County Health Department, Mental Health Association in DuPage, and the United Way of Suburban Chicago, Wheaton, IL.

Parker, J. G., & Asher, S. R. (1987). Peer relations and later personal adjustment: Are low-accepted children "at risk?" *Psychological Bulletin, 102*(3), 357-389.

Roeper, A., & Sigel, I. (1967). Finding the clue to children's thought processes. In W. W. Hartup & N. L. Smothergill (Eds.), *The young child: Reviews of research* (pp. 77-95). Washington, DC: National Association for the Education of Young Children.

Rubin, K. H. (1985). Socially withdrawn children: An "at risk" population? In B. H. Schneider, K. H. Rubin, & J. E. Ledingham (Eds.), *Children's peer relations: Issues in assessment and intervention.* New York: Springer.

Shantz, C. U. (1975). The development of social cognition. In E. M. Hetherington (Ed.), *Review of child development research* (Vol. 5. pp. 257-323). New York: Russell-Sage.

Shure, M. B. (1968). Fairness, generosity and selfishness: The naive psychology of children and young adults. *Child Development, 39,* (3), 875-886.

Shure, M. B. (1992a). *I Can Problem Solve (ICPS): An interpersonal cognitive problem solving program [preschool].* Champaign, IL: Research Press.

Shure, M. B. (1992b). *I Can Problem Solve (ICPS): An interpersonal cognitive problem solving program [kindergarten/primary grades].* Champaign, IL: Research Press.

Shure, M. B. (1992c). *I Can Problem Solve (ICPS): An interpersonal cognitive problem solving program [intermediate elementary grades].* Champaign, IL: Research Press.

Shure, M. B. (1993). *Interpersonal problem solving and prevention* (Research and training final report, No. MH-40801). Washington, DC: National Institute of Mental Health.

Shure, M. B. (1994). *Raising a thinking child: Help your young child to resolve everyday conflicts and get along with others.* New York: Henry Holt.

Shure, M. B. (1996a). *Raising a thinking child: Help your young child to resolve everyday conflicts and get along with others.* New York: Pocket Books. [Paperback]

Shure, M. B. (1996b). *Raising a thinking child: Help your young child to resolve everyday conflicts and get along with others.* New York: Bantam, Doubleday, Dell Audio.

Shure, M. B. (1996c). *Raising a thinking child workbook.* New York: Henry Holt.

Shure, M. B., & Healey, K. N. (1993, August). *Interpersonal problem solving and prevention in urban school children.* Paper presented at the meeting of the American Psychological Association, Toronto.

Shure, M. B., & Spivack, G. (1972). Means-ends thinking, adjustment and social class among elementary school-aged children. *Journal of Consulting and Clinical Psychology, 38*(3), 348-353.

Shure, M. B., & Spivack, G. (1978). *Problem solving techniques in childrearing.* San Francisco: Jossey-Bass.

Shure, M. B., & Spivack, G. (1979, Summer). Interpersonal cognitive problem solving and primary prevention: Programming for preschool and kindergarten children. *Journal of Clinical Child Psychology, 8,* 89-94.

Shure, M. B., & Spivack, G. (1980). Interpersonal problem solving as a mediator of behavioral adjustment in preschool and kindergarten children. *Journal of Applied Developmental Psychology, 1*(1), 29-44.

Shure, M. B., & Spivack, G. (1982). Interpersonal problem solving in young children: A cognitive approach to prevention. *American Journal of Community Psychology, 10*(3), 341-356.

Shure, M. B., Spivack, G., & Gordon, R. (1972). Problem-solving thinking: A preventive mental health program for preschool children. *Reading World, 11*(4), 259-273.

Shure, M. B., Spivack, G., & Jaeger, M. A. (1971). Problem solving thinking and adjustment among disadvantaged preschool children. *Child Development, 42*(2), 1791-1803.

Spivack, G., & Levine, M. (1963). *Self-regulation in acting-out and normal adolescents.* Report M-4351. Washington, DC: National Institute of Mental Health.

Spivack, G., Platt, J. J., & Shure, M. B. (1976). *The problem solving approach to adjustment: A guide to research and intervention.* San Francisco: Jossey-Bass.

Spivack, G., & Shure, M. B. (1974). *Social adjustment of young children: A cognitive approach to solving real life problems.* San Francisco: Jossey-Bass.

Spivack, G., & Shure, M. B. (1975, April). *Maternal childrearing and the interpersonal cognitive problem-solving ability of 4-year-olds.* Paper presented at the meetings of the Society for Research in Child Development, Denver.

Spivack, G., & Shure, M. B. (1982). Interpersonal cognitive problem-solving and clinical theory. In B. Lahey & A. E. Kazdin (Eds.), *Advances in child clinical psychology* (Vol. 5, pp. 323-372). New York: Plenum.

Spivack, G., & Swift, M. (1979). "High risk" classroom behaviors in kindergarten and first grade. *American Journal of Community Psychology, 5*(4), 385-397.

Weddle, K. D., & Williams, F. (1993). *Implementing and assessing the effectiveness of the Interpersonal Cognitive Problem Solving (ICPS) curriculum in four experimental and four control classrooms* (Report to the Faculty Small Research Grant Program). Memphis, TN: Memphis State University.

FOUR

School-Age Programs

• *CHAPTER 9* •

Primary Mental Health Project

A. DIRK HIGHTOWER

The Primary Mental Health Project (PMHP) is a program for the early detection and prevention of school adjustment problems. Such problems are widespread. Consistently national surveys have shown that 20% to 25% of American school children experience moderate to severe school adjustment problems (Namir & Weinstein, 1982). In some urban areas, the figure is almost three times that high (Kellam, Branch, Agrawal, & Ensminger, 1975; Meller, LaBoy, Rothwax, Fritton, & Mangual, 1994). The problems of 1 in 10 children are believed to be serious enough to require immediate professional help. Children who fail to profit from the school experience are often at high risk for developing major mental disorders and many become chronic burdens to society (Mrazek & Haggerty, 1994; Prevention Task Panel Report, 1978).

PMHP identifies young primary grade children with early school adjustment problems. Once identified, they receive prompt, effective helping services. Carefully selected paraprofessional child as-

AUTHOR'S NOTE: The Primary Mental Health Project is supported in part by the New York State Department of Education and the Office of Alcoholism and Substance Abuse Services, the Coordinated Care Services of Monroe County, the United Way of Greater Rochester, and school districts from New York and across the United States. Opinions expressed in this chapter are those of the author and not necessarily of those of the above organizations. This chapter was based in part on material from *School-Based Prevention for At-Risk Children: The Primary Mental Health Project* (Cowen, Hightower, Work, Pedro-Carroll, Wyman, & Haffey, 1996).

sociates, who work under close professional supervision, increase manyfold the number of children who are helped preventively and would otherwise slip between the cracks in our educational system.

PMHP began in 1957 as a small pilot demonstration project in a single school. It was prompted by two observations that remain valid today: first, classroom teachers often reported that about 40% to 60% of their time was preempted by the problems of a few (3-4) children, to the detriment of the whole class; and second and equally remarkable, was the fact that referrals for mental health issues occurred primarily between elementary and high school although a review of cumulative school records of referred students indicated that many had histories of school adjustment problems that went back to kindergarten and the early primary grades. Either helping resources had not been available for those students or the significant adults involved had hoped that the troubles would disappear. Far from vanishing, early problems tend to root and spread to many costly areas, including substance use, delinquency, and serious mental health problems (Cowen, Pedersen, Babigian, Izzo, & Trost, 1973; Ensminger, Kellam, & Rubin, 1983; Kellam, Simon, & Ensminger, 1983; Mrazek & Haggerty, 1994).

These observations pointed to the need for an alternative that provided a prompt, effective preventive intervention—PMHP. The goal of PMHP was to reduce adjustment difficulties as soon as possible within a youngster's life, so that later more serious and more costly difficulties would be prevented.

PMHP's basic program model emerged gradually over a decade. It is best seen as a structural model with four basic elements:

1. It focuses on young, modifiable children before problems become rooted and entrenched. Prekindergarten, kindergarten and primary school grades are ideal for such efforts.

2. It emphasizes an active early screening process of young children, to systematically identify those who are experiencing early school adjustment problems. The target is to find those children who are just beginning to show difficulties and whose prognosis for improvement is the best.

3. It expands geometrically the reach of early effective intervention services for identified children through the use of carefully selected, trained, and supervised paraprofessional child associates. Although relatively inexpensive to hire, such helping services have been found

to be as effective as, if not more effective than, similar types of professional services (Durlak, 1979; Hattie, Sharpley, & Rogers, 1984).

4. It changes traditional, school-based mental health professional's roles to activities such as the selection, training, and supervision of child associates, and consultation and training with school personnel. New resources are not required, but rather a reallocation of existing services is needed.

These structural elements provide an overarching emphasis for PMHP. The approach has been extremely flexible and has been able to accommodate substantial variation in its literal defining practices. Although the PMHP structural model has remained consistent, program implementations have varied in regards to such things as (a) specific measures used in early detection and screening; (b) depth and types of professional staffing patterns; (c) people who serve as child associates (e.g., volunteer versus paid nonprofessionals, students, retired persons, educational levels, etc.); (d) methods of recruiting, selecting, orienting, training, and supervising child associates; (e) how child associates actually work with children (e.g., individual versus group; nondirective versus directive; psychodynamic versus behavioral); and (f) the intensity of parent participation.

Recognizing that for school programs to be effective, they must adapt to the realities of their own specific needs, resources, belief systems, and prevailing practices, PMHP has had a track record of demonstrated success in reducing school adjustment difficulties in a variety of settings. It is a model that has worked effectively in New York, California, Washington, Connecticut, Oklahoma, and Ohio, among others. Similarly, it has been effective in large urban schools such as in New York City and Los Angeles and in small rural schools with a K through 12 population of 400 students. Significant improvement has been demonstrated for both boys and girls, and for African American, Asian American, Hispanic American, and Native American children as well as Caucasian children. Although no single description fully captures how PMHP operates in all schools, the following description provides a reasonable account of how the project works.

I begin with a brief summary of how PMHP works and an overview of how to start a new PMHP program. Next, I describe

PMHP's core defining elements, including the screening and referral processes, clinical conferences, child associate roles and functions, and professional roles and activities.

Starting PMHP

Program Entry

Starting a PMHP program calls for careful planning. Concerned parties must be given essential information about the program and its ways of operating. Relevant school personnel, including administrators, mental health professionals, and teachers need to participate in planning and start-up steps, both to educate them about how PMHP works and to get their input in adapting it to the new setting. Such involvement increases participants' sense of program ownership.

A first step in starting PMHP is for school personnel to learn enough about the project's rationale, goals, and ways of functioning to enable them to form a preliminary judgment about its match with a given setting. These judgments must reflect a setting's needs, resources, and priorities. Because schools differ in these regards, as well as in their due process decision-making mechanisms, time between initial exposure to the PMHP approach and a program's start may range from months to years.

However school personnel learn about PMHP, their familiarity with PMHP is a necessary, but not a sufficient, condition for starting a new program. Important others who must be included are those in decision-making positions in the school, such as superintendents and boards of education as well as those, like parents, who will be significantly involved in the program. These constituents must agree that PMHP is right for them.

Once it has been established that a district is ready to start PMHP, several concrete entry steps follow. These steps go more smoothly when several realities are kept in focus: (a) a school's actual way of functioning may differ considerably from its published table of organization; (b) knowledge of, and respect for *de facto* ways of functioning can facilitate a new PMHP start-up; (c) time, sometimes many months, may be needed to navigate a district's normal procedural and due process mechanisms; (d) patience, persistence, and sensitivity to the needs of relevant school constituencies are needed to build a solid program foundation; and (e) ongoing knowledge and support from multiple levels within a school district or school increases the likelihood that a new program will succeed.

Space

Typically, the building principal designates space for PMHP. The setting should be a safe, comfortable place for children. It should be inviting and welcoming. It is desirable for child associates and children to have individual, semipermanent areas, often partitions in a larger room, that they can call their own. Such space offers a kind of privacy needed to work effectively. Empty classrooms can be converted to meet PMHP space needs by using dividers, book-shelves, and storage bins. The goal, in any case, is to carve out an environment that is comfortable and engaging for young children.

Playroom Equipment

Playrooms are like personalities; no two are exactly alike. However, some materials that engage children in play and expres-sive behavior are found in most playrooms. Examples include a furnished dollhouse with small human figures, puppets, crayons, clay, paints, paper, dolls, stuffed animals, a sandbox with associated tools, and different games.

Personnel

An extremely important step in the start-up process is selection of the personnel who are central to the program's operation (i.e., child associates and school-based mental health professionals). Although those two roles can be extended and made more effective by support from school staff and outside consultants, they are always *the* central elements in a PMHP program. Depending on a school's resources and staffing patterns, different professional cousins, such as school psychologists, school social workers, or elementary counselors, both full-time and part-time, have served as PMHP professionals. These professionals have the skills needed to conduct PMHP and are typically familiar with the school's ecology, needs, personnel, and operating styles.

Child Associates

Child associates are unquestionably central in PMHP. Viewed over the project's long history, the development and refinement of that role is one of PMHP's significant contributions.

Selecting the right child associates with the right characteristics is absolutely crucial. Basic qualities of child associates include personal warmth, empathy, trustworthiness, an ability and a history of working well with both children and adults, flexibility, openness to different types of families and their values, personal stability, and reliability, to name a few (Cowen, Dorr, & Pokracki, 1972). In fact, any program's success depends squarely on the wisdom of those selection decisions. As such, hiring child associates has always been a deeply invested step in PMHP; but accomplishing that step more than justifies the extensive effort that goes into it. Although the principle of hiring maximally able child associates in PMHP is nonnegotiable, the hiring process itself proceeds in several different ways, reflecting a school system's due process mechanisms and natural operating styles. Child associates who have gone through such rigorous selection processes are keenly aware of what they entail. As one newly hired associate put it, "It's like being interviewed for a job at the White House and then getting paid minimum wage."

Child Associate Training. Great care is taken to hire child associates with natural abilities and qualities that make for effective helpgiving with children. Training is intended to build on these positive caring reflexes, to prepare associates for working within the school environment, and to reduce the anxiety associates may feel about taking on their sometimes frightening new role.

Over the past three decades, PMHP has developed, modified, and refined numerous times a comprehensive training program for new child associates. Because the PMHP training program works best when trainers have been trained and supervised by PMHP trainers, PMHP presently limits distribution of these materials to serious professionals interested in providing high quality training. However, PMHP annually provides the essential foundations of PMHP training in a 2-day workshop. If a district remains interested, this can be followed with intensive program consultation. Next, arrangements can be made for a PMHP trainer to go to a school district and model the basic new associate training program, so that a new trainer can participate in a training before becoming a trainer. Finally, it is best when a new trainer provides initial child associate basic training under the supervision of a seasoned trainer. PMHP has found that there are few successful shortcuts in developing and maintaining a high quality training program for new child associates.

Initial child associate training may either precede, or run concurrently with, the child associate's first several months on the job. This training is designed to impart information and skills that facilitate work with children in a school environment and to clarify basic PMHP procedures and intervention strategies. In recent years, most initial associate training cycles have taken between 24 and 36 hours to complete. Some trainers like to provide training for 2 hours per week for 12 to 18 weeks; others like to provide training in 4 to 6 whole days.

Fundamental content for these sessions includes:

1. PMHP's history, rationale, purposes, and procedures; characteristics of children who are served best by PMHP; strategies for building relationships; reporting responsibilities for child abuse;
2. the school environment—roles and relationships within the school environment, clarification of school's actual operating practices, and the culture of schools (Sarason, 1982);
3. typical child development and behavioral norms;
4. the helping relationship, including its importance, communication patterns, and listening skills;
5. understanding children's play as a form of expression and communication;
6. how to equip and use various play materials and activities to facilitate goal achievement;
7. working with aggressive, acting-out children through limit setting; and
8. termination as a natural, yet difficult and important, stage of bringing some closure to the child's work.

Associate training involves activities beyond content coverage. Child associates, like all people, have different learning styles. Some learn well by reading, others by listening and watching; most learn through firsthand experience. Activities such as modeling by the trainer, role plays, videotapes, and active group discussion help to enliven training. Although major portions of associate training are done by a project coordinator or a school mental health professional, it is often helpful to involve relevant others, such as veteran child associates with extensive experience with children. Such veterans are extremely credible to beginning associates.

Child Associate Roles. Child associates' primary responsibility is to the children they serve. A universal goal for child associates is to establish a sound working relationship with a child. A caring, positive relationship, helped by play, creates a framework within which efforts to meet goals to reduce school adjustment problems and promote school competencies can develop.

Child associates are integral to the PMHP team. They are involved in almost all aspects of PMHP, including screening, training activities, and program conferences. They meet with teachers to confer and exchange information about individual students. With additional training, many become skilled enough to work with children in small groups or with parents.

Child associate training in PMHP is an open, ongoing process. It includes initial new associate training and continuing on-the-job training for all associates. Later, more advanced training options are offered to seasoned child associates to broaden their skills. Again, there is flexibility in what ongoing training covers, because such training must be designed to meet a district's needs and beliefs.

The very process of training child associates can be an important team-building element in a PMHP school (Johnson, Carlson, & Couick 1992). Those involved in this process as trainers and trainees work closely with each other and with pupils, teachers, and other school personnel, as part of a cohesive child-serving team.

Professional Roles and Activities

PMHP professionals are intimately involved in the entire program. The professional role in PMHP differs substantially from the traditional school mental health professional role. The essence of that difference is that the PMHP professional's time, rather than doing in-depth diagnostic and therapeutic activities with a few of the school's most troubled children, seeks to promote effective early detection and prevention for many more children than traditional approaches can reach.

One important professional activity is supervising child associates. Other roles and activities of PMHP professionals include team leadership and decision making, consultation with teachers and school staff, child associate recruitment, providing ongoing training experiences for child associates, evaluation-related activities, and public relations presentations.

The PMHP Team

In addition to the central roles of child associates and school mental health professionals, the PMHP team includes the principal and teachers. A principal's positive involvement sets a tone for PMHP to function effectively. Primary grade teachers are central to PMHP. They are the prime source of referrals; moreover, their efforts as part of the team contribute to positive outcomes for children. In some schools, consultants or other school staff have important roles to play. The team, in any case, has responsibility for all aspects of a building's PMHP. In that context, teams often hold weekly or biweekly meetings to review program progress and plan for the future.

Basic PMHP Practices

Children Served by PMHP

PMHP's preventive approach has been to intervene with children as soon as problems are identified. The goal is to optimize their school functioning. In pursuing this goal, PMHP targets young children with incipient school adjustment problems in the mild to moderate range—not children with weighty dysfunction who need professional help. Children most appropriate for PMHP include those who: (a) are shy, withdrawn, not involved, nervous, sad, often fearful in school, or "flat"; (b) become frustrated frequently and act out, lose their tempers easily, fight, seek attention aggressively, or regularly disobey adults; (c) do not get along with peers, are socially isolated, have few friends, or are repeatedly chosen last for games, (d) fail to complete their school work, have limited attention spans, are disorganized, routinely need adult attention, or are frequently off-task; (e) feel inadequate or have low self-esteem, or (f) are experiencing life crises such as parental divorce, sickness or trauma of a parent or sibling, death of a close relative, etc. In summary, PMHP targets and works most effectively with the types of children who are just starting to show a few of these problems, rather than those with numerous or already serious, deeply entrenched difficulties.

Early Detection and Screening

Early detection, screening, and referral are focal in PMHP because they form the base on which the program's early preventive intervention steps rest. Screening in PMHP, like its training, is an ongoing process, that extends over time and reflects informal, as well as formal, components. Personnel in PMHP schools are made aware of the program's presence, scope, and ways of functioning, and become attuned to the importance of early identification and effective early intervention. As in any school, personnel in PMHP schools are witness to daily behavior samples from all children. If and when their concerns about a child reach a certain threshold, they have ready access to the PMHP team for raising such concerns, discussing them, and getting informal feedback about next possible steps. Hence, there is ongoing informal screening in PMHP schools and a mechanism (i.e., team contact) for addressing concerns that arise spontaneously at any time, in any class.

The goal of the PMHP screening process is to develop an accurate representation of all children's early school adjustment; its purpose is to initiate a process of identifying children who stand to benefit most from PMHP. This step also provides a low-cost mechanism by which the PMHP team can review the early school adjustment of all children. It is recognized, however, that not all pertinent emotional and social dimensions can be assessed in an initial screening step. A more realistic goal is to develop a composite sketch of each child's current adjustment situation. The utility of these sketches is enhanced to the extent that they reflect multiple methods, characteristics, input sources, and time-points.

The PMHP screening process begins with the collection of information as soon as school starts. Informally, teachers and other members of the PMHP team observe students in various settings in the school (e.g., classrooms, halls, cafeteria, and playground).

Child associates often arrange with teachers times to observe children in the classroom. Team members review school records and, where pertinent, screening information from prior years. Some teams also do structured observations during standardized testing.

Formally, many schools use rating scales developed or refined by and available from PMHP. For example, the 12-item AML-R Behavior Rating Scale is often completed by the primary grade teacher for each child. This instrument assesses the frequency of acting out, moodiness, and learning-problem behaviors (Primary Mental Health Project, 1995). For children in second grade and above, the Child Rating Scale, a child self-report measure, can be completed by each child. This measure assesses externalized, internalized, and social behaviors, as well as interest in school (Hightower et al., 1987).

Although many of these informal and formal processes are school or district specific, the overall PMHP screening process strives to be systematic, multidimensional, and outreaching. Its prime goal, at least in a preliminary way, is to identify existing problems and competencies in several relevant domains of school functioning for all children, early in their school careers.

Assignment Conference

Most PMHP children first become candidates for intervention as a result of findings from the screening process. After screening steps have been taken, all relevant information is brought together at an assignment conference. The PMHP team meets, reviews this assembled information, creates composite sketches of children's school adjustment, identifies children who seem most appropriate for PMHP services, and begins to formulate an intervention plan for those children. At that point, the referral process starts for children who appear to need PMHP services. Establishing the likelihood of a PMHP referral activates a more extensive information-gathering process.

Although this mass screening process identifies most children who are referred to PMHP, referrals also come from other sources. For some children, initial problems that slipped through the mass-screening "net," or didn't "flower" until later, become apparent. Other children with problems transfer into a school after the formal screening process has ended. Sometimes children who were doing well initially have experiences that adversely affect their school adjustment. And, as PMHP becomes better known within a school, parents initiate a number of referrals.

These realities highlight several points. Referrals to PMHP can, and do, come from many sources and for many reasons; there are multiple routes to services. One of those sources, an important one early on, is the screening process. Referral, however, is always an open option in a PMHP school; it can come up for any child at any time.

Parent Consent

For children identified as candidates for PMHP, written parental consent is required before further steps are taken. If the parent agrees with the referral recommendation, then a more complex, in-depth referral process begins.

Referral

The referral process builds on information already available and gathers additional information from multiple sources so as to formulate an optimal intervention plan for the child. Although schools differ some in the exact nature of the information they gather, as a generalization, it is fair to say that such information is substantial and reflects multiple strands of a child's behavior, occurring in multiple settings, as provided by multiple informants, including teachers, parents, and children themselves.

Direct PMHP Services

Essential to PMHP's preventive approach is the blending of its four key structural elements. Arguably, the most central of those is the ongoing interactive relationship between the child associate and the child in the playroom, a most important ingredient that centrally shapes child outcomes.

Sequentially, after parent permissions are received and the referral process completed, child associates arrange times with teachers and begin to see children in regularly scheduled individual or group contacts, as established by the PMHP Team. The child associate escorts the child to the playroom from the classroom before a session and chaperones him/her back to the classroom after it ends. Most children look forward to meeting with their associate. Classmates sometimes ask if they too can go and when it fits the course of the intervention to do so, a child may be allowed to bring a friend to the playroom. Associate-child meetings, on average, last from 25 to 45 minutes with shorter times for younger children. Although schools also vary in frequency and total number of contacts per child, 20 to 25 sessions is typical for full-year programs and 12 to 15 sessions for one-semester programs. Most part-time child associates see 12 to 18 children per week.

The child associate's first and ongoing responsibility is to develop a healthy relationship with the child. There is no cookbook recipe for doing this. Any effective relationship must reflect the uniqueness of the individuals involved. Child associates, as a matter of course, have different life experiences, interaction styles, and likes and dislikes. Similarly, children have unique life histories, behavioral patterns, and comfort zones. Therefore, each associate-child relationship is special and will require a pinch of this and a smattering of that, depending on what is needed at the time for just the right outcome. By selecting the right child associates, who have skills conducive to working with children and have developed many sound relationships throughout their lives, the relationship balance is tipped toward success. That is why PMHP's recruiting practices place heavy emphasis on an associate's history of effective contacts and skills for establishing warm relationships. If those qualities are present, an associate will get off to a good start with most youngsters.

A warm, trusting, empathic, and mutually respectful associate-child relationship is the foundation on which changes in children are made possible. With this foundation in place, a child associate can use his or her special combination of natural and life-learned skills to help children deal with existing problems and develop needed competencies. Frequently, but not always, less than optimal child progress reflects limitations in the associate-child relationship.

The associate-child relationship is reviewed and considered regularly. Weekly child associate supervision by the mental health professional provides a natural forum for such consideration, as do regularly scheduled conferences with the PMHP team. For more difficult situations, an experienced clinical consultant may be used to provide additional insights and suggestions.

The child associate and child meet in a "playroom." Because play is an enticing medium of expression for young children, they are able to communicate ideas and exchange words with their associates in a naturally conducive child-centered environment. Coupled with a trusting relationship between the associate and the child, the playroom becomes a place where the child feels secure, comfortable, and in control—a place where he or she can feel safe being him or herself.

Child associates are active participants in the playroom. Their actions and words give birth to and maintain an environment of unconditional acceptance of children's feelings, but not necessarily their actions. For example, a child's angry feelings would always be accepted, but limits would be set for actions such as biting, hitting, or spitting. Sometimes, to communicate empathy or understanding, the associate may describe what a child is doing or reflect feelings in ways that can assist the child in dealing with important issues. At other times, an associate may read to the child, play a game with the child, or provide another framework for learning such life skills as taking turns, following rules, attending to a task, and dealing with frustration.

In summary, PMHP provides young children who have incipient signs of school adjustment problems with a warm, caring, supportive, personable, naturally gifted child associate. This special person provides a relationship and environment characterized by security, acceptance, and realistic limits in a playroom. The playroom is designed and outfitted to facilitate age-salient communication so that children can deal with important feelings and issues and acquire appropriate life skills and competencies.

Supervision

A most important checkpoint for child associates is the regularly scheduled weekly or biweekly supervisory meeting. This forum becomes a natural place for reviewing previous events and ongoing processes.

Associates meet regularly, .5 to 1.5 hours per week, with school based mental health professionals for supervision and with teachers to exchange information about the children being seen. These meetings are designed to enhance the program's quality control, to promote communication about the child's functioning in the playroom and classroom, and to maximally coordinate the school's helping efforts in the child's behalf. Supervision in PMHP is ongoing and rests on an established relationship between school professionals and child associates. It serves several purposes, the most important of which is to optimize services to children.

Although there are common elements in all forms of supervision, supervisory formats vary a good deal as a function of time and resources available and the supervisor's professional training. The presence of the same supervisors and associates on a PMHP team for some years builds a foundation of common views, a common vocabulary, and a close, mutually respectful, working relationship—attributes that are all helpful to the supervisory process.

Progress Conferences

About halfway through the PMHP intervention cycle (i.e., January-February for full-year programs), a conference is held to review children's progress in the program. Although most PMHP programs conduct a full set of these midyear progress conferences for all classrooms with involved children, this type of review can be initiated at any time to assess what is happening with a given child. The main purpose of the formal progress conference is to learn about what has been happening with children in the playroom and classroom. The formal, scheduled conference format permits key team members to update each other on the child's status, judge the extent to which initially established goals are being met, and make plans for any in-course corrections.

End-of-Program Conferences

End-of-program conferences are held during the last several weeks of the school year (or semester). As with assignment and progress conferences, all PMHP team members participate. These conferences assess children's overall progress in the program and their current level of functioning. From information provided by teachers and child associates, who know first hand what changes in behavior have occurred, disposition decisions (e.g., terminate from program, continue in PMHP) are made. When pertinent, other information about the child's current adjustment status (e.g., from other school personnel, parents) also enters the end of year conference.

Although most PMHP-seen children are judged at this time to have made significant progress toward established goals and thus no longer need PMHP services, that is not always the case. Indeed, there are always children who evidence limited or no progress toward their goals. Whereas PMHP tended initially to see these children for a second year, our research does not show that it is helpful to do so. In most schools, children seen for a second round are primarily those who have shown some progress and for whom further PMHP contact is seen as a promising option.

Parent Involvement

Open communications with parents and their involvement in the PMHP process make for better child outcomes. Recognizing that point, during the period when PMHP was first developed, the social worker routinely did in-depth interviews with parents of all first-grade children. That practice was helpful because it informed parents about the project, obtained relevant information about the child's early development and family situation, and opened home-school communication lines.

Over the years, this important contact step has lost ground, not because it wasn't helpful, but because it was time-consuming and costly for schools. Although most PMHP programs today still recognize the importance of parent involvement and most try to do all they can to advance that objective, they differ greatly in what they actually do in this respect. Some programs have sufficient resources to arrange for a few individual parent contacts during the year; others conduct weekly parent group meetings. To enhance resources available for home contacts, PMHP has developed a "parent-associate" training program in which associates receive training for work with parents, including home visits to learn more about the child and family and to exchange information about the child's situation at home and school as these relate to the child's PMHP involvement.

The Effectiveness of PMHP

From 1957 until now, PMHP has used a research-service duality in developing, evaluating, and understanding program components and outcomes. Research and service have gone hand in hand. In fact, many of PMHP's key components have been suggested by clinical observations and then carefully researched. Those findings have then been used to shape PMHP so that program services are of highest quality and meet the changing needs of schools and children. Areas included in PMHP's array of studies include (a) assessing school adjustment of children; (b) comparing outcomes of children with different problem types; (c) studies of the selection, characteristics, and performance of child associates; (d) documenting the child associate-child and child associate-supervisor interaction processes; and (e) trying to understand how environmental factors relate to children's school adjustment. A detailed and comprehensive review of these results is not possible within the confines of a small section within a single chapter. Readers interested in more detail are referred to Cowen et al., (1975) and Cowen et al., (1996).

Three early PMHP program evaluation studies, (Cowen et al., 1963; Cowen, Zax, Izzo, & Trost, 1966; Cowen, 1971) followed cohorts of first-grade children and documented clearly that many early problems did not remit spontaneously within the first 3 years of school, but rather such problems increased and resulted in ineffective school functioning. Similarly, longer-term follow-up studies at seventh grade (Zax, Cowen, Rappaport, Beach, & Laird, 1968) and also after more than a decade (Cowen et al., 1973) confirmed that when ignored, children's early adjustment problems resulted in long-term negative outcomes. Such results have been replicated and confirmed by others (Cowen et al., 1983).

One early study (Cowen, 1968) compared adjustment changes among children who were seen by child associates, college students, an after-school program, or not at all. Children seen by the child associates showed significant improvements over and above the other groups.

PMHP's effectiveness has been examined for various subgroups of children. For example, children who are recommended for termination at the end of the school year were found to be less maladjusted and to have gained more from participating in PMHP than those who were recommended to continue (Cowen & Schochet, 1973). More recent studies for the State of California have confirmed the programmatic advantage of focusing PMHP services on less disturbed versus more disturbed children (Cowen et al., 1996).

Lorion, Cowen and Kraus (1974) evaluated the effectiveness of PMHP for children seen once versus twice a week, and found that children seen less often tended to improve more. Lorion, Cowen and Caldwell (1974) compared types of behavioral manifestations in children and discovered that shy-anxious children had the best, whereas acting-out children had the poorest outcomes. This study was followed by Cowen, Orgel, Gesten, & Wilson, 1979, who found that acting-out children could be successfully worked with once specialized training was provided for child associates.

Early research effort in PMHP also focused on the helping process. A series of studies showed that the more successful child associates had significantly higher empathy, affiliation, nurturance, understanding, and less aggression and fewer rejecting responses (Cowen, Dorr, & Pokracki, 1972; Dorr, Cowen, & Sandler, 1973; McWilliams, 1972).

Over the last 20 years there has been a significant growth in PMHP programs and in their evaluations. In New York State, two large program evaluation studies demonstrated consistently positive findings across sites and across years (Weissberg, Cowen, Lotyczewski, & Gesten, 1983; Cowen et al., 1983). Whereas the above studies focused on more rural and suburban districts, Community School District #4 in an East Harlem section of New York City developed and evaluated a PMHP program from 1990 through 1994. All annual evaluations and the combined 4-year evaluation indicated PMHP-involved children had significantly fewer problems and more competencies, showed more initiative and participation, had reductions in shyness, increases in self confidence, and improvements in self-efficacy, social problem solving, and overall participation in school activities (Meller, et al., 1994).

Program evaluations of the Primary Intervention Program (PIP), a program modeled after the Primary Mental Health Project, in both California and Washington demonstrated an effect size that ranged from .37 to .49 with the median of .43. These studies involved more than 50,000 students from over 750 schools. Statistically meaningful improvements have been repeatedly demonstrated in children's school adjustment (Cowen et al., 1996).

Also in California, the Southwest Regional Educational Laboratory conducted a study comparing PIP participants to nonparticipant control groups. PIP children significantly improved compared with the control group in school and social adjustment (Thomas, 1989).

Two follow-up studies (Chandler, Weissberg, Cowen, & Guare, 1984; Work, Lotyczewski, & Raymond, 1995) reported that at-risk children who were seen initially by PMHP were found later to be in the 40th to 50th percentile and were indistinguishable from classmates on teacher- and self-reports of adjustment. Those with PMHP participation had gained more than the groups with whom they were matched and compared.

In sum, "No single study by itself provides definitive confirmation of PMHP short or long term efficacy. Taken together, however, the results of these studies provided weight of evidence in support of the programs effectiveness. This body of evidence has helped established a credibility base that's contributed importantly to PMHP's survival and expansion" (Cowen et al., 1996, p. 249).

Summary

Few programs of any type can trace their history back for 40 years. The success of PMHP exemplifies how prevention programs can root, evolve, and adapt. Without question, one of the reasons PMHP has enjoyed such a history is that its foundation is built on research and program effectiveness data that is sensitive to real-world realities. Second, although the structural elements of the program have remained surprisingly consistent, the structure itself has allowed for changes and modifications by the environments into which it was introduced. Although the above two reasons are necessary, they are not sufficient. Third, PMHP is cost-effective. Children receive excellent services from truly exceptional people in an efficient and timely manner. Parents, teachers, administrators, and elected officials can all enjoy benefits of the program that range from changes in children's behavior to a decrease in the tax burden. Therefore, prevention programs, implemented correctly and considering both individual and environmental conditions, can not only survive, but also flourish in times of wealth as well as in times of downsizing.

As American industry has discovered, short-term gains and outcomes are only a small part of determining long-term success. A long-term vision and plan based on solid research and forward thinking create products and services that people want and need. It is time that those involved with public policy decisions involving the development, evaluation, and dissemination of prevention programs (i.e., governments at all level), recognize the accrued benefits that can be had by investing more heavily in prevention.

References

Chandler, C., Weissberg, R. P., Cowen, E. L., & Guare, J. (1984). The long-term effects of a school-based secondary prevention program for young maladapting children. *Journal of Consulting and Clinical Psychology, 52,* 165-170.

Cowen, E. L. (1968). The effectiveness of secondary prevention programs using nonprofessionals in the school setting. *Proceedings of the 76th Annual Convention of the American Psychological Association, 2,* 705-706.

Cowen, E. L. (1971). Emergent directions in school mental health: The development and evaluation of a program for early detection and prevention of ineffective school behavior. *American Scientist, 59,* 723-733.

Cowen, E. L., Dorr, D. A., & Pokracki, F. (1972). Selection of nonprofessional child aides for a school mental health project. *Community Mental Health Journal, 8,* 220-226.

Cowen, E. L., Hightower, A. D., Pedro-Carroll, J., Work, W. C., Wyman, P. A. & Haffey, W. C. (1996). *School based prevention for at-risk children: The Primary Mental Health Project.* Washington, DC: American Psychological Association.

Cowen, E. L., Izzo, L. D., Miles, H., Telschow, E. F., Trost, M. A., & Zax, M. (1963). A preventive mental health program in the school setting: Description and evaluation. *Journal of Psychology, 56,* 307-356.

Cowen, E. L., Orgel, A. R., Gesten, E. L., & Wilson, A. B. (1979). The evaluation of an intervention program for young schoolchildren with acting-out problems. *Journal of Abnormal Child Psychology, 7,* 381-396.

Cowen, E. L., Pedersen, A., Babigian, H., Izzo, L. D., & Trost, M. A. (1973). Long-term follow-up of early detected vulnerable children. *Journal of Consulting and Clinical Psychology, 41,* 438-446.

Cowen, E. L., & Schochet, B. V. (1973). Referral and outcome differences between terminating and nonterminating children seen by nonprofessionals in a school mental health project. *American Journal of Community Psychology, 1,* 103-112.

Cowen, E. L., Trost, M. A., Lorion, R. P., Dorr, D., Izzo, L. D., & Isaacson, R. V. (1975). *New ways in school mental health: Early detection and prevention of school maladaptation.* New York: Human Sciences Press.

Cowen, E. L., Weissberg, R. P., Lotyczewski, B. S., Bromley, M. L., Gilliland-Mallo, G., DeMeis, J. L., Farago, J. P., Grassi, R. J., Haffey, W. G., Weiner, M. J., & Woods, A. (1983). Validity generalization of a school-based preventive mental health program. *Professional Psychology, 14,* 613-623.

Cowen, E. L., Zax, M., Izzo, L. D., & Trost, M. A. (1966). Prevention of emotional disorders in the school setting: A further investigation. *Journal of Consulting Psychology, 30,* 381-387.

Dorr, D., Cowen, E. L., & Sandler, I. N. (1973). Changes in nonprofessional mental health workers' response preference and attitudes as a function of training and supervised field experience. *Journal of School Psychology, 11,* 118-122.

Durlak, J. A. (1979). Comparative effectiveness of paraprofessionals and professional helpers. *Psychological Bulletin, 86,* 80-92.

Ensminger, M. E., Kellam, S. G., & Rubin, R. B. (1983). School and family origins of delinquency: Comparisons by sex. In K. T. VanDusen & S. A. Mednick (Eds.), *Prospective studies of crime and delinquency* (pp. 17-41). Boston: Kluwer-Nijhoff.

Hattie, J. A., Sharpley, C. F., & Rogers, H. J. (1984). Comparative effectiveness of professional and paraprofessional helpers. *Psychological Bulletin, 95,* 534-541.

Hightower, A. D., Cowen, E. L., Spinell, A. P., Lotyczewski, B. S., Guare, J. C., Rohrbeck, C. A., & Brown, L. P. (1987). The Child Rating Scale: The development and psychometric refinement of a socioemotional self-rating scale for young school children. *School Psychology Review, 16,* 239-255.

Johnson, D. B., Carlson, S. R., & Couick, J. (1992). *Program Development Manual for the Primary Intervention Program.* Sacramento: California Department of Mental Health.

Kellam, S. G., Branch, J. D., Agrawal, K. C., & Ensminger, M. E. (1975). *Mental health and going to school: The Woodlawn program of assessment, early intervention, and evaluation.* Chicago: University of Chicago Press.

Kellam, S. G., Simon, M. B., & Ensminger, M. E. (1983). Antecedents in first grade of teenage substance use and psychological well being: A ten-year community-wide prospective study. In D. F. Ricks & B. S. Dohrenwend (Eds.), *Origins of psychopathology: Research and public policy* (pp. 73-97). New York: Cambridge University Press.

Lorion, R. P., Cowen, E. L., & Caldwell, R. A. (1974). Problem types of children referred to a school based mental health program: Identification and outcome. *Journal of Consulting and Clinical Psychology, 42,* 491-496.

Lorion, R. P., Cowen, E. L., & Kraus, R. M. (1974). Some hidden "regularities" in a school mental health program and their relation to intended outcomes. *Journal of Consulting and Clinical Psychology, 42,* 346-352.

McWilliams, S. A. (1972). A process analysis of nonprofessional intervention with children. *Journal of School Psychology, 10,* 367-377.

Meller, P. J., LaBoy, W., Rothwax, Y., Fritton, J., & Mangual, J. (1994). *Community School District Four: Primary Mental Health Project, 1990-1994.* New York: Community School District No. 4.

Mrazek, P. J. & Haggerty, R. J. (Eds.). (1994). *Reducing risks for mental disorders: Frontiers for preventive intervention research*. Washington DC: National Academy Press.

Namir, S., & Weinstein, R. S. (1982). Children: Facilitating new directions. In L. R. Snowden (Ed.), *Reaching the underserved: Mental health needs of neglected populations* (pp. 43-73). Beverly Hills, CA: Sage.

Prevention Task Panel Report. (1978). *Task panel reports submitted to the Commission on Mental Health* (Vol. 4, pp. 1822-1863; Stock No. 040-000-00393-2). Washington, DC: US Government Printing Office.

Primary Mental Health Project. (1995). *PMHP screening and evaluation measures*. Rochester, NY: Author.

Sarason, S. B. (1982). *The culture of the school and the problem of change* (2nd ed.). Boston: Allyn-Bacon.

Thomas, C. F. (1989). *An evaluation of the effectiveness of the Primary Intervention Program in improving the school and social adjustment of primary grade children: Final report*. Los Alamitos, CA: Southwest Regional Education Laboratory.

Weissberg, R. P., Cowen, E. L., Lotyczewski, B. S., & Gesten, E. L. (1983). Primary Mental Health Project: Seven consecutive years of program outcome research. *Journal of Consulting and Clinical Psychology, 51,* 100-107.

Work, W. C., Lotyczewski, B. S., & Raymond, C. (1995). *Long term effectiveness of an early preventive intervention for rural school children*. Manuscript submitted for publication.

Zax, M., Cowen, E. L., Rappaport, J., Beach, D. R., & Laird, J. D. (1968). Follow-up study of children identified early as emotionally disturbed. *Journal of Consulting and Clinical Psychology, 32,* 369-374.

CHAPTER 10

The Children of Divorce Intervention Program: Fostering Resilient Outcomes for School-Aged Children

JOANNE PEDRO-CARROLL

Very few people in the United States are untouched by divorce these days, if not by personal, firsthand experience, then through the experiences of a close friend or family member. The upsurge in divorce rates over the last three decades has affected 3 million people annually and currently involves half of all marriages. Demographic estimates suggest that approximately 40% of white children and 75% of African American children will experience their parents' divorce by age 16 (Bumpass, 1984). Thus, divorce has become an unwelcome yet common experience for children living in the United States today.

After parental divorce, children spend on average 5 years in a single-parent family before another major transition typically occurs—entering a stepfamily. This poses yet another set of challenging adaptations, often entailing longer readjustment periods than the initial divorce, especially for older children (Hetherington & Clingempeel, 1992). About 75% of divorced mothers and 80% of divorced fathers remarry (Glick & Lin, 1986). And because divorce rates are higher for remarriages for than first marriages, one in four children now experience two or more parental divorces before age 18. These stark realities highlight major changes in patterns of family living over the past 30 years and underscore an ongoing process of transition associated with marital disruption. The latter include a series of changes and family reorganizations that modify many aspects of children's lives and development, ranging from emotional and behavioral changes to markedly different economic and living conditions.

This chapter provides an overview of the social and emotional consequences of divorce for children. These costs, on a societal as well as individual level, provide a compelling rationale for providing multifaceted supports for children, including systematic, preventive interventions designed to reduce the stresses of divorce and teach social competencies that enhance children's adaptive coping and resilience. The Children of Divorce Intervention Program (CODIP), based on this conceptual model, will be described in detail in this chapter, including research findings documenting its efficacy.

Overview

There is substantial variation in children's long-term reactions to divorce. However, in the early stages, most children of all ages experience considerable distress. Sadness, anxiety, anger, resentment, confusion, loyalty conflicts, somatic symptoms, and sometimes guilt are frequent early reactions. A number of studies have found that in the period immediately following the divorce, children may grieve for the absent parent. In our groups, children often rate "missing Dad" as the most difficult aspect of the divorce. National survey data sheds light on the trajectory over time of fathers' diminishing contact with their children. The National Survey of Children found that, 5 years after the divorce, 40% of children haven't had contact with their fathers within the past year (Furstenberg, Nord, Peterson, & Zill, 1983).

The diversity in long-term outcomes means that although some children will fare well, for others there is a lifelong legacy of divorce. The individual and societal costs of divorce for such children can be profound and enduring, including higher rates of high school dropout, earlier marriage, out-of-wedlock childbirth, and disruption of their own marriages (McLanahan & Bumpass, 1988).

Werner and Smith (1992) report similar findings in their book, *Overcoming the Odds*. This longitudinal study monitored the impact of a variety of biological and psychosocial risk and protective factors on development from birth through adulthood. The authors suggest that parental divorce and remarriage can create vulnerabilities that may resurface long after adolescent sons and daughters have come of age when they confront the adult roles of spouse and parent. These authors echo a common concern of clinical investigators (Wallerstein & Blakeslee, 1989) that the psychological effects of parental divorce can extend into adulthood and interfere with the establishment of a strong bond of commitment and intimacy for a significant minority of men and women.

Although these findings certainly warrant concern, it is important to note the limitations of clinical studies, most notably the lack of control groups. Many early studies, which may have overestimated the deleterious impact of divorce on children, had similar limitations of design and methodology. Recent research using more rigorous techniques has shed new light on this topic. Amato and Keith's (1991b) meta-analysis, reflecting many studies, showed that for 72% of uncontrolled studies and 70% of controlled studies, there were small, but statistically significant, negative effects for children of divorce (of all ages) in terms of parent-child relationships, psychological adjustment, academic achievement, self-concept, behavioral conduct, and social adjustment. The strongest of those effects were for conduct and parent-child relationships, followed by psychological adjustment and self-concept. A related study by Hoyt, Cowen, Pedro-Carroll, and Alpert-Gillis (1990) found higher levels of depression, anxiety, and school adjustment problems among second- and third-grade children of divorce than among demographically matched peers from nondivorced families.

A parallel meta-analysis on the impact of divorce on adults (Amato & Keith, 1991a), yielded similar findings. Specifically, for adults, divorce was associated with a decline in socioeconomic status; poorer physical health; diminished psychological well-being, including more depression and less life satisfaction; unhappier marriages; and more frequent future divorce. In summary, these two meta-analyses identified modest but consistent negative effects of divorce on the adjustment of children and adults.

Significant longitudinal data about the effects of the divorce process on children comes from the National Survey of Children, a longitudinal study of a representative sample of 7- to 11-year-old children followed from middle childhood through adolescence and early adulthood (Zill, Morrison, & Coiro, 1993). Children of divorce were found, 8 years after the marital breakup, to have more school adjustment problems than children from intact families (34% vs. 20%). However, the fact that 66% of these children were functioning reasonably well in school highlights the diversity of postdivorce outcomes. Whereas some children land deftly on their feet after the divorce, for others there is a lifelong legacy of negative fallout.

The preceding reality poses the important challenge of identifying factors that shape or mediate children's adjustment to parental divorce over time—an important focus of recent research in this area. In brief, findings from this work suggest that a child's postdivorce adjustment is shaped less by the fact of parental divorce per se, and more by the interplay of diverse risk and protective factors, including characteristics of the child (e.g., age, gender, temperament); coping strategies; additional cumulative stress that the child experiences; continuing qualities of the postdivorce family environment (e.g., parent conflict); and available resources and support beyond the family. The next section considers the role played by such factors in children's postdivorce adaptation and the implications of those findings for developing preventive interventions for children of divorce.

Factors Predicting Risk and Resilience in Children of Divorce

Historically, research on children of divorce has focused more on risk factors for negative outcomes than on protective factors that favor adaptive outcomes (Emery & Forehand, 1994). Although more research is needed identifying pathways to wellness following divorce, some child, family, and extrafamilial factors have been identified that offer important clues for shaping preventive interventions.

On the plus side, family-related factors such as authoritative, nurturant, effective parenting; sound parent-child relationships; parental cooperation in child-related matters; and encapsulated or minimal interparental conflict have been shown to be protective factors that enhance adjustment outcomes for children (Black & Pedro-Carroll, 1993; Emery & Forehand, 1994). Conversely, high interparental conflict has a negative impact on children's postdivorce adjustment (Emery, 1982).

Maladaptive coping styles, such as avoiding the reality of the divorce and attributions of self-blame, are child factors that increase the risk of psychological problems (Kurdek & Berg, 1983, 1987). Research with middle-school and college students highlights the importance of effective coping strategies in facilitating sound postdivorce adjustment (Grych & Fincham, 1992) and hence the need for preventive interventions to teach such strategies. At another level, extrafamilial support sources, including a warm, positive relationship with a teacher or other key adult outside the home, have been found to enhance child adjustment after the divorce (Cowen, Pedro-Carroll, & Alpert-Gillis, 1990).

Children of Divorce Intervention Program

History and Development

As divorce rates rose rapidly in the 1970s, the negative ramifications of divorce posed a challenge for schools to respond to children's need for support. That reality fueled the need to develop a preventively oriented intervention designed specifically for such youngsters. It was out of an awareness of that need that the Children of Divorce Intervention Program (CODIP) was developed in 1982. Although the acronym CODIP has thus far been used in a global, undifferentiated way, it is in reality a generic shorthand for a family of six kindred programs for children of divorce from kindergarten through grade 8 that feature two common goals: (a) minimizing divorce's negative impact on children; and (b) teaching children skills and competencies to help them cope in maximally adaptive ways with the major challenges in the aftermath of divorce.

CODIP is a school-based program, built on the assumption that timely intervention for children of divorce can offer important short and long-term benefits. CODIP's basic goals are *to create a supportive group environment in which children can freely share experiences, establish common bonds, and clarify misconceptions;* and *to teach children skills that enhance their capacity to cope with the stressful changes that divorce often poses.* Wallerstein's (1983) concept of specific psychological tasks confronting children of divorce is reflected in the program's defining features for different age groups.

The initial CODIP model was developed for fourth- to sixth-grade suburban children of divorce (Pedro-Carroll & Cowen, 1985). That program's success laid a sound foundation for adapting the model to children of different ages and sociocultural back-grounds. Through all these many changes, the program's basic goals of providing support and teaching effective coping skills remained constant, though its technologies were modified to reflect the needs and realities of specific age and sociodemographic groups. This long-term evolutionary process has led both to refinement of the initial program and to the development of separate versions of the program tailored specifically to younger (kindergarten-first grade, second-third grade) and older (fourth-sixth grade, seventh-eighth grade) urban and suburban youngsters. Detailed practitioner-oriented manuals have been written for each new version of the program.

Structural Model

A fundamental underpinning of CODIP groups is to provide a safe, supportive environment for children. Thus, CODIP meetings should be scheduled consistently and conducted in a school area that offers privacy. Confidentiality is essential. Although meeting times vary across schools, most CODIP groups convene during the school day. Determinations about optimal group size, session length, and duration of program depend on the developmental characteristics of the target group. For example, with older youngsters, weekly 1-hour sessions for six to eight children balanced by gender have worked well. By contrast, with younger children, 40- to 45-minute weekly sessions with groups of four to six seem ideal.

Children's stage of development has a major influence on their reaction to parental divorce; therefore, CODIP content must also be geared to the attributes of different age groups. For example, issues of loyalty conflicts, anger, stigmatization, and isolation are very salient for 9- to 12-year-olds, whereas feelings of sadness, confusion, guilt, and fear of abandonment are more prominent reactions for younger children (Wallerstein & Kelly, 1980).

Developmental factors also shape the methods used to facilitate group process. Older (fourth- to eighth-grade) children with more advanced cognitive development have a broader understanding of emotions, their own and others, and a clearer awareness of the causes and modes of expression of feelings. Consequently, they are more comfortable than younger children with a discussion format. By contrast, young children's action orientation and shorter attention span limit the effectiveness of lengthy discussion. Given the intrinsic appeal that play and concrete activities hold for young children, CODIP at that age level emphasizes engaging, concrete activities such as puppet play, games, and the interactive use of books and filmstrips as vehicles for advancing key program goals and concepts.

Program Objectives

The development of CODIP was based on generative research documenting the stressors that divorce poses for children and the relationship between social support and children's adjustment. Although support from kindred peers can, in principle, provide a sense of comfort and a common bond for children of divorce, these youngsters often avoid peers precisely because they feel isolated and different. Also, they often lack the experience or skills needed to cope with family changes. These lacks can lead to frustration and withdrawal and can disrupt effective relationships with adults and peers. So viewed, CODIP's prime goals are to provide support and build skills that facilitate adaptive coping and reduce the inherent stresses of parental divorce. Within such a framework, CODIP's five basic objectives are built into a structured, sequential curriculum. Depth of involvement in these five areas and specific program formats and exercises used to advance them vary for different age and sociodemographic groups:

1. *Supportive group environment:* CODIP's format and exercises are designed to maximize supportive interactions. Contact with peers who have had similar experiences helps to reduce children's feelings of isolation and promotes a sense of camaraderie and trust.

From the very first session, a safe, accepting environment is established in which children can respond at their own pace.

2. *Identification and appropriate expression of feelings:* Parental divorce can trigger in children complex feelings that are difficult to cope with or comprehend. Young children especially can be overwhelmed by such feelings because they lack the cognitive understandings and coping skills of adults. Hence, CODIP seeks to enhance children's ability to identify and appropriately express a range of emotions. Leaders seek to create a safe group environment in which all feelings are accepted, and to maintain a balance of emotionally laden and neutral experiences. The program curriculum is sequenced to consider the universality, diversity, and acceptability of feelings before focusing on divorce-related issues.

3. *Clarifying divorce-related misconceptions:* Children's cognitive mastery depends on the accuracy of their perceptions; therefore, clarifying divorce-related misconceptions is an important aspect of the program. Over several sessions, CODIP strives to reduce children's fears of abandonment, feelings of responsibility for the divorce, and unrealistic fantasies about restoring the marriage. The child's ability to attribute the divorce to external realities, rather than something he or she has done, helps to restore self-esteem and overcome feelings of responsibility for the marital rupture.

4. *Enhancing coping skills:* Enhancing children's coping skills is an essential program objective. Several program sessions seek to train children in social problem solving, communication skills, and appropriate ways to express anger, using games and exercises to foster skill acquisition and generalization. These skills help children better cope with many life changes associated with the divorce process (e.g., moving to a new school or neighborhood, being used as a messenger or informant between parents, wanting to spend more time with a parent, or being upset when a parent begins to date), and thus to gain control over situations in which they might otherwise feel helpless. Specifically, children are taught to differentiate between problems that they *can* and *cannot* control. This key distinction helps them to master the psychological task of disengaging from interparental conflicts and redirecting energies to age-appropriate pursuits.

5. *Enhance children's perceptions of self and family:* This final integrative unit emphasizes positive qualities of children and families. Children in the midst of stressful life changes often feel different and defective (i.e., "If I were a better kid, my parents would have stayed together"). Several self-esteem building exercises are used to highlight positive qualities.

The Group Model

All CODIP programs use a group modality for several reasons. Although scarce professional resources in the schools is one reason for doing so, there are more basic and important justifications. Parental divorce alters children's lives profoundly. Despite record-high divorce rates, many children of divorce feel alone and different as a result of their family changes. Hence, one important potential benefit of a group is that it offers children support and comfort by virtue of sharing experiences and feelings with peers who have been through similar experiences, and of learning that they are not alone at a time when it feels as if everything in their life is changing. The group format also provides natural opportunities for exchanging information on common divorce-related issues and for clarifying common misconceptions about divorce.

One of the most comforting aspects of group interaction comes from the reality that children who have gone through common stressful experiences are more credible to peers than those who have not had that experience. A child who fears, deep down, that he or she is responsible for the breakup of her parents' marriage can find much comfort and relief in the words of a peer with exactly the same feelings—indeed, even more so than from the intellectual assurances of an adult. Furthermore, in a group format, children who are further along in the process of adjusting to divorce can serve as credible, important coping models for those in the early stages of readjustment.

Moreover, in CODIP's later, structured, skill acquisition meetings, the group format offers children opportunities to learn about others' efforts to solve problems, deal with anger, disengage from loyalty conflicts, and other interpersonal skills. Thus, children learn from each other's successes and setbacks. The group format also includes discussion and role playing, an engaging, ego-involving format that provides ample opportunities for practice and skill refinement.

Group Leaders

CODIP's success depends on the interest and skills of group leaders. Children's groups may cohere more slowly than adult groups because some children are so absorbed with their own problems that they have difficulty taking the role of others. The group leader's sensitivity and ability to establish a trusting environment, to encourage children's involvement in group activities, and to express feelings all contribute to the development of a cohesive group. The leader's ability to deal comfortably with emotionally laden issues sets a basic tone and climate for the group.

CODIP groups are generally co-led, ideally by a male and female. The two leaders share task and process roles. This arrangement helps children to observe firsthand a positive, cooperative, cross-gender adult relationship. And because most CODIP groups are mixed-gender groups, it also offers children a positive, same-sex adult role model. Having two leaders also facilitates responses to sensitive, emotionally laden issues, nonverbal cues, and behavior management problems. What one leader may miss in the heat of the interaction, the other can pick up.

CODIP leaders are selected more for their interest, skills, and sensitivity than for training in any specific discipline. In practice, leaders have included school psychologists, social workers, and nurses; guidance counselors; principals and teachers; graduate trainees in mental health fields; and a trained paraprofessional teamed with a mental health professional. The leader selection process starts with a meeting for interested school personnel to describe the program and the roles and responsibilities of leaders. At this meeting, time commitments (about 3 hours a week) and role responsibilities are detailed to enable prospective leaders to judge their ability to participate. Also, contact between potential leaders and CODIP staff helps to form two-way judgments about suitability.

Leaders have four to five 2-hour training sessions before the program starts and biweekly 1.5-hour training/supervision meetings while it is in progress. The initial training sessions provide information about the impact of divorce on adults and children;

children's cognitive and emotional growth, including specific, age-related reactions of the target group to parental divorce; factors that shape children's adjustment to parental divorce over time; and group leadership and facilitation skills. Biweekly supervisory meetings review salient aspects of the prior week's meeting(s), including things that went well and problems experienced; provide opportunities to problem solve and modify curricular materials or management strategies; and preview the next week's curriculum.

CODIP for Children of Different Ages: 9- to 12-Year-Olds

The following session summary illustrates how CODIP program objectives are approached in the 12-session curriculum for fourth to sixth graders. At this age, many children react to divorce-related changes and tensions with anger and resentment. They know that divorce, unlike death, is not inevitable; and they may thus align themselves with one parent and blame the other. Also, children at this age often feel embarrassed and different than peers from nondivorced families. Some have lingering fears that they are to blame for their parents' marital strife. The session outline below describes how the CODIP curriculum for 9- to 12-year-olds addresses these common reactions in a supportive environment that focuses on the five general program objectives.

Session 1: Foster a Supportive Group Environment

Social support is a fundamental underpinning of CODIP that extends throughout the program. From the first session, a safe, accepting environment is established, confidentiality is explained and its importance highlighted, and discussion begins of the complex emotions related to parental divorce and things children find helpful in dealing with the challenges it poses. Selecting a group name or symbol helps children develop a common support bond. The names children have chosen reflect the meaning of the group experience for them: Kids Helping Kids, The Confidential Group, and "KICS" Kids Incorporated in Caring and Sharing.

Session 2: Understanding Changes in the Family

Session 2 focuses on divorce-related feelings and experiences and on the clarification of commonly held misconceptions. Filmstrips are used as a catalyst for structured group discussions about common divorce-related scenarios, including loyalty conflicts, visitation, and parental dating. This session's activities stimulate children's involvement and expression of feelings about family changes, often eliciting keenly felt but pent-up emotions.

Session 3: Coping With Changes

The goals of Session 3 are to increase children's understanding of the impact of the divorce for them and their parents, to encourage parent-child communication, and to help children identify appropriate coping strategies for their situation. A filmstrip is preceded by a discussion of why children behave in certain ways after divorce (e.g., "Why do you suppose children might lose their tempers more quickly? worry more? find it harder to talk with their parents?") Those questions stimulate discussion of adaptive ways to cope with concrete, postdivorce challenges.

To increase child-parent communication, the idea of a group newsletter is introduced. Initially conceived by children, the newsletter offers a forum for creative writing, drawing, poetry, and humor that expresses feelings and reaches out to important others to enhance mutual understanding. It is one of several activities designed to strengthen bonds among children; moreover, the creative expression it entails promotes a sense of competence and mastery.

Sessions 4, 5, 6: Social Problem Solving (SPS)

These meetings seek to build social competencies and enhance children's self-control, communication, and problem-solving skills. Problem-solving steps and self-statements are taught to help children recognize that although some things, such as the divorce itself, cannot be controlled, they can control their own behavior and find adaptive solutions to problems. Role playing is used extensively to teach children skills to cope with diverse real-life problems.

Specifically, *Session 4* introduces a six-step procedure for resolving interpersonal problems: (a) problem identification, (b) generating alternatives, (c) analyzing consequences of the solutions generated, (d) choosing an alternative, (e) evaluating its consequences, and (f) implementing the chosen solution. These steps are first applied to non-divorce-related problems with friends or family members. During this session, children receive a cartoon depicting the six problem-solving steps and take turns role-playing those steps. They are encouraged to take the cartoons home and go over them with their parents as a way of increasing parent-child communication. Finally, they are asked to bring to the next session a specific, real-life problem to which the new problem-solving steps can be applied.

Leaders begin *Session 5* by modeling application of the SPS steps to a personal problem of their own. Next, children apply these steps to the divorce-related interpersonal problems they brought in. After an alternative solution is chosen, children role-play its application in the sheltered group setting before trying it out in the "real world." Typical real-life problems include being used as a messenger or informant between parents, wanting to spend more time with a parent, and feeling upset or angry when a parent begins to date.

Session 6 seeks to consolidate and refine newly acquired problem-solving skills, and, importantly, introduces a key distinction between problems children *can* and *cannot* solve. Many children, motivated by the wish to restore interparental harmony and by their own feelings of helplessness, become enmeshed in a futile attempt to solve parental problems that are totally beyond their control. Thus, Session 6 emphasizes the differences between solvable and unsolvable problems and explores ways of disengaging from the latter. Role playing is used to dramatize solvable problems (e.g., whether to tell friends about the divorce) and unsolvable problems (e.g., the divorce itself).

Session 7: Panel of Experts on Divorce: WKID-TV

Session 7 provides an enjoyable way for children to consolidate problem-solving and coping skills thus far acquired and to clarify lingering misconceptions about the divorce. Children take turns as members of a panel of experts on divorce and field questions from the "audience" (i.e., the other group members). This activity (a) underscores common problems of children of divorce; (b) further clarifies misconceptions about divorce; (c) provides practice in solving personal problems; (d) highlights problems that can, and cannot, be controlled; (e) diversifies suggestions for coping with difficult problems; and (f) enhances children's sense of competence and self-esteem by concretizing the fact that they have indeed acquired skills for resolving problems and insights about divorcing families that can help others. Sample questions from this activity include "What are some things kids worry about when their parents separate?" and "My parents still fight even though they're divorced; what can I do to solve this terrible problem?" Children offer spontaneous solutions to the problems posed, often with wit, wisdom, and understanding.

Sessions 8 and 9: Understanding and Dealing With Anger

Sessions 8 and 9 deal with issues of anger, a frequent by-product of parental divorce for children. Emphasis is placed on understanding the causes of anger, identifying it in ourselves and others, and learning about appropriate and inappropriate ways to express it. For example, children are taught to express anger using "I-statements" that communicate a feeling clearly without attacking the other person and intensifying the problem. Again, leaders actively model effective communication and appropriate methods for handling anger. After basic methods of anger control have been considered, children choose anger-provoking scenarios from a "grab-bag" and practice adaptive ways of communicating about, and dealing with, anger.

Session 9 consolidates skills introduced in the problem-solving sessions and deals with the evaluation of alternatives for controlling anger. Children are invited to suggest different ways of coping with the specific anger-provoking events raised in Session 8. The group evaluates the appropriateness of each suggestion, listing them on the board under the headings *Good Control* ("makes things better") and *Poor Control* ("makes things worse"). Leaders also suggest coping strategies (e.g., writing to or talking to the person with whom you're angry, talking to a friend, going to your room to "cool off"). Finally, children take turns in role-playing anger-provoking scenarios, applying the concepts of "I-statements," "good control," and problem-solving.

Session 10: Focus on Families

Session 10 seeks to help children understand the complex nature of family relationships, to promote acceptance of diverse family forms, and to help children learn how to deal with family problems that are within their control. Points highlighted in these discussions are (a) that many different family forms exist; (b) that most families, whatever their form, have some difficult times, but there are ways to problem solve at those times; and (c) that all family forms have potential for love and stability. Children then apply the skills they have learned to family problems by participating in a stage-game (i.e., "Panel of Experts on Families") structurally similar to Session 7's panel, but with a focus on issues of life in a single-parent family, parental dating and remarriage, and the challenges of blended families.

Session 11: "You're A Special Person" Exercise

This session's two main objectives are to bolster children's self-esteem and to identify positive postdivorce changes. Leaders facilitate the discussion by highlighting the fact that although parental divorce is distressing and creates many family changes, some changes may be positive. This helps children to identify sources of hope for the future that are often overlooked in the turmoil of marital disruption. Next comes an exercise designed to underscore children's self-worth and highlight their special strengths. In this activity, all children receive written feedback from peers and leaders about their unique qualities and special contributions to the group. Children enjoy this exercise; some keep their "special person" card long after the group ends.

Session 12: Termination

The last meeting deals primarily with termination. The group experience is reviewed with a focus on children's feelings about its ending. Children are encouraged to identify and seek out people (e.g., parents, friends, teachers) who can provide support after the group ends. After 12 weeks of sharing and learning—and at times crying—together, children are open in talking about the group experience and their reactions to its ending. The following quote conveys their sense of the group experience:

> This group has been a safe place where I could talk about things I've never told anyone before. It's helped me to see that divorce is sad, but it's not the end of the world for my family or me.

CODIP for Kindergarten to Third Grade

The preceding section described the CODIP model for the original fourth- to sixth-grade program. Based on positive results with that age group, a next step was to develop and evaluate a modified CODIP program for younger children. This section describes aspects of that modification, with age-appropriate changes in the CODIP curriculum. Basically, this program revision sought to preserve CODIP's goals and objectives within an approach better suited to the emotional and cognitive realities of younger children.

Although there are separate versions of CODIP for kindergarten to first grades and second to third grades, the two are considered as a unit here because of similarities in objectives and content. However, program activities in each case are tuned to the developmental realities of the targeted age group. Tailoring CODIP to kindergarten to first grade children was challenging. At this age, children are entering the "concrete operations" stage, their verbal skills and capacities for expressive language are limited, and their concepts of emotions don't stretch much beyond a gross "good-bad" polarity. They depend heavily on the family for security and stability and for meeting their physical and emotional needs. Although they need adult support at times of stress or major family change, their limited verbal and interpersonal skills restrict their ability to seek or obtain such support.

At this young age, most children are openly sad about family disruption and a parent leaving home. Wishes for family reunification are frequent and fervent. As one 6-year-old said, "I pray every night that they won't get a divorce." Misconceptions about the reasons for the marital conflict range from confusion (e.g., "because my Mom got up too early to clip coupons") to troublesome self-blame (e.g., "because I wet my bed . . . they were fighting over me"). Themes of loss and sadness, fear of abandonment, deprivation, yearning for the noncustodial parent, and fantasies of reconciliation are prominent in this age group (Wallerstein & Kelly, 1980). The kindergarten through third grade programs address these issues by providing a safe, supportive environment in which children can express feelings and emotions; share experiences; seek needed information, help, and support; and deal effectively with everyday interpersonal problems.

The program's central support and skill-building components unfold in appealing, action-oriented contexts designed to capture young children's active involvement. For example, puppet play is used throughout as one engaging, developmentally appropriate way to convey key program concepts and help children access their feelings. To that end, each group has an honorary member—a puppet named "Tenderheart," who is introduced by the leader at the first meeting. As the children are getting to know each other, Tenderheart explains timidly that this is also his first time in a group like this, so he's a little shy and not sure what to expect. Leaders invite children to tell Tenderheart what they think the group is about and how they can help him feel more comfortable.

The curriculum for younger children also uses interactive games to teach coping skills. For example, one important communication skill for children of this age, especially children of divorce, is *how* to ask for what they need from parents and significant others. The program seeks to promote this skill through an age-appropriate game, "Ask the Dinosaur," and the use of a "Feelings Telegram" that teaches children effective ways to ask for what they need (e.g., how to say "Mom, I need a hug," or "I feel sad when you fight over me; could you please leave me out of it?").

The program also seeks to extend young children's emotional vocabulary. As children learn about a range of emotions and about how to put their feelings into words, they are less likely to develop somatic symptoms or act out in frustration. The program also includes several sessions designed to clarify misconceptions about the divorce and the child's lack of control over reconciliation. Using age-appropriate techniques, including structured puppet and doll play, simple discussion, and interactive books, the message is conveyed that divorce is a "grown-up" problem that children neither cause nor control.

Many children of divorce have limited or no contact with their fathers. For these children, "missing dad" and not understanding his lack of involvement are central program issues. In searching for explanations, children often internalize the belief that they aren't lovable enough to warrant the absent parent's sustained involvement. With young children, puppet and doll play, books, and discussion are used to convey the notion that parents sometimes feel too guilty or upset to visit their children, and that in no way reflects on the child's worth or lovability. Being able to see non-visitation by an absent parent as a product of external, rather than internal, factors is an important precondition for strengthening the child's positive sense of self. The program also uses age-appropriate methods of teaching young children to differentiate between problems they can and cannot control. This differentiation is crucial to the child's mastering the psychological task of disengaging from interparental conflicts and redirecting energies into age-appropriate pursuits (Wallerstein, 1983).

The program for young children also uses games and activities extensively to teach and practice social problem-solving skills. Young children are taught to *"stop"* and *"think"* of various solutions when faced with diverse everyday problems. Puppet plays are used to ease naturally into problem scenarios (e.g., you want to watch your favorite show on TV, but your brother wants to watch something else. What can you do?), to learn relevant problem-solving skills, and to apply them to personal problems. Concrete, age-appropriate games are used to reinforce these skills. The "Red Light-Green Light Game" helps children differentiate between solvable (green light) and unsolvable (red light) problems; and a "Tic-Tac-Toe" game helps them learn to generate alternative solutions, evaluate their consequences, and choose the most appropriate solutions to problems. Semistructured puppet play is used to depict common divorce-related problems, and children are asked to generate alternative solutions to help the puppets deal effectively with those problems. "Kids are Special People" is a board game specially designed to address specific divorce-related concerns and reinforce coping skills and self-esteem in young children.

As with older children, termination issues figure prominently in the last few sessions. Leaders promote discussion of children's feelings about the program ending. The final sessions also provide opportunities for children to review their experience by focusing on special qualities of the group and its members. Concretely, each child is given an "All About Me" book with his or her drawings, feelings posters, problem-solving cartoons, and other program materials. Instant snapshots of each child, as well as an autograph and phone number page, are distributed as mementos of the experience. Ways of identifying supportive adults to whom children can turn are considered. Finally, the group celebrates with a farewell party, and each child is given a certificate of successful participation.

CODIP for Seventh and Eighth Grades

The most recent extension of CODIP—for young adolescents—consists of 12 weekly sessions. The program features the objectives that are important to all CODIP programs (e.g., a supportive group climate; appropriate ways to express feelings, including anger; and problem solving skills) as well as new age-relevant goals such as promoting realistic trust in future relationships.

Understandably, the approaches used to further program goals with seventh and eighth graders differ from those used with younger children. Interactive exercises that highlight unique features of the divorce experience for early adolescents are used to foster a sense of trust and support. Given the program's prime goals of promoting realistic hopes for future relationships and enhancing the capacity to trust, some exercises involve activities that seek to promote trust by taking small risks in a safe setting. In the *Life-Line* exercise, members chart the course of significant events in their lives and talk about those "up" and "down" times in the group. Members also bring in, and talk about, songs with lyrics that convey themes of trust in interpersonal relationships.

Although CODIP for adolescents features teaching effective communication, social problem solving, and anger control skills, it uses more sophisticated, age-appropriate technology for doing so. Group exercises—such as the "One-way, Two-way Communication Experiment"; the "Great Stone Face Exercise"; and the "Total Truth Letter"—and extensive use of role playing and creative dramatics are intended to provide realistic, enjoyable opportunities for skill acquisition and practice in these areas. A final program segment for this age group focuses specifically on feelings about future relationships, hopes, goals, and expectations. One approach used in this context is for group members to give advice to other teens whose parents have just divorced.

Guidelines for Program Implementation

We found it useful to begin CODIP in new schools with a relatively brief meeting to describe the program to relevant school mental health professionals. Because they are the people most likely to be conducting the program, their interest and commitment is an essential precondition for starting. In schools where professionals expressed interest in CODIP, follow-up meetings were held with principals and other school personnel to obtain formal approval and establish preliminary contracts governing how the program would run.

After initial need and contract issues are resolved, recruiting program participants can begin. To that end, we have sent letters on school letterheads describing the program to all parents at the targeted grade levels. The letter includes a consent form. An informational meeting is held at school for parents who want to learn more about the program. There the coordinator describes the program's goals, provides an overview of its activities, and responds to parent questions.

Occasionally, even with parental consent, a child may resist getting involved in CODIP. In such cases, we explain to the parent that the child's hesitation is understandable because not all children know what to expect from the program; and we request permission to meet with the child to explain how the program works. These steps are intended to give parents and children an accurate picture of the program and thus to facilitate informed decisions about participating. Children are free to withdraw from the program at any time; however, fewer than 1% have ever chosen to do so. Before the program begins, leaders meet individually with all children to welcome them, to provide further information about the program, and to answer their questions.

To qualify for CODIP, a child must (a) be within the targeted age range, (b) have parents who are separated or divorced, (c) have written parental consent, and (d) be capable of functioning adequately in a group, i.e., show no evidence of serious acting out, aggressive behaviors in groups or severe emotional problems that require outside referral.

These selection criteria are important. Sometimes there are pressures to include children who are not appropriate for the group. Including such children can be frustrating for all parties if managing the child's inappropriate behavior, rather than the program's central divorce-related objectives, becomes the major focus. Otherwise put, CODIP is designed as a preventive intervention, not as an intensive group therapy experience.

Program Evaluation

Since CODIP began in 1982, it has been evaluated extensively to assess its efficacy with different populations. Research on the initial program with fourth- to sixth-grade suburban children, using a delayed treatment control group design, assessed CODIP's effect on the child's adjustment from four perspectives: parents, teachers, group leaders, and the children themselves. Program children, compared to matched controls randomly assigned to a delayed treatment condition, improved significantly more on teacher-rated adjustment measures (i.e., had fewer problem behaviors and more competencies). Their parents reported improved home adjustment (e.g., better communication, more open about feelings, more age-appropriate behavior, and better able to deal with problem situations). Children reported significant decreases in anxiety and a greater acceptance and understanding of changes in their families. Group leaders reported similar positive outcomes (Pedro-Carroll & Cowen, 1985). A replication study with different group leaders and different schools confirmed these initial findings (Pedro-Carroll, Cowen, Hightower, & Guare, 1986).

Encouraging findings from those early studies fueled extensions of CODIP to children of different ages and sociodemographic backgrounds. Next steps included adaptations of CODIP both for second- to third-grade and fourth- to sixth-grade urban children. Evaluation of these new programs confirmed the adjustment gains previously reported for suburban samples (Alpert-Gillis, Pedro-Carroll, & Cowen, 1989; Pedro-Carroll, Alpert-Gillis, & Cowen, 1992). Overall, these data, involving multiple input sources, demonstrated improved home and school adjustment for CODIP children, reductions in their divorce-related concerns, and gains in their social competencies. Collectively, these data showed that the program model could be modified effectively for young children and for low-income populations in which divorce is but one of many stressors.

A further challenge for CODIP was to identify program components and practices that accounted for positive outcomes (Grych & Fincham, 1992). As noted earlier, CODIP rests on two key components: providing support and teaching coping skills. Others have also found these components to benefit children of divorce (Stolberg & Mahler, 1994). In seeking to disaggregate these components, Sterling's (1986) evaluation of CODIP for second and third graders, assessed the efficacy of a program with, and without, a social problem solving (SPS) component. Sterling found that the support alone (i.e., no SPS) condition was less effective than the full program. She also found that 16 weekly sessions for this group yielded more positive outcomes than a twice weekly, 8-week program format. That information provided a useful foundation for the later adaptation of CODIP for very young children.

Evaluation of the CODIP program for kindergarten to first-grade children provided multisource evidence of the program's efficacy (Pedro-Carroll & Alpert-Gillis, in press). Teachers reported gains in participants' school-related competencies and their ability to ask for help when needed, and decreases in their school-related problem behaviors, compared to a nonparticipant control group. Similarly, leaders reported gains for participants in their understandings of the reasons for divorce (e.g., "divorce is a grown-up problem and not children's fault"), being able to talk about, and deal with, divorce-related feelings, getting along with peers, and thinking of ways to solve interpersonal problems. Parents reported similar improvements in participants' home adjustment (e.g., ability to deal with feelings, behave appropriately, and cope with problems). They also reported that their children were less moody and anxious, more open to sharing feelings, and that parent-child communication had improved. Finally, participating children reported feeling more positive about themselves and their families, being less worried about the changes in their families, and talking more, and enjoying talking more, about their feelings with their parents (Pedro-Carroll & Alpert-Gillis, in press).

The positive findings cited reflect children's adjustment status when the program ended. Pedro-Carroll, Sutton, and Wyman

(1996) assessed the stability of these outcomes over a 2-year follow-up period. New teachers, blind to children's initial group status, rated CODIP children as having significantly fewer school problems and more competencies than comparison children. Parent interview data showed that their improvements at home and in school endured over the 2-year period. They also had fewer visits to the school health office than divorce-controls in the follow-up period. Spontaneous parent comments in the follow-up interview highlighted the value of the program's support and skill-training components. These findings suggest that CODIP gains had staying power and helped children of divorce cope more effectively over time.

An evaluation of a pilot CODIP program for seventh and eighth graders (Pedro-Carroll, Sutton, & Black, 1993) again reflected the perspectives of parents, leaders, and children. Although findings from this study are tempered by relatively small sample sizes, agreement about important gains for participants was again found across diverse perspectives. Parents, for example, reported improvements in children's overall adjustment and their ability to cope effectively with family changes. Leaders found program children better able to express feelings, manage anger, solve interpersonal problems, and differentiate between controllable and uncontrollable problems. In the latter context, children had acquired strategies for disengaging from parent conflict and refocusing on age-appropriate activities. In addition, children reported gains in friendship formation, anger control, and communication effectiveness.

A further finding of special interest for this age group was the significant improvement in participants' hopes and expectations for the future—a finding with implications for choices and decisions that shape their lives. Concretely, they saw themselves as having better futures in such areas as personal responsibility and interpersonal relationships, staying out of trouble, and having people who care about them. Such self-views facilitate responsible decision making and the formation of trusting, enduring, satisfying relationships. In this context, Wyman, Cowen, Work, and Kerley (1993) found that the presence of positive future expectations among 10- to 12-year-old, highly stressed urban children related to resilient outcomes 3 years later. Such views functioned as a protective factor in reducing the negative effects of major life stress.

Summary

Significant stressors associated with marital disruption are experienced by millions of children every day in the United States. Although these stressors increase the risk for psychological problems, research on risk and protective factors shows that long-term maladaptation is not an inevitable outcome for children of divorce. Sometimes the protective elements needed to deflect maladaptive outcomes exist in the child's natural life situation. However, because that is not uniformly the case, prevention programs are needed to reduce the risk that stems from marital disruption. The CODIP model represents a persistent effort to develop, field-test, and evaluate such a prevention program over time. CODIP findings to date testify to the promise that preventive interventions hold for children of divorce of all ages and for their parents.

The individual and societal costs of divorce are far-reaching and in some cases have dramatic emotional and economic consequences. An overwhelming majority of referrals for outpatient mental health treatment are children of divorce. Moreover, children of divorce are at risk for longer term outcomes with serious intergenerational consequences, including high school dropout, lower life satisfaction and achievement, and the demise of their own marriages. Preventive interventions provide a low-cost, effective support for those at risk. If divorce is to provide a solution to a failed marriage, with opportunities for family members to thrive as well as survive, then our efforts must focus on the promotion of health, resilience, and psychological well-being. The findings reported in this chapter strongly suggest that preventive interventions are a promising part of that formula for wellness.

References

Alpert-Gillis, L. J., Pedro-Carroll, J. L., & Cowen, E. L. (1989). Children of Divorce Intervention Program: Development, implementation and evaluation of a program for young urban children. *Journal of Consulting and Clinical Psychology, 57,* 583-587.

Amato, P. R., & Keith, B. (1991a). Parental divorce and adult well-being: A meta-analysis. *Journal of Marriage and the Family, 53,* 43-58.

Amato, P. R., & Keith, B. (1991b). Parental divorce and the well-being of children: A meta-analysis. *Psychological Bulletin, 110,* 26-46.

Black, A. E., & Pedro-Carroll, J. L. (1993). The role of parent-child relationships in mediating the effects of marital disruption. *Journal of the American Academy of Child and Adolescent Psychiatry, 32,* 1019-1027.

Bumpass, L. (1984). Children and marital disruption: A replication and update. *Demography, 21,* 71-82.

Cowen, E. L., Pedro-Carroll, J. L., & Alpert-Gillis, L. J. (1990). Relationships between support and adjustment among children of divorce. *Journal of Child Psychology and Psychiatry, 31,* 727-735.

Emery, R. E. (1982). Interparental conflict and the children of discord and divorce. *Psychological Bulletin, 92,* 310-330.

Emery, R. E., & Forehand, R. (1994). Parental divorce and children's well-being: A focus on resilience. In R. J. Haggerty, L. R. Sherrod, N. Garmezy, & M. Rutter (Eds.), *Stress, risk and resilience in children and adolescents* (pp. 64-99). New York: Cambridge University Press.

Furstenberg, F. F., Nord, C. W., Peterson, J. L., & Zill, N. (1983). The life-course of children of divorce: Marital disruption and parental contact. *American Sociological Review, 48,* 656-668.

Glick, P. C., & Lin, S. (1986). Recent changes in divorce and remarriage. *Journal of Marriage and the Family, 48,* 737-747.

Grych, J. H., & Fincham, F. D. (1992). Interventions for children of divorce: Toward greater integration of research and action. *Psychological Bulletin, 111,* 434-454.

Hetherington, E. M., & Clingempeel, W. G. (1992). Coping with marital transitions. *Monographs for the Society for Research in Child Development, 57,* 1-299.

Hoyt, L. A., Cowen, E. L., Pedro-Carroll, J. L., & Alpert-Gillis, L. J. (1990). Anxiety and depression in young children of divorce, *Journal of Clinical Child Psychology, 19,* 26-32.

Kurdek, L. A., & Berg, B. (1983). Correlates of children's adjustment to their parents' divorces. In L. A. Kurdek (Ed.), *New directions in child development: Vol. 19. Children and divorce* (pp. 47-60). San Francisco: Jossey-Bass.

Kurdek, L. A., & Berg, B. (1987). Children's beliefs about parental divorce scale: Psychometric characteristics and concurrent validity. *Journal of Consulting and Clinical Psychology, 55,* 712-718.

McLanahan, S. S., & Bumpass, L. (1988). Intergenerational consequences of family disruption. *American Journal of Sociology, 94,* 130-152.

Pedro-Carroll, J. L., & Alpert-Gillis, L. J. (in press). Preventive interventions for children of divorce: A developmental model for 5 and 6 year old children. *Journal of Primary Prevention.*

Pedro-Carroll, J. L. Alpert-Gillis, L. J., & Cowen, E. L. (1992). An evaluation of the efficacy of a preventive intervention for 4th-6th grade urban children of divorce. *Journal of Primary Prevention, 13,* 115-130.

Pedro-Carroll, J. L., & Cowen, E. L. (1985). The children of divorce intervention program: An investigation of the efficacy of a school-based prevention program. *Journal of Consulting and Clinical Psychology, 53,* 603-611.

Pedro-Carroll, J. L., Cowen, E. L., Hightower, A. D., & Guare, J. C. (1986). Preventive intervention with latency-aged children of divorce: A replication study. *American Journal of Community Psychology, 14,* 277-290.

Pedro-Carroll, J. L., Sutton, J. L., & Black, A. E. (1993). *The Children of Divorce Intervention Program: Preventive outreach to early adolescents* (Final report). Rochester, NY: Rochester Mental Health Association.

Pedro-Carroll, J. L., Sutton, J. L., & Wyman, P. A. (1996). *A two year follow-up investigation of a preventive intervention for children of divorce.* Manuscript submitted for publication.

Sterling, S. E. (1986). *School-based intervention program for early latency-aged children of divorce.* Unpublished doctoral dissertation, University of Rochester.

Stolberg, A. L., & Mahler, J. (1994). Enhancing treatment gains in school-based intervention for children of divorce through skill training, parental involvement and transfer procedures. *Journal of Consulting and Clinical Psychology, 62,* 147-156.

Wallerstein, J. S. (1983). Children of divorce: The psychological tasks of the child. *American Journal of Orthopsychiatry, 53,* 230-243.

Wallerstein, J. S., & Blakeslee, S. (1989). *Second chances: Men, women, and children a decade after divorce—Who wins, who loses, and why?* New York: Ticknor & Fields.

Wallerstein, J. S., & Kelly, J. B. (1980). *Surviving the breakup: How children cope with divorce.* New York: Basic Books.

Werner, E. E., & Smith, R. S. (1992). *Overcoming the odds: High risk children from birth to adulthood.* Ithaca, NY: Cornell University Press.

Wyman, P. A., Cowen, E. L., Work, W. C., & Kerley, J. H. (1993). The role of children's future expectations in self-system functioning and adjustment to life stress. A prospective study of urban at risk children. *Development and Psychopathology, 5* 649-661.

Zill, N., Morrison, D. R., & Coiro, M. J. (1993). Long-term effects of parental divorce on parent-child relationships, adjustment, and achievement in young adulthood. *Journal of Family Psychology, 7,* 91-103.

• *CHAPTER 11* •

The Improving Social Awareness-
Social Problem Solving Project

LINDA BRUENE-BUTLER

JUNE HAMPSON

MAURICE J. ELIAS

JOHN F. CLABBY

TOM SCHUYLER

Society pays a high price when students lack social and emotional competence. *Social competence* refers to the ability to establish acceptable and productive relationships with others. It has been linked with many areas of success in adulthood, such as vocational competence (Goleman, 1995b; Krackhardt & Hanson, 1993; U.S. Department of Labor, 1991); marital satisfaction (Davis & Oathout, 1987; Gottman, 1993, 1994); and parenting socially adjusted children (Cohen, Patterson, & Christopoulos, 1991; Putallaz & Heflin, 1990; Rubin, Booth, Rose-Krasnor, & Mills, 1994). A strong and growing body of research also links social and emotional functioning in childhood to a wide variety of life outcomes (Asher & Parker, 1989; Bierman, 1993; Parker & Asher, 1987; Parker, Rubin, Price, & DeRosier, 1995; Putallaz & Gottman, 1982; Rubin, Booth, Rose-Krasnor, & Mills, 1994), including academic functioning (Abrams & Kaslow, 1977; Ollendick, Weist, Borden, & Greene, 1992), school dropout (Cairns, Cairns, & Neckerman, 1989), teen pregnancy (Underwood &

Albert, 1989), juvenile delinquency, and mental health problems (Bye & Jussim, 1993).

Over two decades of research has established peer relationships as the most reliable and sensitive predictor not only of life success, but also of problems during childhood and later life (e.g., Asher & Parker, 1989; Kupersmidt, Coie, & Dodge, 1990; Ollendick et al., 1992; Parker & Asher, 1987; Putallaz & Gottman, 1982). In December 1993, the technical planning group of the National Educational Goals Panel targeted social and emotional development as a necessary dimension of learning. The report noted that poor peer relationships correlate with aggression, poor social skills, and lack of empathy for the thoughts and feelings of others. They concluded that the adequacy with which a child gets along with other children may well be the single best predictor of adult adaptation.

Because schools are where students spend the most time with a group of peers, they can be an ideal on-the-job training site for learning and practicing these essential life skills. At a White House briefing on the subject, expert panelists emphasized that given the host of problems youths face—from AIDS and violence to early sex and drugs—comprehensive, realistic school-based prevention efforts are urgently needed (DeAngelis, 1994). The current educational climate, however, is one of urgent reform, recognizing the need for technological and economic competitiveness. Given these educational priorities, it is critical that school-based efforts to promote social and affective skills set meaningful instructional objectives and implement proven strategies that are effective and cost efficient in promoting these skills in a school-based context.

Identifying skills with an empirical link to social competence provides a strong and informed base for intervention, but finding effective methods to instill these skills is just as critical. To develop strategies that positively influence social behavior and learning and then to institutionalize these strategies into the fabric of children's everyday lives is the essential challenge.

The following chapter describes an approach that was designed to address this challenge. The Improving Social Awareness-Social Problem Solving (ISA-SPS) Project is a comprehensive, action research, primary prevention program designed for elementary and middle school-aged students at all levels of risk. The ISA-SPS Project defines a collaborative relationship among Rutgers University, the University of Medicine and Dentistry of New Jersey, and a number of New Jersey's public school systems. The approach developed by this project received the Lela Rowland Award in 1988, was validated by the Program Effectiveness Panel of the U.S. Department of Education's National Diffusion Network in 1989, and was revalidated in 1995. Much of the success of this initiative can be attributed to the use of action research methods that allow for multiyear collaboration and direct input from teachers and students. This approach enables educators and parents to equip children with skills linked with clear thinking, social competence, and the avoidance of high-risk behaviors.

Conceptual Framework and Theoretical Roots

The conceptual model developed by the ISA-SPS Project has many roots from advances in child development, child clinical psychology, the cognitive sciences, organizational and community psychology, and action research methodologies. An extensive discussion of this background is available for the interested reader in **Building Social Problem Solving Skills: Guidelines From a School-Based Program** (Elias & Clabby, 1992). For the present, key underlying features from which the ISA-SPS approach is drawn will be summarized.

Primary Prevention

Primary prevention efforts are designed to proactively create conditions that promote well-being. The focus is shifted to showing and teaching children what we want them to do rather than what we do not want them to do. As stated by Elias, "an absence of problem behaviors is not the presence of health" (in DeAngelis, 1994, p. 33).

Successful prevention requires sustained commitment and comprehensive intervention. Weissberg reports that when children are immersed in a prevention program for several years, they improve over time; but if they are exposed for only a year, they show washout effects (in DeAngelis, 1994). Goleman (1995a) explained this phenomenon in a recent article: "like good child rearing at home, the lessons imparted are small but telling, delivered regularly and over a sustained period of years. That is how emotional learning becomes ingrained; as experiences are repeated over and over, the brain reflects them as strengthened pathways, neural habits to apply during times of duress, frustration and hurt" (p. 48). In the context of our work, this means creating active methods and conditions in all aspects of school life to build social competence skills.

Organizational-Community Systems Theory

An organizational perspective was an essential foundation for this project and helped in planning strategies for program acceptance, implementation, and growth. This literature also provided us with frameworks for conceptualizing the developmental process and stages involved in organizational change. Schools are organic social systems (Bertalanffy, 1968); therefore, we designed the program based on established relationships, roles, rules, formal and informal hierarchies, boundaries, and established norms for communication and negotiations of school systems. A grounding in basic organizational-community systems theory was a key foundation for the ISA-SPS project. The work of Sarason (1982) and Hord, Rutherford, Haling-Austin, and Hall (1987) has provided important insights. Sarason cautions that schools are structurally arranged to resist genuine change, particularly if such changes seem at variance with defined, academic-related goals. Schools may also lack effective coordinating mechanisms, particularly around nonacademic issues. Programs of a social-affective nature that occur in isolation or in competition or within a single content area (such as health) preclude any lasting impact (Devlin, 1983; Elias & Clabby, 1984; Elias & Clabby, 1992). We learned from these caveats that the ISA-SPS approach had to "fit" into diverse school ecologies.

Action Research

Action research methods were adopted as the framework for program development. *Action research* refers to a methodology used to develop and test programs through a sustained collaboration between researchers, program developers, and an action research setting. It involves entering a system, developing a planned change in the system, and a conducting a continuous research cycle of testing, refinement, and development of the plan. These research methods were developed for use in "turbulent" real-life settings to develop and refine effective procedures (Billington, Washington, & Trickett, 1981; Lewin, 1951; Munoz, Snowden, & Kelly, 1979; Price, 1987; Price & Smith, 1985; Sanford, 1970; Sarason, 1978). A cornerstone of the ISA-SPS Project is ongoing feedback and input from students, teachers, administrators, other pupil services providers, and ISA-SPS team members across sites around the United States. This input contributes to the ongoing refinement and development of the program.

Social Skills/Social Competence Promotion Training

The ISA-SPS approach is a skills-based approach. As such, it draws from work over the past two decades that has shown that despite the fact that children's behavior and peer acceptance is influenced by many factors—such as culture, social context, physical attractiveness, social ability (Putallaz & Gottman, 1982), reputation (Hymel, Wagner, & Botter, 1990), attributions (Crick & Dodge, 1994; Dodge, 1986; Dodge, Pettit, & Bates, 1994; Hymel, 1986), and peer rejection (Parker et al., 1995)—two facts are clear: (a) Specific behaviors and cognitions reliably predict acceptance and rejection in the peer group (Parker & Asher, 1987; Parker et al., 1995), and (b) these skills can be enhanced through training and practice (Ladd & Mize, 1983).

Interpersonal Problem-Solving Skills

We owe a great debt to the work of George Spivack and Myrna Shure, who began as traditional psychodynamic therapists who realized that to handle problems in their everyday lives, their troubled young clients needed skills such as the ability to generate alternative solutions, to consider consequences, and to plan. Their extensive program of research has demonstrated that Interpersonal-Cognitive Problem Solving Skills can be taught in ways that prevent poor social adjustment in children (Shure & Spivack, 1978; 1988).

Among the most long-standing projects has been the work of Emory Cowen and colleagues at the University of Rochester (Cowen, 1994). Cowen's prevention efforts began with a secondary prevention effort called the Primary Mental Health Project, which provided tutoring and special attention to at-risk youngsters in the early elementary grades. The data around this program, as well as its frequency of adoption, have been impressive. Cowen then began to shift his work toward primary prevention, instituting a series of studies of school-based, social problem-solving interventions in the elementary school. Evaluations by Weissberg and others showed relatively consistent short-term gains for interventions lasting from 3 months to a full school year. Most recently, Cowen has again extended his focus, adding the Children of Divorce Project, which involves short-term social problem-solving and social support-based interventions in schools for elementary school-aged children of parents undergoing divorce. Compared to controls, children participating in these programs have shown decreased likelihood to display signs of internalizing and externalizing disorders (Pedro-Carroll, Alpert-Gillis, & Cowen, 1992). All told, Cowen's prevention efforts have extended the reach of social problem-solving interventions and have substantiated the efficacy of this approach.

Problem-solving skills also have been key components of projects targeted at substance abuse and problem behavior, such as the Life Skills Training Program (Botvin & Tortu, 1988). The main focus has been to provide junior high-aged children with the knowledge, motivation, and skills needed to resist influences to smoke. Smoking has been identified as a link in a chain of behaviors likely to extend to the use of alcohol and other illegal substances. General training in prosocial skills such as stress management and problem solving is combined with application of these skills in the area of refusal and assertion skills. A review of findings indicates that recipients of social influence approaches show significant reductions in the onset and prevalence of cigarette smoking, as well as marijuana and alcohol use, when compared to untreated controls. The most consistent effects are on smoking and marijuana use, and less so with regard to alcohol, probably because social norms against the use of alcohol are inconsistent (Botvin, Schinke, & Orlandi, 1995).

Many aspects of our design were also developed after consideration of the difficulties these projects reported in long-term retention once the program terminated. We also know that no problem solving can occur if children do not feel that they can act effectively. If children attribute failure and success to external loci of control (Rotter, 1966), problem-solving efforts will be viewed as irrelevant.

Bandura's (1986) concept of self-efficacy helped us to realize the need to shift the emphasis from teaching isolated cognitive skills, to focusing on the contexts within which children actually perform problem solving. We also owe a large debt to Irving Sigel for his theory of "distancing" as a means of facilitating children's representational competence. According to Sigel, teachers and other adults should ideally respond to children with open-ended questions, which will lead children to consider alternatives for themselves. This results in the strengthening of children's cognitive abilities (Barell, Liebmann, & Sigel, 1988).

Description of the Social Decision Making and Problem Solving Program for the Elementary Grades

The ISA-SPS Program targets four competency areas. These four areas form the basis for what the ISA-SPS team called the Social Decision Making/Problem Solving Approach. It includes the following:

1. Skills linked with self-control, such as attending, turn taking, impulse control, and regulation of emotions and communication style
2. Behaviors linked with peer acceptance and the ability to work cooperatively in a group
3. Problem-solving/decision-making skills
4. The ability to apply these skills in response to changing social situations

In 1979, a multidisciplinary team of educators, community and child clinical psychologists, and researchers began a collaborative effort to build students' social competence proactively. The goal was to make these protective skills operational and to incorporate them into a family of interventions to promote social competence at individual, dyadic, small group, classroom, school, and district levels. We also felt that it was necessary to generate a simplified skill array that would reflect historical, cross-cultural, and long-term adaptation that could feasibly be implemented with high quality in diverse school settings (Elias & Clabby, 1992).

Most school prevention programs address specialized areas by programs and curricula. Although many of these are, individually, excellent, and some districts place a high value on curricular integration, the predominant situation is jumbled confusion. Few students are able to integrate the diverse elements into a whole. The guiding vision of the ISA-SPS Project is that the way children learn best is through a consistent framework that allows students to overlearn and to practice applying the social competencies of self-control, social awareness, group participation, and social problem-solving and decision skills in all areas of life. This approach allows diversity to become synergy.

Because curricula are the building blocks used by schools to set forth an organizational plan for teaching objectives, a curriculum was chosen as the vehicle for integrating social and affective development into the natural heart of formalized and regulated school operations. The use of a curriculum also provides an ideal focal point for extended action research. To be successful within the educational community, however, the curriculum had to be linked with larger organizational mandates, be accepted by elementary school educators and their students as our front-line consumers, and prove effective in demonstrating lasting knowledge and skill gains in students.

In the following sections, we will describe the approach developed by the ISA-SPS team, called Social Decision Making and Problem Solving, which has accomplished the criteria for success outlined above. This approach uses a research-validated curriculum, *Social Decision Making Skills: A Curriculum Guide for the Elementary Grades* (Elias & Clabby, 1989), as a base for institutionalizing social-affective education in the school setting. The curriculum contains a set of coordinated, sequenced, and scripted lesson materials and follow-through activities for grades K-6 (or K-5, or K-4, if an elementary school is so configured). This document aids our dissemination efforts, which are now conducted out of the Social Problem Solving Program of the University of Medicine and Dentistry, University Behavioral Health Care at Piscataway. The curriculum contains a set of procedures that are the basis for staff development activities, ongoing program monitoring, feedback gathering, expansion to parent and whole-school and community involvement, and methods for program evaluation. The framework and validated methods have also served to launch extended action-research projects that continue to develop out of the ISA-SPS Program in the Department of Psychology of Rutgers

University and the Social Problem Solving Program of the University of Medicine and Dentistry of New Jersey.

In what follows, the content of curriculum-based activities will first be described, then an introduction will be provided to a few examples of action-research developments that extend the use of skills to computer-based applications, practice in after-school clubs and activities, and approaches for involving parents. These examples only illustrate the variety of program extensions that have emerged from using a decision-making and action-research framework for building a comprehensive school-based program.

Overview of the Curriculum

Social Decision Making Skills: A Curriculum Guide for the Elementary Grades (Elias & Clabby, 1989) has made operative a set of skills linked empirically with social competence and peer acceptance.

Systematic skill-building procedures are used to teach self-control, social awareness, and group participation skills while emphasizing critical thinking skills. Skills are organized into three domains: Readiness for Decision Making, Instruction in a Social Decision Making Process, and Application of Social Decision Making. A description of each follows.

Readiness for Decision Making

This domain targets a repertoire of skill areas that are "tools" for social decision making. The Readiness domain includes Self-control and Improving Social Awareness units. The Self-control Unit refers to personal skills necessary for self-regulation and monitoring of emotion and communication style, whereas the Social Awareness Unit focuses on social skills and awareness linked with successful participation in a group.

As can be seen in the overview (Table 11.1) the Self-control Unit includes skills such as listening, turn-taking, and remembering and following a series of directions. The heart of this unit focuses on skills for regulating emotional reactions and impulsivity. Children learn to recognize physical cues and situations that put them at risk of "fight or flight" reactivity, which can result in negative consequences and poor decisions. They are also taught specific strategies for gaining emotional control. Regulating emotions is then linked to the self-monitoring of body language, eye contact, use of words, and tone of voice. Because emotional reactivity is a natural human tendency, the objective is to develop the ability to self-regulate and self-monitor emotional reactions and communication skills. The Self-control Unit provides students with repeated practice in concrete strategies that interrupt "fight or flight" reactions that block access to clear thinking.

The Improving Social Awareness Unit teaches skills characteristic of children who are accepted by their peers. Children respond positively to peers who express positive emotions and appreciation of their peers. Children who are accepted by their peers also recognize and respond when peers need help, recognize when they need help and appropriately ask for it, and give criticism by clearly stating what they do not like, giving the reasons they don't like it, and offering new ideas. They also develop the ability to accept constructive criticism appropriately and take another's perspective. Lessons in this unit target these skills and also include activities for group building, expressing feelings and thoughts in a group, and exploring characteristics and behaviors of friendship.

The Readiness Phase uses systematic skill-building procedures. Each skill concept is introduced and presented in terms of *concrete behavioral components* that are clarified by descriptions, modeling of skill use, and examples of *not* using the skill. Repeated practice of the skill is provided by "kid-tested," enjoyable activities that allow for corrective feedback and reinforcement by the teacher until skill mastery is approached. Skills are labeled with a prompt or cue that establishes a "shared language" used to call for the skill in future situations. Assignments for skill practice outside of the structured lesson and follow-up activities are provided for use in academic and real-life situations.

An example of an activity from the self-control topic "Resisting Provocation and Keeping Control" is a worksheet called the "Problem Diary." This is one of the first in a series of tools designed to encourage children to be self-reflective, thoughtful, and responsible about their behaviors. At the time that this is introduced, the children have already been taught a self-calming breathing technique and the importance of attending to tone of voice, eye contact, speech, and appropriate body posture in their interpersonal presentations.

Table 11.1 Social Decision Making and Problem Solving Skills: Phases of Instruction and Target Skill Areas

	Self-Control	*Social Awareness*
Readiness phase (skill training and establishing prompts and cues)	Listening Paying attention Following directions Keeping calm Vent or BEST (assertive communication) Resisting provocation Sharing ways to cope with hassles	Sharing ideas and feelings with a group Asking for, giving, and receiving help (cooperation) Giving and receiving praise Conversation skills Giving criticism Choosing friends Perspective taking

An Eight-Step Strategy for Thinking Through Problems

Instructional phase (overlearning of thinking steps)	1. Look for signs of different feelings. 2. Tell yourself what the problem is. 3. Decide on your goal. 4. Stop and think of as many solutions to the problem as you can. 5. For each solution, think of all the things that might happen next. 6. Choose your best solution. 7. Plan it and make a final check. 8. Try it and rethink it.

Interpersonal and Academic Practice

Application phase (practice applying and using steps to think through problems)	Repeated practice in applying problem solving skills to a wide variety of interpersonal and academic situations

SOURCE: Adapted from *Social Decision Making Skills: A Curriculum Guide for the Elementary Grades,* by M. Elias and J. Clabby, Aspen Publishers, Inc. 1989, pp. 33-34.

The Problem Diary begins to anticipate the emphasis in the instructional phase of the curriculum on a step-by-step social decision-making strategy. As a beginning effort at problem definition, students are oriented by their teacher to track their experience by responding to these questions: "Briefly describe a difficult situation that you were involved in this week. What happened? Who were you with? When and where did this take place?" To engage the students in the process of thinking about their own contributions to interpersonal encounters, they are asked on the worksheet: "What did you say and do?" And to begin some consequential thinking, they respond to a worksheet item: "What happened in the end?" Youngsters are also reminded on the worksheet to use skills that they have been taught in the program—such as the "Keep Calm" breathing technique—by rating themselves on a 1 to 5 scale, answering the questions, "How calm and under control were you before you said or did something?" and "How satisfied were you with what you did?"

The worksheet continues with several similar questions. In professional development experiences with teachers, we share with them different adaptations and versions of this worksheet that have been developed over the years in the areas of language, structure, and process. And, importantly, we encourage all teachers to adapt such tools to fit the needs of their own classes.

The Instructional Phase of Decision Making

This domain targets an eight-step framework for organizing clear thinking. The eight thinking skills are worded in language designed to provide children with self-talk they can use to think through a problem or make a decision. The eight steps are

1. *Look for signs of different feelings.* The skills developed include the ability to identify and describe the feelings of self and feelings of others.
2. *Tell yourself what the problem is.* This refers to the ability to develop objective problem statements and clearly put problems into words.
3. *Decide on your goal.* This refers to the ability to translate a problem into a clear objective statement about what it would look like if the problem were solved, or what one wants to achieve.
4. *Think of as many solutions to the problem as you can.* This skill involves the ability to brainstorm a wide range of diverse alternative solutions.
5. *For each solution, think of what might happen next.* This skill is the ability to anticipate possible negative and positive consequences of alternative actions.
6. *Choose your best solution.* Here, students learn to select a solution based on consideration of possible consequences and with a focus on their goal.

7. *Plan it and make a final check.* Students learn to consider the steps and details necessary to carry out their solutions. "Final check" refers to the ability to anticipate and plan for possible obstacles.

8. *Try it, and rethink it.* This refers to the ability to follow through on a decision, reflect and learn from the outcome, and if necessary, cycle back to the problem-solving process if the problem was not solved.

The objective of the Instructional Phase is for students to develop a metacognitive understanding of their decision-making process and to internalize a framework for thinking through a problem or making a decision. Because of this, continual review and recitation is built into the program. Each of the skill steps is recognized as a complex, yet identifiable skill, which is explored and practiced in a variety of hypothetical, age-appropriate, and open-ended conflict stories. Each skill is introduced and practiced and then cumulatively linked within the eight-step framework to maximize its retention and use.

The instructional procedures used in a 22-topic breakdown of the eight social decision-making skills include the following elements:

1. Define a purpose for the lesson. A focusing organizational goal statement is provided and explored through a brief discussion.

2. The new skill step is added to a list of the social problem-solving steps that have been taught so far. For example, in Lesson 11 in the sequence, "Think of More Than One Consequence for Your Action," teachers would actively review the steps of identifying signs of different feelings, describing the problem, selecting goals, and brainstorming alternative solutions. After asking the children to animatedly recite the steps, which are posted prominently, students would be asked to share how one or more of the steps may have been helpful to them recently.

3. Following the Leaders Guide, the instructor
   a. Begins with an opening "sharing circle" (or "team huddle," as our action research feedback advised this be called for urban settings). This is an opportunity for the children to say hello to one another and briefly respond to an opening question or to state what is on their minds. The sharing circle (team huddle) may be introduced in the readiness phase as a skill-building lesson in and of itself.

    b. Reviews the previous lesson. This reminds the students of what has been covered thus far, similar to what a teacher does when introducing a new skill in math or science.

    c. Provides an introduction and explanation of the new concept, which in this case is anticipating both positive and negative consequences to actions.

    d. Provides a practical rationale to emphasize "Why should I pay attention to this lesson? What's in it for me?" Here the teacher explores with the class practical reasons why looking ahead at consequences can make their lives better.

    e. Introduces a structured experiential activity, which usually consists of the presentation of a hypothetical social conflict (presented by either recommended video segments or a story) involving school issues or peer situations that are appropriate for the grade level and group. Some example vignettes provided in this topic include asking students to think of the positive and negative consequences that might occur if "everyone at school got into a fight every time they had an argument" or "if there were no classroom rules." If a complete story is presented, the students select a focal character and review the story with the primary focus of discussion on the new step of consequences.

4. Students participate in follow-through activities:

    a. Social applications: Students are given assignments for skill practice life situations.

    b. Academic applications: Teachers are provided with suggestions for integrating skill practice into academic content areas and objectives.

5. Teachers are provided with a compilation of hints and suggestions compiled by feedback from teachers over the years, concerning how to overcome problems in teaching a particular skill or how to maximize the children's learning experience.

The Application Phase of Decision Making

This domain of instruction focuses on structured opportunities to apply the skills students are learning to real-life problems and decisions and within the context of academic content areas. This area of instruction and teacher training stresses two areas: structured lessons and facilitative questioning.

Application Phase Lesson Outlines. Teachers are provided with sample lesson plans and worksheets for integrating the practice of the skills children are learning into a wide variety of topic areas, such as A Decision Making Approach to Social Studies, Problem Solving and Creative Writing, A Problem Solving Strategy for Starting and Completing Projects, Keeping Track of Everyday Problem Solving, Alternatives to Stereotyping and Prejudice, Recognizing and Changing Academic and Interpersonal "Weak Points," and Thinking About What We Hear and See in the Media.

The Application Phase Curriculum materials are example structures to help teachers infuse a decision-making approach into the way they teach. The lessons are easily adapted and modified to address specific instructional objectives. For example, an adapted version of "Taming Tough Topics," a worksheet from the Application Phase of the Social Decision Making Skills curriculum (Elias & Clabby, 1989, pp. 151-158) was used as a base for integrating decision-making skills into a thematic project for studying environmental problems in one of our participating school districts. Students developed projects and plans for solving environmental problems that surpassed their teachers' expectations: for example, making presentations to the City Council that led to plastic recycling in their town, making presentations to the State Assembly, starting recycling in the school cafeteria, writing editorials published in the local newspaper. Students' efforts received local, regional, and national news coverage; a write-up in *Environmental Magazine*; and a President's Environmental Youth Award in 1989 (Johnsen & Bruene-Butler, 1993).

Adaptations of other lessons were used to develop a paradigm for analyzing literature in middle school (Naftel & Elias, 1995), a Comprehensive Health Curriculum (Poedubicky, 1996), and a project to bring model education programs to teachers working with incarcerated youth in juvenile correctional institutions (Columbia Education Center, 1995), among others.

Facilitative Questioning. A primary focus of our adult training sessions is teaching adults to facilitate and coach children to use and develop their readiness and thinking skills. This is done through exercises and practice with a series of questions designed to involve individual students or groups in a thinking process. Using the same eight-step strategy, we train adults to use modeling of their own thinking and to translate the eight steps into questions that prompt an individual or group to think through a problem. Teachers are trained in a variety of specific applications tailored to common situations such as corrective discipline, mediating conflict, motivating children to develop plans for reaching a goal identified by the adult, strategies for diagramming the thinking of a group when working to solve a problem or make a decision, and working through the steps as applied to real-life situations or a situation confronted by a character or group the class is thinking about in history, current events, or a story in language arts.

Verbal and nonverbal strategies to promote thinking are practiced repeatedly in training through the use of live and videotape modeling, processing what was observed, and then repeated participant practice, with positive corrective feedback. As shown in the evaluation findings that follow, our data demonstrate that teachers who have undergone training significantly increase their use of questioning strategies and become less inhibitory of children's thinking by the end of the year.

Comprehensive School-Based Programs

Once students have had training in the skills targeted in the curriculum, the opportunities for extending the use or practice of these skills is almost endless. The eight steps and the readiness prompts and cues become a "shared language" to call for the use of skills, and to promote generalization and maintenance of skills beyond the classroom walls. Playground aides, bus drivers, school nurses, and other school staff as well as parents and other adults in the community can be trained to use the prompts and cues and in strategies to promote children's thinking.

To illustrate only a few examples, three areas of extended application will be described below: computer-based programs, structured activities designed for use in after-school and community-based clubs and activities, and strategies used to involve parents in efforts to extend skill applications to home and community situations.

Computer-Based Technology

A computer program, *The Student Conflict Manager/Personal Problem Solving Guide* (Friedlander, 1993; Elias, Tobias, & Friedlander, 1994), has become a valuable tool for helping students to apply their problem-solving skills to personal situations that are causing them life difficulties. Designed for use with children who have discipline-related, peer, or emotional problems, academic difficulties, problems with teachers, or other personal or interpersonal issues, the program has two tracks: one for "trouble," which allows a constructive, self-directed review process; and another for "problem," which can be useful for any other time when students could benefit from structured time to think through a problem. The program has been used effectively with peer partners or mediators, as a tool to focus the thinking of cooperative learning groups, as a method for providing individualized practice of skills, as a supplement to large- or small-group instruction, and with both regular and special education students.

After-School Clubs and Activities

In our experience, one of the most difficult areas in which to promote the transfer of skills is in less structured peer situations, such as after-school teams, clubs, and activities. In many of our school communities, these endeavors are run by adults or college students from the community with little professional training for the job and working either for little pay or as a volunteer. There is usually a high staff turnover each year. Because of this, it has been one of the most difficult situations in which to adequately train individuals in the skills necessary to promote peer relationships.

We have been experiencing recent gains in this area, however, thanks to a program developed by the Hallmark Corporate Foundation in collaboration with youth organizations such as the Boys and Girls Clubs, 4-H, and the Girl and Boy Scouts, and employing child development experts, including Dr. Maurice Elias, from our team. The programs are video-based, leader-friendly, group activities and games that help students develop skills for working as a team: *Talking with T. J.: Teamwork Series* (Halper & Richardson, 1993) and for resolving conflicts and problems without violence: *Talking with T. J.: Conflict Resolution Series* (Halper, London, &

Richardson, 1994). This program is highly compatible with the goals and language of our classroom curriculum and helps adults establish guidelines for group interaction. These activities serve as a base and complement to other objectives of the group, such as free play, team sports, or club activities.

Parent Involvement

A critical area of extension is the involvement of parents. In this area, we have collaborated in the development of a wide variety of outreach activities and materials, based on the creative problem solving of educators and our staff. For example, local cable video programs have been successful in reaching many parents in the community (Wedam, 1988). A parent survey to assess the best times for parents to tune in can help set a schedule so that busy parents can be given as many viewing times as possible. No baby-sitter or other logistical planning is needed for participation. Copies of the video can also be distributed by the school for home viewing. Parents are reached as well through the book *Teach Your Child Decision Making* (Clabby & Elias, 1986), and through "Refrigerator Notes" (Hett & Krikorian, 1993), which isolate and describe specific skills and ways parents can help children practice skills at home. Both of these can be sent home by the classroom teacher.

A wide variety of school-based events have also been effective, such as evening sessions that included dinner and baby sitters, and bagel breakfasts where parents are invited to join a morning class session in which children help their teachers to share what they are learning. Many other events have been designed and marketed in collaboration with our school colleagues, who are knowledgeable regarding the local needs and obstacles in the community.

Program Management

Two of the biggest challenges we face as districts move toward institutionalization of our program are (a) developing a coordinated and comprehensive strategy for system-wide participation and (b) developing internal mechanisms for program management, leadership, and planned expansion. In our experience, institutionalizing a comprehensive program generally takes 3 to 7 years. Because of this, a critical aspect of our training involves a Leadership and Management component for a representative team of school personnel and parents. We facilitate the team's planning and decision making to address key issues regarding long- and short-term goal setting, developing a scope and sequence of skills across grade levels, program management, evaluation, providing technical support to front-line implementers, outreach to parents, and other aspects of a plan for institutionalization.

A detailed description of methods used to address this area of training is beyond the scope of this chapter; however, those interested are encouraged to read Heller and Firestone (1995) for a description of leadership functions that have led to successful institutionalization of our program in multiple school sites.

Our confidence in presenting this intervention approach stems from the extensive action research, program planning, and evaluation history of our project. In the section that follows, we outline our most significant and most recent findings.

Evidence of Program Effectiveness

1989 Validation by the Program Effectiveness Panel of the U. S. Department of Education

The Social Decision Making and Problem Solving Program has been thoroughly evaluated during the 15 years since its initial demonstration phase. The primary development site was a lower-middle to middle-class suburban community in central New Jersey with a predominantly white, blue-collar population. In 1989 the program demonstrated conclusively to the Program Effectiveness Panel of the U.S. Department of Education that it effectively changed the behaviors of both teachers and students. Specifically, we proved that teachers improve in their ability to build children's social decision-making and problem-solving skills by increasing their own use of facilitative questioning strategies, following training in the program. In addition, in a series of studies, we found that compared with controls, students trained in the SPS program developed improved skills in the areas of self-control, interpersonal sensitivity, problem analysis, planning, and gains in knowledge of detailed problem solving concepts. Moreover, in two studies we demonstrated real-life applications of these skills. Students who had been trained in the SPS program in elementary school coped more effectively with the stress of middle school transition (Elias, Gara, Ubriaco, Rothbaum, Clabby, & Schuyler, 1986) and displayed significantly more prosocial behaviors and fewer self-destructive and aggressive acts in high school (Elias, Gara, Schuyler, Branden-Muller, & Sayette, 1991).

1995 Revalidation by the U.S. Department of Education

In 1995, we once again submitted our research to the rigorous scrutiny of a Program Effectiveness Panel of the U.S. Department of Education, which revalidated our program. Although space does not permit a full report of the data, we would like to focus on some of the studies from our recent revalidation application (Hampson, 1995).

Claim 1: Following training, teachers improve in their ability to facilitate children's social decision making and problem solving.

As noted in Table 11.2, teachers representing suburban, urban-suburban, and rural sites participated in this study. The New Jersey teachers included a sample from a newly trained site, teachers from schools that have certified trainers; whereas our out-of-state sites represent data collected by newly certified trainers. As a result, the data set includes second-generation results. In these studies, teachers were given a series of hypothetical school-based problem situations derived from the work of Irving Sigel, and George Spivack and Myrna Shure. In his extensive research with regular and special education students, Sigel has developed a hierarchy of types of teacher responses to decision-making situations faced by students. This hierarchy ranges from responses that are *inhibitory* of children's representational competence (e.g., authoritarian responses), through those that are *moderately facilitative* (e.g., providing consequences or alternatives to choose from), to those that are *highly facilitative* of children's cognitive abilities (e.g., open-ended questions that encourage reflection on the possibilities and options). On the basis of Spivack and Shure's operationalization of Sigel's work, we presented teachers with vignettes and a choice of seven responses, each structured to reliably and objectively

Table 11.2 Summary of Change in Teachers' Inhibitory and Highly Facilitative Responses following SPS Training

	N	Site[a]	Inhibitory			Facilitative		
			Pre (%)	Post (%)	– %	Pre (%)	Post (%)	+ %
Original validation	8	S	25	15	–40	37	50	+35
NJ 1	9	U/S	17	6	–65	46	81	+76
NJ 2	7	U/S	22	9	–59	32	52	+63
NJ 3	13	U/S	29	14	–52	33	46	+39
AK	16	R	20	11	–45	52	60	+15
OR	4	S	17	8	–53	29	63	+117
Mean			21	10	–52	38	60	+58

a. Site: S = suburban; U/S = urban/suburban; R = rural.

represent a point in Sigel's hierarchy of responses (Copple, Sigel, & Saunders, 1979; Sigel, 1985) that facilitate or inhibit cognitive development. The results showed that after training, teachers significantly increased their use of questioning strategies found to be highly facilitative of problem-solving thinking. Across sites, 6 to 10 months following training, teachers' inhibitory responses were reduced by a mean of 52%, and highly facilitative responses showed a mean increase of 58%. This pattern of response change corresponds to our original validation data; in fact, the current results actually exceed the original results in magnitude.

Claim 2: Children receiving the program improve their social decision-making and problem-solving skills.

The Instructional and Application phases of the curriculum were evaluated with the Group Social Problem Solving Assessment (GSPSA), a criterion-referenced, developmentally based instrument for which reliable scores have been derived through replicated factor and multitrait-method analyses. Coefficient alphas for the three subscales—Interpersonal Sensitivity, Problem Analysis, and Specificity of Planning—are around .75. Scores from the GSPSA have discriminated behaviorally and emotionally disordered middle school children from other subgroups in their school and are not correlated with a child's academic abilities.

In Table 11.3, are the results of two fourth-grade studies from our revalidation application, using our original validation data for comparison purposes. SPS is taught districtwide in both sites, and therefore within-district controls could not be obtained. Site A is an urban/suburban district that introduced SPS in 1989 with the training of 14 teachers and phased the program into all first-through fifth-grade classrooms by 1993, serving approximately 3,000 children. The fourth grade has a 29% minority population, with 27% of the students qualifying for free or reduced meals. Site B is a suburban district with a 15% minority population, serving students from the upper middle class. The SPS program was introduced to Site B in 1984, and the district has had multiple-year training contracts leading to complete implementation of the program in the district for grades 2 through 6. The nonparametric Wilcoxon rank sum test was used to obtain approximate t-test results, with two-tailed tests; and interrater reliability exceeded 90%. The results presented in Table 11.3 indicate that children

Table 11.3 Change in Fourth Graders' Mean Interpersonal Sensitivity (IS), Problem Analysis (PA), and Planning (PLAN) Scores Following Training in the Instructional Phase of SPS

Original Validation	(N = 120)			Site A (N = 147)				Site B (N = 77)			
	PRE	POST	ES	PRE	POST	Z	ES	PRE	POST	Z	ES
IS	9.89	10.29	.18	9.95	10.70	3.31*	.34	10.99	11.96	4.03**	.60
(SD)	2.20	1.54		2.19	1.88			1.62	1.09		
PA	10.37	12.47	.58	9.86	12.16	4.95**	.58	10.42	15.81	7.68**	1.31
(SD)	3.62	3.72		3.95	3.56			4.13	2.82		
PLAN	4.83	5.51	.42	5.55	6.56	4.06**	.49	6.20	7.61	4.65**	.80
(SD)	1.63	1.27		2.08	1.91			1.76	1.72		

*p <.001; **p < .0001.

trained in SPS continue to make substantial gains in Interpersonal Sensitivity, Problem Analysis (which reflects a child's ability to examine a problem, define it, set goals, and consider alternative solutions), and Planning (which includes evaluating consequences and realistically assessing obstacles to problem resolution). The magnitude of effects for the current data exceeds that found in our original study.

In addition, our recent validation presented data that proved that students receiving the program in elementary school show more prosocial behavior. Taken together, the results give potential implementers grounds for some confidence in implementing programs such as ours to address social decision-making skills. School-based program choices, however, are rarely, if ever, made solely on the basis of data. Considerations such as cost-effectiveness are being raised more and more often, particularly in this era of shrinking financial resources.

Costs-Benefits

Weissberg and Elias (1993) have addressed the difficulties inherent in casting the discussion of costs and benefits of prevention into some sort of numeric or financial framework. There are certain key elements, such as "human capital," for which a quantitative value cannot be validly assigned. Nor is it possible to truly unpack the unique costs of comprehensive programs that are infused into classroom and school routines and structures.

Nevertheless, it is possible to get a sense of the preventive impact if one looks at the impact of the Social Decision Making and Problem Solving Program as diverting students from special education placements. In a typical implementation in a 300-student school with 15 teachers and various support and pupil services staff, a full unit of intervention would consist of full-staff training and follow-up consultation over a 3-year period. The cost of such an effort would be about $4,000, plus about $1,500 in curriculum materials.

In a school of 300 students, 3 to 15 students per year will be classified as being in need of special education services. At an average cost of $20,000 per student, this ranges from $60,000 to $300,000. In districts using the Social Decision Making approach, referral rates to special services have been reduced as part of an overall reduction in disciplinary incidents. Even by the most conservative estimates of 1 to 3 students per year being diverted from special education, the costs are more than offset by the financial gains. And the benefit in human terms can be added as well.

Conclusion

We agree with the National Commission on the Role of the School and the Community in Improving Adolescent Health (1990) that "in today's world, schools can only accomplish their education mission if they attend to student's emotional, social, and physical problems" (p. 38).

This is not something that we have done as a nation, a society, or in the vast majority of instances, as individual communities. Only when we have instituted such efforts in a dedicated and extensive way, can we begin to understand the costs and the benefits. Until then, we need only look at the media headlines, the correctional system, and the child and adolescent treatment system and visit our schools to see the vacant look in too many children's eyes. Only then can we compute the cost of continuing on the current path. This alone should be enough to spur caring people to action.

Ultimately, primary prevention is a developmental right. It aims to ensure that all children possess the skills needed for everyday interpersonal success in school and at home. The Social Decision Making and Problem Solving Program has been presented as a research-validated approach to primary prevention that can be implemented in any school in a way that captivates the participation of students, teachers, and parents.

References

Abrams, J. C., & Kaslow, F. (1977). Family systems and the learning disabled child: Intervention and treatment. *Journal of Learning Disabilities, 10,* 86-90.

Asher, S. R., & Parker, J. G. (1989). Significance of peer relationship problems in childhood. In B. H. Schneider, G. Attili, J. Nadel, & R. P. Weissberg (Eds.), *Social competence in developmental perspective* (pp. 5-23). Dordrecht: Kluwer.

Bandura, A. (1986). *Social foundations of thought and action.* Englewood Cliffs, NJ: Prentice Hall.

Barell, J., Liebmann, R., & Sigel, I. (1988, April). Fostering thoughtful self-direction in students. *Educational Leadership*, pp. 14-17.

Bertalanffy, L. Von (1968). *General systems theory: Foundation, development, applications.* New York: George Braziller.

Bierman, K. L. (1993, March). *Social adjustment problems of aggressive-rejected, aggressive, and rejected boys: A longitudinal analysis.* Paper presented at the biennial meeting of the Society for Research in Child Development, New Orleans, LA.

Billington, R. J., Washington, L. A., & Trickett, E. J. (1981). The research relationship in community research: An inside view from public school principles. *American Journal of Community Psychology, 9,* 461-480.

Botvin, G., Schinke, S., & Orlandi, M. (1995). School-based health promotion: Substance abuse and sexual behavior. *Applied and Prevention Psychology, 4,* 167-184.

Botvin, G., & Toru, S. (1988). Preventing adolescent substance abuse through life skills training. In R. Price, E. Cowen, R. Lorion, & J. Ramos-McKay (Eds.), *Fourteen ounces of prevention: A casebook for practitioners* (pp. 89-110). Washington, DC: American Psychological Association.

Bye, L., & Jussim, L. (1993). A proposed model for acquisition of social knowledge and social competence. *Psychology in the Schools, 30*(2), 143-159.

Cairns, R. B., Cairns, B. D., & Neckerman, H. J. (1989). Early school dropout: Configurations and determinants. *Child Development, 60*(6), 1437-1452.

Clabby, J. F., & Elias, M. J. (1986). *Teach your child decision making.* New York: Doubleday. (Available from Maurice J. Elias, Ph.D., Department of Psychology, Tillett Hall/Rutgers University, Livingston/Kilmer Campus, New Brunswick, NJ 08903)

Cohen, D. A., Patterson, C., & Christopoulos, C. (1991), The family and children's peer relations. *Journal of Social and Personal Relationships, 8,* 315-346.

Columbia Education Center. (1995). [Unpublished curriculum developed at the Summer Institutes of Understanding the Law, Selves, and Others (ULSO).] Contact Bob Kramer, Columbia Education Center, Tualatin, OR.

Copple, C., Sigel, I., & Saunders, R. (1979). *Educating the young thinker.* New York: Van Nostrand Reinhold.

Cowen, E. L. (1994). The enhancement of psychological wellness: Challenges and opportunities. *American Journal of Community Psychology, 22,* 149-178.

Crick, N. R., & Dodge, K. A. (1994). A review and reformulation of social information-processing mechanisms in children's social adjustment. *Psychological Bulletin, 115,* 74-101.

Davis, M. H., & Oathout, H. A. (1987). Maintenance of satisfaction in romantic relationships: Empathy and relational competence. *Journal of Personality and Social Psychology, 53*(2), 397-410.

DeAngelis, T. (1994, June). Government should support realistic prevention projects. *APA Monitor,* pp. 32-33.

Devlin, N. (1983, June 19). The vicious circle of educational mediocrity. *New York Times,* p. NJ-22.

Dodge, K. A. (1986), A social information processing model of social competence in children. In M. Perlmutter (Ed.), *Minnesota Symposium on Child Psychology* (Vol. 18, pp. 77-125). Hillsdale, NJ: Lawrence Erlbaum.

Dodge, K. A., Pettit, G. S., & Bates, J. E. (1994). Socialization mediators of the relation between socioeconomic status and child conduct problems. *Child Development, 65*(2), 649-665.

Elias, M. J., & Clabby, J. F. (1984). Integrating social and affective education into public school curriculum and instruction. In C. A. Maher, R. J. Illback, & J. E. Zins (Eds.), *Organizational psychology in the schools: A handbook for professionals* (pp. 143-172). Springfield, IL: Charles C Thomas.

Elias, M. J., & Clabby, J. F. (1989). *Social decision-making skills: A curriculum guide for the elementary grades.* Rockville, MD: Aspen Publishers.

Elias, M. J., & Clabby, J. F. (1992). *Building social problem-solving skills: Guidelines from a school-based program.* San Francisco: Jossey-Bass.

Elias, M. J., Gara, M., Ubriaco, M., Rothbaum, P., Clabby, J., & Schuyler, T. (1986). Impact of a preventive school problem-solving intervention on children's coping with middle-school stressors. *American Journal of Community Psychology, 14*(3), 259-275.

Elias, M. J., Gara, M. A., Schuyler, T. F., Branden-Muller, L. R., & Sayette, M. A. (1991). The promotion of social competence: Longitudinal study of a preventive school-based program. *Journal of Orthopsychiatry, 61*(3), 407-417.

Elias, M. J., Tobias, S. E., & Friedlander, B. S. (1994). Enhancing skills for everyday problem solving and conflict resolution in special needs students with the support of computer-based technology. *Special Services in the Schools, 8*(2), 22-52.

Friedlander, B. (1993). Incorporating computer technologies into social decision making: Applications to problem behavior. In M. J. Elias (Ed.), *Social decision making and life skills development* (pp. 315-318). Gaithersburg, MD: Aspen.

Goleman, D. (1995a, September 27). Beyond IQ: Why some schools are adding "Emotional Intelligence" to their definition of what it means to be smart. *Education Week,* pp. 48, 40.

Goleman, D. (1995b). *Emotional intelligence: Why it can matter more than IQ.* New York: Bantam.

Gottman, J. (1993). *What predicts divorce: The relationship between marital processes and marital outcomes.* Hillsdale, NJ: Lawrence Erlbaum.

Gottman, J. (1994). *Why marriages succeed or fail.* New York: Simon & Schuster.

Halper, A., London, M., & Richardson, S. (1994). *Talking with T. J.: Trainers guide* (Conflict Resolution Series: Helping Children Work Out Problems without Violence). Kansas City, MO: Hallmark Corporate Foundation.

Halper, A., & Richardson, S. (1993). *Talking with T. J.: Trainers guide* (Teamwork Series: Helping Children Work and Play Together). Kansas City, MO: Hallmark Corporate Foundation.

Hampson, J. (1995). [Technical report submitted to the Program Effectiveness Panel of the U.S. Department of Education.] (Available from the author at University of Medicine and Dentistry of New Jersey, Social Problem Solving Program, 240 Stelton Road, Piscataway, NJ 08854-3248)

Heller, M. F., & Firestone, W. A. (1995). Who's in charge here? Sources of leadership for change in eight schools. *Elementary School Journal, 96*(1), 65-85.

Hett, C. H., & Krikorian, L. A. (1993). Fostering communication through school and home newsletters. In M. J. Elias (Ed.), *Social decision making and life skills development* (pp. 261-271). Gaithersburg, MD: Aspen.

Hord, S. M., Rutherford, W. L., Haling-Austin, L., & Hall, G. E. (1987). *Taking charge of change*. Alexandria, VA: Association for Supervision and Curriculum Development.

Hymel, S. (1986). Interpretations of peer behavior: Affective bias in childhood and adolescence. *Child Development, 57*(2), 431-445.

Hymel, S., Wagner, E., & Botter, L. J. (1990). Reputational bias: View from the peer group. In S. R. Asher & J. D. Cole (Eds.), *Peer rejection in childhood* (pp. 156-186). New York: Cambridge University Press.

Johnsen, R. L., & Bruene-Butler, L. (1993). Promoting social decision-making skills of middle school students: A school/community environmental services project. In M. J. Elias (Ed.), *Social decision making and life skills development* (pp. 241-249). Gaithersburg, MD: Aspen.

Krackhardt, D., & Hanson, J. R. (1993, July-August). Informal networks: The company behind the chart. *Harvard Business Review,* p. 104.

Kupersmidt, J. B., Coie, J. D., & Dodge, K. A. (1990). The role of poor peer relationships in the development of disorder. In S. R. Asher & J. D. Coie (Eds.), *Peer rejection in childhood* (pp. 274-305). Cambridge, UK: Cambridge University Press.

Ladd, G. W., & Mize, J. (1983). A cognitive-social learning model of social skills training. *Psychological Review, 90*(2), 127-157.

Lewin, K. (1951). *Field theory in social science*. New York: Harper & Row.

Munoz, R. F., Snowden, L. R., & Kelly, J. G. (1979). *Social and psychological research in community settings*. San Francisco: Jossey-Bass.

Naftel, M. I., & Elias, M. J. (1995). Building problem solving and decision making skills through literature analysis. *Middle School Journal, 26*(4), 7-11.

National Commission on the Role of the School and the Community in Improving Adolescent Health. (1990). *Code blue: Uniting for healthier youth*. Alexandria, VA: National Association of State Boards of Education.

Ollendick, T. H., Weist, M. D., Borden, M. G., & Greene, R. W. (1992). Sociometric status and academic, behavioral, and psychological adjustment: A five-year longitudinal study. *Journal of Consulting and Clinical Psychology, 60,* 80-87.

Parker, J. G., & Asher, S. R. (1987). Peer relations and later personal adjustment: Are low-accepted children at risk? *Psychological Bulletin, 102*(3), 357-389.

Parker, J. G., Rubin, K. H., Price, J. M., & De Rosier, M. E. (1995). Peer relationships, child development and adjustment: A developmental psychopathology perspective. In. D. Cicchetti & D. J. Cohen (Eds.), *Developmental psychopathology: Vol. 2. Risk, disorder and adaptation* (pp. 96-161). New York: John Wiley.

Pedro-Carroll, J., Alpert-Gillis, L., & Cowen, E. L. (1992). An evaluation of the efficacy of a preventive intervention for 4th-6th grade urban children of divorce. *Journal of Primary Prevention, 13,* 115-130.

Poedubicky, V. (1996). *Comprehensive health: Social decision making and problem solving curriculum (grades 3-6)*. Unpublished district curriculum, Bartle School, Highland Park, NJ.

Price, R. (1987). Linking intervention research and research and risk factor research. In J. Steinberg & M. Silverman (Eds.), *Preventing mental disorders: A research perspective* (pp. 48-56; DHHS Publication No. ADM 87-1492). Rockville, MD: National Institute of Mental Health.

Price, R., & Smith, S. (1985). *A guide to evaluating prevention programs in mental health* (DHHS Publication No. ADM 85-144). Washington, DC: Government Printing Office.

Putallaz, M., & Gottman, J. (1982). Conceptualizing social competence in children. In P. Kardy & J. J. Steffen (Eds.). *Advances in child behavior analyses and therapy* (Vol. 2, pp. 1-3). New York: Gardner.

Putallaz, M., & Heflin, A. H. (1990). Parent child interaction. In S. R. Asher & J. D. Coie (Eds.), *Peer rejection in childhood* (pp. 189-216). Cambridge, UK: Cambridge University Press.

Rotter, J. B. (1966). Generalized expectancies for internal versus external control of reinforcement. *Psychological Monographs, 80,* (1 Serial No. 609).

Rubin, K. H., Booth, C., Rose-Krasnor, L., & Mills, R. S. L. (1994). Family relationships, peer relationships, and social development: Conceptual and empirical analyses. In S. Shulman (Ed.), *Close relationships and socio-emotional development* (pp. 64-94). New York: Ablex.

Sanford, N. (1970). Whatever happened to action research? *Journal of Social Issues, 29*(1), 3-23.

Sarason, S. B. (1978). The nature of problem solving in social action. *American Psychologist, 33,* 370-380.

Sarason, S. B. (1982). *The culture of the school and the problem of change* (2nd ed.). Boston: Allyn & Bacon.

Secretary's Commission on Achieving Necessary Skills. (1991). *What work requires of schools: A SCANS report for America 2000.* Washington, DC: U.S. Department of Labor.

Shure, M. B., & Spivack, G. (1978). *Problem solving techniques in childrearing.* San Francisco: Jossey-Bass.

Shure, M. B., & Spivack, G. (1988). Interpersonal cognitive problem solving. In R. Price, E. Cowen, R. Lorian, & J. Ramos-McKay (Eds.), *Fourteen ounces of prevention: A casebook for practitioners* (pp. 69-82). Washington, DC: American Psychological Association.

Sigel, I. (Ed.). (1985). *Parental belief systems: The psychological consequences for children.* Hillsdale, NJ: Lawrence Erlbaum.

Underwood, M., & Albert, M. (1989, April). *Fourth-grade peer status as a predictor of adolescent pregnancy.* Paper presented at the meeting of the Society of Research on Child Development, Kansas City, MO.

Wedam, K. (1988). *Parent involvement in school-based prevention programs: A method for improving home-school partnership utilizing cable television.* Unpublished dissertation, Graduate School of Applied and Professional Psychology, Rutgers University.

Weissberg, R. P., & Elias, M. J. (1993). Enhancing young people's social competence and health behavior: An important challenge for educators, scientists, policymakers, and funders. *Applied and Preventive Psychology 2,* 179-190.

• *CHAPTER 12* •

The Social-Competence Promotion Program for Young Adolescents

ROGER P. WEISSBERG

HEATHER A. BARTON

TIMOTHY P. SHRIVER

An unprecedented adolescent health crisis is facing our nation (National Commission on the Role of the School and the Community in Improving Adolescent Health, 1990). Psychosocial and health problems among America's youth are due, in large part, to significant changes that have occurred in families and communities during the last few decades (National

AUTHORS' NOTE: We express our appreciation to the New Haven Public Schools for their commitment to developing and implementing high-quality programming to enhance the social development of children and youth. Special thanks go to our primary collaborators on the SCPP-YA: Marlene Caplan, Karol DeFalco, Alice Jackson, and Mickey Kavanagh. We also appreciate the helpful editorial comments of Mary Hancock and Eva Patrikakou, who reviewed an earlier draft of this paper.

We acknowledge NIMH's Prevention Research Branch and Office on AIDS for their support and funding of the University of Illinois at Chicago (UIC) Prevention Research Training Program in Urban Children's Mental Health and AIDS Prevention (1-T32-MH19933) directed by Roger Weissberg. We also appreciate the support of this Training Program by the Irving B. Harris Foundation in Chicago, Illinois. Finally, the work of the first author was supported, in part, with funds from the Mid-Atlantic Laboratory for Student Success.

Correspondence concerning this chapter should be addressed to: Roger P. Weissberg, Department of Psychology (M/C 285), the University of Illinois at Chicago, 1007 West Harrison Street, Chicago, IL 60607-7137.

Commission on Children, 1991). Dual-career couples and single parents who work outside the home have become the norm. Divorce is more prevalent. Extended families that live close to children are less common. Record numbers of women and young children live in poverty. These social and environmental changes have reduced the extent to which positive adult role models are able to support the development of young people and monitor their behavior. Stressful conditions are even greater for youth living in urban, poverty-ridden neighborhoods (Panel on High-Risk Youth, National Research Council, 1993).

Research indicates that 25% to 50% of American youth engage in multiple high-risk behaviors—such as drug use, unprotected intercourse, and violence—that can interfere with their development into constructive family members, workers, and citizens (Dryfoos, 1990). Although many American youth do not currently engage in these behaviors, they still require adult support and guidance to avoid such involvement and to protect themselves from the antisocial acts of others. In summary, current societal conditions and the prevalence of high-risk behavior among young people prompt calls for effective school-based prevention programs to address children's social and health needs (DeFriese, Crossland, Pearson, & Sullivan, 1990; National Mental Health Association, 1986).

Many researchers and educators recognize the need to establish effective school-based health-promotion and social competence enhancement programs for early adolescents (Carnegie Council on Adolescent Development, 1989, 1995; Hamburg, 1992). Young adolescents are notably at risk for developing behavioral and emotional problems. Individuals between the ages of 10 and 15 experience many predictable stressors and dramatic life changes. During these years, puberty transforms the child, at least physically, into a young adult. Rapid bodily changes, cognitive maturation, and increased social pressures profoundly influence, and in some instances disrupt, the psychosocial functioning of young adolescents. The transition from self-contained, single-teacher, elementary school classrooms to the less structured and less protective middle school culture is often difficult and introduces new stresses and challenges to compound those connected with growing up (Carnegie Council on Adolescent Development, 1989). All adolescents face decisions about resolving conflicts with peers, choosing appropriate friends, negotiating increased independence from parents, experimenting with alcohol or drugs, and having sex. Although these are common experiences, the negative consequences of poor decision making can lead to serious health and emotional problems that negatively affect the quality of adolescents' lives.

Failure to prevent violence, substance use, and high-risk sexual behavior incurs tremendous costs to society each year. An estimated $33 billion is spent annually on medical and mental health treatment, emergency response, employment productivity losses, and health insurance and disability payments for victims of violence (Miller, Cohen, & Rossman, 1993). In addition, the loss in quality of life among victims of violence is associated with an additional $145 billion annually (Miller et al., 1993). According to *Healthy People 2000,* the economic costs associated with alcohol problems are staggering, with more than $70 billion spent annually (U.S. Department of Health and Human Services [DHHS], 1990). Drug problems accounted for an additional $44 billion annually. Teenage pregnancy is associated with an estimated $16.6 billion in public funds spent annually to support families headed by teenage mothers (U.S. DHHS, 1990). In reality, the total economic impact of adolescents' involvement with violence, substance use, and high-risk sexual behavior is even greater because these problems have ripple effects in other domains such as mental health, juvenile justice, special education, and social services. The human costs of these problems are also profound in terms of how violence, substance use, and high-risk sexual behavior affect the quality of life of adolescents and their families.

To reduce these costs, it is imperative to develop and disseminate effective, theory-driven, school-based health-promotion approaches that reduce adolescent high-risk behavior. As compulsory institutions that reach large numbers of children and youth during their formative years of development, schools are especially well suited to teach students life skills and critical-thinking abilities to provide a foundation for responsible behavior and positive interactions at school, with peers and families members, and in the community.

The Social-Competence Promotion Program for Young Adolescents (SCPP-YA) is a school-based prevention program that teaches students cognitive, behavioral, and affective skills and encourages them to apply these skills in dealing with daily challenges, problems, and decisions (Caplan & Weissberg, 1990; Kavanagh, Jackson, Gaffney, Caplan, & Weissberg, 1990; Weissberg, Caplan, Bennetto, & Jackson, 1990). SCPP-YA was developed collaboratively by Roger Weissberg, his colleagues at Yale University, and educators from the New Haven, Connecticut Public Schools over a 10-year period. New Haven is an urban community with approximately 130,000 people and a public school system that serves approximately 19,000 kindergarten through 12th-grade students. Approximately 56% of the students are black, 24% are Hispanic, and 20% are white. New Haven is among the poorest cities in the country, with approximately 21% of its children living in poverty and 34% living in single-parent homes. The New Haven Public Schools have implemented SCPP-YA systemwide with all 6th graders attending regular-, special-, or bilingual-education classrooms since 1989. SCPP-YA has also been disseminated to many schools around the United States. The 45-session program provides classroom-based instruction and establishes environmental supports aimed at (a) promoting social competencies such as self-control, stress management, responsible decision making, social problem solving, and communication skills; (b) enhancing the quality of communication between school personnel and students; and (c) preventing antisocial and aggressive behavior, substance use, and high-risk sexual behaviors.

Conceptual Framework and Previous Research

Two core areas of person-centered competence are (a) behavioral effectiveness in dealing with the environment, such as attaining adaptive goals in school, at work, and in interpersonal relationships; and (b) possessing positive self-perceptions and feelings of efficacy when addressing developmental challenges and situations (Ford, 1985). Behavioral effectiveness and a sense of personal well-being are hallmarks of mental health; therefore, a goal of prevention programs should be to enhance them. A socially competent individual is able to make use of personal and environmental resources to achieve prosocial goals (Waters & Sroufe, 1983). Modifiable personal resources often targeted in prevention programs include cognitive, affective, and behavioral skills; personal beliefs and social attitudes; tacit knowledge and acquired knowledge about developmentally and culturally relevant social issues and situations; self-perceptions of performance efficacy in specific social domains; and the ability to elicit the support of parents, teachers, and peers when needed.

To enhance children's personal resources for coping adaptively with decisions, social interactions, and life stresses, SCPP-YA follows a social-information-processing framework to guide the content of its lessons (e.g., Dodge, Pettit, McClaskey, & Brown, 1986). According to social-information-processing models, individuals who behave competently in particular contexts have the capacities to (a) control impulses and manage affect in order to engage in responsible problem solving; (b) perceive the nature of a task and the feelings and perspectives of the people involved; (c) feel motivated to establish an adaptive goal to resolve a situation; (d) feel confident in their ability to achieve a goal successfully; (e) access or generate goal-directed alternatives and link them with realistic consequences; (f) decide on an optimal strategy and when necessary, develop elaborated implementation plans that anticipate potential obstacles; (g) carry out solutions with behavioral skill; (h) self-monitor behavioral performance with the capacity to abandon ineffective strategies, try alternative plans, or reformulate goals as needed; and (i) provide self-reinforcement for successful goal attainment or engage in emotion-focused coping when a desired goal cannot be reached. Thus, one central component of SCPP-YA involves enhancing the abilities of young people to coordinate cognition, affect, and behavior so that they may more effectively handle relevant social tasks.

Even programs effectively addressing these competencies will fall short of their potential benefits without also concentrating on the people and systems in which young people function (Bronfenbrenner, 1979; Perry, Kelder, & Komro, 1993). Hawkins (1995) emphasized that these programs must also afford young people opportunities to apply newly learned skills and assure that those who interact with young people consistently recognize and reinforce skillful performance. According to his protective-factor model, prevention programs must create system resources that reward children's daily application, generalization, and maintenance of adaptive cognitive, behavioral, and affective skills. Furthermore, when involved adults have healthy beliefs and clearly articulated standards of behavior, these serve as additional protection against the adoption of high-risk, maladaptive behaviors (Hawkins, 1995). Therefore, a second major emphasis of SCPP-YA emphasizes the fostering of environmental settings, resources, and opportunities that support real-life applications of adaptive skills and behavior.

The content, instructional strategies, and structure of SCPP-YA stem from four major findings of research about high-quality health education (Consortium on the School-based Promotion of Social Competence, 1994; DeFriese et al., 1990; Dryfoos, 1990; National Commission on the Role of the School and the Community in Improving Adolescent Health, 1990; Weissberg & Elias, 1993). First, the most efficacious programs enhance students' cognitive, affective, and behavioral skills; promote prosocial attitudes, values, and perceptions of norms; and provide accurate, socioculturally relevant information about targeted social and health domains. Second, they employ teaching methods that ensure student engagement, foster application of positive behavior in real-life situations, and transform the ways in which children and adults communicate about problem situations. Third, to address adequately the widespread social and health problems of children, multiyear, multilevel, multicomponent interventions—in which peers, parents, the school, and community members reinforce classroom instruction—are realistically needed. Fourth, systemwide policies, practices, and infrastructures are required to support the systematic, coordinated implementation and institutionalization of effective school-based prevention programs. These considerations were integral to every phase of SCPP-YA program development from design through implementation and institutionalization (Elias & Weissberg, 1990; Weissberg, Caplan, & Sivo, 1989).

Program History and Design

University researchers and New Haven Public School educators have collaborated for more than a decade to create and evaluate SCPP-YA and other school-based prevention initiatives. What began as a series of small-scale pilot program development and evaluation efforts has grown into a systemwide, comprehensive, institutionalized effort to enhance children's health and social development. Actually, SCPP-YA is a core component of a much larger kindergarten through high school effort known as the New Haven Social Development Project. Although the main focus of this chapter is on SCPP-YA, we are quick to assert that schools should develop coordinated multiple-year, multiple-component programs to foster enduring, positive social and health behaviors in young people (Weissberg, 1991). SCPP-YA's benefits to children and its staying power in the New Haven schools have been enhanced because of concerted efforts to contextualize this 1-year program in a larger, coordinated system of related programs.

A Brief History and the Larger Program Context for SCPP-YA

Although Dr. Roger Weissberg had developed social competence promotion programs for elementary school children before moving from Rochester to New Haven in the early 1980s (e.g., Weissberg, Gesten, Carnrike, et al., 1981; Weissberg, Gesten, Rapkin et al., 1981), New Haven school administrators and teachers encouraged him to focus his new collaborative efforts on middle school children. Consequently, in 1984-1985 classroom teachers and undergraduate teaching assistants piloted a 12-session social competence promotion program for middle school students in one New Haven school. With the input of teachers, school personnel, and students, the program was expanded and improved during 1985-1986 when we initiated a large-scale longitudinal study with fifth to eighth graders from four schools to assess a new 16-session program. Between 1986 and 1988, we designed a follow-up training program for students and also broadened the program to include a new unit on the prevention of substance abuse.

In 1987, the Superintendent of Schools convened a task force to examine high-risk behaviors of New Haven students in the areas of drug use, teen pregnancy and AIDS, delinquency and aggressive behavior, truancy, and school failure. This task force was comprised of teachers, parents, administrators, students, pupil personnel staff, community leaders, university researchers, and human service providers. The task force indicated that a significant proportion of New Haven students engaged in high-risk behaviors that jeopardized their academic performance and health. In addition, they noted that many of these problems had common roots such as poor problem-solving and communication skills, low self-esteem, limited constructive after-school opportunities, and a lack of monitoring and guidance by positive adult role models.

To address these concerns, the task force recommended the creation of a comprehensive kindergarten through high school social development curriculum. The Superintendent and the Board of Education endorsed this recommendation and established a Social Development District Steering Committee and broadly representative elementary, middle, and high school curriculum committees to accomplish the following tasks: (a) articulate the broad mission and goals for the Social Development Project; (b) identify a scope and sequence of the curriculum with student learning objectives at each grade level; (c) design or select social development and health promotion programs to address these learning objectives; (d) coordinate school, parent, and community activities to support classroom instruction; and (e) design professional development programs to train and support school teachers, administrators, and pupil personnel staff who implemented these programs.

Within a year, the Superintendent and Board further strengthened the organizational infrastructure to support the successful systemwide implementation of social development initiatives by forming a Department of Social Development with Tim Shriver as district-level supervisor and a staff of facilitators. This structure insured broad involvement by school, parents, and community members in the creation of the kindergarten through high school Social Development Curriculum. Furthermore, the Department of Social Development provided high-quality training, support, and on-site coaching to teachers who implemented the curriculum and to school-based planning and management teams who coordinated classroom instruction with school and community programming to promote health and social competence. Between 1989 and 1993, the Social Development Department's efforts to design, implement, monitor, and evaluate coordinated prevention programming were assisted through a close, collaborative working relationship with Roger Weissberg and his staff at Yale University. Since Roger Weissberg moved from Yale University to the University of Illinois at Chicago, an active core of New Haven Public School Social Development staff has continued to support program implementation and to coordinate new program initiatives. In addition, Dr. Mary Schwab-Stone from the Yale Child Study Center and her colleagues have provided consultative support to New Haven about program development and evaluation efforts.

The mission of the Social Development Project is to educate students so that they (a) develop a sense of self-worth and feel effective as they deal with daily responsibilities and challenges; (b) engage in positive, safe, health-protective behavior practices; (c) become socially skilled and have positive relationships with peers and adults; (d) feel motivated to contribute responsibly to their peer group, family, school, and community; and (e) acquire a set of basic skills, work habits, and values as a foundation for a lifetime of meaningful work.

Between 1989 and 1993, the Department of Social Development accomplished three main goals. First, it phased in a K through 12 curriculum with 25 to 50 hours of classroom-based instruction at each grade. The curriculum emphasized self-monitoring, problem solving, conflict resolution, and communication skills; values such as personal responsibility and respect for self and others; and content about health, culture, interpersonal relationships, and careers. Second, it created educational, recreational, and health promotion opportunities at the school and community levels to reinforce classroom-based instruction. These include programs such as mentoring, peer mediation and leadership groups, an Extended Day Academy with after-school clubs, and an outdoor adventure class. Third, each school's mental health team—composed of pupil personnel staff, school teachers and administrators, and parents—focused on attention to the climate of the school and coordinated planning and implementation of school-based social development initiatives supported by all segments of the school community.

The SCPP-YA has been a core element of New Haven's systemwide social development curriculum instruction since 1989. During the 1988-1989 school year, New Haven's Middle-School Social Development Curriculum Committee conducted a national search to identify curricula to implement systemwide during the subsequent year with every sixth-grade student in regular education and special education. The Middle-School Committee selected the SCPP-YA. All program materials were translated into Spanish so that bilingual-education students could receive SCPP-YA training as well. For the last 7 years, SCPP-YA has been taught annually in approximately 50 New Haven classrooms to more than 1,000 students.

SCPP-YA Program Design

The 45-session SCPP-YA has three modules. The first module includes 27 lessons of intensive instruction in social problem-solving (SPS) skills (Weissberg et al., 1990). These foundational lessons are followed by two 9-session programs that teach students to apply SPS skills to the prevention of substance use (Caplan & Weissberg, 1990) and high-risk sexual behavior (Kavanagh et al., 1990). Next we provide more detailed descriptions of each module and how these components fit together within the school experience to form an integrated overall program.

Social Problem-Solving Module
(Weissberg et al., 1990)

The main goal of this module is to teach students to employ a six-step social information processing framework for solving a wide range of real-life problems. A traffic light poster is used to display the following sequential six-step process: (1) stop, calm down, and think before you act, (2) say the problem and how you feel, (3) set a positive goal, (4) think of lots of solutions, (5) think ahead to the consequences, and (6) go ahead and try the best plan. The traffic light links a familiar image to three central, sequential phases of problem solving. The red light—or "stop" phase—symbolizes stopping to calm down in preparation for problem-solving thinking and action (Step 1); the yellow light—or "thinking" phase—offers a process for identifying problems and evaluating options for implementation (Steps 2 to 5); and the green light—or "go" phase—represents taking action to resolve the problem (step 6). Through explicit instruction in the six steps, teachers and students learn a common language and framework for communicating about problems. Furthermore, the traffic light poster may be used as a visual reminder to prompt students to apply the problem-solving steps throughout the school (e.g., in the cafeteria, on the playground) and at home.

The 27-session SPS curriculum is divided into eight units allowing students ample time to learn the six steps and practice applying them to a variety of situations. These units are structured around the SPS steps: Unit 1 overviews the entire SPS process; units 2 to 7 each focus on one problem-solving step and concepts related to it; and unit 8 emphasizes integration of the entire SPS process and using it in daily interactions. Sessions are designed to be taught by classroom teachers in 45-minute class periods. Teacher training manuals provide detailed guidelines and scripted lesson plans as well as student worksheets and other materials (Weissberg et al., 1990). Next, we present brief summaries of major concepts for each unit.

In unit 1 ("Introducing Social Problem Solving"—two sessions) students define stress, discuss common situations that cause stress, and identify stress-related physical symptoms. The six-step SPS process is offered as a method to handle stressful situations and interpersonal conflicts effectively. The teacher sends parents a letter describing the program and laying the foundation for subsequent activities that can be used to reinforce problem solving at home.

The second unit ("Stop, Calm Down, and Think Before You Act"—3 sessions) introduces students to a variety of self-control and stress management strategies. Students discuss the value of stopping to calm down before acting in stressful situations and learn that inhibiting impulsive, angry responses may reduce the likelihood of making problems worse. A "stress thermometer" activity helps students monitor and regulate their levels of stress. Taking slow deep breaths is highlighted as an effective way to calm down, and students work in small groups to share other effective "calm-down" strategies they typically employ in stressful situations.

Unit 3 ("Say the Problem and How You Feel"—4 sessions) expands students' "feeling-word" vocabularies, associates feelings with positive and negative experiences, and encourages students to recognize and respect that people may feel differently about the same situation. Students also learn to describe problems and feelings that they experience in one or two sentences, enabling them to stand back and analyze situations more objectively. In one crucial activity, small working groups of students review a list of 13 commonly experienced adolescent problems, add important missing problems to the list, and vote to identify problems that they hope the program will emphasize in future sessions. Subsequent sessions incorporate concerns expressed by the students.

The fourth unit ("Set a Positive Goal"—2 sessions) teaches students that a goal is "how you want things to end up." Students learn to distinguish between constructive goals and those that are harmful or worsen situations. Teachers encourage students to try, whenever possible, to establish prosocial goals that are not harmful to themselves or others. In a homework assignment, students reflect on difficult situations they have experienced during the past week and identify the problem, the feelings of all involved, the goal they set, and whether they reached it. In addition, the assignment encourages students to talk with the teacher or another responsible adult if they need help with the situation.

The fifth unit ("Think of Lots of Solutions"—3 sessions) offers students opportunities to brainstorm alternative solutions to diverse problem situations. This process expands students' repertoire of coping strategies beyond the limited range they typically employ. Teachers convey that generating many solutions increases the likelihood that one will come up with a really good one and provides backup strategies if the first solution fails. Students also learn the benefits of working with or seeking input from other peers or an adult when they have trouble generating solutions.

Unit 6 ("Think Ahead to the Consequences"—2 sessions) encourages students to predict realistic consequences of the solutions they generate. Through a series of structured questions (e.g., What would probably happen next if I tried that solution? What effects would the solution have now and also a little while from now? How would others feel?), students learn to anticipate better both the short- and long-term effects of their solutions, as well as the impact potential solutions are likely to have on themselves and others. By answering these "consequential-thinking" questions, students increasingly think ahead to the likely results of their actions instead of behaving unreflectively and impulsively.

The seventh unit ("Go Ahead and Try the Best Plan"—3 sessions) teaches students how to select a good solution from multiple alternatives and to develop a step-by-step plan for its successful implementation. Because even the best of solutions will fail if carried out ineffectively, students learn about (a) the best tone of voice or body language to use when implementing solutions,

(b) timing or when it is best to enact solutions, and (c) planning ahead to overcome obstacles if their initial actions fail to resolve a situation to their satisfaction. By the end of this unit (session 19), the curriculum has completed the introduction of all six SPS steps. Teri Kazmier, a middle school music teacher, who has taught SCPP-YA for many years, created the following Problem-Solving Rap for session 19 that summarizes the SPS process (Weissberg et al., 1990; p. 205):

> If you have a problem, don't muddle through.
> Here's a simple rap about what to do.
> **Stop, calm down** before you act.
> You'll think more clearly—that's a fact.
> **Say the problem** and how you **feel.**
> Set a **positive goal** (and try to be real).
> Now for some "brainy" contributions,
> make out a list with **lots of solutions.**
> Slow down, though, and use some sense
> 'cause you gotta consider each **consequence.**
> Now if you've done your thinking and you're planning ahead,
> you can face your problem with a little less dread.
> So knowing you've done everything that you can,
> **go ahead**—try the **very best plan.**

The final unit ("Mastering Problem Solving"—8 sessions) guides students to apply their SPS knowledge to a variety of role-play and real-life situations. Major emphases involve (a) encouraging class members to share "101 ways that they use social competency skills to make the world a better place," (b) group meetings in which students work together cooperatively to resolve important individual, class, or school problems, (c) individual use of a structured worksheet to guide the systematic solving of interpersonal difficulties and conflicts, and (d) identifying resources that students may use for help, guidance, and support when they face difficult problems. In the final session, students reflect on their growth and evaluate the program through a survey and class discussion.

Substance Use Prevention Module
(Caplan & Weissberg, 1990)

This module conforms to federal guidelines for drug and alcohol prevention and education. The four-unit, nine-session program (a) offers current, accurate information about the health, social, and legal consequences of substance use; (b) corrects mistaken beliefs that students have about substance use; (c) enhances awareness of social and media influences that contribute to substance use; (d) teaches assertiveness and critical-thinking skills to resist pressures and influences to experiment with alcohol and other drugs; (e) identifies ways to involve peers, parents, school staff, and community members in prevention education; and (f) provides information on appropriate referral services for personal and family drug-related problems.

In the first module ("Establishing Goals for Healthy Life Styles"— 1 session), students set personal short- and long-term goals for themselves and identify positive role models. For homework, students interview people they admire about goals they have accomplished, obstacles they overcame, how substance use can negatively affect future dreams and aspirations, and advice for someone trying to succeed in life. The second unit ("Substance and Health Information"—2 sessions) provides students with accurate information about substance use and health. Students play cooperative and competitive games to review a series of myths and realities about the effects of tobacco, alcohol, and illicit substances on one's social, physical, and emotional health. They also learn to think more critically about information provided in cigarette and alcohol advertisements. Students begin to develop and role-play reasons for remaining drug free. For homework, they interview parents regarding the dangers of drug use, the benefits of being drug free, and family rules about drug use. The third unit ("Applying Social Problem-Solving Skills to Peer Pressure Situations"—2 sessions) uses video modeling and role playing to promote student awareness about social influences that contribute to drug experimentation and to enhance student use of effective peer resistance strategies to avoid substance use. The final unit ("Family, School, and Community Supports to Prevent Substance Use"—4 sessions) begins by informing students about school and community resources to help children and families in which someone has a drug problem and teaches them how to access such services. Session 7, "Ask the Experts," provides students with opportunities to hear various community speakers' views on substance use, to learn more about the consequences of substance use from a community perspective, and to reinforce the fact that resources are available for students who experience drug-related problems. Students conclude the module by working individually or with a team to create a service project that conveys to others the negative effects of substance use or the positive features of drug-free living. Students use the SPS framework to identify a problem, generate alternative ways to address it, and then implement their service project plan.

Human Growth and Development, AIDS Prevention, and Teen Pregnancy Prevention Module (Kavanagh et al., 1990)

This nine-session module informs students that it is important to study about puberty, reproduction, and AIDS to learn accurate information and to develop comfort discussing these topics so that it will be easier to ask questions and get correct facts when they need it. Session 1 begins with a series of "Dear Jamal" letters that model questions about puberty and sex that many young adolescents have. Students discuss where they go to find out answers to these questions and discuss the pros and cons of seeking information from various sources. The teacher and students also work together to establish guidelines for conducting class sessions with respect for other students' opinions and privacy. In addition, teachers create a "question box" and encourage students to use it anonymously throughout the module. Subsequent sessions begin by addressing any questions placed in the box. Session 2 ("What Happens During Puberty?") uses films and discussion to convey information about the physical, emotional, social, and cognitive changes of puberty. The teacher emphasizes that students mature at different rates and that this is perfectly normal. In Session 3 ("Learning the Language of Reproduction") students hear and say the proper names for reproductive anatomy and locate each body part on diagrams. Students are also introduced to some typical adolescent problem situations that may cause embarrassment or self-consciousness and are taught ways to get help or information when they need it. During Session 4 ("Human Reproduction— What's It All About?"), students study basic information about male and female roles in reproduction, recognize that there are myths and realities regarding what they hear about human sexuality, and generate a list of reliable sources of accurate and relevant information. In Session 5 ("Thinking About Relationships"), students work in small groups to identify ways to express affection and love in relationships without having intercourse and apply social competency skills to real situations involving social relationships and human sexuality. Session 6 ("Sexually Transmitted Diseases/AIDS") emphasizes how AIDS and other sex-related diseases are transmitted, the importance of seeking health care if you suspect you have a sexually transmitted disease, and how to contact specific sources for health care. Sessions 7 ("Ask the Experts"), 8 ("Solving Common Problems"), and 9 ("Sharing Solutions") provide further training about ways to apply problem solving to personal concerns and reinforce messages about the benefits of seeking support and information from others to address human sexuality issues effectively.

Beyond the Curriculum: Reinforcing
Prosocial Behavior and Competence

It is critical to extend environmental support of social competency skills beyond class instruction to enhance enduring positive behavior change. To foster the application and generalization of SPS concepts to daily life, teachers are trained to model problem solving to students in situations other than formal classroom lessons and to guide and encourage students to try out problem-solving strategies in everyday situations. One way that teachers help students apply problem-solving skills outside of the regular curriculum is through "problem-solving dialoguing" (Spivack, Platt, & Shure, 1976). The dialoguing technique is employed spontaneously when a problem occurs in the classroom. Instead of solving a students' problems for them, the teacher facilitates student thinking about situations and planning a step-by-step course of action. Teachers also use a "Becoming a Successful Problem Solver" worksheet to help students think independently about their problems (Weissberg et al., 1990). This worksheet guides children through the six steps of the "traffic light" model with a structured sequence of questions that are followed by dialogue with the teacher. Another effective way to help students maintain and apply their problem-solving skills is through teacher modeling. As teachers encounter certain problems during the course of a normal school day, they occasionally model their problem-solving thought process aloud for students rather than unobtrusively solving these problems on their own. Some teachers also invite students to participate with them in brainstorming solutions to resolve various classroom problems. Finally, teachers also help students practice their social competency skills by applying them to academic subjects and incorporating them into classroom activities. Many teachers use their regular academic curriculum materials with an emphasis on critical-thinking and problem-solving skills. History, social studies, current events, science, and language arts curriculum are especially amenable to incorporating problem-solving skills. Teachers have invented a range of creative ways to incorporate SCPP-YA skills into their daily classroom activities, including a problem-solving box, class problem-solving meetings, problem solver of the week awards, student diaries, projects to "make the school or world a better place," and teaching family members about problem solving (Weissberg et al., 1990).

Social competency skills are also used throughout the school to maximize the program's impact on student behavior. All school personnel are trained to help children use the six-step traffic light framework to solve problems. For instance, several New Haven schools restructured their in-house suspension program to include SCPP-YA skills. In-house suspension is now used as a place for children to think about how to handle problems more constructively. School staff dialogue with students to facilitate their thinking about the problem and to formulate action plans. To ensure that students follow through, they create a contract or agreement detailing how they will behave in the future if confronted with a similar problem (Weissberg et al., 1990). Some social workers and counselors make presentations about their services to Social Development classes and then use the SPS framework when working with high-risk students in individual or small-group treatment sessions. Finally, social competency skills are also emphasized and reinforced by school staff in the lunch room, on the playground, during after-school clubs, and on field trips.

Evaluation Data That Document the Effectiveness of SCPP-YA

Several controlled outcome studies have evaluated SCPP-YA's effects on students' skills, attitudes, and behavior (Arthur, Weissberg, & Caplan, 1991; Caplan et al., 1992; Weissberg & Caplan, 1996). In addition, process evaluations have assessed student, teacher, and parent reactions to the program as well as program implementation issues (Caplan, Weissberg, & Shriver, 1990; Weissberg & Caplan, 1996). The outcome research indicates that SCPP-YA training improves students' problem-solving skills, social relations with peers, and behavioral adjustment (Arthur et al., 1991; Caplan et al., 1992; Weissberg & Caplan, 1996). Program students made greater gains than control students in the number, effectiveness, and planfulness of alternative solutions they generated to problem situations. Furthermore, program students' alternatives included fewer aggressive and passive alternatives and more nonconfrontational and compromise solutions than controls. Program students also employ more adaptive stress management strategies when faced with situations that make them upset or anxious.

SCPP-YA training also enhanced positive involvement with peers, as measured by self-report and teacher ratings. In addition, teacher ratings indicated that program students improved more than controls in constructive conflict resolution with peers, in impulse control, and in popularity. These positive changes are reflected both in ratings by program teachers and by teachers who observed students in other class settings such as music and gym. Whereas the frequency of self-reported antisocial and delinquent behavior increased 36.8% in pre- to postassessments for control students, such behavior was stable for program students. Our substance abuse prevention efforts have also been quite successful. Results from confidential self-report surveys indicate that relative to controls, program students become less inclined to use drugs and are less likely to engage in excessive alcohol use. Program teachers reported that SCPP-YA classes most positively affected students in the following areas: feeling good about themselves, recognizing the negative effects of drugs and avoiding them, recognizing behaviors that may lead to pregnancy and AIDS, and identifying behaviors that reduce the risk of pregnancy and AIDS (Kasprow et al., 1991).

Arthur et al. (1991) assessed the long-term effects of these interventions in a 1-year follow-up study in which 6th and 7th graders who received 2 years of social development training were compared with those who received 1 year or no training. Students with 2 years of intervention maintained improvements in problem-solving skills, prosocial values, and teacher-rated peer relations and behavioral conduct. These findings suggest that although 1 year of intervention may produce short-term benefits for students, multiple years of instruction may be needed to promote more enduring improvements.

We also have evaluated how consumers feel about the program. Results of anonymous postprogram surveys consistently indicate that students enjoy the program and find it worthwhile. For example, Caplan et al. (1992) reported that almost all students (98%) liked the program and believed they learned by participating. Typically, more than 90% of the students report that they (a) apply SPS skills to issues in their daily lives, (b) are better able to handle stress and problems, (c) learned ways to resist alcohol and drug offers as well as other pressures from peers, and (d) would recommend the program to a friend.

New Haven parents have been extremely supportive of Social Development programming for children. Kasprow et al. (1991) reported that approximately 95% of their parent sample agreed that the school system should include classroom-based Social Development instruction. In addition, many parents have been willing to attend special information sessions to learn about SCPP-YA and ways to promote responsible social and health behavior at home.

Finally, program teachers have reacted positively on multiple levels. Most teachers (96%) indicated that the curricula address issues that are important for their students. More than 90% of the teachers enjoyed teaching the lessons and felt confident about their ability to teach the program. Interestingly, Caplan, Weissberg, and Shriver (1990) reported that 31% of teachers indicated (on an anonymous survey) that they initially were *not* happy about teaching the SCPP-YA curriculum the first year the program was disseminated systemwide in New Haven; however, by the end of the first year of implementation, 96% of the teachers reported feeling favorable about the experience, and 91% said they would like to teach the program again next year. A key reason for the positive response by teachers is their belief that both they and their students benefit from the Social Development programs. Importantly, Caplan et al. (1990) found that 89% of the teachers said the program helped them to communicate better with students; 85% indicated that the program helped them to deal with stress better in their own lives; and 96% believed the program had positive effects on them in application of problem solving to their own problems.

SCPP-YA is also remarkable for its sustainability. Due to the truly collaborative nature of the program's development and implementation, SCPP-YA has become institutionalized as a vital part of the school system's curriculum. The program has continued despite the departure of several staff persons, at both Yale and New Haven Public Schools, who were instrumental in creating the Social Development Program.

Summary

The importance and value of the Social-Competence Promotion Program for Young Adolescents is supported by several observations: (a) many young adolescents are at risk for behavior problems and school maladjustment as they face the physical, cognitive, and psychosocial changes brought about by puberty; (b) the transition from elementary to middle school sometimes exacerbates the difficulties connected with growing up; (c) statistics about stress-related problems (e.g., substance use, unwanted pregnancy, violence) for this age group demand that young adolescents be trained to cope with the daily problems and decisions; (d) schools represent the most logical site for systematically and effectively training large groups of children in life skills to deal adaptively with interpersonal stresses and developmental challenges; and (e) social competence promotion represents a highly promising and appropriate educational strategy for preventing high-risk behaviors.

SCPP-YA has positive effects on students' problem-solving skills, social relations with peers, and school adjustment, and also reduces participation in high-risk behavior. In addition, the program enhances teachers' capacity to communicate effectively with students. Realistically speaking, however, a single year of intervention cannot completely turn adolescents' lives around in terms preventing aggression, substance use, and high-risk sexual behavior. To have more enduring positive effects on adolescents' social, emotional, and physical health, there must be comprehensive and coordinated efforts throughout the school years. Classroom programs, such as SCPP-YA, are most beneficial when implemented in the context of systematic instruction at each grade level and reinforced by supportive activities and opportunities at school, at home, and in the community. In addition, school personnel must receive high-quality training, coaching, and organizational support to implement social, emotional, and health education programs effectively. SCPP-YA and the New Haven Social Development Project continue to contribute to the goal of educating students to fulfill their potential to become healthy, productive, and socially responsible citizens.

References

Arthur, M. W., Weissberg, R. P., & Caplan, M. Z. (1991, August). *Promoting social competence in young urban adolescents: A follow-up study.* Paper presented at the annual meeting of the American Psychological Association, San Francisco, CA.

Bronfenbrenner, M. (1979). *The ecology of human development: Experiments by nature and design.* Cambridge, MA: Harvard University Press.

Caplan, M., & Weissberg, R. P. (1990). *The New Haven Social Development Program: Sixth-grade substance use prevention module.* Chicago: University of Illinois at Chicago.

Caplan, M., Weissberg, R. P., Grober, J. S., Sivo, P. J., Grady, D., & Jacoby, C. (1992). Social competence promotion with inner-city and suburban young adolescents: Effects on social adjustment and alcohol use. *Journal of Clinical and Consulting Psychology, 60,* 56-63.

Caplan, M., Weissberg, R. P., & Shriver, T. (1990). *Evaluation summary for the 1989-1990 Social Development Project.* New Haven, CT: New Haven Public Schools.

Carnegie Council on Adolescent Development. (1989). *Turning points: Preparing American youth for the 21st century.* New York: Author.

Carnegie Council on Adolescent Development. (1995). *Great transitions: Preparing adolescents for a new century.* New York: Author.

Consortium on the School-Based Promotion of Social Competence. (1994). The school-based promotion of social competence: Theory, research, practice, and policy. In R. J. Haggerty, L. R. Sherrod, N. Garmezy, & M. Rutter (Eds.), *Stress, risk, and resilience in children and adolescents: Processes, mechanisms, and interventions* (pp. 268-316). New York: Cambridge University Press.

DeFriese, G. H., Crossland, C. L., Pearson, C. E., & Sullivan, C. J. (1990). Comprehensive school health programs: Current status and future prospects. *Journal of School Health, 60,* 127-190.

Dodge, K. A., Pettit, G. S., McClaskey, C. L., & Brown, M. M. (1986). Social competence in children. *Monographs of the Society for Research in Child Development, 51,* (2, Serial No. 213).

Dryfoos, J. G. (1990). *Adolescents at risk: Prevalence and prevention.* New York: Oxford University Press.

Elias, M. J., & Weissberg, R. P. (1990). School-based social competence promotion as a primary prevention strategy: A tale of two projects. *Prevention in Human Services, 7,* 177-200.

Ford, M. E. (1985). Primary prevention: Key issues and a competence perspective. *Journal of Primary Prevention, 5,* 264-266.

Hamburg, D. A. (1992). *Today's children: Creating a future for a generation in crisis.* New York: Times Books.

Hawkins, J. D. (1995). Controlling crime before it happens: Risk-focused prevention. *National Institute of Justice Journal, 229,* 10-18.

Kasprow, W. J., Weissberg, R. P., Voyce, C. K., Jackson, A. S., Fontana, T., Arthur, M. W., Borman, E., Marmorstein, N., Zeisz, J., Shriver, T. P., DeFalco, K., Elder, W., & Kavanaugh, M. (1991). *New Haven Public Schools Social Development Project: 1990-91 evaluation report.* New Haven, CT: New Haven Public Schools.

Kavanagh, M., Jackson, A. S., Gaffney, J., Caplan, M., & Weissberg, R. P. (1990). *The New Haven Social Development Program: Sixth-grade human growth and development, AIDS prevention, and teen pregnancy prevention module.* Chicago: University of Illinois at Chicago.

Miller, T., Cohen, M., & Rossman, S. (1993). Victim costs of violent crime and resulting injuries. *Health Affairs, 12,* 187-198.

National Commission on Children. (1991). *Beyond rhetoric: A new American agenda for children and families.* Washington, DC: Government Printing Office.

National Commission on the Role of the School and the Community in Improving Adolescent Health. (1990). *Code blue: Uniting for healthier youth.* Alexandria, VA: National Association of State Boards of Education.

National Mental Health Association. (1986). *Report of the NMHA Commission on the Prevention of Mental-Emotional Disabilities.* Alexandria, VA: Author.

Panel on High-Risk Youth, National Research Council. (1993). *Losing generations: Adolescents in high-risk settings.* Washington, DC: National Academy Press.

Perry, C. L., Kelder, S. H., & Komro, K. A. (1993). The social world of adolescents: Family, peers, schools, and the community. In S. G. Millstein, A. C. Petersen, & E. O. Nightingale (Eds.), *Promoting the health of adolescents* (pp. 73-97). New York: Oxford University Press.

Spivack, G., Platt, J. J., & Shure, M. B. (1976). *The problem-solving approach to adjustment.* San Francisco: Jossey-Bass.

U.S. Department of Health and Human Services, Public Health Service. (1990). *Healthy People 2000: National health promotion and disease prevention objectives.* Washington, DC: Government Printing Office.

Waters, E., & Sroufe, L. A. (1983). Social competence as a developmental construct. *Developmental Review, 3,* 79-97.

Weissberg, R. P. (1991). Comprehensive social-competence and health education (C-SCAHE): An urgently needed educational reform for the 1990's. *Child, Youth, and Family Services Quarterly, 14*, 10-12.

Weissberg, R. P., & Caplan, M. (1996). *Promoting social competence and preventing antisocial behavior in young urban adolescents.* Manuscript submitted for publication.

Weissberg, R. P., Caplan, M. Z., Bennetto, L., & Jackson, A. S. (1990). *The New Haven Social Competence Promotion Program for Young Adolescents: Social problem-solving module.* Chicago, IL: University of Illinois at Chicago.

Weissberg, R. P., Caplan, M. Z., & Sivo, P. J. (1989). A new conceptual framework for establishing school-based social competence promotion programs. In L. A. Bond & B. E. Compas (Eds.), *Primary prevention and promotion in the schools* (pp. 255-296). Newbury Park, CA: Sage.

Weissberg, R. P., & Elias, M. J. (1993). Enhancing young people's social competence and health behavior: An important challenge for educators, scientists, policymakers, and funders. *Applied & Preventive Psychology, 2*, 179-190.

Weissberg, R. P., Gesten, E. L., Carnrike, C. L., Toro, P. A., Rapkin, B. D., Davidson, E., & Cowen, E. L. (1981). Social problem-solving skills training: A competence building intervention with second- to fourth-grade children. *American Journal of Community Psychology, 9*, 411-423.

Weissberg, R. P., Gesten, E. L., Rapkin, B. D., Cowen, E. L., Davidson, E., Flores de Apodaca, R., & McKim, B. J. (1981). The evaluation of a social problem-solving training program for suburban and inner-city third-grade children. *Journal of Consulting and Clinical Psychology, 49*, 251-261.

CHAPTER 13

Going for the Goal: A Life Skills Program for Adolescents

STEVEN J. DANISH

Adolescents are taking more risks with their health, their lives, and their future than ever before. The number of illegitimate births to teenage girls has risen by more than half since 1980; marijuana use among eighth graders has doubled in just the past three years; arrests of young people for murder and

AUTHOR'S NOTE: This chapter was, in part, supported by Grant H84-AD00489 from the Center for Substance Abuse Prevention and Grants S184A90001 from the U.S. Department of Education. The contents of the chapter are solely the responsibility of the author and do not necessarily represent the views of CSAP or the Department of Education.

Many individuals and groups have been instrumental in the success of the Going for the Goal (GOAL) program. They include the program's coauthors: Mark Mash, Cathy Howard, Sherman Curl, Aleta Meyer, Susanna Owens and Kathy Lindstrom; Albert Farrell, my collaborator on the original project and the individual who, along with Aleta Meyer, has directed our evaluation efforts; and the schools and community groups and coordinators in the different cities in which GOAL has been taught. They have ensured the success of the Program. Without the financial and moral support of the Athletic Footwear Association and the Sporting Goods Manufacturing Association, especially Gregg Hartley, and Anheuser-Busch, GOAL would not have been able to reach out into different sites. Sandy McElhaney, Director of Prevention for the National Mental Health Association, has been invaluable in supporting our efforts. Alice Westerberg, Administrative Assistant for the Life Skills Center, has been the mainstay of the Life Skills Center. It is her organization and unwavering good cheer that keeps our operation going smoothly. Finally, I would like to thank Valerie Nellen and Aleta Meyer for their suggestions and help in the completion of this manuscript.

manslaughter has gone up 60% since 1980; and the drop out rate in some of our city schools approaches 50%. The cost of these actions to our society is staggering not only in the present, but for years to come. Despite our best efforts to develop programs that reduce these actions, the involvement of adolescents in these activities is not abating.

In this chapter, a life skills program developed by the Life Skills Center at Virginia Commonwealth University will be described. Going for the Goal (GOAL) (Danish et al., 1992a, 1992b) is designed to teach adolescents to develop a sense of personal control and confidence about the future so that they can make better decisions and ultimately become better citizens. To be successful in life, it is not enough to know what to avoid; one must also know how to succeed. For this reason, our focus is on teaching youth "what to say yes to" as opposed to "just say no." It is often stated that learning the "3R's" is a passport for future success; however, without the concomitant life skills, this passport is likely to be little more than a piece of paper symbolizing unrealized potential. As Comer (1988) has so aptly stated, schools must recognize that social and personal development are as important as academic development; in fact, changes in students' personal behavior are likely to affect their academic performance.

Theoretical and Empirical Basis
for a Life Skills Framework

Early adolescence is an appropriate time to teach life skills. During this period, ages 10 to 15, adolescents are at an age when they are experiencing a number of stressful concurrent life changes. These changes include biological changes with the onset of puberty, a reference change from a child to an adolescent and then to a teenager, and physical relocation from elementary school to middle or junior high school (Crockett & Petersen, 1993). Until a child reaches early adolescence, family members are usually the strongest influence. With the onset of adolescence, significant social changes occur. Perhaps the most important is that peer groups become the largest and most influential source affecting behavior and values (Petersen & Hamburg, 1986). Consequently, because adolescents spend a large percentage of their day in school, what happens in school will influence their behavior (Weissberg, Caplan, & Sivo, 1989). However, the importance of after-school settings cannot be minimized because youth spend more time out of school than in school. For example, researchers have found that eighth graders who are unsupervised for 11 or more hours per week are at twice the risk of substance abuse as are those who are supervised (Richardson et al., 1989) and that after-school hours are the most common time for adolescents to engage in sexual intercourse, usually at the home of the male while family members are at work (Zelnik & Kantner, 1977). For these reasons, involving youth in meaningful after-school programs is important.

It is during adolescence that youth begin to display evidence of precursors to problem behaviors (e.g., smoking, skipping school). In a longitudinal study of middle school students, a strong relationship among drug use, unsafe sexual activity, violent behavior, school attendance, and school disciplinary problems was found. Correlations among these behaviors were statistically significant and had an average value of .30 (Farrell, Danish & Howard, 1992).

Interventions for early adolescents must simultaneously increase health-enhancing behaviors and decrease health-compromising behaviors. A conceptual model for adolescent health promotion proposed by Perry and Jessor (1985) identifies four domains of health: physical health, psychological health, social health, and personal health. Within each domain, adolescents are involved in *health-compromising behaviors* (behaviors that threaten individual well-being) and *health-enhancing behaviors* (behaviors that promote individual well-being). Among the health-compromising behaviors that researchers have targeted are the ones identified at the beginning of the chapter: drug and alcohol abuse, violent and delinquent behaviors, engaging in premature and unsafe sexual activity that may result in pregnancy or diseases such as AIDS, and dropping out of school. Youth who have problems in one of these areas are likely to experience problems in other areas. The result is a "lifestyle syndrome" of health-compromising behaviors.

As a result of this research, some important conclusions can be drawn. First, there is a strong relationship among substance abuse, unsafe sexual activity, violent behavior, school attendance, and school disciplinary problems. Second, adolescents involved in one behavior are likely to be involved in one or more of the other behaviors, and it is unclear which behavior occurs first and how the cycle develops. Third, focusing only on preventing one of these behaviors to the exclusion of the others is likely to be ineffective and time-consuming. Consequently, we developed a life skills program for adolescents that is designed to *reduce* a number of health-compromising behaviors, and at the same time *promote* life-enhancing behaviors.

The future is important to youth, and those who do not have positive future expectations are at high risk for engaging in health-compromising behaviors. Much of the previous research on adolescent behavior has focused on variables related to youths' past or present, as opposed to their future. This focus is surprising, considering how much time adolescents spend thinking about the future. For example, Erikson (1968) believed that the adolescent "identity crisis" propels youth to look ahead to their projected future. Moreover, to form a healthy self-identity, adolescents must integrate their appraisal of their past, present, and future into a coherent self-concept.

Researchers have found a significant relationship between health-compromising or problem behavior and aspects of future thinking. Jurich and Andrews (1984) found that rural, early adolescent delinquent youth had a negative view of their personal future in comparison with their nondelinquent peers. In a longitudinal study, Newcomb, Bentler, and Collins (1986) found that adolescents' dissatisfaction about their perceived future opportunities predicted increased alcohol use from adolescence to adulthood. Research has also consistently shown that youth with low educational goals are at a higher risk for substance use (Johnston, O'Malley, & Bachman, 1987), unsafe sexual activity (Jones & Philliber, 1983), and delinquency (Catalano, Hawkins, White, & Padino, 1985).

Gullotta (1990) believes that youth who have developed negative future expectations are less concerned about engaging in problem behaviors because they do not feel valued by society. Until they feel valued and have opportunities to contribute to society, their operative response regarding involvement with problem behavior may become "Why not?"

On the other hand, youth with positive expectations for their personal futures tend to be at a lower risk for engaging in problem behavior because they view their participation in conventional society as having long-range rewards. For these youth, problem behavior may be seen as future-compromising and therefore as less attractive.

High-risk youth are not responsive to traditional health promotion programs; if behavior and cognition are to be changed, skills must be taught. Information taught about health is often ignored by adolescents. Millstein (1993) contends that knowledge about health is important only if health is a motivating factor for a given individual. Individuals who feel powerless in controlling their future do not value health as much as those who perceive themselves as powerful (Klerman, 1993). They believe that people achieve goals and success through luck rather than planning. Persons telling these youth about the dangers of engaging in health-compromising behaviors are likely to be disregarded, if not actually derided.

Teaching skills makes more sense. Skills are easily taught and learned; and when they are directed toward everyday life, they are empowering. By behavioral skills we are referring to such things as learning how to communicate effectively with peers and adults; by cognitive skills we mean learning such things as how to make effective decisions. Skills are taught differently than is knowledge. A Chinese proverb states, "I listen—and forget. I see—and remember. I do—and understand." Just as learning to drive a car, dance, or play a sport cannot occur solely through listening to a tape or reading a book, skills for living cannot be taught in a passive manner. Skills are learned through instruction, demonstration, and supervised practice (Danish & Hale, 1983).

The skills taught should have utility across problems; they should be skills for effective living. These skills are called life skills. Life skills are those skills that enable us to succeed in the environments in which we live. Life skills are both behavioral and cognitive. Some of the environments in which we live are families, schools, workplaces, neighborhoods, and communities. Most individuals must succeed in more than one environment. As one becomes older, the number of environments in which one must be successful increases. For example, a child need only succeed within the family;

an adolescent must succeed within the family, at school, and in the neighborhood. Environments will vary from individual to individual; thus, the definition of what it means to succeed will differ across individuals, as well as across environments (Danish, 1995; Danish & Donohue, 1995).

Individuals in the same environment are likely to be dissimilar from each other as a result of the life skills they have already mastered; their other resources; and their opportunities, real or perceived (Danish, 1995). For this reason, the needed life skills are likely to be different for individuals of different ages, ethnic or racial groups, or economic status.

Having peers—high school-aged adolescents—teach life skills is beneficial to both the older peer and the younger peer. To teach health behaviors to youth, it is important that the message and the teacher be credible. Because peers are important role models during adolescence, they can be effective in teaching younger students about the value of health and the importance of thinking about the future (Aloise-Young, Graham, & Hansen, 1994; GAO, 1992). In their 1992 report, the GAO concluded that it was important to involve local role models as mentors for youth, especially peer role models.

Very few high school-aged students have given a great deal of thought to the impact that they can have on their younger peers, and by extension, on their community as a whole. An awareness of this potential to lead, the development of a sense of responsibility for those who follow them, and the knowledge and skills that they gain by being effective leaders are valuable learning experiences and heighten their self-esteem (Hines, 1988; Snyder & Omoto,1992). There is still another benefit: Educational psychologists have long concluded that teaching is one of the best ways of learning. Thus, when "students" serve as "teachers" they learn as much or more about the subject being taught as the "students" they teach. Peer teaching, then, provides the peer teacher with benefits of both a psychological and a content nature. By teaching others how to succeed, the teacher's ability to succeed is enhanced.

In summary, to assist youth in developing positive expectations about the future, we must unleash their feelings and abilities to be self-directing; we must empower them. This process involves enhancing well-being by promoting healthy choices—including learning how to set personal goals and achieve these goals in the immediate future, and coming to believe in a valuable future. In the GOAL program, our intent is to teach personal competence, which we define as doing life planning, being self-reliant, and being able to seek help from others (Danish, D'Augelli, & Ginsberg, 1984). If we are successful in teaching these skills, the adolescent will be self-directed and will have positive expectations about life.

The GOAL Program

The Content of the Program

Early adolescents who are taught GOAL learn how to (a) identify positive life goals, (b) focus on the process (not the outcome) of goal attainment, (c) use a general problem-solving model, (d) identify health-promoting behaviors that can facilitate goal attainment, (e) identify health-compromising behaviors that can impede goal attainment, (f) seek and create social support, and (g) transfer these skills from one life context to another.

To learn these skills, ten 1-hour skill-based workshops are taught. After the first workshop, each subsequent session begins with a review of what has been taught in the previous workshop, followed by a brief skit introducing the new material. Skits feature "Goal Seeker," "Goal Buster," "Goal Keeper," and "Goal Shooter." The participants assume the roles of these characters during the skits. The skits in the GOAL program tell a story of a young person who has a goal to become a computer programmer. In each workshop, this protagonist faces some sort of obstacle to goal attainment. By using the skill taught in the workshop that day, goal attainment becomes more certain. The story line of the skits, therefore, serves as a metaphor for how to transfer educational material to real-life situations. Such metaphors have been found to enhance the transfer of learning from experiential, professional development courses to the work setting (Gass, 1984). Following the skits, the skills are taught and practiced.

In the first workshop, *Dare to Dream,* the program and the leaders are introduced. Participants discuss the importance of dreams and learn to dream about their future. There are two major activities in this workshop: first, participants are taken on a trip to their future and asked to identify their dreams and to write a brief story or draw a picture that depicts this future; and second, they are asked to identify goal keepers in their lives—people who serve as role models to them—and goal busters—people who try to impede them from a positive future.

In the second workshop, *Setting Goals*, participants are taught that a goal is a dream they work hard to reach. They learn the value of goal setting and the importance of setting reachable goals. The four characteristics of a reachable goal are that it is stated positively, it is specific, it is important to the goal setter, and it is under the goal setter's control. The major activity of this workshop is to learn how to distinguish goals that are reachable (have the essential four characteristics) from those that are not.

In Workshop 3, *Making Your Goal Reachable*, participants apply what they learned in the second workshop. They are asked to write a reachable goal to be attained within the next month or two and to make sure that it meets the characteristics of a reachable goal. The participants discuss and evaluate in small groups each characteristic individually as it pertains to their goal statement and receive feedback from the leader on whether the goal is stated correctly. By the end of the session, participants develop a goal statement that meets the criteria and that they will work with for the rest of the program.

In the fourth workshop, *Making a Goal Ladder*, participants learn how to make a plan to reach their goal. Participants put their goal at the top of the goal ladder, identify the steps (all of which must meet the characteristics of a reachable goal), and then place them in the order needed to reach the goal at the top of the ladder. Finally, they identify target dates by which each step/rung will be completed and sign a statement making a commitment to work hard to reach the goal.

In the fifth workshop, *Roadblocks to Reaching Goals*, participants learn how various roadblocks such as drug abuse, teen pregnancy, violence, dropping out of school, and lack of self-confidence can prevent them from reaching their goals in life. They read brief stories of others who encounter roadblocks, write stories about what happens to the characters in these stories, and identify some of their own possible roadblocks to their current goals.

In the sixth workshop, *Overcoming Roadblocks,* participants learn a problem-solving strategy called STAR (Stop and chill out; Think of all your choices; Anticipate the consequences of each choice; and Respond with the best choice). They practice using STAR in a number of simulated situations that they may encounter at school, after school, or at home.

In the seventh workshop, *Seeking Help From Others,* participants learn the importance of seeking social support to achieve goals. Two types of help, "doing" help and "caring" help, are described. Activities include engaging in a game that requires helping each other, identifying a "dream team" of 10 individuals (family members, very close friends, good friends, and older friends and role models) who can help them reach their goals, and practicing how to ask for help in several simulated situations.

In the eighth workshop, *Rebounds and Rewards,* participants learn how to rebound when a goal or a step on the goal ladder becomes too difficult to reach. They are asked to respond to simulated letters that depict individuals who have not reached their goals and to suggest strategies to help them be successful. Participants also identify a rebound plan for themselves if they are having trouble reaching their goal. Finally, they are asked to share their accomplishments to date with the rest of the group and how they plan to reward themselves for these accomplishments.

In the ninth workshop, *Identifying and Building on Your Strengths,* participants identify their personal strengths, including those learned through the GOAL program, and delineate how they can develop these strengths. They are then asked to identify an area in which they want to improve and list ways they can undertake this improvement. In addition to ways they list, several additional steps, based on other workshops, are suggested. This process is designed to help them transfer skills they have learned from one life domain to another.

In the tenth and final workshop, *Going for Your Goal,* participants play a game, "Know-It-All-Baseball," which provides an opportunity for them to integrate and apply the information covered in the nine other workshops.

Throughout the program, there is little discussion about health-compromising behaviors and how to avoid them. Some recent research conducted on social competence programs has suggested that to change behavior in specific areas, such as a specific health-compromising behavior, these areas must be specifically addressed by the intervention (Caplan, et. al, 1992). Although our own research is seemingly coming to a different conclusion, we recognize that GOAL may not be a stand-alone intervention and may be complementary to other interventions targeting specific health-compromising behaviors.

Who Delivers the Program and How It Is Delivered

The GOAL program is delivered using what Seidman and Rappaport (1974) called an educational pyramid. The structural premise of the model we use is that if life skills are taught at all levels of participation, it will maximize the positive effect that these skills can have for all the levels of participants involved in the program.

Life Skills Center staff are at the top of the pyramid. These individuals are skilled at training others. The next level of the pyramid is comprised of community and school personnel who coordinate the program in their setting. They participate in a condensed version of GOAL during which they perform all of the exercises that they will be teaching their students. Recently, college students have become part of this level. We have found college students to be effective teachers and supervisors. Often these college students participate as part of a service-learning course.

The third level on the pyramid is a group of high school student-leaders. These students are selected on criteria that suggest that they are positive role models for the younger students; they have a good academic record, leadership qualities, involvement in extracurricular activities, and a history of exemplary conduct both in and out of school.

Peer leaders are especially effective at teaching skills because they are able to use their own experiences and successes as an example. Because these high school students have grown up in the same neighborhoods, attended the same schools, and confronted similar roadblocks, they serve as important role models and are thus in an ideal position to be effective teachers.

The student-leaders are taught the GOAL program by the school and community personnel. If college students are involved, they can become the primary teachers as they serve as role models for the high school students. The student-leaders learn the concepts taught in the program and how to apply them to their own lives. In addition, they learn how to teach these skills to younger students, the program's ultimate audience. Leaders participate in sessions such as how to speak to groups, how to organize a class or lecture, how to be a good listener, how to transfer skills between different but similar areas (thus increasing the leaders' awareness of their competence in many dimensions), and how to work effectively with teams comprised of both peers and adults. The content of the training is skills oriented. Leaders also receive a detailed Leader Manual (Danish et al., 1992a) that provides information on how to teach skills, encourage discussion, communicate effectively, and give feedback and how to manage a group. For each workshop, the Leader Manual provides a checklist of what to accomplish and guidelines on what to say and how long each activity should take. Leaders are asked to complete all activities within the program themselves and to share their experiences and answers with the participants.

As the middle of the pyramid, the high school student-leaders come to a realization that they have been entrusted with influencing the future of students who are just a few years their junior. Not only do they have positive role models in the adults who work with the program, but they have guidance and an opportunity to take their first steps in the direction of becoming community leaders themselves. We believe it is critical to prepare a new generation of leaders from today's adolescents. Our perspective on leadership is based on DePree's (1989) definition: Leaders are people who facilitate others (individuals, families, organizations, and communities) in reaching their potential. This process involves (a) helping others identify goals related to their potential, (b) instilling in them the confidence to reach these goals, (c) teaching them to develop and implement a plan to attain these goals, and (d) encouraging them to share with others in their community what they have learned. In other words, leaders have the requisite life skills necessary to succeed, and the commitment and vision to use their skills and knowledge to help others succeed.

Following this training, the high school students teach GOAL in middle and junior high school or in after-school programs in groups of 2 to 3 high school leaders per 15 younger students. Supervision of their teaching is generally done by the college students who observe the sessions, provide feedback to the leaders, and meet with them prior to the session to review what is to be taught.

At the widest part of the pyramid, the middle/junior high school students are provided with not only the program's content, but with leaders they can relate to—people who were recently their age and who have managed to make the most of their time since then to reach their current level of success. These younger students can see the direct connection between themselves and their student-leaders, and can envision the day in a few years when they could be leaders themselves. So far, we have seen an encouraging number of these younger students return in several years to be high school student-leaders—a signal that the program is working.

Program Dissemination

Effective program implementation and dissemination require that the program developer become an instructional technologist. An effective intervention should be able to be replicated across sites and by different intervention agents. For replication to occur, the program must be formalized. When programs depend exclusively on the charisma of the leader, they are less likely to be successful. Issues such as how to train staff, implement and evaluate the program, and adapt it to the local needs of the setting must be addressed.

The GOAL program started in 1987 in Richmond, Virginia, as a result of a grant from the Center for Substance Abuse Prevention. Since 1987, we have also received grants from The Virginia's Governor's Council for Drug and Alcohol Prevention and the U.S. Department of Education to further develop GOAL and assess its effectiveness in Richmond. It was as a result of grants from the Athletic Footwear Association, the Sporting Goods Manufacturing Association, the U.S. Olympic Training Center, and the U.S. Diving Federation starting in 1992, however, that the GOAL program really started to be disseminated nationally.

The Athletic Footwear Association (AFA) and the Sporting Goods Manufacturing Association (SGMA) funded the Life Skills Center to disseminate GOAL to a number of cities nationally and to make it as transportable as possible. To facilitate dissemination, a Leader Manual (Danish, et. al, 1992a), a Student Activity Guide (Danish, et. al, 1992b) and an Operations Manual (Nellen & Goff, 1996) were developed. We also decided not to give or sell the program to communities, but to work with the communities to implement it. This decision was based on our belief that the more an intervention becomes removed from those who designed it, the more likely it is to lose some (if not all) of its essence. By "removed," we are referring to either lower levels of the pyramid or settings geographically separate from the Life Skills Center. By having high school students teach the program, early adolescents are being taught by the most credible source available; by offering the program to other communities, we are meeting our obligation as community psychologists to "give psychology away."

With the support of AFA and SGMA, we began to discuss implementing the GOAL program in Atlanta, Boston, Los Angeles, and New York. In each city, Life Skills Center staff initiated contact with school systems and with colleagues at local colleges and universities. In all four settings, we were able to establish and conduct programs in the schools during 1993-1994. Because of the commitment of one school system in Los Angeles County and the involvement of Dr. Margaret Gatz and her students at the University of Southern California, we have not only maintained the program for 3 years in Los Angeles, but have expanded it to several other schools in the area. It has even been translated into Spanish to meet the needs of students in several Los Angeles area schools.

The higher education institutions are involved in the training and supervising of the local high school student-leaders and overseeing the project in their individual cities. Our higher education partners include Georgia State University (Atlanta), Boston University (Boston), Michigan State University (Lansing), University of Southern California (Los Angeles), Columbia University (New York) and Norfolk State University (Virginia Beach). In New London, Connecticut, where the community decided to have college students, instead of high school students serve as leaders, five colleges are involved—the Coast Guard Academy, Connecticut College, Eastern Connecticut State University, Mitchell College, and the University of Connecticut. We believe that by involving colleges and universities committed to their communities, we can better ensure the development and maintenance of an ongoing program.

For the most part, GOAL has been taught in schools, usually by integrating it into the health curriculum. However, as a result of a grant from the U.S. Diving Federation, GOAL has been taught at

18 diving clubs throughout the country. High school-aged divers were trained at four regional USDF meets, and then these youth taught GOAL to younger divers in 2-day sessions at the 18 clubs. Combining sport activities and the GOAL program has also been done at some summer camps and Saturday morning programs in Richmond. Linking sports and life skill programs is a natural. First, life skills are similar to physical skills in the way that they are learned, through demonstration and practice. Second, many of the skills learned in sport are transferable to other life domains. These skills include the ability to perform under pressure, solve problems, meet deadlines or challenges, set goals, communicate, handle both success and failure, work with a team and within a system, and receive feedback and benefit from it. Third, sport is a pervasive activity throughout our society. Fourth, sport is a major influence in the development of identity and competence for adolescents (Danish, Nellen, & Owens, 1996).

In addition to after-school, sports-related programs, we are also developing other school-based components. Among the other components we have piloted in Richmond are Teachers Enhancing Adolescents' Competence and Hope (TEACH) and Creating Opportunities for Preventive Education (COPE). TEACH is a component to be taught the semester or year after GOAL is taught. Teachers are taught to review the skills taught in GOAL and then implement an expanded set of life skills as a means of reinforcing the skills taught earlier by the high school students. COPE is a component taught by counselors to prepare middle school and junior high school students for the transition to high school.

For several years, GOAL was taught under the auspices of AFA and SGMA. More recently, support has come from the private sector; and in the case of New London, Connecticut, from a human service agency. For example, in Richmond we have received support for different aspects of the Program from IBM, Broughton Systems, NationsBank, and Anheuser-Busch. Other communities have had similar private sector support. Such support is critical for a number of reasons. First, and perhaps foremost, having private sector support enables the community to feel a sense of local control—that is, that they are doing a program *with* the Life Skills Center, not that the Life Skills Center is doing a program *for* or *to* the community. Such a perspective results in a greater likelihood that the

GOAL program will continue and expand. Second, we cannot rely on the federal government to continue to develop and support these programs, because it doesn't have the resources. Moreover, many Americans don't want the federal government to run "social" programs; they feel government is inefficient and out of touch with the needs of the local community. The private sector is viewed as more responsive to communities in which they have a stake. Third, it is in the best interest of the private sector to be involved because they rely on well-trained and motivated employees, intelligent and successful customers, and thriving communities. Businesses are beginning to realize that if they are to succeed in the long run, their involvement in such activities is necessary.

To obtain support from the private sector, we have found the following guidelines to be helpful:

1. A program curriculum must be developed, printed, and available for dissemination so that interested private sector sponsors can see how the program operates. Some sponsors like to see that there is an operations manual as well.

2. When establishing relationships with other systems, either in the public or private sector, it is critical that a credible local person assist in developing contacts and serve as a champion for the program.

3. The cost of the dissemination must be reasonable and specific. The costs of some programs are so great that some have suggested, only somewhat sarcastically, that it would be better to give the money, rather than the program, to the participants. We like to use a per-person cost. In this way a local organization can sponsor or cosponsor a program, and if the cost is reasonable, make an ongoing commitment.

4. When a program focuses on life skills or some generic concept rather than on an individual health-compromising behavior, it significantly increases the attractiveness of the program. In some cities violence prevention has become the "hot" topic; in other cities it is pregnancy prevention or drug abuse prevention. Having a life skills focus enables one to meet a number of needs and to complement other programs often mandated by the state or local school boards. A life skills program is also less controversial in terms of its content. Finally, programs that have the potential to

enhance life skills are much more likely to be supported by private businesses as they see these skills as essential for future employees (Danish, 1995).

We receive numerous requests for information about the GOAL program. This is especially true because we have developed a partnership with the National Mental Health Association to offer their 325 affiliates the opportunity to implement GOAL in their communities. As a result, if schools or community groups contact us, we have developed a set of procedures. We ask that the groups identify school and community personnel to serve as a coordinating group for GOAL in their community. It is helpful for this group to include someone from a local college, if one exists. If the program is to be conducted in school, this group should also include school liaisons at each participating high school and junior high or middle school. Liaisons from the high schools are responsible for the selection of the GOAL leaders and for some of the training of the students as GOAL leaders. We have developed an application process and interview format to help schools in their selection process. Liaisons from the junior high or middle school facilitate the implementation of the delivery of the GOAL program in their schools. These organizational procedures help ensure that the program runs smoothly and enhances the chances that it will continue beyond the first year.

Life Skills Center staff then meet with the local GOAL group and any other staff involved in the implementation to train them how to teach the GOAL program. This training usually requires a day. Following the training, the local GOAL group implements the training program for the selected high school leaders. The training of the high school leaders generally takes two days and is often done at the campus of the participating college. Sometimes the high school students are taught the complete program, which requires a longer period of time.

Studies of Effectiveness

Rationale for Our Procedures

According to several researchers who have done primary prevention in school settings, the priorities of the researchers must be balanced with the priorities of administration and staff in the school whenever these programs are evaluated (Linney, 1989; Meyer, Miller, & Herman, 1994; Weissberg, Caplan, & Sivo, 1989). From the schools' perspective, the main purpose of any evaluation in a school is to assess how well the school meets academic expectations. Because of this, the value of any additional evaluation is weighed by how much it interferes with the priorities of academics. For example, the time it takes for students to complete self-report measures can interfere with time needed for attending class and doing homework. Therefore, to maintain a positive relationship with schools, those who evaluate prevention programs must think of the most nonintrusive, yet valid, methods of measurement possible. These recommendations are similar to the recent report of the Institute of Medicine concerning prevention (Mrazek & Haggerty, 1994).

Evaluation Results

Since 1992 when the current GOAL program was developed, process evaluations have occurred at sample schools in Richmond, Los Angeles, and New London. Data were collected in Richmond in 1992-1993, 1993-1994, and 1994-1995. During the first year, 173 sixth graders participated in the evaluation; during the second year, 187 sixth graders participated; and during the third year, 152 sixth graders were involved. During these years, the ethnicity of the students was 91% African American, 8% Caucasian American, and .5% each of Latino American and Asian American. These demographics are similar to the entire sixth-grade population in Richmond.

A total of 197 New London sixth graders received the program in 1993, and 230 in 1994. The population in the New London schools was approximately 30% African American, 30% Latino American, and 40% Caucasian American.

In Los Angeles, almost 1100 students have been taught GOAL, 367 of them in 1994-1995. In one school, the ethnicity of the students was 92% Latino American and 7% Asian American, with the remaining percentage divided between Caucasian and African Americans. In the second school, the ethnic breakdown was 70% Latino American and 30% African American. As a result of the large number of Latino Americans being taught the program, it has been translated into Spanish; however, the books used are bilingual.

Some of the major statistically significant findings were (a) participants learned the information the program teaches; (b) participants were able to achieve the goals they set, found the process easier than they expected, and thought they had learned quite a bit about how to set goals; (c) participants had better school attendance (as compared to a control group); (d) participants did not report the same increase in health-compromising behaviors including getting drunk, smoking cigarettes, drinking beer, and drinking liquor as was found in the control group (for boys only); (e) participants reported a decrease in violent and other problem behavior as compared to a control group who reported an increase in these behaviors (for boys only); and (f) participants thought the GOAL program was fun, useful, important, and something that would be helpful for their friends.

Focus groups of sixth-grade GOAL participants were used in Richmond in the Spring of 1993 to solicit the perceptions of the participants themselves (Meyer, 1994). The students who participated in these focus groups were a diverse group that paralleled the larger sample. The overall picture presented from the focus groups was of young individuals who viewed the process of working on, and reaching for, their goals as something they had developed during the sixth grade. The participants attributed their participation in GOAL with facilitating this process. They also reported that GOAL had helped them focus on the steps needed to reach a goal, instead of focusing only on the outcome. The students wanted to continue to use these abilities throughout their lives. They thought that GOAL provided the right type of learning environment for them to explore their options with older peers who cared about them. Often, the settings they described in their daily lives in school and at home did not provide role models who cared about the students' personal goals

The GOAL program, then, has been well received in the cities where it has been taught and evaluated. We believe that the results of the focus groups are extremely important for demonstrating what occurs in a peer-led health promotion program. For example, the focus group participants reported that they currently focused more on the learning process of reaching a goal than they had prior to participating in GOAL. We are presently examining other instruments to help us measure the impact of the intervention.

Implications and Perspectives for the Future

All the interventions in the world are not going to eliminate adolescents' involvement in health-compromising behaviors. However, there are effective programs that can *reduce* such behaviors. The implementation of these programs will be well worth the expense, given the tremendous costs that health-compromising behaviors exact from our society in terms of health care, lost productivity in the workplace, and welfare participation. Unfortunately, too often it seems that society looks for easy answers, such as teaching adolescents to "just say no." For programs to be effective, they must be comprehensive; *telling* adolescents what to do and what not to do just won't work. Life skills are *taught* not *caught*.

Although the importance of preventing health-compromising behavior should not be minimized, when we focus primarily on problems, we tend to lose sight of what young adolescents need to succeed in life. Indeed, this type of negative focus in programs tends to limit their effectiveness (Keefe, 1994). Successful programs teach participants not just what to avoid, but more important, how to succeed. As noted earlier, the definition of "success" will differ for different individuals. However, in general terms, successful adolescents have attained the life skills necessary for effective functioning in the family, school, and community. These skills are similar to those described by the Task Force on Education of Young Adolescents (1989) as the five desired outcomes or characteristics for every young adolescent: to process information from multiple sources and communicate clearly; to be en route to a lifetime of meaningful work by learning how to learn and therefore being able to adapt to different educational and working environments; to be a good citizen by participating in community activities and feeling concern for, and connection to, the well-being of others; to be a caring and ethical individual by acting on one's convictions about right and wrong; and to be a healthy person (Task Force on Education of Young Adolescents, 1989).

However, it is not just well-meaning but naive community members who are holding us back from helping develop healthier adolescents. Developers of effective interventions have been short-sighted. Many of us have focused on applying our interventions in one community and have ignored one of the keys concepts in psychology—replication. Initially, the issue of replication related only to research. However, if we are to develop a science of primary prevention, we need to be concerned about this issue too. We need interventions that are not only effective in the domains or settings in which they are initially implemented, but that can be replicated and transferred to other settings as well, and that are sufficiently cost-effective that they can be transferred without the need for a significant outlay of federal funds (Danish, 1995).

Clearly, we need to make certain that our programs are effective. However, we have allowed the pursuit of federal funds to subvert our task—to design, implement, evaluate, *and* disseminate effective prevention programs. Until we expend as much effort on dissemination as we do on the other areas, we have not achieved our mandate as community intervention agents.

References

Aloise-Young, P., Graham, J., & Hansen, W. (1994). Peer influences on smoking initiation during early adolescence: A comparison of group members and group outsiders. *Journal of Applied Psychology, 79*(2), 281-287.

Caplan, M., Weissberg, R., Grober, J., Sivo, P. Grady, K., & Jacoby, C. (1992). Social competence promotion with inner-city and suburban young adolescents: Effects on social adjustment and alcohol use. *Journal of Consulting and Clinical Psychology, 60*(1), 56-63.

Catalano, R. F., Hawkins, J. D., White, H., & Padino, R. (1985). *Predicting marijuana use and delinquency in two longitudinal studies.* Paper presented at the annual meeting of the American Society of Criminology, San Diego, CA.

Comer, J. (1988). Educating poor minority children. *Scientific American, 250*(5), 42-48.

Crockett, L., & Petersen, A. (1993). Adolescent development: Health risks and opportunities for health promotion. In S. Millstein, A. Petersen, & E. Nightingale (Eds.), *Promoting the health of adolescents* (pp. 13-37). New York: Oxford.

Danish, S. (1995). Reflections on the status and future of community psychology. *Community Psychologist, 28*, 16-18.

Danish, S., D'Augelli, A., & Ginsberg, M. (1984). Life development intervention: Promotion of mental health through the development of competence. In

S. Brown & R. Lent (Eds.), *Handbook of counseling psychology* (pp. 520-544). New York: John Wiley.

Danish, S., & Donohue, T. (1995). Understanding media's influence on the development of antisocial and prosocial behavior. In R. Hampton, P. Jenkins, & T. Gullotta (Eds.), *Preventing violence in America* (pp. 133-156). Thousand Oaks, CA: Sage.

Danish, S. J., & Hale, B. D. (1983). Sport psychology: Teaching skills to athletes and coaches. *Journal of Physical Education, Recreation, and Dance, 54*(8), 11-13, 80-81.

Danish, S. J., Mash, J. M., Howard, C. W., Curl, S. J., Meyer, A. L., Owens, S., & Kendall, K. (1992a). *Going for the Goal leader manual.* Department of Psychology, Virginia Commonwealth University.

Danish, S. J., Mash, J. M., Howard, C. W., Curl, S. J., Meyer, A. L., Owens, S., & Kendall, K. (1992b). *Going for the Goal student activity manual.* Department of Psychology, Virginia Commonwealth University.

Danish, S., Nellen, V., & Owens, S. (1996). Community-based programs for adolescents: Using sport to teach life skills. In J. L. Van Raalte & B. W. Brewer (Eds.), *Exploring sport and exercise psychology* (pp. 205-228). Washington, DC: APA Books.

DePree, M. (1989). *Leadership is an art.* New York: Doubleday.

Erikson, E. H. (1968). *Identity, youth and crisis.* New York: Norton.

Farrell, A. D., Danish, S. J., & Howard, C. W. (1992). Relationship between drug use and other problem behaviors in urban adolescents. *Journal of Consulting and Clinical Psychology, 60*(5), 705-712.

Gass, M. (1984). Programming the transfer of learning in adventure education. In R. Kraft & M. Sakofs (Eds.), *The theory of experiential education* (2nd ed.). Boulder, CO: Association for Experiential Education.

GAO Report. (1992). *Adolescent drug use prevention.* U.S. General Accounting Office (GAO/PEMD-92-2).

Gullotta, T. (1990). Preface. In T. P. Gullotta, G. R. Adams, & R. Montemayor (Eds.), *Developing social competency in adolescence* (pp. 7-8). Newbury Park, CA: Sage.

Hines, M. H. (1988). The effect of first year of matching on the self-esteem of big and little brothers. *Journal of Humanistic Education and Development, 27,* 61-68.

Johnston, L. D., O'Malley, P. M., & Bachman, J. G. (1987). *National trends in drug use and related factors among American high school students and young adults, 1975-1986.* Rockville, MD: National Institute on Drug Abuse.

Jones, J. B., & Philliber, S. (1983). Sexually active but not pregnant: A comparison of teens who risk and teens who plan. *Journal of Youth and Adolescence, 12,* 235-251.

Jurich, A. P., & Andrews, D. (1984). Self-concepts of rural early adolescent juvenile delinquents. *Journal of Early Adolescence, 4*(1), 41-46.

Keefe, K. (1994). Perceptions of normative social pressure in attitudes toward alcohol use: Changes during adolescence. *Journal of Studies on Alcohol, 35*(1), 46-54.

Klerman, L. (1993). The influence of economic factors on health-related behaviors in adolescents. In S. Millstein, A. Petersen, & E. Nightingale (Eds.), *Promoting the health of adolescents* (pp. 38-57). New York: Oxford.

Linney, J. (1989). Optimizing research strategies in the schools. In L. Bond & B. Compas (Eds.), *Primary prevention and promotion in the schools* (pp. 50-76). Newbury Park, CA: Sage.

Millstein, S. (1993). A view of health from the adolescent's perspective. In S. Millstein, A. Petersen, & E. Nightingale (Eds.), *Promoting the health of adolescents* (pp. 97-118). New York: Oxford.

Meyer, A. (1994). *The effectiveness of a peer-led positive youth development program for sixth graders.* Unpublished dissertation, Penn State University, State College, PA.

Meyer, A., Miller, S., & Herman, M. (1994). Balancing the priorities of evaluation with the priorities of the setting: A focus on positive youth development programs in school settings. *Journal of Primary Prevention, 12*(4), 95-113.

Mrazek, P., & Haggerty, R. (Eds.). (1994). *Reducing risks for mental disorders.* Washington, DC: National Academy Press.

Nellen, V., & Goff, A. (1995). *Operations manual for the GOAL program.* Richmond, VA: Department of Psychology, Virginia Commonwealth University.

Newcomb, M. D., Bentler, P. M., & Collins, C. (1986). Alcohol use and dissatisfaction with self and life: A longitudinal analysis of young adults. *Journal of Drug Issues, 16,* 479-494.

Perry, C., & Jessor, R. (1985). The concept of health promotion and the prevention of adolescent drug abuse. *Health Education Quarterly, 12*(2), 169-184.

Petersen, A., & Hamburg, B. (1986). Adolescence: A developmental approach to problems and psychopathology. *Behavior Therapy, 17,* 480-499.

Richardson, J., Dwyer, K., Hansen, W., Dent, C., Johnson, C., Sussman, S., Brannon, B., & Flag, B. (1989). Substance use among eighth-grade students who took care of themselves. *Pediatrics, 84*(3), 556-566.

Seidman, E., & Rappaport, J. (1974). The educational pyramid: A paradigm for training, research, and manpower utilization in community psychology. *American Journal of Community Psychology 2,* 119-130.

Snyder, M., & Omoto, A. (1992). Who helps and why? The psychology of AIDS volunteerism. In S. Spacapan & S. Oskamp (Eds.), *Helping and being helped: Naturalistic studies* (pp. 231-239). Newbury Park, CA: Sage.

Task Force on Education of Young Adolescents (1989). *Turning points: Preparing American youth for the 21st century.* New York: Carnegie Corporation.

Weissberg, R., Caplan, M., & Sivo, P. (1989). A new conceptual framework for establishing school-based social competence promotion programs. In L. Bond & B. Compas (Eds.), *Primary prevention and promotion in the schools* (pp. 255-296). Newbury Park, CA: Sage.

Zelnik, M., & Kantner, J. (1977). Sexual and contraceptive experience of young unmarried women in the United States, 1976. *Family Planning Perspectives, 9,* 55-71.

CHAPTER 14

Teen Education and Employment Network

LAURIE J. BAUMAN

SUSAN M. COUPEY

CHERYL KOEBER

JENNIFER L. LAUBY

ELLEN J. SILVER

RUTH E. K. STEIN

Epidemiologic estimates of the number of children and adolescents affected by chronic health conditions range from 5% to 30% (Cadman et al., 1986; Gortmaker & Sappenfield, 1984; Newacheck, McManus, & Fox, 1991; Newacheck & Taylor, 1992; Pless & Pinkerton, 1975; Pless & Wadsworth, 1988; Starfield & Pless, 1980). Although estimates vary due to differences in the definition and measurement of chronic health conditions (Stein, Bauman, Westbrook, Coupey, & Ireys, 1995), most experts believe that between 15% and 20% of children are affected. Thus, a substantial proportion of children grow up with an ongoing health condition such as asthma, diabetes, sickle cell disease, epilepsy, or cancer, or with a physical disability from an illness, birth defect, or injury. Due to advances in medical technology and treatment, the large majority of youngsters with chronic conditions and disabilities live into adulthood.

Many studies have described the psychological and physical burdens that a serious illness or handicap can place on children, adolescents, and their families (Haggerty, 1981; Klerman, 1981; Newacheck et al., 1991; Fox, 1991; Newacheck & Taylor, 1992; Pless & Nolan, 1991; President's Commission on Mental Health, 1978; Select Panel on the Promotion of Child Health, 1981; Stein, 1988). The Isle of Wight studies (Rutter, Tizard, & Whitmore, 1970) and the Rochester Child Health Study (Haggerty, Roghmann, & Pless, 1975) were among the first to show that the prevalence of psychological disorder in youngsters with chronic health conditions was higher than among healthy children. Since that time, data have accumulated showing that the psychological and social dysfunction accompanying chronic health conditions may be more disabling than the conditions themselves (Pless & Pinkerton, 1975; Stein, 1988; Steinhauser, Mushin, & Rae-Grant, 1974). Adolescents and young adults with chronic illnesses tend to experience higher than expected rates of psychological problems (Gortmaker et al., 1989; Sanger, Copeland, & Edwards, 1991; Sawyer, Crettenden, & Toogood, 1986; Siegel, Golden, & Gough et al. 1990), including poorer adjustment and lower self-esteem (Beck & Carpenter, 1986; Campbell, Hayden, & Davenport, 1977; Stern, Norman, & Zevon, 1993); lack of initiative, underachievement, less future directedness, and less independence (Orr, Weller, & Satterwhite, 1984; Pless & Wadsworth, 1988); more behavioral problems (Apter, Aviv, & Kaminer et al., 1991); and poorer social competence (Apter et al., 1991).

If, in the face of chronic illness, an adolescent's competence and self-esteem can be sustained and enhanced, prevention of poor social and psychological outcome may be possible. According to LeCroy and Rose (1986), the highest form of primary prevention is the active promotion or enhancement of generic components of competence. The adolescent patient, according to Hamburg and Varenhorst (1982), may be especially responsive to efforts to raise the overall level of competence and to develop a sense of mastery that may be generalized to other life tasks. "The effects of competent interchanges with the environment are clear—one achieves, is promoted, rewarded. . . . But the internal, self-reward consequences of self-perceived competence are likely to be even stronger" (Ricks, 1980, p. 131). Adolescents with a strong sense of internal and external competency are better prepared to engage in the struggle for autonomy and to prepare for their future.

As a result of our work with adolescents with chronic illnesses, we designed a preventive intervention designed to promote self-esteem and competence and prevent mental health problems. The Teen Education and Employment Network (TEEN) aimed to enhance the competency of adolescents with chronic health conditions and ultimately to help them more successfully accomplish developmental tasks and achieve psychological well-being. The TEEN Program is a low-cost, short-term intervention consisting of two parts: a 12-session social and communication skills program, and a 4-month, part-time job internship in a community agency in a helping role. The program is based on our belief that the psychological distress that can occur in this population may be preventable through building competence, teaching communication skills, and providing a concrete job experience. TEEN was developed especially for adolescents served by two large hospitals in the Bronx. These adolescents were vulnerable not only because they had a chronic illness, but also because they had other risk factors for poor mental health, particularly poverty. Because this population was at high risk for many different reasons, the TEEN intervention was designed to build resources and provide skills that could protect against different kinds of threats to their mental health.

Previous Research

Effects of Chronic Illness on Psychological Status

Although adolescence is no longer considered a time of inevitable crisis (Simmons & Blyth, 1987; Smith, 1983), it is still acknowledged as a stressful transition (Coleman, 1978; Rutter, 1979). According to Erikson (1985), it is a pivotal developmental stage during which identity formation takes place, preparing the way for future tasks of young adulthood (Driscoll, 1986; Erikson, 1985; Smith, 1983). Evidence suggests that having a chronic physical illness can interfere with normal development (Abrahamson, Ash, & Nash, 1979; Drotar & Bush, 1985; Gunther, 1985; Pless &

Pinkerton, 1975; Sussman, Hollenbeck, Nannis, & Strope, 1980). Lindemann (1981) points out that the developmental tasks of identity formation, desire for independence, and experimentation with new lifestyles is especially complicated for chronically ill teens. For example, teens with a chronic illness may alter medication and diet out of pure curiosity, the need to achieve control and independence, or to "test limits" (Partridge, Garner, Thompson, & Cherry, 1972). In our view there are two mechanisms through which having a chronic illness can threaten mental health and the achievement of normal developmental tasks: by internal processes, and by having limitations imposed on them by adults.

Internal Processes

Although both healthy and chronically ill teens can respond similarly to the developmental demands of adolescence (Kellerman, Zeltzer, Ellenberg, Dash, & Rigler, 1980; Orr, Weller, & Satterwhite, 1984), the stress of a chronic illness may create additional risk (Blumberg, Lewis, & Susman, 1984; Orr et al., 1984). Typical adolescent concerns about body image can be aggravated in chronically ill teenagers (Richardson, Hastorf, & Dornbusch, 1964; Smith, 1983; Sullivan, 1979; Swift, Seidman, & Stein, 1967) leading to a sense of vulnerability, damage, and an impaired sense of self (Hamburg & Varenhorst, 1982). Boyle, Sant'Agrese, Sack, Millican, and Kulczycki (1976) found four sources of psychological stress that could lead to emotional disturbance for young adults with cystic fibrosis: altered physical appearance, strained interpersonal relationships, conflicts in upbringing, and increased awareness of death.

Imposed Limitations

An adolescent's illness takes on new meaning under the pressure for increased autonomy and independence. Movement away from the family may be hindered by actual dependence on caretakers and family members. Identity consolidation may also be obstructed by the generally negative or paternalistic response of the community to people with disabilities. Opportunities for normal peer group interaction may be limited or altered. The presence of disability or visible stigmata may inhibit normal experimentation and otherwise preempt the trial and error investigations that ordinarily provide a pathway toward developmental maturation. In addition, adolescents' struggle for independence may be compromised by the protectiveness of those around them (Dodrill, 1983; Lesser, Luders, Wyllie, Dinner, & Morris, 1986; Ziegler, 1981). Concerned parents may actively deter independent strivings, subverting adolescents' confidence about their ability to handle the responsibilities of their own health care.

Competence as a Protective Factor

Recent work indicates that competence is a useful construct for understanding adaptive human behavior (Danish & D'Augelli, 1980; Harter, 1983; LeCroy & Rose, 1986; Ricks, 1980, Tyler & Gatz, 1977). Three general approaches to the study of competency have been taken. The first, growing from behaviorist and social learning traditions, views competency as a set of behaviors or responses (social skills) (Goldfried & D'Zurilla, 1969); the second defines competence as coping behavior (Hamburg & Varenhorst, 1982; Ricks, 1980); and the third, arising from developmental psychology, focuses on a sense of perceived competence as an important component of an individual's self-worth. Harter (1983, 1986) argues that competence is a collection of "domain-specific judgments about one's competency," and that *perception* of competence is related to global self-esteem. Furthermore, people who like themselves are likely to perform well in areas they value (Harter, 1986).

Chronic illness can compromise self-esteem as well as interfere with the attainment of social competence. Self-judgments about one's physical appearance and competence contribute to one's sense of perceived competency (Harter, 1986). Both of these dimensions may be compromised in youngsters with a chronic illness. Furthermore, having an illness that imposes restrictions or numerous medical regimens can interfere with an adolescent's ability to participate in normal activities, which, in turn, limits the opportunity to develop social skills. Finally, chronic illness may be associated with reduced sense of control over health and future, which makes the development of competence problematic (Kellerman et al., 1980). Wolman, Resnick and Harris et al. (1994) found that, in contrast to their healthy peers, adolescents with a wide range of chronic conditions had poorer emotional well-being. The most important predictors of well-being were body image, family connectedness, having a disability, worry about peer relationships, and worry about school and future work.

Adolescent identity and self-concept can be developed through vocational experiences (Jordaan & Super, 1974). However, a chronic disorder may interfere with employability (Smith, 1983). Several studies of chronically ill adults have demonstrated difficulties in obtaining or holding a job. Teta et al. (1986) found substantial evidence that long-term survivors of child and adolescent cancer had experienced more rejection from the armed forces, college, and employment than their siblings. Juul-Jensen (1974) found that 27% of patients with epilepsy encountered occupational difficulties. Although some employment problems are associated with physical limitations, most chronically ill teenagers and adults are able to work. When given suitable employment, the job performance, absence rate, and on-the-job accident record of employees who have epilepsy, diabetes, or hemophilia are not different from others (Epilepsy Foundation of America, 1975; Risch & Rose, 1957). Underemployment is due in part to erroneous stereotypes held by employers and insurance carriers about employability, and in part to patients' negative self-image or poor social adaptation (Lindemann, 1981).

Causal Model
for Intervention

Several general theoretical stress models guided our research and intervention with adolescents with chronic health conditions (see Wheaton, 1991 for a more complete review of these models). The *Differential Vulnerability* model emphasizes that people have different coping resources based on their location in the social structure, interpersonal networks, or personality characteristics. This literature has generated the tradition of research on the buffering effect of social support. The *Trait Theory* approach to stress claims that stressors vary in their effects on mental health because the events differ in their characteristics (e.g., undesirability, uncontrollability, unpredictability, event magnitude). This position focuses on the importance of stress characteristics for identifying stress potential.

The *Contextual* approach to stress emphasizes that stress does not occur in a vacuum. One must consider other facts about an individual's life circumstances to understand the stressfulness of events. *Crisis Theory* suggests that normal personality growth occurs through resolution of normative developmental crises and stressors in the environment. Resolution does not imply permanent solution so much as a reconciliation or "settling" of the meaning of the event. This literature, which argues that stressful events represent a challenge and an opportunity for growth, has been used in some measure to incorporate notions of social competence and mastery into stress research.

Each of these theoretical models contributed to the conceptual model that guided the development and evaluation of TEEN. A simplified version of this model is presented in Figure 14.1. The context box (based on Contextual and Differential Vulnerability theories) includes background and social variables that may influence psychological risk status. Many of the adolescents in the TEEN program come from minority ethnic groups and low income families. Others may have been raised in single-parent families or have experienced a large number of stressful life events.

Trait Theory is reflected in the box marked "Illness Factors." We hypothesized several direct and indirect ways or "paths" through which having a chronic health condition in adolescence might increase psychological morbidity. For example, adolescents with chronic health conditions are at risk for psychological morbidity due to physical disability, unpredictability of symptoms, or other characteristics of their condition. They are also more likely to experience employment problems due to employer reluctance to hire those with chronic diseases, lack of a job history, and poor job skills. Because employment in the teenage years is one way adolescents learn about adult roles and responsibilities, the lack of opportunity to rehearse such roles may in turn inhibit developmental progress.

Chronic illness may also directly reduce internal competence (self-esteem). Many adolescents, already sensitive to body image and perceived individual inadequacy, see their illness as stigmatizing, which diminishes them in the eyes of their major reference group, their peers. Thus, in addition to the negative effects that a chronic health condition can have on psychological health, it can also affect potential resources (competence) that can be mechanisms

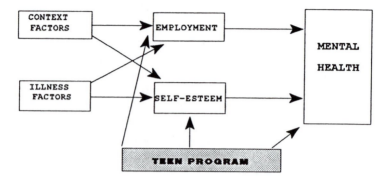

Figure 14.1. Teen Conceptual Model

mechanisms mediating the relationship between chronic illness and psychological disability. This box is based in part on Crisis Theory.

The TEEN program (the intervention box in the model) aimed to influence both directly and indirectly the *process* that the model describes. TEEN was hypothesized to increase competence and also have a direct effect on mental health. Although we describe one specific outcome, mental health, in this chapter, we hypothesized that TEEN would facilitate the achievement of developmental tasks of adolescence. We also thought that other benefits might accrue to participants in TEEN. These were not explicit program goals, yet because we were aiming to increase internal resources available to teenagers and to provide skills that are generalizable, these new competencies and experiences could have multiple effects beyond those noted—for example, decreased school dropout rates, decreased rates of "irresponsible" alcohol and drug use, later initiation of sexual intercourse, increased use of contraception, and fewer unplanned pregnancies. These outcomes have been found in other similar competence-building programs.

Competence-Building Programs

Competence Through Skills Training

A large literature has documented that a sense of competency can be developed by teaching adolescents social skills (Le Croy & Rose,

1986; Sarason & Sarason, 1981; Simmons & Parsons, 1983; Tyler & Gatz, 1977). Ricks (1970) described more than 20 ways to enhance competency in teenagers, ways he describes as "slow going and unglamourous," such as assisting with reading, vocational guidance, and teaching simple social skills (p. 143). The aim of such efforts is to strengthen the adolescent and provide areas of competence that can compensate for areas of incompetence or weakness.

Competence Through a Helping Job

The impact of part-time work for adolescents has been the subject of some study. Some voice concerns that working during the school year can interfere with academic achievement and reduce opportunities for peer interaction and socializing. Others point to the opportunity work provides to build self-esteem, self-reliance, social responsibility, and job skills such as punctuality and attendance. The Carnegie Commission Report (1980) recommended that teenagers increase their participation in employment to decrease crime and delinquency. In a study of adolescent work, Greenberger and Steinberger (1986) found that although work has the potential to teach self-reliance and self-management and decision-making skills, the typical jobs teenagers hold do not provide these opportunities. Instead, their work generally involves highly routinized activity with little task variety.

In contrast, considerable evidence exists that the experience of being involved or employed in a helping relationship facilitates personal growth. The "helper therapy" principle (Riessman, 1965) states that the person who helps—be it tutor, counselor, or provider of service of any kind—benefits as much or more than one helped. Both empirical and clinical evidence suggests that Riessman's concept works in many contexts—mental health (e.g., Cowen, Leibowitz, & Leibowitz, 1968; Greenblatt & Kantor, 1962; Holzberg, Gewirtz, & Ebner, 1964; Schiebe, 1965); social services; and education (Gartner, Kohler, & Riessman, 1971). McManus (1982) evaluated a peer counselor program and found extensive evidence of personal growth in counselors via the helper therapy principle. In addition to personal growth, those who participated in mental health training and service programs benefit in a wide range of ways, including increased positive self-image, confidence, assertiveness, and independence (Dineen, Clark, & Risley, 1977; Durlak, 1973); identity formation (Schiebe, 1965); formation of career choice (Greenblatt & Kantor, 1962); greater self-understanding (Reinherz, 1962; Stollak, 1969); greater self acceptance (Holzberg et al., 1964); and increased social interaction skills and empathy (Woudenberg & Payne, 1978). Buck (1977) reported a peer counseling program implemented in an urban high school in which counselors perceived an increase in their communication and problem-solving skills. By using skills to help others, individuals' progress in social, academic, and emotional areas may be enhanced (Zunker & Brown, 1966).

Peer Counseling Programs

We chose peer counseling as the program strategy for our preventive intervention because it is designed to enhance social competence. One part of social competence is *social cognition* (Shantz, 1975); that is, how adolescents infer and understand others' feelings and behavior. Aspects of social cognition include problem solving (Spivak & Shure, 1973) and role taking (Piaget, 1954). Social competence also includes empathy, control of impulsive behavior, and building social skills (Sarason, 1981), all topics that traditionally are included in peer counseling programs.

Prior to developing TEEN, we developed and piloted a peer counseling program that provided listening, communication, and counseling skills to adolescents with and without chronic health conditions. Successful graduates were hired for 6 months to counsel hospitalized teenagers with various health problems. The training program we used had been conducted successfully in a suburban high school setting with significant enhancement of ego development occurring among its participants (Cosse, 1985). We evaluated the effectiveness of the program in several ways (Silver, Coupey, Bauman, Doctors, & Boeck, 1992). Trainees ($n = 29$) completed pre- and posttests of psychiatric symptoms and were evaluated for counseling skills by the group leader, who was unaware of their illness status or their scores on any measure. A comparison sample of adolescents under 18 years also was assessed before and after an equivalent 3-month time period ($n = 28$). Psychological status did not change in the comparison sample or for two subgroups of graduates: (a) those judged adequate in counseling skills but who declined to take counseling jobs and (b) those not invited to become counselors after training. Only the subgroup who later accepted jobs exhibited improved mental health. All follow-up testing was done before trainees knew if they would be offered counseling jobs, so eventual participation was not a factor that could have influenced these measures. Chronic illness was not related to success in training or to mental health outcomes for any group. The results suggested that, for adolescents who were psychologically ready for the emotionally demanding role of becoming a peer counselor, the opportunity to become involved in the training program may have enhanced their mental health.

There are many other examples of peer counseling programs. Although some have been evaluated, the outcomes usually focus on academic achievement, achievement of particular counseling skills or empathy (e.g., Cooker & Cherchia, 1976; Rapp, Dworkin, & Moss, 1978). A few programs have systematically examined the benefits of peer counseling programs for mental health, self-esteem, or competence. Thompson (1986) found that high school students trained as peer group facilitators were less dogmatic, more open, and more self-confidant after participating in training to develop communication behaviors. In an earlier study, Cognetta and Sprinthall (1978) described a program in which high school students were taught instructional, listening, and communication skills and then were allowed to take on the actual teacher role with younger students. Participants improved significantly on two measures of psychological and ethical maturity, whereas a comparison group of students showed no growth on either measure. Woudenberg and Payne (1978) examined the psychological effects of a peer counseling training program that involved both formal presentations and role-playing sessions with the goal of teaching college student volunteers to become effective listeners and advocates for other students. The counselor trainees showed significant decreases in interpersonal problems and increases in empathy, whereas a comparison group of undergraduates did not change on these same measures.

The TEEN Program

The TEEN program aimed to provide a variety of skills and experiences that would build internal and external competence in inner-city adolescents with chronic health conditions. These included social and communication skills; formation of a peer support group while in training; availability of the trainer as a role model and mentor; the experience of rehearsing adult job roles in a safe environment; successful completion and graduation from the training program, which was a marker of achievement; and the experience of being in a helping relationship with others.

Program Structure

The TEEN program was composed of two parts: a formal communication and social skills *training,* and a part-time job *internship*. The training consisted of twelve 90-minute sessions, held over a 2-month period. Approximately 20 to 35 adolescents were trained together as a cohort. Adolescents were paid $4.50/hour during training, with $1.75 from each session withheld and paid as a bonus at the last session if attendance was adequate to graduate (minimum 10 sessions). Adolescents were not paid for missed sessions.

Session Content and Training Techniques

The training devoted 10 sessions to social and communication skills and 2 sessions to job-related skills. The skills provided in the first 10 sessions were communication and interpersonal skills (e.g., open- vs. closed-ended questions, reflective questions, clarification, body language, making requests, speaking to adults) as well as problem-solving skills (Carkhuff, 1987; Hamburg & Varenhorst, 1972; LeCroy & Rose, 1986). These 10 sessions built on one another so that skills became more integrated and sophisticated as time went on. The two sessions on employment applied the general skills provided in the first part of the training to the world of work, including the job interview (e.g., how to give a positive summary of one's eligibility and how to answer questions clearly, concisely, and pleasantly). We also covered self-presentation and etiquette, dress and grooming, work expectations, and potential problem situations on the job such as conflict with one's boss or coworkers, and illness-related decisions (Azrin, Flores, & Kaplan, 1975; Schinke, Gilchrist, Smith, & Wong, 1978a, 1978b). During this time, teenagers were guided through the process of obtaining working permits and helped to open a bank account.

The trainers opened each session with a presentation of a skill and then modeled the particular behavior during the session. Trainees practiced the behavior in dyads or triads using techniques such as modeling, role playing, coaching, feedback, and positive and negative reinforcement. Because level of adjustment correlates with adolescents' effectiveness in the groups in which they participate (Chester & Fox, 1966; Himber, 1970; Schmuck, 1968), during the first few sessions, trainers facilitated the formation of a peer support group (i.e., a peer community). Peer groups were formed through teaming up three or four participants to share feelings, better understand their own and others' behaviors, and develop higher levels of empathy (Buck, 1977). Trainers worked hard to gain participants' trust and become confidants and mentors. They also helped facilitate individual progress and troubleshoot with program and personal concerns. The experience of successfully completing and graduating from the training program had enormous meaning to the participants. Completion of the program was a marker of achievement and was formally acknowledged in a graduation ceremony. This can have ego-enhancing effects independent from skills learned.

The Job Experience

All adolescents who completed the training program (i.e., attended 10 of 12 sessions) were offered job internships, regardless of skill level. Participants were given a paid position in a community agency after school or on weekends for 4 to 10 hours per week for approximately four months. Adolescents were placed in one of four types of helping positions: homework helper for younger children in community centers, teacher's aide in day care centers, geriatric visitors in nursing homes, and peer counselors in an adolescent pregnancy program.

All job internships had several criteria in common. First, each adolescent was supervised by both the TEEN coordinator and a supervisor from the job site. This model permitted the continued direct support of the TEEN coordinator during the job experience.

Second, job supervisors were oriented by the coordinator about the adolescent's skills, our expectations, and appropriate duties on the job. Third, all jobs involved relationships with others in which the TEEN participant was in a helping role. We limited the job opportunities to "helping" positions for two reasons: It was an important aspect of the theoretical rationale for the program's potential efficacy; and it was important methodologically that the job experiences be as similar as possible, so that idiosyncratic aspects of the jobs themselves did not add error to the evaluation of the program's outcomes. Fourth, adolescents worked between 4 and 10 hours per week at a consistent hourly wage of $5.00/hour, which was paid by the TEEN program. We paid the salaries of TEEN participants (rather than the placement site) to assure availability of quality placements, to guarantee that TEEN participants would actually perform helping roles, and to retain control over job content.

Once each month during the job sequence, participants were invited back as a group for booster sessions and a discussion of how the jobs were working out. This allowed participants to use the peer community they had established during the training period for problem solving and support. They also were encouraged to call the program coordinator should any problems arise.

The Evaluation of TEEN'S Effectiveness

Design

The evaluation of TEEN employed a pretest multiple posttest randomized experimental design (Coupey, Bauman, Lauby, Koeber, & Stein, 1991). Assessment occurred five times: at baseline (before assignment to the intervention) and at four follow-ups conducted at 2 months (equivalent to posttraining for the experimental group), at 6 months (after completion of the 4-month job experience for the experimental group), and at 12 and 18 months postbaseline.

Sample

Adolescents who were 14 through 17 years old were eligible for TEEN if they had an ongoing physical health condition and spoke

English. Adolescents were identified as having a chronic health condition through hospital discharge and clinic records. We excluded those with a serious sensory deficit, speech impairment, motor disability, or mental retardation and adolescents under treatment for a behavioral or psychiatric condition. To normalize the TEEN program and avoid stigmatizing these adolescents any further, healthy adolescents also were recruited by allowing index adolescents to bring a same-sex friend to participate in the study. This strategy had the additional benefit of increasing participation, because many adolescents resist joining new activities without their friends. Prior to randomization, we excluded those who scored higher than two standard deviations above the mean on the Global Symptom Inventory of the BSI (Derogatis, 1977), and those who were functionally illiterate based on a brief reading screen using the Wide Range Achievement Test (WRAT). Six cohorts of adolescents were enrolled in the study, giving us a total of 428 eligible subjects.

Measures

Data were collected using face-to-face interviews and self-administered questionnaires. The interview covered medical care and illness, schooling, previous employment, household composition, risk behaviors, and demographic characteristics. Self-esteem was measured using the Rosenberg Self-Esteem Scale, a 10-item scale designed for adolescents (Rosenberg, 1965). It has been used extensively in the literature and has impressive validity and reliability. Social competence was measured using the Harter Self-Perception Profile for Adolescents (Harter, 1986) which consists of 45 items divided into nine subscales (scholastic competence, social acceptance, athletic competence, physical appearance, conduct/morality, job competence, romantic appeal, close friendship, and global self-worth). The subscales are used separately and have adequate internal consistency reliabilities (.80 or higher). Mental health was measured using the Brief Symptom Inventory (BSI) a self-administered 58-item version of the SCL-90-R. It includes nine symptom subdimensions (somatization, obsessive-compulsive, interpersonal sensitivity, depression, anxiety, phobic anxiety, psychoticism, paranoid ideation, and hostility). The Global Severity Index (GSI) is a summary score reflecting the number and intensity of symptoms. The scale has a high level of internal consistency and temporal stability (Derogatis, 1977).

Results

Sample Characteristics and Study Participation.

Descriptive data about study participants are presented in Table 14.1. Of the 428 eligible adolescents, 278 were randomized to the experimental group and 150 to the control group. We randomized a larger number of adolescents to the experimental group because we expected that not all adolescents would participate fully in the intervention, and we wanted to make sure that the number of program graduates would be sufficient for analysis. Index adolescents and their healthy friends were randomized in pairs. There were no significant differences between the experimental and control groups at baseline in demographic characteristics. They were similar on all but one psychological measure; the experimental group was lower than the control group on the Harter Romantic Appeal Scale (2.6 vs. 2.8, $p < .05$).

We were successful in retaining a minimum of 89% of adolescents at each follow-up data collection point, including Time 5, 18 months after recruitment. This is an unusually high retention rate for a study focusing on inner-city, minority group adolescents. The retention rates did not differ between the experimental and control groups, or by ethnic group. We compared characteristics of those who dropped out and those who were retained. Boys were more likely to drop out of the research than were girls, but there were no significant differences on the psychological measures.

Rate of Program Participation

Of the 278 adolescents invited to join TEEN, 140 (50%) graduated from the training and 109 (83% of training graduates) completed the job internship. The pattern of participation in the TEEN program by gender was similar to that found with participation in the research study above: Girls were more likely than boys to graduate from the program or to attend some sessions and drop out. Boys were more likely not to attend any session. Graduates tended to be younger, whereas those who dropped out tended to be older. Those who dropped out were more likely to come from a family on public assistance, whereas those who did not attend were the least likely to receive public assistance. Graduates of the skills training had significantly **more** psychological symptoms at baseline as measured by the BSI than those who did not attend. In addition, graduates started out with lower scores on two of nine Harter subscales (Scholastic Competence and Athletic Competence). These findings indicate that the TEEN intervention attracted and graduated teens with poorer mental health at baseline, who seem at greater risk for future problems. Those who were doing well on their own were less likely to enroll in the program.

Program Effects

Table 14.2 presents the results of a repeated measures MANOVA for all six cohorts using scores at baseline (T1), post intervention (T3), and eighteen months postbaseline (T5) ($N = 343$). The MANOVA tests whether changes in the experimental group over time were significantly different from the changes occurring in the control group. A significant Time × Group interaction is evidence that the groups did change differently over time.

Building Internal Resources. We first examined effects of the intervention on increasing internal resources. There was a significant Time × Group interaction for the Rosenberg Self-Esteem Scale, indicating that the intervention group experienced enhanced self-esteem compared to the control group. The intervention effect was strongest during the period from T1 to T3, the time when TEEN was ongoing. There were no significant MANOVA interactions for any of the Harter subscales; however, there were significant T1 to T3 differences on Scholastic Competence, Athletic Competence, and Romantic Appeal.

Effects on Mental Health. There was a significant Time × Group effect on the Global Severity Index of the BSI. In addition, on every subscale of the BSI, the experimental group mean scores declined from T1 to T5, whereas those of the control group remained the same or showed a smaller decline. Thus, the differences between the groups were always in the hypothesized direction.

Table 14.1 Characteristics of Experimental and Control Groups at Baseline

Demographic Characteristics	Experimental	Control	Total
N	278	150	428
Sex			
Female	53%	54%	53%
Male	47	46	47
Ethnic group			
African American	24%	20%	22%
West Indian	11	13	12
Puerto Rican	37	42	39
Other Hispanic	8	6	7
White	9	7	8
Asian	1	1	1
Mixed	12	12	12
Age			
14	36%	30%	34%
15	25	32	27
16	21	25	22
17	18	14	17
Grade			
8 or less	11	7	9
9	30	31	31
10	33	27	31
11	13	26	18
12	14	9	12
Repeated a grade	39%	32%	36%
Family type			
Both parents	33%	32%	32%
Mother only	46	44	45
Other	21	24	23
Family receiving welfare	32%	32%	32%

NOTE: Difference between groups significant at $p = .05$.

Subgroup Differences in Intervention Effects. We also examined whether TEEN had different effects in various subgroups. In most cases, the effects shown in Table 14.2 remained when we used MANCOVA to control for demographic and illness characteristics. However, it appears that the intervention had stronger effects for certain groups. Analysis by sex indicated a significant Group × Sex × Time interaction on the GSI ($p = .008$). Examination of the means showed that the intervention effect on the mental health of girls was much stronger than the effect on boys. There was also a Group × Age × Time interaction on Global Self-Worth ($p = .01$) with Global Self-Worth increasing among younger (14- to 15-year-old) but not older (16- to 17-year-old) adolescents. A similar interaction on Global Self-Worth by ethnic group ($p = .02$) indicated that black teens in the experimental group improved on this measure, whereas those in the control group stayed the same. Hispanic teenagers in both groups tended to improve.

Conclusion

The evidence suggests that although the TEEN program did not increase social competence as measured by the Harter Self-Perception Profile, it did increase adolescents' internal resources, particularly self-esteem, and promoted mental health. Effects of the intervention were strongest when measured directly after the intervention, but most short-term differences that were achieved were maintained through the last data collection point, a year after the program ended. The program had significant benefits for all kinds of adolescents, but girls and younger teens were more likely to benefit than others.

The TEEN intervention was successful in attracting and retaining adolescents who were at most risk for mental health problems. The combination of interesting group activities, a supportive atmosphere, the opportunity to prepare for a job, and monetary compensation made this program an attractive one for adolescents, especially those without an after-school job or other extracurricular activities. We have since repeated the TEEN intervention with a particularly high-risk group of adolescents without chronic illnesses, and we have also modified its content to serve a group of adolescents with epilepsy. The program appears highly amenable to

TABLE 14.2 Mean Scale Scores T1 to T5, Experimental and Control Groups (Significance Tested by Repeated Measures MANOVA)[a]

Resources	T1	T3	T5
Rosenberg Self-Esteem Scale			
Experimental	3.08	3.21*	3.28**
Control	3.17	3.17	3.26
Harter Subscales			
Scholastic competence			
Experimental	2.82	3.06*	3.14
Control	3.00	3.12	3.19
Social acceptance			
Experimental	3.04	3.22	3.26
Control	3.15	3.19	3.26
Athletic competence			
Experimental	2.44	2.55*	2.62
Control	2.69	2.67	2.77
Physical appearance			
Experimental	2.67	2.86	2.98
Control	2.72	2.85	2.96
Job competence			
Experimental	3.10	3.22	3.31
Control	3.06	3.18	3.30
Romantic appeal			
Experimental	2.58	2.82*	3.05
Control	2.81	2.89	3.15
Conduct morality			
Experimental	2.81	2.92	3.01
Control	2.78	2.91	2.98
Close friendship			
Experimental	3.08	3.15	3.18
Control	3.10	3.17	3.19
Self-worth			
Experimental	3.03	3.12	3.20
Control	3.12	3.08	3.15
Mental Health Global Severity Index (GSI)			
Experimental	0.75	0.59*	0.52**
Control	0.70	0.67	0.59

a. $N = 343$.
* T3: significant group effect on T1 to T3 change;
** T5: significant p value for MANOVA Time × Group interaction.

these modifications. In fact, the intervention was offered to healthy adolescents as well and appears to work well with them. We believe that TEEN is a generic model of intervention that can be adapted to serve many different high-risk teen populations.

Our analyses of the study data also lend support to our conceptual model. The intervention seemed to work directly on improving self-esteem, and through this pathway decreased psychiatric symptoms. These results support the effectiveness of a mental health promotion intervention that strengthens the resources of adolescents before they show symptoms of a psychiatric disorder.

References

Abrahamson, M., Ash, M., & Nash, W. (1979). Handicapped adolescents—A time for reflection. *Adolescence, 55,* 557-565.

Apter, A., Aviv, A., Kaminer, Y., Weizman, A., Lerman, P., & Tyano, S. (1991). Behavioral profile and social competence in temporal lobe epilepsy of adolescence. *Journal of the American Academy of Child and Adolescent Psychiatry, 30,* 887-892.

Azrin, N. H., Flores, T., & Kaplan, S. J. (1975). Job-finding club: A group assisted program for obtaining employment. *Behavior Research and Therapy, 13,* 17-27.

Beck, I. L., & Carpenter, P. A. (1986). Cognitive approaches to understanding reading: Implications for instructional practice. *American Psychologist, 41,* 1098-1105.

Blumberg, B. D., Lewis, M. J., & Susman, E. J. (1984). Adolescence: A time of transition. In M. G. Eisenberg, L. C. Sutkin, & M. A. Jansen (Eds.), *Chronic illness and disability through the lifespan* (pp. 133-150). New York: Springer.

Boyle, I., Sant'Agrese, P., Sack, S., Millican, F., & Kulczycki, L. (1976). Emotional adjustment of adolescents and young adults with cystic fibrosis. *Journal of Pediatrics, 88,* 318-326.

Buck, M. (1977). Peer counseling in an urban high school setting. *Journal of School Psychology, 15*(4), 362-366.

Cadman, D., Boyle, M., Offord, D., Szatmari, P., Rae, N., Crawford, J., & Byles, J. (1986). Chronic illness and functional limitation in Ontario children: Findings of the Ontario child health study. *Canadian Medical Association Journal, 135,* 761-767.

Campbell, M., Hayden, P. W., & Davenport, S. L. H. (1977). Psychological adjustment of adolescents with myelodysplasia. *Journal of Youth and Adolescence, 6,* 397.

Carkhuff, R. R. (1987). *The art of helping* (Vol. 6). Amherst, MA: Human Resources Development Press.

Carnegie Commission on Policy Studies in Higher Education. (1980). *Giving youth a better chance.* San Francisco: Jossey Bass.

Chester, M., & Fox, R. (1966). *Role-playing methods in the classroom.* Chicago: Science Research Associates.

Coleman, J. (1978). Current contradictions in adolescent theory. *Journal of Youth and Adolescents, 7,* 1-11.

Cognetta, P., & Sprinthall, N. (1978). Students as teachers: Roletaking as a means of promoting psychological and ethical development during adolescence. *Character Potential: A Record of Research, 8,* 188-195.

Cooker, P., & Cherchia, P. (1976). Effects of communication skills training on high school students' ability to function as peer group facilitators. *Journal of Counseling Psychology, 23,* 117-126.

Cosse, W. J. (1985). Deliberate psychological education: A study of two ways of enhancing the normal ego development, self-esteem, and internal locus of control of middle adolescent females. *Dissertation Abstracts International, 46,* 323.

Coupey, S., Bauman, L., Lauby, J., Koeber, C., & Stein, R. (1991, May). *Mental health effects of a social skills intervention for adolescents with chronic illness.* Paper presented at the annual meeting of the APS/SPR, New Orleans, LA.

Cowen, E. L., Leibowitz, E., & Leibowitz, G. (1968). Utilization of retired people as mental health aids with children. *American Journal of Orthopsychiatry, 38,* 900-909.

Danish, S. J., & D'Augelli, A. R. (1980). Promoting competence and enhancing development through life development intervention. In L. A. Bond & J. C. Rosen (Eds.), *Competence and coping during adulthood.* Hanover, NH: University Press of New England.

Derogatis, L. R. (1977). *SCL-90-R: Administration scoring and procedures manual I.* Baltimore, MD: Clinical Psychometrics Research.

Dineen, J. P., Clark, H. B., & Risley, T. R. (1977). Peer tutoring among elementary students: Education benefits of the tutor. *Journal of Applied Behavior Analysis, 10,* 231-238.

Dodrill, C. (1983). Psychosocial characteristics of epileptics. *Journal of Nervous and Mental Disease, 61,* 341-353.

Driscoll, P. T. (1986). Early adolescence: Identity formation. In E. V. Lapham & K. M. Shevlin (Eds.), *The impact of chronic illness on psychosocial stages of human development.* Washington, DC: Georgetown University Hospital Medical Center.

Drotar, D. & Bush, M. (1985). Mental health issues and services. In N. Hobbs & J. M. Perrin (Eds.), *Issues in the care of children with chronic illness: A sourcebook on problems, services, and policies.* San Francisco: Jossey-Bass.

Durlak, J. (1973). Ninth graders as student aides: Making use of the helper therapy principle. *Psychology in the Schools, 10,* 334-339.

Epilepsy Foundation of America. (1975). *Basic statistics on the epilepsies.* Philadelphia: Davis.

Erikson, E. H. (Ed.). (1985). *The challenge of youth.* New York: Doubleday.

Gartner, A., Kohler, M. C., & Riessman, F. (1971). *Children teach children.* New York: Harper.

Goldfried, M. R., & D'Zurilla, T. J. (1969). A behavioral-analytic model for assessing competence. In C. D. Speilberger (Ed.), *Current topics in clinical and community psychology* (Vol. 1). New York: Academic Press.

Gortmaker, S., & Sappenfield, W. (1984). Chronic childhood disorders: Prevalence and impact. *Pediatric Clinics of North America, 31,* 3-18.

Gortmaker, S., Walker, D. K., Weitzman, M., & Sobol, A. M. (1989). Chronic conditions, socioeconomic risk and behavioral problems in children and adolescents. *Pediatrics, 85,* 267-276.

Greenberger, E., & Steinberg, L. (1986). *When teenagers work.* New York: Basic Books.

Greenblatt, M., & Kantor, P. (1962). Student volunteer movement and the manpower shortage. *American Journal of Psychiatry, 118,* 809-814.

Gunther, M. S. (1985). Acute-onset serious chronic organic illness in adolescence: Some critical issues. *Adolescent Psychiatry, 12,* 59-76.

Haggerty, R. J. (1981). Challenges to maternal and child health: Research in the 1980's. In L. V. Kerman (Ed.), *Research priorities in maternal and child health.* Report of a conference sponsored by Brandeis University and the Office for Maternal and Child Health, Health Services Administration, Public Health Services, U.S. Department of Health and Human Services, 245-251.

Haggerty, R. J., Roghmann, K. J., & Pless, I. B. (1975). *Child health and the community.* New York: John Wiley.

Hamburg, B., & Varenhorst, B. (1982). Peer counseling in the secondary schools: A community mental health project for youth. *American Journal of Orthopsychiatry, 42,* 566-581.

Harter, S. (1983). Development perspectives on the self-system. In P. H. Mussen (Ed.), *Handbook of child psychology* (Vol. 4). New York: John Wiley.

Harter, S. (1986). *Self-perception profile for adolescents.* University of Denver.

Harter, S. (1988). Causes, correlates and the functional role of global self-worth: A life span perspective. In J. Kolligan & R. Sternberg (Eds.), *Perceptions of competence and incompetence across the life-span.* New Haven, CT: Yale University Press.

Himber, C. (1970). Evaluating sensitivity training for teenagers. *Journal of Applied Behavioral Science, 6,* 307-322.

Holzberg, J. D., Gewirtz, H., & Ebner, E. (1964). Changes in moral judgment and self-acceptance as a function of companionship with hospitalized patients. *Journal of Consulting Psychology, 28,* 299-303.

Jordaan, J. P., & Super, D. E. (1974). The prediction of early adult vocational behavior. In D. Ricks, A. Thomas, & M. Roff (Eds.), *Life history research in psychopathology* (Vol. 3). Minneapolis: University of Minnesota Press.

Juul-Jensen, P. (1974). Social prognosis. In O. Magnus & A. M. Lorentz de Haas (Eds.), *The epilepsies* (pp. 800-814). Amsterdam: North Holland.

Kellerman, J., Zeltzer, L., Ellenberg, L., Dash, J., & Rigler, D. (1980). Psychological effects of illness in adolescence: I. Anxiety, self-esteem and perception of control. *Journal of Pediatrics, 97,* 126-131.

Klerman, L. V. (Ed.). (1981). *Research priorities in maternal and child health* (Report of a conference). Waltham, MA: Brandeis.

LeCroy, C. G., & Rose, S. D. (1986). Evaluation of preventive interventions for enhancing social competence in adolescents. *Social Work Research and Abstracts,* 8-16.

Lesser, R. P., Luders, E., Wyllie, E., Dinner, D. S., & Morris, H. H., III. (1986). Mental deterioration in epilepsy. *Epilepsia, 27*(Suppl. 12), 102-123.

Lindemann, J. E. (Ed.). (1981). *Psychological and behavioral aspects of physical disability: A manual for health practitioners.* New York: Plenum.

McManus, J. L. (1982). Comprehensive psychological services at the secondary level utilizing student paraprofessionals. *Journal of School Psychology, 20,* 280-298.

Newacheck, P. W., & Taylor, W. R. (1992). Childhood chronic illness: Prevalence, severity, and impact. *American Journal of Public Health, 82,* 364-371.

Newacheck, P. W., McManus, M. A., & Fox, H. B. (1991). Prevalence and impact of chronic illness among adolescents. *American Journal of Diseases of Children, 145,* 1367-1373.

Orr, D., Weller, S., & Satterwhite, B. (1984). Psychosocial implications of chronic illness in adolescence. *Journal of Pediatrics, 104,* 152-157.

Piaget, J. (1954). *The moral judgment of the child.* New York: Free Press.

Partridge, J. W., Garner, A. M., Thompson, C. W., & Cherry, T. (1972). Attitudes of adolescents toward diabetes. *American Journal of Diseases in Children, 124,* 226.

Pless, I. B., & Nolan, T. (1991). Revision, replication and neglect: Research on maladjustment in chronic illness. *Journal of Child Psychology and Psychiatry and Allied Disciplines, 32,* 347-365.

Pless, I. B., & Pinkerton, P. (1975). *Chronic childhood disorders: Promoting patterns of adjustment.* Chicago: Yearbook Medical Publishers.

Pless, I. B., & Wadsworth, M. E. J. (1988). The unresolved question: Long term psychosocial sequelae of chronic illness in childhood. In R. E. K. Stein (Ed.), *New direction in care of children with chronic illness.* New York: United Hospital Fund.

President's Commission on Mental Health. (1978). *Report on the task panel on community support systems* (Vol. 2). Washington, DC: Government Printing Office.

Rapp, H. M., Dworkin, A. L., & Moss, J. L. (1978). Student-to-student helping program. *Humanistic Educator, 18,* 88-98.

Reinherz, A. (1962). Group leadership of student volunteers. *Mental Hospitals, 13,* 600-603.

Richardson, S. A., Hastorf, A. H., & Dornbusch, D. M. (1964). The effects of a physical disability on a child's description of himself. *Child Development, 35,* 93-97.

Ricks, D. F. (1970). Life history research in psychopathology: Retrospect and prospect. In M. Roff & D. F. Ricks (Eds.), *Career development and counseling of women.* Springfield, IL: Charles C Thomas.

Ricks, D. F. (1980). A model for promoting competence and coping in adolescents and young adults. In L. A. Bond & J. C. Rosen (Eds.), *Competence and coping during adulthood.* Hanover, NH: University Press of New England.

Riessman, F. (1965). The "Helper Therapy" principle. *Social Work, 10,* 27-31.

Risch, F., & Rose, A. (1957). A community plan for epileptics. *Public Health Reports, 72,* 813-817.

Rosenberg, M. (1965). *Society and the adolescent self-image.* Princeton, NJ: Princeton University Press.

Rutter, M. (1979). *Changing youth in a changing society.* Abingdon, Oxfordshire, England: Nullfield Provincial Hospital Trust.

Rutter, M., Tizard, J., & Whitmore, K. (Eds.). (1970). *Education, health, and behavior.* London, UK: Longman.

Sanger, M. S., Copeland, D. R., & Edwards, D. R. (1991). Psychosocial adjustment among pediatric cancer patients: A multidimensional assessment. *Journal of Pediatric Psychology, 16,* 463-474.

Sarason, B. R. (1981). The dimensions of social competence: Contributions from various research areas. In J. D. Wine & M. D. Smye (Eds.), *Social competence.* New York: Guilford.

Sarason, I. G. & Sarason, B. R. (1981). Teaching cognitive and social skills to high school students. *Journal of Consulting and Clinical Psychology, 49(6),* 908-918.

Sawyer, M., Crettenden, A., Toogood et al. (1986). Psychological adjustment of families of children and adolescents treated for leukemia. *American Journal of Pediatric Hematology and Oncology, 8,* 200-207.

Schiebe, K. E. (1965). College students spend eight weeks in a mental hospital: A case-report. *Psychotherapy: Theory, Research and Practice, 2,* 117-120.

Schinke, S., Gilchrist, L., Smith, T., & Wong, S. (1978a). Group interpersonal skills training in a natural setting: An experimental study. *Behavioral Research and Therapy, 17,* 149-154.

Schinke, S. P., Gilchrist, L. D., Smith, T. E., & Wong, S. E. (1978b). Improving teenage mothers' ability to compete for jobs. *Social Work Research and Abstracts, 14,* 25-29.

Schmuck, R. (1968). Helping teachers improve classroom process. *Journal of Applied Behavioral Science, 4,* 401-435.

Select Panel on the Promotion of Child Health. (1981). *Better health for our children: A national strategy* (Vols. 1-4). Washington, DC: Government Printing Office.

Shantz, C. V. (1975). The development of social cognition. In E. M. Hetherington (Ed.), *Review of child development research* (Vol. 5). Chicago: University of Chicago Press.

Siegel, W. M., Golden, N. H., Gough, J. W. et al. (1990). Depression, self-esteem and life events in adolescents with chronic diseases. *Journal of Adolescent Health Care, 11,* 501-504.

Silver, E., Coupey, S., Bauman, L., Doctors, S. R., & Boeck, M. A. (1992). Effects of a peer counseling training intervention on psychological functioning of adolescents. *Journal of Adolescent Research, 7(1),* 110-128.

Simmons, C. H., & Parsons, R. J. (1983). Developing internality and perceived competence: The empowerment of adolescent girls. *Adolescence, 18(72),* 917-922.

Simmons, R. G., & Blyth, D. A. (1987). *Moving into adolescence: The impact of pubertal change and school context.* New York: Aldine De Gruyter.

Smith, M. S. (Ed.). (1983). *Chronic disorders in adolescence.* Boston: John Wright-PSG.

Spivak, G., & Shure, M. B. (1973). *Social adjustment of young children.* San Francisco: Jossey-Bass.

Starfield, B., & Pless, I. B. (1980). Physical health. In O. G. Brim & J. Kagen (Eds.), *Constancy and change in human development.* Cambridge, MA: Harvard.

Stein, R. E. K. (Ed.). (1988). *Caring for children with chronic illness: Issues and strategies.* New York: Springer.

Stein, R. E. K., Bauman, L. J., Westbrook, L. E., Coupey, S. M., & Ireys, H. T. (1995). A framework for identifying children who have chronic conditions: The case for a new definition. *Journal of Pediatrics, 122*(Special Article), 342-347.

Steinhauser, P. D., Mushin, D. N., & Rae-Grant, Q. (1974). Psychological aspects of chronic illness. *Pediatric Clinics of North America, 21,* 825.

Stern, M., Norman, S., & Zevon, M. A. (1993). Adolescents with cancer: Self-image and perceived social support as indexes of adaptation. *Journal of Adolescent Research, 8,* 124-142.

Stollak, G. E. (1969). The experimental effect of training college students as play therapists. In B. G. Guerney, Jr. (Ed.), *Psychotherapeutic agents: New roles for nonprofessionals, parents and teachers.* New York: Holt, Rinehart & Winston.

Sullivan, B. (1979). Adjustment in diabetic adolescent girls: II. Adjustment, self-esteem and depression in diabetic teenage girls. *Psychosomatic Medicine, 41,* 127.

Sussman, E. J., Hollenbeck, A. R., Nannis, E. D., & Strope, B. H. (1980). A developmental perspective on psychosocial aspects of childhood cancer. In J. L. Schulman & J. Kupst (Eds.), *The child with cancer.* Springfield, IL: Charles C Thomas.

Swift, C., Seidman, F., & Stein, H. (1967). Adjustment problems in juvenile diabetes. *Psychosomatic Medicine, 29*(6), 555.

Teta, M., Del Po, M., Kasl, S., Meigs, J., Myers, M., & Mulvehill, J. (1986). Psychosocial consequences of childhood and adolescent cancer survival. *Journal of Chronic Diseases, 39,* 751-759.

Thompson, R. A. (1986). Developing a peer group facilitating program on the secondary level: An investment with multiple returns. *Small Group Behavior, 17,* 105-112.

Tyler, F. B., & Gatz, M. (1977). Development of individual psychosocial competence in a high school setting. *Journal of Consulting and Clinical Psychology, 45,* 441-449.

Wheaton, B. (1991, August). *Chronic stress: Models and measurement.* Paper presented at the annual meeting of the Society for the Study of Social Problems, Cincinnati, Ohio.

Wolman, C., Resnick, M. D., Harris, L. J., Blum, R. W. (1994). Emotional well-being among adolescents with and without chronic illness. *Journal of Adolescent Health, 15,* 199-204.

Woudenberg, R. A., & Payne, P. A. (1978). An examination of the training therapy principle. *Journal of College Student Personnel,* 141-145.

Ziegler, R. G. (1981). Impairment of control and competence in epileptic children and their families. *Epilepsia, 22,* 339-346.

Zunker, V. G., & Brown, W. F. (1966). Comparative effectiveness of student and professional counselors. *Personnel and Guidance Journal, 44,* 738-743.

FIVE

Adult Programs

CHAPTER 15

From Job Loss to Reemployment: Field Experiments in Prevention-Focused Coping

ROBERT D. CAPLAN

AMIRAM D. VINOKUR

RICHARD H. PRICE

In an age of organizational downsizing, restructuring, and outsourcing, the long-term relationship between employer and employee is disappearing (Reich, 1991). Rapid changes in technology are leading to predictions that careers will last only half as long for the next generation as they do now (Handy, 1989; Price, in press). In this turbulent climate, skill in transporting one's generic talents between employers, jobs, industries, and sectors will become a central component of lifelong career development. Such changes will increase the stakes that job seekers, employers, educators, and government will have in how well people manage what is often a stressful and challenging transition from job loss to reemployment.

Although numerous attempts are being made to promote effective transitions in employment, little has been established ex-

AUTHORS' NOTE: This program of research and preparation of this chapter were made possible by a series of grants from the National Institutes of Mental Health including NIMH grant # 5P30MH38330 to the Michigan Prevention Research Center, The University of Michigan, and NIMH grant # R10 MH52817 to the Center for Family Research and the Department of Psychology, The George Washington University.

perimentally regarding the components of a successful program. Through grants from NIMH to the Michigan Prevention Research Center (MPRC) and its investigators, it has been possible to develop, test experimentally, and establish the components of effective programs of early, client-focused preventive intervention. These interventions, known as the JOBS Programs, are designed to help job seekers manage the challenging transition from job loss to reemployment. Early intervention is required to prevent the harmful effects of job loss on mental and physical health. This chapter summarizes the results of this research and examines the generic principles of intervention theory that have guided the design of its prevention-focused trials.

Brief Introduction to the JOBS Program

This chapter explores how the JOBS Program research has pursued three programmatic aims. These aims are represented schematically in Figure 15.1. The first aim is to contribute to and test basic theory regarding the determinants of effective coping, in which effectiveness is judged in terms of outcomes such as mental health and economic and social well-being. Etiological research addressing this aim is designed to identify antecedents of successful coping that intervention might strengthen, antecedents such as self-efficacy.

The second aim is to develop and test theories of preventive intervention. Such experiments provide a basis for the third aim, the development of theory and methods for helping employers and other organizations in the community adopt and successfully implement the resulting social technologies.

In Figure 15.1, the economic and social environment of community and society are listed as important contextual variables. Elements of this broader environment, including public policy, financial resources, and norms can influence (a) the readiness of host organizations to institute preventive interventions, (b) the availability of such organizations to use tested social technologies for promoting coping, and (c) the resultant attitudes, knowledge, coping behaviors, and coping outcomes.

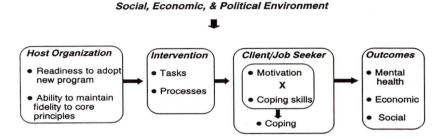

Figure 15.1. Programmatic Model of the Multiple Levels of Influence on Economic and Psychological Well-Being for Persons Coping With Job Loss

The text begins with a brief summary of the psychosocial sequelae of job loss and of effects of the JOBS intervention on economic and psychological well-being. As part of the economic effects, we describe the cost effectiveness of the intervention. Next, we examine the theories of coping and intervention that lie behind the success of the JOBS interventions. Finally, we explore ways in which employers and other organizations in society can generate these same successes. Those ways include steps that can maximize the readiness of the host organization to launch such a program (D'Aunno, 1986) and can maximize the likelihood that, once launched, the program will generate the same successes as it has during its formal testing.

The JOBS intervention includes both short-term and long-term goals. The short-term goals focus on the enhancement of productive job-seeking skills and on the self-confidence to use those skills. These short-term goals also include fortifying the job seeker's ability to resist demoralization and to persist in the face of barriers and common setbacks that are inherent in the search for a new job.

The long-term goals focus on providing the job seeker with the confidence and skills to achieve reemployment in stable settings that maximize economic, social, and psychological rewards from reemployment. The findings indicate that the JOBS intervention meets these goals, and in addition, it generates significant economic benefits for society. At the end of this chapter, we describe how the goals of this prevention-oriented research program are being programmatically extended to target the well-being and self-sufficiency of the family as well as the job seeker.

Why Is Preventive Intervention Needed? Job Loss, Mental Health, and the Effective Recovery of Employment

Numerous studies show that loss of employment is one of the most consistent antecedents of depressive symptoms (e.g., Catalano, 1991; Dew, Penkower, & Bromet, 1991; Kessler, House, & Turner, 1988; Vinokur, Caplan, & Williams, 1987). Studies suggest that job loss increases the likelihood of risk of alcohol abuse (Catalano, Dooley, Wilson, & Hough, 1993), poor physical health (Cobb & Kasl, 1977; Catalano & Serxner, 1992), violent behavior (Catalano, Dooley, Novaco, & Wilson, 1993), child abuse (Krishnan & Morrison, 1995; Harris & Kotch, 1994), marital disruption (Atkinson, Liem, & Liem, 1986; Rook, Dooley, & Catalano, 1991), and suicide (e.g., Heikkinen, Isometsa, Aro, & Sarno, 1995; Dooley, Catalano, Rook, & Serxner, 1989).

The financial strain of job loss exacerbates the effects of other costly negative life events, such as illness in the family (Kessler et al., 1988). When economic loss occurs, tensions among family members increase in response to disagreements regarding the allocation of scarce financial resources (e.g., Conger et al., 1990). In addition, the tensions and disagreements undermine the quality and stability of the relationship between spouses and spouse mental health (Vinokur, Price, & Caplan, in press).

When reemployment occurs, it can reverse the harmful emotional and social sequelae of job loss by reducing economic hardship and financial strain (Kessler et al., 1988). There are, however, exceptions. When people use the wrong job-seeking strategies, the benefits of reemployment may be short-lived. For example, job seekers suffering from depressive symptoms may take the first job that comes along, whether the fit is good or not, to short-circuit the pain of depression (Kessler et al., 1988). Such job seekers are likely to experience subsequent job loss and risk a return of depressive symptoms. In these cases, finding reemployment may be an especially uphill battle because studies suggest that depression prolongs unemployment (Hamilton, Broman, & Hoffman, 1990; Hamilton, Hoffman, Broman, & Rauma, 1993). To prevent such occurrences, preventive intervention needs to take place *before* job seekers become emotionally disabled.

Etiological research indicates that both the risk of depressive symptoms and the motivation to engage in job seeking are potentially amenable to social influence (e.g., Vinokur & Caplan, 1987). Consequently, preventive intervention can provide both the attitudinal armament and the behavioral strategies for persevering beyond setbacks when they occur and for finding stable reemployment. Recent studies suggest that such interventions can accomplish these goals while increasing the efficiency with which job seekers and employers find one another (Bloom, 1987; Fischer & Cordray, 1995). Furthermore, such programs can accelerate the reemployment of program participants without displacing the employment opportunities of nonparticipants. Labor market analysis indicates that programs designed to promote reemployment have minimal effects on the displacement of other job seekers (Davidson & Woodbury, 1993). Any small displacement effects are offset by overall improvement in the economy that results from reducing the duration of job vacancies. The acceleration of job filling, in turn, leads to the creation of additional job opportunities. Thus, if programs that promote faster reemployment succeed in generating quicker reemployment or in helping people obtain jobs more suitable for their skills, those programs enhance the efficiency of the labor market and, ultimately, contribute to economic growth.

Key Psychological, Behavioral, and Economic Effects of the JOBS Preventive Intervention

Scientific Design

The results summarized below are derived from both the initial long-term project, JOBS I (Caplan, Vinokur, Price, & van Ryn, 1989; Price, van Ryn, & Vinokur, 1992; van Ryn & Vinokur, 1992; Vinokur, Price, & Caplan, 1991; Vinokur, van Ryn, Gramlich, & Price, 1991) and its replication, JOBS II, which focused on a comparison of job seekers at high and low risk of poor coping (Vinokur, Price, & Schul, 1995).

JOBS I and II were randomized field experiments in which recently unemployed job seekers were assigned to either a control group or the preventive intervention. Following random assignment, the inspection of baseline characteristics of the job seekers has demonstrated that the control and preventive intervention groups were essentially the same on a wide variety of demographic variables, attitudes about job seeking and work, and measures of mental health symptomatology.

At the baseline pretest, about one week before these interventions took place, participants completed standardized measures of demographic attributes and psychological characteristics thought to influence successful coping. These attributes and characteristics included the amount and quality of employment in the last steady job, attitudes toward job seeking, and mental health. These attributes were also assessed in posttests at 1 to 2 months and 4 to 6 months after the baseline measure was obtained and at long-term follow-up 2 to 2.5 years after the pretest.

Who Participated?

JOBS I included 928 recently unemployed male and female job seekers. In JOBS II, 1801 job seekers participated. In both experiments, participants were primarily European American and African Americans from a wide range of occupations (i.e., unskilled and skilled, blue and white collar, professional and technical), between the ages of 18 to 60. These job seekers were seeking services at State of Michigan offices of employment compensation. As detailed in Caplan et al. (1989), job seekers were approached and recruited by professional interviewers. In both JOBS I and II, two out of every three volunteers were randomly assigned to the intervention, and one out of three was assigned to the control group.

Who Responded?

Of those persons assigned to the intervention program, 59% failed to appear in JOBS I and 46% in JOBS II. Once job seekers entered these field experiments, it was possible to follow up 88% and 80% of the JOBS I and II participants respectively at the 1 to 2 month posttest, 80% and 87% respectively at the 4 to 6 month posttest, and 76% and 80%, respectively at the 2.5 and 2 year long-term follow-up.

Experimental Conditions

In JOBS I, the intervention program initially consisted of a set of eight 3.5-hour sessions held during the first half of the day and spanning 2 weeks. In JOBS II, the program was successfully shortened to five half-day sessions spanning 1 week. A male-female pair of trainers ran each set of sessions for groups of 12 to 22 participants, the average group size being 16 job seekers.

The content focused on providing behavioral skill training in how to seek reemployment effectively and included active methods for raising job seeker self-confidence and providing attitudinal and behavioral repertoires (inoculation) for dealing with barriers and setbacks effectively. The control group received a brief (8-page) booklet with tips on how to find a new job. The tips covered the same content that was included in the intervention (the importance of discovering transferable skills, the use of social networks to locate job leads, and so on).

Measurement

The measures used in these studies came from past etiological research in our program (e.g., Vinokur & Caplan, 1987; Vinokur et al., 1987) and from other studies that focused on stress and coping, job seeking, and mental health. All measures met acceptable statistical standards for internal reliability and demonstrated evidence of predictive validity in previous research.

Analyses

Two types of analyses were used. One type maintained complete randomization by comparing 100% of the job seekers in each condition, including the show and no-show participants in the intervention. This type of analysis provides a lower bound, conservative estimate of program impact.

The second type of analysis compared those who actually did show up and complete the intervention program with persons in the control group who were similar to them and, therefore, would be likely to show up were they allowed to participate in the intervention (Bloom, 1984; Vinokur et al., 1991). This second type of analysis is more likely to generate significant treatment differences because it focuses on those persons who participated in the intervention, rather than on those who were assigned, of which a large proportion failed to show up. The scientific conclusions drawn about the JOBS intervention are consistent, regardless of which method of analysis was used. The difference in magnitude of the effect sizes using the two methods indicates that the full-group, conservative method of estimating program effects may underestimate the intervention's efficacy by nearly half (Vinokur et al., 1991; Vinokur, Price, & Schul, 1995, pp. 66-68).

The Findings

Mental Health and Attitudes

An immediate need was to prevent poor mental health and discouragement while job seekers remained unemployed. At the 1- and 4-month follow-up surveys, job seekers who had completed the intervention program and were still looking for work had higher levels of confidence in their job-seeking ability and a greater sense of self-efficacy than their counterparts in the control group. These effects were detectable even among unemployed job seekers up to six months after losing their jobs.

Further evidence of the power of attitudinal inoculation against setbacks came from analyses of levels of depression among job seekers still unemployed at 1 and 4 months after the intervention. Analyses of the full intervention and control groups showed no differences in level of depression. When, however, the intervention participants were compared to their statistically matched counterparts in the control group, they showed consistently lower levels of depression.

Among job seekers who became reemployed, these same analyses showed that although participants in the intervention had *higher* levels of depressive symptoms at 1 month after the intervention, these effects reversed by 4 months after. The intervention was particularly beneficial for persons at *high risk* of developing depressive symptoms at later follow-up interviews. High-risk participants were characterized by a high combined index of depression, financial hardship, and low social assertiveness at the first interview. High-risk participants who participated in the prevention program showed significantly lower levels of both the incidence and prevalence of severe depressive episodes, even 2.5 years after the intervention (Price et al., 1992).

These results were replicated in JOBS II using a completely new staff of trainers and supervisor of the trainers and a program that involved fewer hours of intervention. On the basis of JOBS I, the number of program hours was shortened by 30%; and the overall duration was reduced from 2 weeks to 1 week with greater emphasis on the enhancement of self-efficacy. JOBS II was designed to test if the program could be made more efficient by targeting high-risk persons who were considered most likely to benefit from the intervention program. Screening was used to assign high risk job seekers and a comparison group of low-risk job seekers to the prevention and control conditions (Vinokur et al., 1995b).

The high-risk job seekers had significantly higher levels of depressive symptoms prior to entering the study. Among these job seekers, only those who were assigned to the preventive intervention showed a drop in symptoms both at 2 and 6 months after the intervention. Low-risk participants entered the study with low levels of depression. Those levels remained unchanged regardless of whether they were in the control group or in the intervention. In sum, the original JOBS intervention and its replication suggest that preventive intervention benefits those facing the greatest threats to their emotional, economic, and social well-being.

Reemployment and Job Security

As intended, the benefits of the JOBS intervention extend to finding reemployment as well as to reducing depressive symptomatology. In JOBS I, participation in the intervention program enhanced a range of employment-linked outcomes. Program participants found reemployment sooner than job seekers in the control group. Analyses comparing actual participants with their counterparts in the control group showed that by 4 months, 53% of the intervention participants, compared to only 29% of the control group, found reemployment. This more than 20% advantage by intervention participants was evident as soon as 1 month after the intervention.

Subsequent analyses of the pathways through which the intervention had its strongest effects on job seeking showed that changes in self-efficacy were the most important determinant of job seeking behavior (van Ryn & Vinokur, 1992). This finding has been replicated in experimental work conducted in Israel with job seekers (Eden & Aviram, 1993) as well as in the second replication of the JOBS intervention. The effect is consistent with major theories of behavior change cited below. Those theories played a critical role in determining how the intervention would be designed.

The quality of reemployment was also higher for job seekers who participated in the prevention program (Caplan et al., 1989). Compared to the jobs found by control group members, intervention program participants' jobs were more likely to be in what they characterized as their main occupation. At the 4-month posttest, the intervention group rated the quality of their working life as significantly better than the control group rated theirs. The measure of quality of working life included items assessing a wide range of conditions, including use of skills and abilities, effective supervision, overall work load, and pay. Consequently, even though job seekers in the intervention program were finding jobs sooner, they were not taking *any* job that came along. The quality of the jobs that they found suggests that they were more effective than control group job seekers in exploiting the best opportunities in the job market.

At 2.5 years, most participants were reemployed, regardless of whether they were in the intervention or control group. Intervention participants, however, had experienced significantly fewer work transitions with new employers than their counterparts in the control group (Vinokur et al., 1991). These findings suggest that the intervention was successful in teaching the participants to get better, more stable jobs. In a world of increasingly temporary commitments between employer and employee, a world in which job seeking may become a frequently used skill, this long-term effect suggests that single interventions of the type developed in the JOBS program may yield career-long coping skills.

In the JOBS II replication, all intervention participants, whether high-risk or not, were more likely to be reemployed by the 2-month follow-up. By the 6-month follow-up, the low-risk job seekers from the intervention and control groups were equally likely to find reemployment. Once again, it was the high-risk job seekers in the prevention program who benefited more.

Earnings and Other
Economic Outcomes

As early as 4 weeks after completing the intervention program, its job seekers had established a lead with regard to salary that increased and then persisted through the 2.5-year follow-up (Vinokur et al., 1991). By 4 weeks after the intervention, the intervention participants had an advantage of $178 per month; by 4 months, $227 per month; and by 2.5 years, $239 per month. Analyses currently being completed indicate that findings on salary from the JOBS II study replicate this basic pattern of results, particularly for high-risk participants.

The long-term follow-up in JOBS I suggests that these effects may continue for a substantial period of time and may have beneficial economic effects on society as well as on the job seeker. Benefit/cost analyses showed that the JOBS I intervention resulted in net benefits of $6,420 per respondent at the end of the 2.5-year follow-up. This advantage is projected to yield a conservative net benefit of $12,619 at the end of 5 years, and $48,151 by the time the respondents are likely to begin retiring at the estimated age of 60 years old.

The intervention group's higher projected contributions to taxable income, coupled with their lower use of unemployment compensation, suggests that implementation of the JOBS program would generate notable net economic benefits to government as well. Using a conservative discount rate (5%), the lifetime earning payout was estimated at nearly $7000 per participant to the federal government and more than $2000 per participant to the state government. These findings suggest that prevention-oriented programs focused on promoting mental health and effective coping skills can make good economic sense both for the job seekers and the society.

Summary

Two replications of the JOBS intervention tell the same story. Preventive intervention can have beneficial effects on the mental health, reemployment, and economic well-being of job seekers. Analyses of the experiences of job seekers who vary in their economic and social-emotional resources suggest that high-risk job seekers are particularly likely to benefit in terms of the prevention of continued depression, unemployment, and economic hardship. Regardless of risk, however, the findings suggest that job seekers who participate in such interventions are likely to experience a higher sense of self-confidence about the road ahead. Additional analyses suggest that such mastery and self-efficacy and the lower levels of depressive symptoms found among intervention participants provide the motivational energy that leads to reemployment.

What Makes the JOBS Program Tick?
The Theories Behind the Intervention

In this section we describe how generic theory, principles, and findings from the behavioral and social sciences formed the crucial foundation on which the intervention was designed. The incorporation of such theory makes it possible to establish general principles for preventive intervention, principles that are likely to guide a wide variety of interventions, whether aimed at people dealing with job loss or at people experiencing other major life events, such as a life-threatening illness.

The heading for this section refers to "theories" rather than just one theory because a theory of intervention puts together two bodies of scientific knowledge. *Etiological* theory deals with the malleable characteristics of people that determine how well they cope with adversity. *Intervention* theory deals with methods for helping people *change* those characteristics in ways that enhance their capacity for effective coping. Figure 15.2 provides a schematic of the etiological theory and its intersection with the theory of the intervention. In the following sections, we examine the elements of these theories and how we translated those elements into the JOBS design for preventive intervention.

The Theory of What Should Be
Targeted for Preventive Intervention

Figure 15.2 depicts the general hypothesis that a job seeker (or any other person facing a stress) who is well equipped to cope with a stressful situation needs three critical internal resources. The first

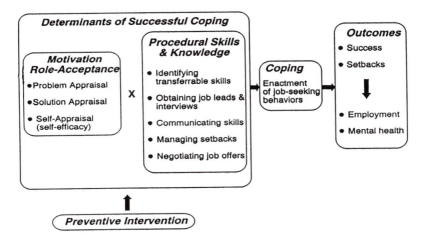

Figure 15.2. The Michigan JOBS Program: Interventions Targeting the Confluence of Motivation, Procedural Knowledge, and Skill in Coping with Job Loss

resource consists of knowledge of the procedures that are effective (e.g., how to find job leads or how to conduct a job interview). The second resource involves the behavioral skills to use the knowledge. The third internal resource is the energizing motivation to put knowledge and skills into action. This combination is expected to lead to effective coping, and thereby, to a wide range of outcomes. Small successes along the path to reemployment are likely to further energize motivation to continue job seeking. Setbacks and perceived barriers, however, are likely to have the opposite effect, undermining self-confidence.

Motivation, the Energizer of Coping

According to theory and research on human motivation and on coping (e.g., Atkinson & Feather, 1966; Bandura, 1989; Lawler, 1973; Lazarus & Folkman, 1984; Zimmerman & Bonner, in press), motivation to cope is made up of three components: (a) Do I believe I have a *problem* to solve, and have I accepted problem solving as part of my role? (Baker & Faulkner, 1991; Callero, 1994. (b) Do I have the knowledge of possible solutions? That is, am I aware of any *paths* for addressing the problem (referred to as the "instrumentality" of a possible solution)? And (c) Do I *personally* believe I have the skills to apply the solutions successfully? That is, have I a general sense of confidence and mastery, and a specific self-efficacy to follow the action path successfully? The theory states that these elements generally combine in a multiplicative fashion to increase the motivation to use active coping. Consequently, the closer the answer to any one of these three questions is to a categorical "no" (e.g., instrumentality = 0), the more likely the job seeker's allocation of effort to carrying out that coping tactic will be zero.

These types of belief regarding having a problem, having a solution, and having the skills to use the solution can be either supported or undermined by others (Vinokur & Caplan, 1987). Such support or undermining can have significant effects on how much effort the job seeker mobilizes in looking for reemployment. A problem must be appraised, as well as a solution and personal ability to overcome the problem, to energize effective coping. Consequently, preventive interventions must seek to maximize all three elements. If people differ in the elements that constitute their stumbling blocks, then preventive intervention has to enable clients to take an active role in clarifying and deciding which elements of motivation need work. The theory of intervention described below includes the need for that active role.

Procedural Knowledge and Skilled Use of That Knowledge, the Content of Coping

In addition to motivation, sustained effective coping requires knowledge of what steps and principles to apply. Highly motivated but inadequately trained job seekers are as unlikely to exhibit effective coping as inadequately motivated but highly trained job seekers.

What should be the content of that procedural knowledge and skill? Books on how to find employment (e.g., Bolles, 1995, Granovetter, 1974; Jackson, 1991) suggest that there are at least six tasks that a well-prepared job seeker must be able to handle: (a) identification of transferable skills and (b) of the market for them, (c) procurement of interviews with employers, (d) skill in communicating one's value to prospective employers, (e) emotional, attitudinal, and behavioral management of setbacks and barriers, and (f) when receiving a job offer, ability to negotiate and make the best choice.

A Working Theory of Intervention Tasks and Processes

Enhancing Role Taking

The overall task of the intervention is to reinforce self-acceptance of the transitional role of job seeker as well as the skills and motivation required to enact that role successfully. The claiming of this new role is crucial to effective coping (Baker & Faulkner, 1991; Callero, 1994; Ezzy, 1993). Role acceptance allows the job seeker to legitimize tasks that ordinarily fall outside the realm of daily behavior (Price, Vinokur, & Friedland, 1996). Such legitimated tasks can include asking friends, relatives, and others for job-lead information and seeking help from a spouse or others for child care. Formal acceptance of the job-seeking role can officially legitimize the job seeker's right to apply for government-sponsored employee assistance programs such as job retraining, career planning seminars, and job search workshops.

Targeting Malleable Attributes of the Job Seeker: Coupling Generic Intervention Goals to Generic Intervention Processes

Research on the acquisition of knowledge and behavioral skills indicates that there are effective methods of influencing the acquisition of such roles (e.g., Ajzen & Fishbein, 1980; Goldstein, 1994). Effective methods target potentially malleable attitudes, knowledge, and behaviors that comprise the job-seeking role. Once such elements are identified, theories of intervention can be used to generate specific goals and processes for enhancing these malleable elements. This strategy of identifying and targeting malleable aspects of the job seeker was instrumental in generating the JOBS I and II interventions.

There are both goals and processes for influencing malleable aspects of coping. Those goals and processes combine to form a matrix of intervention goals in Table 15.1. The cells of the table

Table 15.1 The Intersection of Generic Goals and Processes in Preventive Interventions

Goals	Active Learning (All elements in this table are examples of active learning.)	Social Modeling	Graded Exposure	Reinforcement of Self-Efficacy and Role Taking
		Processes		
Recruit participants	Elicit reasons why participation would be beneficial (vs. tell participants why)	Present examples of similar others participating	Indicate that the participant can make a final decision after trying out the first session	Indicate that participation in seminar is part of job-seeker role and that the participant has the capacity to overcome potential barriers to participation
Establish and maintain trust and social influence of trainers and peers	As a form of moderate self-disclosure, ask participants to interview one another and present each other to the group (vs. let acquaintance happen informally or give everyone a prepared list of participant names and interests)	Have trainers demonstrate how to engage in moderate self-disclosure by interviewing each other	Have trainers self-disclose before participants do	Have trainers praise participants for how well they introduced one another, noting that these are exactly the skills that are important in interviewing for a job

Enhance motivation to cope	Engage participants in identifying how the *trainers* can improve a role play of a poor approach to coping such as interviewing for a job (vs. tell the participants the best way to interview)	Have trainers model the suggestions made by the participants	Have participants observe the trainers role-play, then role-play, and then enact outside of the seminar	Have peers as well as trainers provide efficacy-building feedback to the participants on their role performances and contributions
Enhance procedural knowledge and skills	Engage participants in generating this knowledge (vs. give them a handout, a lecture, or a video)	Have trainers model the suggestions made by the participants	Have trainers model, followed by participants role-playing the application of the same principles and then trying them out outside the seminar	Have peers as well as trainers provide efficacy-building feedback to the participants on their role performances and contributions
Promote transfer, inoculation against setbacks, and coping with barriers	Engage participants in considering what might go wrong when they try new coping behaviors	Have trainers model the suggestions made by the participants	Have trainers model, followed by participants role-playing the application of the same principles and then trying them out outside the seminar	Have peers as well as trainers provide efficacy-building feedback to the participants on their role performances and contributions

represent transformations of the intersecting goal and process into a set of actions for preventive intervention.[1]

The JOBS program focuses on five goals:

1. Recruit participants—that is, persuade them to participate.
2. Establish and maintain each participant's trust in the trainers and the peers or other participants.
3. Enhance the participant's motivation to use methods of coping that are known to be effective.
4. Enhance the participant's knowledge of the correct coping procedures and his or her skill in using those procedures.
5. Promote transfer of that coping and its generalization to a variety of settings.

The program focuses on four generic processes that apply equally well to each task: (a) active learning, (b) social modeling, (c) graded exposure, and (d) the reinforcement of self-efficacy (also referred to as self-confidence and sense of mastery). The elements in this list of processes are not necessarily mutually exclusive, but they each represent an important component from the literature on behavioral and attitudinal learning and development.

Active Learning. The most overlapping process is active learning. As we examine examples of how process is linked to each of the intervention goals, elements of active learning will appear repeatedly. Active learning redefines teacher-student roles. The client-as-student learns how to become a client-as-self-teacher. The trainer or teacher becomes a facilitator of this process. To illustrate, learning how to think like the employer is active; being told how employers think is passive. Role playing how to handle conflicts is active; watching a multimedia presentation on how to handle conflicts is passive. Generating the do's and don'ts of interviewing is active; being shown a list of do's and don'ts is passive.

Active learning leads to better skill acquisition and utilization by reducing client resistance to the adoption of new skills (e.g., Cunningham, Davis, Bremner, Dunn, & Rzasa, 1993; McKeachie, 1969). By contrast, didactic instructional strategies may increase resistance to learning new skills (e.g., Cunningham et al., 1993; Patterson & Forgatch, 1985).

In active learning modes, the client "owns" or controls the process of discovery. Such ownership means that the client can control the extent to which new areas of learning are considered. It also means that interventions can avoid providing inappropriately rigid doses of education whether or not the client needs or is ready for them.

When active learning is combined with social modeling and graded exposure to increasingly more realistic settings, such learning has the added effect of helping the client transform procedural knowledge to behavioral skill. Applied to the JOBS interventions, job seekers can move from being *aware* of the best procedures for job seeking to being able to *perform* those procedures in a way that allows them to correctly attribute responsibility for, and success of learning, to themselves. Such attribution is expected to promote self-sustained learning and problem-solving skills that will transfer beyond the time and place of the intervention.

The Use of Peer Groups. The JOBS intervention is designed for use with small groups of clients. Group interventions are more economical to deliver. Groups also relieve the solo participant from having to perform all of the active generation of ideas. At the same time, groups increase the range of ideas and experience on which each client can draw.

The use of peers has the added advantage of lowering resistance to change by providing normative support for the exploration of new ideas. Peers maximize the power of social influence and source credibility for the client because peers close the gap between client and sources of social influence (e.g., Baekelund & Lundwall, 1975; Moscovici, 1985).

*Examples of the Integration of Intervention
Goals With Intervention Processes*

Goal 1: Persuading the Right People to Participate. JOBS I and II research suggests that not everyone necessarily benefits from an intervention; indeed, some people may do nearly as well without intervention (Price et al., 1992; Vinokur et al., 1995b). As a result, the first component of goal 1 consists of *identifying* persons with the greatest need for, and likelihood of benefiting from, preventive intervention. The second component is to *persuade* these people to participate in the intervention.

Persuading people to come to the very first session may be substantially more than half the battle. Although this is hardly conclusive regarding the importance of the first session, our experience with both JOBS I and II shows that as many as 85% of those persons who show up at the first session complete the program.

Recruiting people to the first session, however, remains a major challenge. Our experience across four different projects, one currently ongoing in another state, is that only about half the persons who indicate that they will participate actually show up.

This recruitment task may be the most difficult one in the intervention. The recruiter must persuade unemployed persons, who are shaken by their recent job loss, uncertain about their financial and career futures, and frequently haunted by self-doubts about their marketability, to come to the intervention. In terms of role claiming, these persons may fall somewhere between the *negative* self-identity of job loser and the more positive self-identity of temporary job seeker. Consequently, the recruiter should be viewed as the front line of intervention. The role-claiming perspective is relevant to success both in this goal and in the others listed in Table 15.1. That perspective, combined with the models of motivation and intervention shown in Figure 15.2 and Table 15.1, provide the elements of a sound theory of recruitment. Such a theory suggests that the recruiter needs three types of persuasive armament in the form of methods for (a) enhancing the unemployed person's acceptance of the role of job seeker and of the need to address the task of competing successfully in the job market, (b) increasing the perception that attending such interventions will lead to effective and successful job search (instrumentality), and (c) increasing the perception that the job seeker is capable of attending and benefiting from the intervention. If possible, the intervention program must be prepared to remove barriers to attending that are not under the client's control (e.g., needs for transportation or child care).

To influence malleable antecedents of program participation, the interventionist should consider principles, such as the following, all of which derive from theories of motivation and behavior change (e.g., Bandura, 1989; Janis, 1983; Meichenbaum, 1985): social modeling (perhaps a videotape or recording of similar persons discussing the program, their initial doubts about its value, and the benefits that they accrued); reinforcement of self-efficacy in attending important meetings (e.g., elicitation from the client of previous instances and praise for having that quality); and inoculation against setbacks (e.g., elicitation of possible barriers that might come up at the last minute, such as "feeling too tired," and strategies for overcoming them). These strategies fit with findings from the more general literature on persuasion and attitude change (e.g., Ajzen & Fishbein, 1980; Cialdini, 1988), on participation in preventive health care (i.e., tests of the Health Beliefs Model; e.g., Janz & Becker, 1984), and on related models such as the precaution-adoption process (e.g., Weinstein, 1993).

Goal 2: Establishing and Maintaining Trust in the Trainers, Peers, and Process. Research suggests that social influence that is based on referent and expert power is the most likely to help recruit people into the intervention as well as facilitate their acceptance of what the intervention has to offer (French & Raven, 1959). Referent power occurs when a relationship of trust is established because the target person identifies with, likes, or admires the source of the social influence. Not surprisingly, peers, because of their high referent power, are powerful sources of social influence. An effective way of building up such trust is by engaging in moderate self-disclosure of attributes or about experiences of the self that others will identify with (Jourard, 1968). Accordingly, the Michigan JOBS intervention has its trainers begin the intervention by engaging in moderate self-disclosure about their own experiences in coping with job loss. These disclosures emphasize the normal experience of self-doubt, the experience with barriers and setbacks, persistence in the face of these conditions, and, ultimately, success. For example, a trainer might say "I once was unemployed myself. I found that a lot of my friends didn't really understand what being unemployed was like. Some of them told me I'd do OK. But there were times when I wasn't sure I'd succeed. Still, I told myself that I had to keep plugging away. It was that persistence that led to success."

To build up the referent power of group members with each other, participants are asked to engage in moderate self-disclosure with other group members. Although participants are only asked to describe the type of job they are looking for and something special about themselves, such as a hobby, they frequently share feelings of distress and worry. Such disclosure encourages other members of the group to feel comfortable making similar disclosures such as "I thought I was the only person experiencing these thoughts and feelings. It's good to find out all this is normal. I thought that maybe there was something wrong with me." These comments normalize the stressful experiences of job loss for participants, create a bond based on shared experience, and signal a safe environment for further disclosure and participation.

To establish the trainer's expert power, the trainers refer to the scientific evidence that the program works. The trainers also refer to their own special training in running the program.

Goals 3 and 4: Enhancing Motivation to Cope and Enhancing Procedural Knowledge and Skills. Rigorous scientific tests of social influence theory (e.g., Bandura, 1989; Eden, 1990) demonstrate that procedural knowledge and skilled performance can be influenced in tandem. Social modeling theory (Bandura, 1989; Marlatt & Gordon, 1985; Meichenbaum, 1985) has generated useful tools for achieving these goals. The JOBS program incorporates those tools in steps that move the participant into successively more challenging situations where performance of the new skill is required. To take a concrete example, job seekers learn how to conduct networking telephone calls first by watching the trainers model the wrong way, next by generating suggestions to improve the trainers' modeling, then by role-playing the correct approaches themselves, and finally by applying these repertoires of action outside the program.

At each step, efficacy-enhancing feedback is used to increase self-confidence. For example, the protocols are structured so that once the trainers follow the participants' suggestions, and the participants see how useful those suggestions are, the trainers point out that "you have demonstrated that you already know what experts know about the best way to network." As participants role-play various job seeking behaviors, the intervention is structured so that their peers combine positive feedback about the effective application with feedback about ways in which the participant can make the performance even better. The trainers model the methods for giving positive feedback and practice those methods in providing feedback to the participants.

Goal 5: Promoting Transfer and Inoculation Against Setbacks. Studies of people attempting to engage in new behaviors indicate that slips and lapses into previous behaviors, attitudes, and moods are normal, not the exception (e.g., Janis, 1983; Marlatt & Gordon, 1985; Meichenbaum, 1985). When such setbacks occur, people may make extreme and disabling self-attributions. "I'll *never* be good at networking." "I'll *always* be a failure." "I'm *basically* lousy at making good impressions." This type of negative self-talk has been shown to be a key aspect of depressive symptoms (Beck & Freeman, 1990; Ellis & Dryden, 1987). Consequently, the prevention of such talk is a particularly important benefit for high-risk participants who already experience relatively low levels of self-esteem.

Such findings have generated methods for helping people build up repertoires of thought and action that can be called on in the face of setbacks and barriers, slips, and lapses. Once participants have practiced a new coping strategy, trainers encourage them to generate a list of things that could go wrong. Consider, for example, participants who have just practiced telephone techniques for getting connected directly with the employer rather than with a personnel department. The trainers will ask these participants to suggest (a) what could go *wrong* (e.g., the secretary might say the job has been filled, or that the person is on another line), (b) how a job seeker is likely to feel (e.g., angry, helpless), (c) what the job seeker is likely to think (e.g., "I *knew* I'd never be able to do this"), and (d) how to deal with what could go wrong and with the dysfunctional thoughts and actions that are normally elicited by the setback.

With regard to suggestions for coping with setbacks, respondents might say "You've got to tell yourself, 'these things will happen. It's normal.'" Or "Sure I feel low, but that won't get me a job. I've got to turn to the next number on my phone list and make the next call." In addition, if the group has not done so, the trainer may help reframe the rejection by saying, "One writer has pointed out that successful job seeking is a long string of *no's* followed by a *yes*. So the idea is to collect as many *no's* as possible, as quickly as possible, to reach that *yes* in the shortest amount of time" (Jackson, 1991).

How Can Employers and Other Organizations Get the Results That Were Generated in the JOBS Studies?

No intervention manual can ensure that one group's successful program will be replicated by others. Two additional ingredients are required: methods for ensuring the fidelity with which the program staff deliver the program, and organizational readiness to introduce a new program into its portfolio of functions.

Ensuring Fidelity

The recommendations in this section come from two intervention trials, JOBS I and II. In both cases, the investigators and other staff observed the adherence of the trainers to the procedures prescribed in the training manual and rated the trainers on their adherence. The results indicate that the trainers delivered the procedures with high fidelity to the intervention protocol. The procedures and practices that led to such high-quality program delivery by our staff in both trials are generally associated with high employee productivity and corporate financial performance in work organizations (e.g., Huselid, 1995; Jones & Wright, 1992).

Fidelity is likely to be threatened when there is a poor fit between the demands of the program to be delivered (for example, ability to adhere to the procedures) and the abilities of the staff to carry out those demands. It is also likely to be threatened when the trainer's needs (e.g., for interesting work or feedback) are not met by procedures and resources of the workplace (French, Rogers, & Cobb, 1974). We have identified the following four requirements that need to be addressed by host organizations to prevent these types of poor fit and promote fidelity:

1. A manual or documentation of the intervention protocol and procedures so that *a consistent and concrete standard* exists for defining the nature of the role staff are expected to fulfill[2]

2. A *valid selection procedure* that will maximize the likelihood that the staff hired and assigned to run the intervention have the capacity to learn the procedures in the manual

3. A *training program* that will raise staff skill and motivation to perform according to the standard set by the manual

4. *Processes to maintain performance at or above the standard*

Each of these four requirements is a necessary condition. The absence of any one component can be sufficient to undermine the fidelity of the program.

The manual for the JOBS intervention addresses all of these requirements (Curran, 1992). It contains principles and standards for performance including methods for assessing staff performance, an identification of required staff skills and abilities, how to search for qualified staff during the selection process, methods for training the staff, and procedures for maintaining high performance on a long-term basis. For example, to achieve long-term maintenance of performance, we recommend ongoing monitoring of, and feedback to, staff about their performance; supplementary training to address lapses in performance; the use of rewards (e.g., compensation, verbal, symbolic); and the addressing of other needs, such as for task enrichment (see discussion below regarding task complexity). Researchers and practitioners interested in interventions with other types of clients can view the manual as a useful launching point for the design and standardization of procedures.

Fitting Program Complexity to the Capacities of the Staff

Research indicates that the more complex the program protocol, the greater the risk that it will outstrip the capacity of the staff to deliver the program (e.g., Yeaton & Sechrest, 1981). The JOBS program reduces the risk of such complexity by installing a training program that focuses the staff on (a) following a small number of fundamental principles, (b) following the same format conventions from session to session, and (c) providing a concrete and predictable, rather than ambiguous, structure for each session. Complexity is further reduced by using the same set of principles for training the staff in their new attitudes and behaviors as for training the job seekers in theirs—active learning, social modeling, and so on. This parallel is pointed out to the staff when they are trained.

As trainers become more experienced in carrying out such interventions, what was initially a challenging and interesting job may become repetitious and boring. What may have been initially too complex may become too simple, too lacking in stimulation. We have observed programs in which the latter was the case. Under such conditions, staff diverge from the manualized procedures to enrich their own jobs and to fill the growing gap between need for stimulation and inadequate supplies of it.

The JOBS manual describes methods of job enrichment for counteracting this threat to fidelity. Within each pair of trainers, members can rotate responsibilities for different sections of the protocol. Every 2 to 3 weeks, pairs of trainers are rotated off delivering the sessions for a week. During the off week, the trainers take on responsibility for observing and providing postsession feedback to the other trainers, for designing the agenda for weekly skill maintenance meetings of all the trainers, and for helping to recruit new job seekers. The routine of trainer can also be further enriched by pairing trainers with new cotrainers.

In organizations that specialize in preventive interventions across a variety of life challenges, it may also be possible to rotate generically trained staff from one type of intervention to another. Trainers might be rotated between interventions for job seekers and interventions for people facing life-threatening health problems, and so on, while varying the composition of trainer pairs from intervention to intervention.

Maximizing Organizational Readiness

The term *organizational readiness* (D'Aunno, 1986) refers to a set of preconditions for adopting innovative practices. On the basis of a review of the literature on such readiness, Price and Lorion (1989) conclude that organizational interventions are more likely to succeed in host organizations that have five critical attributes. These attributes are presented in Figure 15.3. The first step in introducing a new innovation such as the JOBS program is to assess the presence of these attributes. Where they are not in place, they are likely to undermine program introduction and survival.

Pressures and Resources From the External Environment

The organization's external environment may either facilitate or hinder such adoption. For example, corporate decision makers may be more ready to adopt the JOBS program for outplacement purposes if key agencies in the environment of the organization produce incentives for corporate outplacement. Community-based

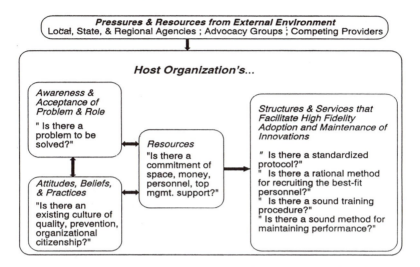

Figure 15.3. Determinants of Organizational Readiness to Adopt the JOBS Program.
SOURCE: After Price and Lorion (1989).

institutions may find support from advocacy groups for a proactive, preventive orientation in providing services.

Awareness and Acceptance of the Problem by the Host Organization

Awareness, acceptance, and ownership of the problem by top managers in the organization are hypothesized to be critical components of readiness. For example, a vice president for human resources may recognize that there are major corporate costs associated with downsizing efforts that do not include an effective outplacement program. Knowing that the lack of an outplacement program may result in demoralization of those workers who remain (e.g., Brockner et al., 1994), the vice president may be more likely to champion a program such as JOBS. Where such awareness does not exist, external as well as internal sources (e.g., professional associations, personnel departments, employee assistance programs, psychiatric hospitals, and local, state, and federal government agencies) may seek to remedy the situation.

Attitudes, Beliefs, and Practices in the Local Organization

Attitudes, beliefs, and practices of corporate managers and staff or public agency officials in the local organization can also be a critical dimension of readiness. If local human resource staff, for example, feel that the problem of job search and reemployment is not part of their roles and responsibilities, the likelihood of successful implementation is much lower.

A key practice component in influencing these attitudes as well as the resources that will be made available is *how* decisions to implement a new program or service are made. Particularly in organizations faced with scarce resources—of budget, office and meeting space, or otherwise—the unilateral introduction by top management of a new program may stir turf battles. Staff who are left out of the process may attempt to sabotage the process and are likely to make life miserable for the newcomer program. Accordingly, organizational psychologists recommend that decisions to introduce new programs be made via participation and with a problem-solving orientation (e.g., Argyris, 1993; Senge, 1990). In this way, stakeholders can express their concerns; and threats to program survival can be addressed openly, with the aim of achieving commitment from all stakeholders to protect the new program.

Resources

There may be organizational structures, services, and values already in place in organizations that can facilitate adoption of interventions such as the JOBS program (Galbraith, 1982; Van de Ven, 1986). Organizations with high levels of flexibility in their structures and work roles may be more likely to adopt and implement novel programs (Hasenfeld, 1983; Katz & Kahn, 1978; Lawrence & Lorsch, 1967; Thompson, 1967). Organizations that already allow staff to support effective job transitions within the organization, using available internal labor markets, may also be more likely to adopt an outplacement program such as JOBS. In such cases, persons with a stake in introducing the new social technology should identify and involve such resources in mapping out the strategy for introducing the innovation.

In sum, there are a series of steps that organizations can take to maximize the productivity of preventive intervention programs such as JOBS. The care taken in strengthening organizational readiness ensures that there will be adequate resources to launch the program. The next step is management of those resources to maximize the fidelity with which staff deliver intervention services. The steps that we have listed for achieving fidelity make sense on two grounds: They have worked well with two separate staffs, and organizational research indicates that they are among the most fundamental components of sound management practice.

The Future: Continuing the Agenda

The Cycle Between Survey and Field Trial

The first studies in the JOBS program focused on identifying malleable characteristics of job seekers and their environments that made a difference in how well they coped with job loss. Research from these studies formed a basis for field trials testing whether we could impart the advantages of successful copers to persons with a need for such resources. The JOBS program is continuing this cycle of longitudinal panel surveys and field trials along two paths: providing communities and organizations with the enhanced ability to launch programs such as JOBS; and broadening the focus to the family.

Providing Communities With the Ability to Launch Programs Such as JOBS

Initial studies in this cycle will examine the impact of naturally occurring variations in the readiness of organizations that introduce programs such as JOBS and in the methods they use to manage fidelity on program outcomes. Later studies will examine these effects in field trials that experimentally attempt to prevent loss of fidelity.

Investigators in other countries have translated the JOBS Manual into Russian and Finnish. These translations are likely to contribute to research that will examine what is generic in the current models of intervention and what needs further specification to take into account the role of culture.

Broadening the Focus to the Family

Since the Great Depression, there has been evidence that job loss affects the entire family (e.g., Jahoda, 1982; Atkinson et al., 1986). The JOBS program's investigators made the explicit decision to initially target preventive intervention only at the job seeker because including the spouse or partner would add too much complexity in the initial stages of field trials. Based on the success of the JOBS trials, the research program is turning its attention to the family as a target of preventive intervention.

This work brings together two lines of work, one by members of the Center for Family Research at George Washington University (Howe, Caplan, Foster, Lockshin, & McGrath, 1995) and the other at the Michigan Prevention Research Center (Vinokur, Price, Caplan, van Ryn, & Curran, 1995). Their joint studies will allow simultaneous constructive replications (Lykken, 1968) in their respective labor market areas.

Initial-stage etiological research conducted in the Center for Family Research is identifying the determinants of successful couple-focused coping and is providing a platform for the development of measures of couples' coping behavior. The findings are intended to guide field trials aimed at helping couples manage the challenges to the family of job loss and recovery. These trials will merge the social technology of the JOBS program with that for helping couples deal with relational challenges of job loss (for example, Markman, Renick, Floyd, Stanley, & Clements, 1993).

The Identification of Basic Principles: What Is Generic?

The programmatic aim of the JOBS research is to contribute to the development of basic theory and principles of preventive intervention. A basic theory should apply across a wide range of stressful life events, including job loss. Such theory should also include guidelines for when modifications should be made to accommodate event-specific crises. For example, serious illness in the family, loss of property, and unemployment may all call for interventions that include the raising of self-efficacy regarding survival skills. At the same time, there may be significant variance among these events with regard to their impact on family roles, the cognitive reframing of loss, and the time frame over which the event unfolds and generates different sequelae. Such variance is likely to require tailoring of the intervention to the event.

To maximize the likelihood that the JOBS focuses on fundamental principles and contributes to a general theory of preventive intervention, we derived the elements of the program's theoretical models from a variety of basic literatures. Those literatures include social, clinical, community, and industrial/organizational psychology as well as health and family psychology. Theory and findings from these sources were integrated with those from the literatures on job loss and well-being.

Future application of the principles that guided the JOBS interventions to preventive interventions for other stressful life events can provide a direct test of the generalizability of those principles. Drawing on Figures 15.1 through 15.3 and Table 15.1, we will conclude with a dozen of those principles, all of which are linked to broader theory and applications cited in this text. The first nine principles address the design of the intervention, whereas the last three address the successful implementation of that design by host organizations.

Principles of Intervention Design

1. *View recruitment as the start of the intervention.* Client acceptance of the role of "successful" or "potentially successful coper" is key to entering a preventive intervention. Successful copers maximize their resources (Pearlin & Schooler, 1978). However, unless potential clients perceive a need for intervention and accept their own role to be an active pursuer of such services, they will not participate. Accordingly, recruitment should attempt to make the role of successful coper a salient one. Recruitment should be treated as an intervention—the first and perhaps most critical one.

2. *View intervention as social influence.* For interventionists to achieve such social influence, they must initially establish a relationship of trust with the client (i.e., staff will act in the client's best interest and respect the client's needs). Interventionists must

also provide a basis for client beliefs that the interventionist has expertise in running the procedure and that the procedure is efficacious. Once these perceptions are established, the intervention must maintain them.

3. *Target motivation, skills, knowledge, and resources,* because all of these elements are required for successful coping. If coping is required to obtain resources (e.g., financial aid, referrals and leads, information), then build declarative knowledge on what skills need to be used, the procedural skills that enact appropriately performed repertoires, and the self-confidence to enact those skills.

4. *Build self-sufficiency.* An intervention need not provide all the resources for successful coping, but it needs to enhance whatever motivation, skills, and knowledge the person requires to acquire key resources that are not presently available. The intervention needs to provide the skill and motivation to pursue such resources beyond the time and place of the intervention. As an illustration, the JOBS intervention does not provide job leads, but it provides the motivational foundation and behavioral tools for uncovering such leads, once the job seekers are on their own.

5. *No one succeeds unless he or she has the confidence to try to succeed.* In some cases, the beneficial effects of preventive intervention on successful coping may result more from the enhancement of a sense of mastery than from the acquisition of new skills. In the JOBS experiments, for example, the likelihood of gaining reemployment may depend more on having the self-confidence to search for, locate, and pursue job leads than on the skills used in doing so. A sense of mastery, however, results from the performance of skills coupled with positive feedback about that performance. Consequently, interventions should view skill building and positive feedback as inseparable requirements for successful future coping.

6. *Within the structure of the intervention, allow for individual differences in levels and modes of participation.* To prevent resistance to change and to maximize individual achievement, interventions should allow clients to find their own levels of challenge within each component of intervention. This approach recognizes that (a) there are basic sequences in developing coping skills (e.g., build trust, generate felt need, build skills, raise self-efficacy, and inoculate against setbacks), but that (b) there are individual differences in people's expression of their needs and abilities to benefit from the intervention.

7. *Use active teaching and learning methods to maximize fit between the demands of the intervention and the learning capabilities of the participants.* The incorporation of active teaching methods that involve peers as sources of feedback can maximize the likelihood that each participant will proceed at the rate that is best for that person. Peer feedback in one-on-one exercises can maximize instruction that is individualized to the needs of each client.

8. *Select components of active methods to maximize the experience of success.* When active learning incorporates social modeling, graded exposure, and reinforcement of self-efficacy, the combination increases the likelihood that the person will both learn and use new coping techniques. Together, these intervention elements should appear to (a) minimize the experience of failure, (b) maximize the experience of success, (c) maximize the attribution that success is the result of internal stable attributes, and (d) minimize the attribution that success is tied to external sources such as the presence of the trainer or the support group. The deletion of such elements could lead to experiences of failure, participant dropout, and failure to generalize beyond the setting of the intervention (e.g., Abramson, Seligman, & Teasdale, 1978; Feather & Davenport, 1981).

9. *Build expectancies of setbacks and barriers and inoculate against them.* Lapses, setbacks, and slips in the performance of new as well as established coping methods are normal. Interventions should prepare people for these contingencies by having participants generate repertoires of thought and action for dealing with them.

Principles of Design Implementation

10. *Pursue program fidelity with a passion.* Successful application of a tested program of intervention is limited by the fidelity with which the staff apply the program's generic principles. If you have to make modifications, make them quantitative (e.g., reduce the number of minutes), not qualitative (e.g., omit the practice of reinforcing self-efficacy).

11. *Select the right staff and take care of them.* Fidelity to the original principles of an intervention depends on careful identification of desired staff attitudes, skills, and behaviors; the selection

and training of the staff; and the maintenance of the desired types of performance. For example, to maintain staff teamwork, pay systems should recognize team-relevant as well as individual performance.

12. *Do your organizational homework.* The achievement of all of the preceding goals depends fundamentally on the successful introduction of the program into the host organization. The context of preexisting priorities and values, contests, pressures, scarcities, and strengths influences the host organization's decision to implement and support new programs and services. Failure to recognize, respect, and capitalize on that context may lead to short-lived programs. Doing one's organizational "homework" is shorthand for organizational networking, information-seeking, trust- and coalition-building, and negotiating and a variety of related tasks. Give yourself an "A" on such homework if, by time the decision to implement the new program comes up for a vote, the vote is pro forma, and the answer is "approve."

In sum, such prescriptions represent an accruing set of ideas regarding the ingredients for successful programs of preventive intervention. The field of preventive intervention research is still relatively young, and the empirical literature on the conditions under which interventions such as JOBS are successfully transferred to new host organizations is in its infancy. Consequently, we would not be surprised if a number of these elements are modified or reframed by subsequent theory and research on what constitutes best practice for preventive intervention.

Notes

1. *JOBS: A Manual for Teaching People Successful Job Search Strategies.* (Curran, 1992), provides complete instructions for implementing these principles for the JOBS intervention. Each session is described in 12 to 15 pages of detailed instructions. For readers interested in developing new interventions, the manual can be used as a template for what should be included.

2. It is likely that identical replication of a program such as the JOBS from site to site will be impossible. Differences in resources and other contextual demands will force adaptation of procedures rather than faithful adoption. The more that adaptation preserves the generic principles of the core design, the greater the likelihood that the delivered intervention will generate the beneficial outcomes of

the original social technology. There is a need for research that examines the effects of, and limits to, such adaptations.

References

Abramson, L. Y., Seligman, M. E. P., & Teasdale, J. D. (1978). Learned helplessness in humans: Critique and reformulation. *Journal of Abnormal Psychology, 87*(1), 49-74.

Ajzen, I., & Fishbein, M. (1980). *Attitudes, personality, and behavior.* Englewood Cliffs, NJ: Prentice Hall.

Argyris, C. (1993). *Knowledge for action: A guide to overcoming barriers to organizational change.* San Francisco: Jossey-Bass.

Atkinson, J. W., & Feather, N. T. (1966). *A theory of achievement motivation.* New York: John Wiley.

Atkinson, T., Liem, R., & Liem, J. (1986). The social costs of unemployment: Implications for social support. *Journal of Health and Social Behavior, 27*(4), 317-331.

Baekelund, F., & Lundwall, L. (1975). Dropping out of treatment: A critical review. *Psychological Bulletin, 82,* 738-783.

Baker, W. E., & Faulkner, R. R. (1991). Role as resource in the Hollywood film industry. *American Journal of Sociology, 97*(2), 279-309.

Bandura, A. (1989). Human agency in social cognitive theory. *American Psychologist, 44*(9), 1175-1184.

Beck, A. T., & Freeman, A. T. (1990). *Cognitive therapy for depression.* New York: Guilford.

Bloom, H. S. (1984). Accounting for no-shows in experimental evaluation designs. *Evaluation Review, 8*(2), 225-246.

Bloom, H. S. (1987). What works for whom? CETA impacts for adult participants. *Evaluation Review, 11*(4), 510-527.

Bolles, R. N. (1995). *What color is your parachute? A practical manual for job hunters and career changers.* Berkeley, CA: Ten Speed Press.

Brockner, J., Konovsky, M., Cooper-Schneider, R., Folger, R., Martin, C., & Bies, R. J. (1994). Interactive effects of procedural justice and outcome negativity on victims and survivors of job loss. *Academy of Management Journal, 37*(2), 397-409.

Callero, P. L. (1994). From role-playing to role-using: Understanding role as resource. *Social Psychology Quarterly, 57*(3), 228-243.

Caplan, R. D., Vinokur, A. D., Price, R. H., & van Ryn, M. (1989). Job seeking, reemployment, and mental health: A randomized field experiment in coping with job loss. *Journal of Applied Psychology, 74*(5), 759-769.

Catalano, R. (1991). The health effects of economic insecurity. *American Journal of Public Health, 81*(9), 1148-1252.

Catalano, R., Dooley, D., Novaco, R. W., & Wilson, G. (1993). Using ECA survey data to examine the effect of job layoffs on violent behavior. *Hospital and Community Psychiatry, 44*(9), 874-879.

Catalano, R., Dooley, D., Wilson, G., & Hough, R. (1993). Job loss and alcohol abuse: A test using data from the Epidemiological Catchment Area Project. *Journal of Health and Social Behavior, 34*(3), 215-225.

Catalano, R., & Serxner, S. (1992). The effect of ambient threats to employment on low birthweight. *Journal of Health and Social Behavior, 33*(4), 363-377.

Cialdini, R. B. (1988). *Influence: Science and practice.* Glenview, IL: Scott, Foresman.

Cobb, S., & Kasl, S. V. (1977). *Termination: The consequences of job loss* (DHEW NIOSH Publication No. 77-224). Cincinnati, OH: NIOSH.

Conger, R. D., Elder, G. H., Lorenz, F. O., Conger, K. J., Simons, R. L., Whitbeck, L. B., Huck, S., & Melby, J. N. (1990). Linking economic hardship to marital quality and instability. *Journal of Marriage and the Family, 52,* 643-656.

Cunningham, C. E., Davis, J. R., Bremner, R., Dunn, K. W., & Rzasa, T. (1993). Coping modeling problem solving versus mastery modeling: Effects on adherence, in-session process, and skill acquisition in a residential parent-training program. *Journal of Consulting and Clinical Psychology, 61*(5), 871-877.

Curran, J. (1992). *JOBS. A manual for teaching people successful job search strategies.* Ann Arbor, MI: Michigan Prevention Research Center, Institute for Social Research, University of Michigan.

D'Aunno, T. (1986). *AIDS prevention among intravenous drug users: Organizational factors.* Unpublished manuscript, University of Michigan School of Public Health, Ann Arbor, MI.

Davidson, C., & Woodbury, S. A. (1993). The displacement effect of reemployment bonus programs. *Journal of Labor Economics, 11*(4), 575-605.

Dew, M. A., Penkower, L., & Bromet, E. J. (1991). Effects of unemployment on mental health in the contemporary family. *Behavior Modification, 15*(4), 501-544.

Dooley, D., Catalano, R., Rook, K., & Serxner, S. (1989). Economic stress and suicide: Multilevel analyses: II. Cross-level analyses of economic stress and suicidal ideation. *Suicide and Life-Threatening Behavior, 19*(4), 337-351.

Eden, D. (1990). *Pygmalion in management.* Lexington, MA: Lexington Books.

Eden, D., & Aviram, A. (1993). Self-efficacy training to speed reemployment: Helping people to help themselves. *Journal of Applied Psychology, 78*(3), 352-360.

Ellis, A., & Dryden, W. (1987). *The practice of rational emotive therapy.* New York: Springer.

Ezzy, D. (1993). Unemployment and mental health. A critical review. *Social Science and Medicine, 37*(1), 41-52.

Feather, N. T., & Davenport, P. R. (1981). Unemployment and depressive affect: A motivational and attributional analysis. *Journal of Personality and Social Psychology, 41*(3), 422-436.

Fischer, R. L., & Cordray, D. S. (1995). *Job training and welfare reform: A policy-driven synthesis.* Unpublished manuscript.

French, J. R. P. Jr., & Raven, B. (1959). The bases of social power. In D. Cartwright (Ed.), *Studies in social power* (pp. 150-167). Ann Arbor, MI: Institute for Social Research.

French, J. R. P. Jr., Rogers, W., & Cobb, S. (1974). Adjustment as person-environment fit. In G. V. Coelho, D. A. Hamburg, & J. E. Adams (Eds.), *Coping and adaptation*. (pp. 316-333). New York: Basic Books.

Galbraith, J. R. (1982). Designing the innovating organization. *Organizational Dynamics, 10*(3), 3-24.

Goldstein, I. L. (1994). *Training in organizations* (3rd ed.). Belmont, CA: Brooks/Cole.

Granovetter, M. (1974). *Getting a job.* Cambridge, MA: Harvard University Press.

Hamilton, V. L., Broman, C. L., & Hoffman, W. S. (1990). Hard times and vulnerable people: Initial effects of plant closing on autoworkers' mental health. *Journal of Health and Social Behavior, 31*(2), 123-140.

Hamilton, V. L., Hoffman, W. W., Broman, C. L., & Rauma, D. (1993). Unemployment distress and coping: A panel study of autoworkers. *Journal of Personality and Social Psychology, 65*(2), 234-247.

Handy, C. B. (1989). *The age of unreason.* Boston: Harvard Business School Press.

Harris, M. J., & Kotch, J. B. (1994). Unintentional infant injuries: Sociodemographic and psychosocial factors. *Public Health Nursing, 11*(2), 90-97.

Hasenfeld, Y. (1983). *Human service organizations.* Englewood Cliffs, NJ: Prentice Hall.

Heikkinen, M. E., Isometsa, E. T., Aro, H. M., & Sarna, S. J. (1995). Age-related variation in recent life events preceding suicide. *Journal of Nervous and Mental Disease, 183*(5), 325-331.

Howe, G. W., Caplan, R. D., Foster, D., Lockshin, M., & McGrath, C. (1995). A research strategy for developing preventive interventions. In G. Keita & S. Sauter (Eds.), *Stress in the 90s.* Washington, DC: American Psychological Association.

Huselid, M. A. (1995). The impact of human resource management practices on turnover, productivity, and corporate financial performance. *Academy of Management Journal, 38*(3), 635-672.

Jackson, T. (1991). *Guerilla tactics in the new job market.* New York: Bantam.

Jahoda, M. (1982). *Employment and unemployment: A social-psychological analysis.* Cambridge, UK: Cambridge University Press.

Janis, I. L. (1983). The role of social support in adherence to stressful decisions. *American Psychologist, 38*(2), 143-160.

Janz, N. K., & Becker, M. H. (1984). The Health Belief Model: A decade later. *Health Education Quarterly, 11*(1), 1-47.

Jones, G. R., & Wright, P. M. (1992). An economic approach to conceptualizing the utility of human resource practices. In K. Rowland & G. Ferris (Eds.), *Research in personnel and human resources management* (pp. 271-299). Greenwich, CT: JAI.

Jourard, S. M. (1968). *Disclosing man to himself.* Princeton, NJ: Van Nostrand.

Katz, D., & Kahn, R. L. (1978). *The social psychology of organizations* (2nd. ed.). New York: John Wiley.

Kessler, R. C., House, J., & Turner, B. (1988). The effects of unemployment on health in a community survey: Main, modifying, and mediating effects. *Journal of Social Issues, 44*(4), 69-86.

Krishnan, V., & Morrison, K. B. (1995). An ecological model of child maltreatment in a Canadian province. *Child Abuse & Neglect, 19*(1), 101-113.

Lawler, E. E. (1973). *Motivation in work organizations.* Belmont, CA: Wadsworth.

Lawrence, P. R., & Lorsch, J. W. (1967). *Organization and environment.* Boston: Harvard Business School, Division of Research.

Lazarus, R. S., & Folkman, S. (1984). *Stress, appraisal, and coping.* New York: McGraw-Hill.

Lykken, D. T. (1968). Statistical significance in psychological research. *Psychological Bulletin, 70*(3), 151-159.

Markman, H. J., Renick M. J., Floyd, F. J., Stanley, S. M., & Clements, M. (1993). Preventing marital distress through communication and conflict management training: A four- and five-year follow-up. *Journal of Consulting and Clinical Psychology, 61*(1), 70-77.

Marlatt, A. G., & Gordon, J. R. (1985). *Relapse prevention.* New York: Guilford.

McKeachie, W. J. (1969). *Teaching tips.* Boston: D. C. Heath.

Meichenbaum, D. (1985). *Stress inoculation training.* New York: Pergamon.

Moscovici, S. (1985). Social influence and conformity. In G. Lindzey & E. Aronson (Eds.), *The handbook of social psychology* (pp. 347-412). New York: Random House.

Patterson, G. R., & Forgatch, M. S. (1985). Therapist behavior as a determinant for patient noncompliance: A paradox for the behavior modifier. *Journal of Consulting and Clinical Psychology, 53*(6), 846-851.

Pearlin, L. I., & Schooler, C. (1978). The structure of coping. *Journal of Health and Social Behavior, 19*(1), 2-22.

Price, R. H. (in press). Unemployment. In J. Rappaport & E. Seidman (Eds.), *Handbook of community psychology.* New York: Plenum.

Price, R. H., & Lorion, R. P. (1989). Preventive programming as organizational reinvention: From research to implementation. In D. Shaffer, I. Phillips, N. B. Enzer, M. M. Silverman, & V. Anthony (Eds.), *Prevention of mental disorders, alcohol and drug use in children and adolescents* (pp. 97-123; DHHS Publication No. ADM 89-1646). Rockville, MD: Office of Substance Abuse Prevention and American Academy of Child and Adolescent Psychiatry.

Price, R. H., van Ryn, M., & Vinokur, A. D. (1992). Impact of preventive job search intervention on the likelihood of depression among the unemployed. *Journal of Health and Social Behavior, 33*(2), 158-167.

Price, R. H., Vinokur, A. D., & Friedland, E. S. (1996). *The job seeker role as resource: Achieving reemployment and enhancing mental health.* Unpublished manuscript, Institute for Social Research, Ann Arbor, MI.

Reich, R. B. (1991). *The work of nations: Preparing ourselves for 21st century capitalism.* New York: Knopf.

Rook, K., Dooley, D., & Catalano, R. (1991). Stress transmission: The effects of husbands' job stressors on the emotional health of their wives. *Journal of Marriage and the Family, 53*(1), 165-177.

Senge, P. M. (1990). *The fifth discipline: the art and practice of the learning organization.* New York: Doubleday/Currency.

Thompson, J. D. (1967). *Organizations in action.* New York: McGraw-Hill.

Van de Ven, A. H. (1986). Central problems in the management of innovation. *Management Science, 32*(5), 590-608.

van Ryn, M., & Vinokur, A. D. (1992). How did it work?: An examination of the mechanisms through which a community intervention influenced job-search behavior among an unemployed sample. *American Journal of Community Psychology, 20*(5), 577-597.

Vinokur, A., & Caplan, R. D. (1987). Attitudes and social support: Determinants of job-seeking behavior and well-being among the unemployed. *Journal of Applied Social Psychology, 17*(12), 1007-1024.

Vinokur, A., Caplan, R. D., & Williams, C. C. (1987). Effects of recent and past mental health: Coping with unemployment among Vietnam veterans and non-veterans. *Journal of Applied Social Psychology, 17*(8), 710-730.

Vinokur, A. D., Price, R. H., & Caplan, R. D. (1991). From field experiments to program implementation: Assessing the potential outcomes of an experimental intervention program for unemployed persons. *American Journal of Community Psychology, 19*(4), 543-562.

Vinokur, A. D., Price, R. H., & Caplan, R. D. (in press). Hard times and hurtful partners: How financial strain affects depression and relationship satisfaction of unemployed persons and their spouses. *Journal of Personality and Social Psychology.*

Vinokur, A. D., Price, R. H., Caplan, R. D., van Ryn, M., & Curran, J. (1995). The JOBS I preventive intervention for unemployed persons: Short and long-term effects on reemployment and mental health. In G. P. Keita (Eds.), *Job stress interventions: Current practices and new directions* (pp. 125-138). Washington, DC: American Psychological Association.

Vinokur, A. D., Price, R. H., & Schul, Y. (1995). Impact of the JOBS intervention on unemployed workers varying in risk for depression. *American Journal of Community Psychology, 232*(1), 39-74.

Vinokur, A. D., van Ryn, M., Gramlich, E. M., & Price, R. H. (1991). Long-term follow-up and benefit-cost analysis of the JOBS Program: A preventive intervention for the unemployed. *Journal of Applied Psychology, 76*(2), 213-219.

Weinstein, N. D. (1993). Testing four competing theories of health-protective behavior. *Health Psychology, 12*(4), 324-333.

Yeaton, W. H., & Sechrest, L. (1981). Critical dimensions in the choice and maintenance of successful treatments: Strength, integrity, and effectiveness. *Journal of Consulting and Clinical Psychology, 49*(2), 156-157.

Zimmerman, B. J., & Bonner, S. (in press). A social cognitive view of strategic learning. In C. E. Winstein & B. L. McCombs (Eds.), *Strategic learning: Skill, will, and self-regulation.* Hillsdale, NJ: Lawrence Erlbaum.

CHAPTER 16

The San Francisco Depression Prevention Research Project

RICARDO F. MUÑOZ

The San Francisco Depression Prevention Research Project (DPRP) is part of a research program dedicated to the development and evaluation of methods to prevent clinical depression; that is, depression such as major depression and dysthymia that interferes significantly with an individual's life or activities. Depression is a highly common disorder that can ruin lives and disrupt families and work, and that contributes to several other public health problems. Our society must recognize the need for developing reliable methods of identifying groups and individuals at risk for depression and providing them with strategies to manage their mood levels so that they do not become clinically depressed. In this chapter, we will review the impact of depression itself, the influence that depression has on several other public health problems, and the directions that our work and that of other researchers are taking to reduce the number of new cases of depression.

Depression

The word *depression* is used in many ways. It most often refers to a passing mood state that is a normal part of human life. It can also mean a symptom that is part of some physical and emotional disorders. And it is the name of one of the most common of mental disorders. Technically called "major depression," this disorder affects 17% of U.S. adults sometime during their lives, and more than 10% in any 1-year period (Kessler et al., 1994). The disorder is more common in women: 21% of women have major depression sometime in their lives, compared to 12% of men (Kessler et al., 1994). Depression costs the nation $44 billion dollars in 1990 dollars (Greenberg, Stiglin, Finkelstein, & Berndt, 1993). But this cost is often overlooked, partly because most people do not recognize the role that depression plays in their own lives, the lives of their loved ones, or the lives of their students, patients, or supervisees.

For example, there are more suicides than homicides in the United States (U.S. Bureau of the Census, 1994); and depression is implicated in the majority of suicides. Most people find this fact surprising, underscoring the way in which depression's impact on our society is greatly underestimated. And this underestimation extends even to individuals whose job is to be aware of national issues. As part of their coverage of gun control issues, *Time* magazine recently did a story on all the people killed by guns during one week in the United States (Magnuson, 1989). The writers expressed great surprise at the fact that over half of those killed by guns had killed themselves.

The taking of one's own life is clearly connected to the fact that depression can be an intensely painful human experience. In a study in which depressed individuals who had a history of life-threatening medical illnesses were asked to compare the pain of the two conditions, the pain of depression was rated as worse (Osmond, Mullaly, & Bisbee, 1984). In a separate study, persons with terminal illnesses generally did not wish to die unless they also had clinical depression (Brown, Henteleff, & Barakat, 1986). Depressed people consider suicide not so much because they want to die, but because they want the emotional pain they are experiencing to stop. Depression makes it difficult for them to see any way to stop or diminish the emotional pain other than through death.

The impact of depression on human functioning is comparable to, or worse than, several of the most debilitating physical disorders. A large-scale study of over 11,000 individuals measured physical, social, and role functioning; number of days in bed; perceived current health; and amount of pain felt. The individuals in the study suffered one or more of the following problems:

hypertension, diabetes, current advanced coronary artery disease, angina, arthritis, back problems, lung problems, gastrointestinal disorder, depressive disorder, and high symptom levels of depression. In general, patients with either depressive disorder or high levels of depressive symptoms had impaired functioning as bad or worse than those with the other disorders (Wells et al., 1989).

The Role of Depression in the Health of the Public

In 1990, there were approximately 2,148,000 deaths in the United States. Over half of these deaths were caused by nine external (nongenetic) factors. These factors, the estimated number of deaths due to each factor, and the percentage of total deaths from each were as follows: tobacco (400,000, 19%), diet/activity patterns (300,000, 14%), alcohol (100,000, 5%), microbial agents (90,000, 4%), toxic agents (60,000, 3%), firearms (35,000, 2%), sexual behavior (30,000, 1%), motor vehicles (25,000, 1%), and illicit use of drugs (20,000, <1%) (McGinnis & Foege, 1993). Take a moment to consider these causes of death and make a mental estimate of what proportion of them might be related to depression. We have already seen that over half of deaths due to firearms are self-inflicted, and most of those probably take place when the individual is in a depressed state of mind. Could other major causes of death be related to depression?

Attributable Risk

The field of epidemiology studies the distribution and determinants of disease frequency in humans (Fletcher, Fletcher, & Wagner, 1988). One of the concepts developed in epidemiology is that of *attributable risk*; that is, the proportion of cases of a specific condition that are attributable, or due, to a specific factor. I find it easier to understand this concept when considering the following example: It is now commonly known that tobacco smoking is related to lung cancer. However, lung cancer can also be caused by other factors. If we were to eradicate tobacco, some proportion of lung cancer would be prevented, but not all cases. The proportion prevented would be the proportion of cases attributable to smoking, or the attributable risk.

Some proportion of the major causes of death in the United States are attributable to depression. If we could estimate these proportions, we could determine the effect that reducing the prevalence of depression would have on preventing premature deaths and the impaired quality of life that often precedes them. Although no such estimates have been made, there is substantial evidence that several of the major causes of death are related to depression. Let's consider some.

Depression, Smoking, and Alcohol

The National Health Interview Survey of Health Promotion and Disease Prevention interviewed 43,732 adults 18 years or older in 1991 and found that adults who were often depressed were about 40% to 50% more likely to smoke than persons who were never depressed. Persons who were often lonely were about 60% to 70% more likely to smoke than persons who were never lonely. Men with the highest levels of negative moods were three times as likely to be heavy drinkers than those with no negative moods. (Heavy drinking in women was not related to negative moods, however.) And men with the highest levels of negative moods were four times as likely to combine smoking with heavier drinking than men reporting no negative moods (Schoenborn & Horm, 1993).

Other studies have shown depressive symptoms can predict ability to quit smoking. Anda and colleagues (1990) analyzed data from the Health and Nutrition Examination Survey, another national study, and found that only 9.9% of respondents with a score of 16 or above on the Center for Epidemiological Studies Depression Scale had been able to quit in a 9-year period, compared to 17.7% of those with scores of 15 or below. Persons with a history of major depression are more likely to have smoked sometime during their lives, and if they smoke, are less likely to quit (Glassman et al., 1990).

The conclusion is relatively straightforward: depressive symptoms and depressive disorders are related to use of tobacco and alcohol, the two most-used legal drugs. They are likely to be related to the use of illicit drugs as well. Tobacco, alcohol, and illicit use of drugs together cause approximately 25% of deaths in the United States or 520,000. If the risk of drug use attributable to depression were as low as 20%, the effect of preventing depression would be a reduction of over 100,000 premature deaths a year. Note that deaths from drug use are but the final outcome. At least as important are the disruption in individuals' lives and those of their families, and the curtailment of their contributions to their communities either because of being under the influence of the drugs or because of the debilitating disease process which eventually leads to their death.

Depression, Diet, and Activity Patterns

The role of depression in self-care patterns is well-recognized at a clinical level. Persons who are depressed often exhibit appetite problems, either eating less or more than their usual amount. They are prone to a vicious cycle that includes a tendency to reduced activity levels, reduced energy, and reduced mood levels. The reduction in motivation to live fully that accompanies a depressed state of mind leads to the phenomenon of "letting oneself go." Interestingly, increasing activity levels, as well as establishing a healthy sleeping and eating routine, often have positive effects on mood levels (Sime & Sanstead, 1987). There are currently no estimates regarding what proportion of unhealthy diet/activity patterns are related to depression.

Depression, Firearms, Sexual Behavior, and Motor Vehicles

The latter three factors often involve either actively self-destructive behavior or more passive disregard for personal safety. Self-destructive behavior can include suicidal use of guns or motor vehicles. Over half of deaths from guns are self-inflicted (U.S. Bureau of the Census, 1994). Estimates of the number of fatal accidents in which a suicidal driver is involved would be harder to ascertain. Actively self-destructive behavior can also include reckless sexual encounters that can lead to life-threatening sexually transmitted diseases, including AIDS.

More passive disregard for personal safety includes engagement in lifestyles that place persons at risk for being shot, such as gang-related activities, drug dealing, or engaging in violent encounters. It can include unsafe driving, for example, under the influence of alcohol or other drugs. And it can also include unprotected sex. Clinical impressions suggest that persons who have lost hope are more likely to either develop a "what the hell" attitude, or to be unable to extricate themselves from such dangerous situations. Sometimes acts stemming from desperation born of despair can hurt or kill others, thus having an effect beyond the depressed individual's personal well-being.

Depression and the Major Causes of Death

We have now examined seven of the nine major causes of death in the United States and found that depression appears not only to be related to each, but is most likely to have a substantial impact in at least two of the top three: smoking and alcohol. Thus, in addition to the pain, suffering, and life disruption that major depression causes directly, it is very likely that it is also involved in the major causes of death in the nation.

The Role of Depression in Intergenerational Misery

The effects of depression and its related problems do not remain only with individuals who suffer from this condition. They can also affect those around them, including their progeny. Let us follow one such trajectory to illustrate the insidious nature of this problem. Consider a young woman having problems with depressive moods. To attempt to change her mood state, she begins using a psycho-active substance (say alcohol or an illicit drug). Under the influence of this substance, she engages in unprotected sex. An unplanned pregnancy results. In having the baby, she begins a high-risk, single-parent household, which increases her stress level and likely leads to dysfunctional parenting. Later on, the daughter born from this pregnancy develops mood problems that continue into childhood and adolescence, at which time this young woman, having problems with depressive moods, considers, as her mother did, ways to change her mood state by using psychoactive substances.

Obviously, intervention at any point in this cycle might prevent the cycle from continuing. It is important to note that cycles similar to this are occurring constantly in our communities. And a significant factor in the cycle is the feeling of helplessness and hopelessness that is so common in depressed states.

The Limits of Treatment
Approaches to Depression

Many professionals readily agree that depression is a major public health problem. Their response to the problem, however, is to call for more resources to be allocated to the *treatment* of depression. There is no doubt that more resources should be allocated to treatment. Mental disorders, in general, receive fewer treatment resources than physical disorders, including very limited insurance coverage. The reduction in human suffering and dysfunction that would ensue if more treatment were available would be substantial; however, treatment approaches are unlikely to be sufficient to address the pervasive effect of depression itself and its impact on other public health problems.

In the first place, most depression goes unrecognized. Several studies have found that even when individuals seek help from health care providers, depression is likely not considered as the reason for help seeking. Primary care providers recognize only between a third and a half of cases of depression (Pérez-Stable, Miranda, Muñoz, & Ying, 1990). Although this state of affairs is partly due to lack of knowledge and to underestimating psychological issues as important elements in health care, it is also possible that both individuals and care providers are reluctant to attribute health problems to mental health issues. There is still stigma associated with having "mental problems." A preventive approach, such as an educational offering focused on mood management, might be more acceptable to individuals and health care providers.

Even when recognized, depression often goes untreated or is undertreated. The Agency for Health Care and Policy Research recently released Clinical Practice Guidelines focused on the treatment of depression in primary care settings to counteract the tendency toward inadequate treatment of depression. Such treatment involves subtherapeutic doses of antidepressants as well as lack of sufficient monitoring and patient education. The latter can result in stopping the use of medication because of side effects or because patients do not understand how to use them properly. There is also the likelihood that patients will not be referred for psychological treatments that have been found useful in the treatment of depression, such as cognitive-behavioral therapy and interpersonal psychotherapy (Depression Guideline Panel, 1993b).

Even when provided under carefully monitored conditions, treatment is far from universally successful. Clinical trials of depression treatments, which include carefully selected, well-motivated individuals suffering from depression, still result in dropout rates of 20 to 52% (DiMascio et al., 1979; Simons, Levine, Lustman, & Murphy, 1984). In the National Institute of Mental Health Collaborative Study (Elkin et al., 1989), 35% dropped out; and of those who completed treatment, 51 to 70% improved. In another study by Murphy and Simons (Murphy, Simons, Wetzel, & Lustman, 1984; Simons, Murphy, Levine, & Wetzel, 1986), out of 95 randomized to treatment, 26% (25) dropped out, 63% (44) of those who completed treatment recovered, and 64% (28) of the latter did not relapse after one year. Thus, of 95 randomized only 29% were remitted at 1-year follow-up.

In addition to limitations in effectiveness, current treatments for depression also have some risk attached, from minor side effects to the use of antidepressants to commit suicide (Muñoz, Hollon, McGrath, Rehm, & VandenBos, 1994).

Potential Benefits of a Prevention Perspective

The Agency for Health Care Policy and Research Clinical Practice Guidelines for Depression (Depression Guideline Panel, 1993a) report that once a person develops a clinical episode of major depression, he or she has a 50% chance of developing a second episode. After two episodes, the likelihood of having a third goes up to 70%, and after three episodes, the likelihood of having an additional one climbs to 90%. The authors of the Clinical Practice Guidelines use this information to encourage active identification of depression and aggressive treatment of this condition. However, these data seem to me to be a clear call for preventing the first episode.

Why might preventing the first episode be strategically preferable? Some theorists believe that once the human organism goes through the massive and pervasive dysregulation of functioning associated with major depression, the organism is "kindled;" that is, a permanent change in its physiology occurs that makes it more likely to enter this state in the future. Post, Rubinow, and Ballenger (1984) reviewed several models based on animal experimentation that may have relevance to the course of depressive disorder in humans. Kindling originally referred to the potentiation of motor seizures in response to electrical or chemical stimulation of the brain, so that eventually levels of stimulation that were originally insufficient to produce these seizures now trigger them. The animal can be described as becoming sensitized to what were originally minor influences on its functioning, so that eventually even these minor stimuli produce massive dysfunctioning. These authors suggest that a similar process might be occurring in depression. Clinical depression is a state in which many of our physiological systems, such as our sleep mechanism, digestive system, and motivational, memory, and attention mechanisms, become altered. The first time this happens, it may have been the result of a major negative life event. Once the organism becomes dysregulated, however, less severe life events can trigger this condition. This could explain the increased likelihood of depressive episodes once one has experienced the first.

Effective preventive interventions might prevent this kindling process by avoiding the organism's entry into the initial dysregulated condition. By providing alternative ways to manage one's mood states, the gradual entry into a clinical depression might be averted. Continuous use of these alternative methods of emotion regulation could have long-term preventive effects.

The kindling hypothesis addresses the possible physiological effects of clinical depressive episodes on the human body. However, the presence of clinical depression in humans has more wide-ranging effects. Clinical depression can cause major disruptions in people's lives that are often hard to correct. Marital, parental, or job-related dysfunction can be difficult to "patch up" after a bout of depression. For example, the unpredictability of depressed behavior can change the way in which our loved ones or our coworkers perceive us. This perception can be hard to normalize after periods of disability caused by depression. In addition, in the case of children of depressed parents, the depressive state could cause long-lasting changes in the way children process information and react to their environment. Depressive episodes are related to increased aggressive or neglectful behavior toward children (Zuravin, 1989). Infants of depressed mothers show different patterns of behavior toward strangers as early as 3 months old (Field et al., 1988). If these children develop psychological or behavioral problems in the future, the increased stress on the parent could in turn trigger another depressive episode, thus creating a vicious cycle. Once again, the development and implementation of effective preventive interventions might reduce these long-lasting sequelae of depression.

The San Francisco Depression Prevention Research Project

The San Francisco Depression Prevention Research Project (DPRP) was part of a programmatic research effort intended to develop feasible and effective interventions to prevent major depression in populations at risk. It focused on public sector primary care patients, including Spanish-speaking Latinos. The DPRP also implemented a pilot study in which Chinese language (Cantonese and Mandarin) interventions were developed and tested. Detailed reports of the DPRP can be found in Muñoz, Ying, Armas, Chan, and Gurza (1987); Muñoz and Ying (1993); and Muñoz et al. (1995). In this chapter, I will give a brief description of the steps that were taken in planning, implementing, and evaluating its effects. I recommend that future prevention programs consider each of these steps as they are planned and executed.

Identifying the Target: What Do You Intend to Prevent?

The DPRP set as its goal the prevention of new cases of major depression and dysthymia. Both of these depressive disorders were defined strictly in terms of diagnostic criteria as put forth in the *Diagnostic and Statistical Manual of Mental Disorders* (American Psychiatric Association, 1987). Thus, what we intended to prevent was specific depressive disorders.

At the same time, the DPRP was intended to reduce high depressive symptoms in the individuals taking part in the study. The reduction in depressive symptoms would occur if the methods for mood management taught to participants actually helped them to reduce feelings of depression. Our thinking went as follows: To reach a clinical level of depression, individuals must first go through a spell of gradually worsening depressive symptoms. As the duration, intensity, and frequency of these depressive symptoms increases, the individual becomes more likely to develop a full-blown clinical episode of depression. Thus, providing individuals with strategies to modulate their mood should result in both lower depressive symptom scores and fewer cases of major depression.

Choosing a Theory to Guide the Intervention: What Mechanisms Are Involved?

Depression appears to involve several mechanisms, including genetic and other biological factors, psychological factors, and social and other environmental factors. We chose to intervene at the psychological level, using a social learning conception (Bandura, 1977) of depression derived primarily from the work of Peter M. Lewinsohn (Lewinsohn, 1975; Zeiss, Lewinsohn, & Muñoz, 1979), and that of other cognitive behavioral theorists (Beck, Rush, Shaw, & Emery, 1979; Ellis, 1962; Kelly, 1955; Mahoney & Thoresen, 1974). This approach to depression has been found effective in the treatment of major depression: depressed patients exhibit major improvement in their mood state comparable to that produced by antidepressant medications. Thus, there was empirical evidence for the success of this type of approach to depression at the clinical level. Our task was to apply the general theory at a preventive level.

A reciprocal process was hypothesized involving mood, thoughts, and behaviors: specific thoughts and behaviors increase or decrease the likelihood of depressed mood; and depressed mood, in turn, increases the likelihood that depressive thinking and behavior will occur. Participants who learn to identify the elements in this process would be able to modify the thoughts and behaviors that lead to depressive mood states. By reducing the likelihood of these states, they would reduce the likelihood of falling into a clinical episode of depression.

Identifying High-Risk Groups

Data clearly show that about half of the treated cases of depression are treated by the general health care sector, not by the mental health sector. Most persons who begin to experience clinical depression and who choose to go for help do not go to a mental health professional. They go to their primary care doctor (Regier et al. 1993). Thus, a large proportion of those meeting diagnostic criteria for depression are found in primary care clinics. We extrapolated from this information that the likelihood of seeking help would increase as depressive symptoms increased, even if individuals did not meet criteria for a full-blown depressive episode. Therefore, we expected that persons at risk for depression would be likely to frequent primary care clinics.

High symptoms of depression have also been found in low-income and minority populations. For example, Roberts (1987) reported the highest proportions of symptomatology in African American and Latino samples. Poverty has been found to be an attributable risk factor for depression in about 10% of new cases (Bruce, Takeuchi, & Leaf, 1991). Moreover, Mexican Americans are half as likely to seek mental health care as non-Hispanic whites (Hough et al., 1987). Focusing on low-income minorities using public sector primary care clinics was therefore hypothesized to result in finding a substantial group of persons with high symptom levels, with the high-risk markers of poverty and self-perceived health problems. It would also result in finding many who, if they became clinically depressed, would be unlikely to seek help for their depression. Such a population would be both at high risk for depression and a good target for prevention.

Designing the Intervention: The Depression Prevention Course

Our intent was to provide an educational intervention that would not require individuals to take on the role of a "patient." Rather, the participants would be students being taught the latest from the psychological literature on mood management skills. The intervention, labeled the "Depression Prevention Course," consisted of eight weekly 2-hour sessions with no more than 10 students in the class. Participants were taught to identify their mood states and to learn to keep track of how specific thoughts, level of pleasant activities, and interpersonal contacts either improved or worsened their mood. Then, they were taught to increase those thoughts, activities, and contacts with others that led to positive mood states. The primary source for these methods was the book *Control Your Depression*, by Peter M. Lewinsohn, Ricardo F. Muñoz, Mary Ann Youngren, and Antonette M. Zeiss (1978, 1986). However, the Depression Prevention Course was simplified to be used with individuals with lower levels of education than the population on which the material in the book had been originally tested. It was also prepared in Spanish and Chinese.

The Depression Prevention Course materials included two sections: an outline for participants, and lecture notes for the instructors (see Appendix A in Muñoz & Ying, 1993). The outline included homework forms on which the participant could document daily mood levels, frequencies of mood-related thoughts, activities, and contacts with people. These forms were reviewed in class to illustrate the relationship among these events.

Designing the Study:
Measuring the Effects of the Intervention

The study took place in the primary care clinics at San Francisco General Hospital and the University of California, San Francisco. Patients who had appointments during the time of our recruitment campaign were asked if they were interested in a study about mood and health, and, if they agreed to participate, were asked to participate in two 2-hour interviews. (Consent forms were signed by participants, and they received a small "subject fee" for their participation in the research interviews.) To make sure that the study was truly a preventive trial, we used a diagnostic instrument to screen for individuals who already met criteria for major depression, dysthymia, or other major disorders. These persons were referred for treatment and screened out of the study. The study was intended to include those portions of the community that were generally underserved, including those who were not English speaking.

To determine how long the effects of the intervention lasted, we followed participants at posttreatment, 6 months, and 12 months after the initial screening. In addition to testing the depressive symptom levels and the number of new cases, we also attempted to determine whether we had an effect on changing the participants' thoughts, activity levels, and social activities and whether changes in these variables were related to changes in depressive symptoms. We also examined whether other factors, such as social support and life events, had an effect on the results.

Finally, participants were randomly assigned to either the Depression Prevention Course or to a control condition, to determine whether attendance at the course, rather than purely self-selection factors, would be responsible for any observed changes. In all, 150 participants entered the randomized part of the study, with 78 assigned to the control condition and 72 to the Depression Prevention Course.

Results of the SF DPRP

At the 1-year follow-up, we were able to find 139 (93%) of the participants, 72 from the control group and 67 from those assigned to the Depression Prevention Course. Of the latter, 42 had come to at least 4 out of 8 sessions of the course and were considered to have received enough of a "dose" of the intervention to be considered "completers." The other 25 were considered "dropouts."

Symptoms of depression as measured by the Beck Depression Inventory were significantly lowered by the Depression Prevention Course.

The number of new cases of major depression during the 1-year follow-up was 4 (out of 72) in the control group, and 2 (out of 67) from those assigned to the Depression Prevention Course. However, both of the latter 2 were from the 25 "dropouts." One had attended none of the sessions, and the other only two. One person who attended all eight sessions met criteria for dysthymia (a less severe, but longer-lasting form of depression) at the 1-year follow-up. The small number of new cases of major depression did not allow for a good statistical test of differences between the two conditions because of what is known as lack of sufficient "statistical power."

This is one important lesson from the DPRP: Future depression prevention trials ought to recruit individuals who are at higher imminent risk for major depression. Although our participants belonged to a group that *is* at higher risk than the general population as individuals, their risk extends beyond the current year. In other words, they have a high lifetime risk, but not necessarily a high current risk.

In the terminology recommended by the Institute of Medicine's Committee on Prevention of Mental Disorders (Mrazek & Haggerty, 1994), the DPRP was a "selective" preventive intervention; that is, it differed from a "universal" preventive intervention in that it did not target the population as a whole, but rather selected for intervention the segment of the population using public sector primary care clinics. This segment was indeed at higher risk than the general population. For purposes of relatively short prevention trials, however, a subsegment at even higher risk is advisable. Such a preventive intervention would be termed an "indicated" intervention, and could consist of participants who have some sort of individualized "marker" of high risk, but do not meet criteria for the disorder that is to be prevented. For example, in the area of depression, individuals with a family history of either major depression or bipolar disorder, with a weak social support system, and with particular thinking and activity patterns might be at even higher risk than other primary care patients. Ways to identify those at imminent high risk might include assessing stressful life events or high (but subthreshold) levels of depressive symptoms. The former have been shown to be related to onset of physical illness as well as depressive episodes. The latter could be seen as evidence that the individual's mechanisms to regulate his or her mood state is inadequate at this time. Thus, providing additional mood management methods might preclude continuing descent into a clinical depression.

After the Depression Prevention Research Project was completed, another depression prevention trial has been successful in demonstrating that this approach can, indeed, result in a statistically significant reduction in new cases of major depression. Clarke and his colleagues (1995), working with high school students in Portland, Oregon, recruited only those students who scored 24 or above on the Center for Epidemiological Studies-Depression Scale (CES-D). Any student who met criteria for major depression at the start of the study was screened out (and referred for treatment). The rest were randomly assigned to the "Coping with Depression Course" for adolescents or to a control condition. At one year, those students who took the course had an incidence (number of new cases of depression) of 15%, compared to 26% for the control group. We can deduce from these figures that over a quarter of high school adolescents (at least in Portland) who score 24 or above in the CES-D and who do not already meet criteria for major depression, will do so within one year. If a feasible intervention can reduce that proportion to 15%, we might be able to save a substantial number of young people from a most upsetting and potentially long-lasting condition.

Going back to the results of the DPRP, we also examined whether the participants had learned and put into practice what we had taught them, and whether these changes were related to the lowering of depressive symptoms. For example, was there evidence that they had changed the way they thought, or engaged in a higher number of healthy activities? Our data provided evidence that those in the class condition became less pessimistic, had more self-rewarding and less self-punishing thoughts, and engaged in more pleasant and social activities. Moreover, greater declines in depressive symptoms were generally related to changes in thoughts and activity levels in the hypothesized direction.

Future Directions

These data provide encouragement for continuing to develop this line of intervention for preventing depression. It will be important to make advances in the following areas:

1. We must develop methods to identify those at high imminent risk in a fairly routine and inexpensive way (Miranda, Muñoz, & Shumway, 1990). One method that we have begun to develop is an automated voice recognition system that could be used in primary care settings at the time that vital signs are usually taken, and that would accommodate persons who do not read, or who are not English speaking (Muñoz, González, & Starkweather, 1995). An ideal system would identify three groups: first, those already meeting criteria for major depression, who would be referred for treatment; second, those at high imminent risk for major depression, who would be referred to preventive interventions; and third, those for whom mood problems do not appear to be an issue, and who would receive no intervention.

2. We must develop methods to provide the preventive intervention in a manner that is effective and feasible (Muñoz, 1995). For example, there is now evidence that bibliotherapy can be effective in reducing depressive symptoms in older persons with mild to moderate clinical depression (Scogin, Jamison, & Davis, 1990; Scogin, Jamison, & Gochneaur, 1989). By extrapolation, individuals with evidence of mood problems, but no clinical depression, ought to be able to use printed materials at least as well. The use of other adjuncts to delivery of preventive mental health services must also be examined.

ADULT PROGRAMS

3. We must develop policy that incorporates preventive interventions focused on depression as an accepted part of the armamentarium of public health agencies and health insurance coverage. Preventive care is now routinely provided in dental coverage. This is probably because there are methods that have been clearly shown to be effective in the prevention of cavities and other dental problems, and because the prevention of such problems is considered important and economically feasible. The task for the mental health field is to provide similar evidence for depression.

Conclusion

In this chapter, I have attempted to provide evidence that depression is not only a painful and disruptive influence in the life of individuals; but, because it has impact on several other public health problems, it also has a pervasive and substantial effect on our society. Secondly, I have described a concerted effort to develop and evaluate interventions to prevent depression that is taking place at the University of California, San Francisco, Department of Psychiatry at San Francisco General Hospital. One of the studies stemming from this line of research, the Depression Prevention Research Project, was chosen for the Lela Rowland Prevention Award in 1994. This line of research has systematically focused on primary care patients in public sector clinics, including Spanish-speaking medical patients.

I encourage professionals, policymakers, and members of our communities to seriously consider the effect that depression has in our society and to devote resources to develop and evaluate interventions designed to prevent depression.

I suggest envisioning communities in which that portion of drug use that stems from hopelessness, helplessness, and demoralization is curtailed; where sexual activities take place primarily out of romantic feelings instead of out of loneliness and pain, and thus lovers are careful not to place one another at risk of sexually transmitted diseases or unintended pregnancies; where new mothers have the support and, if needed, the professional interventions that reduce the risk of having to care for an infant while suffering from a clinical depressive episode, and thus the mother and child can enjoy the process of infancy and childhood without depleting the mother's energy and placing the child at risk for future depression. If we could reduce the level of clinical depression in our society, we would immeasurably reduce unnecessary pain and suffering. This is a worthy goal that could dramatically transform human experience.

References

American Psychiatric Association. (1987). *Diagnostic and statistical manual of mental disorders (DSM-III-R)* (3rd ed. revised). Washington, DC: American Psychiatric Association.

Anda, R. F., Williamson, D. F., Escobedo, L. G., Mast, E. E., Giovino, G. A., & Remington, P. L. (1990). Depression and the dynamics of smoking: A national perspective. *Journal of the American Medical Association, 264*(12), 1541-1545.

Bandura, A. (Ed.). (1977). *Social learning theory.* Englewood Cliffs, NJ: Prentice Hall.

Beck, A. T., Rush, A. J., Shaw, B. F., & Emery, G. (1979). *Cognitive therapy of depression.* New York: Guilford.

Brown, J. H., Henteleff, P., & Barakat, S. (1986). Is it normal for terminally ill patients to desire death? *American Journal of Psychiatry, 143*(2), 208-211.

Bruce, M. L., Takeuchi, D. T., & Leaf, P. J. (1991). Poverty and psychiatric status: Longitudinal evidence from the New Haven Epidemiological Catchment Area Study. *Archives of General Psychiatry, 48*(5), 470-474.

Clarke, G. N., Hawkins, W., Murphy, M., Sheeber, L. B., Lewinsohn, P. M., & Seeley, J. R. (1995). Targeted prevention of unipolar depressive disorder in an at-risk sample of high school adolescents: A randomized trial of a group cognitive intervention. *Journal of the American Academy of Child and Adolescent Psychiatry, 34*(3), 312-321.

Depression Guideline Panel. (1993a). *Depression in primary care: Detection, diagnosis and treatment: Quick reference guide for clinicians* (Clinical Practice Guideline No. 5, AHCPR Publication No. 93-0552). Rockville, MD: Department of Health and Human Services, Public Health Service, Agency for Health Care Policy and Research.

Depression Guideline Panel. (1993b). *Depression in primary care: Vol. 2. Treatment of major depression* (Clinical Practice Guideline No. 5, AHCPR Publication No. 93-0551). Rockville, MD: Department of Health and Human Services, Public Health Service, Agency for Health Care Policy and Research.

DiMascio, A., Weissman, M. M., Prusoff, B. A., Neu, C., Zwilling, M., & Klerman, G. L. (1979). Differential symptom reduction by drugs and psychotherapy in acute depression. *Archives of General Psychiatry, 36*(13), 1450-1456.

Elkin, I., Shea, M. T., Watkins, J. T., Imber, S. D., Sotsky, S. M., Collins, J. F., Glass, D. R., Pilkonis, P. A., Leber, W. R., Docherty, J. P., Fiester, S. J., & Parloff, M. B. (1989). National Institute of Mental Health Treatment of Depression Collaborative Research Program: General effectiveness of treatments. *Archives of General Psychiatry, 46*(11), 971-982.

Ellis, A. (1962). *Reason and emotion in psychotherapy*. New York: Stewart.

Field, T., Healy, B., Goldstein, S., Perry, S., Bendell, S., Schamberg, S., Zimmerman, E., & Kuhn, G. (1988). Infants of depressed mothers show "depressed" behavior even with non-depressed adults. *Child Development, 60*(6), 1569-1579.

Fletcher, R. H., Fletcher, S. W., & Wagner, E. H. (1988). *Clinical epidemiology: The essentials* (2nd ed.). Baltimore, MD: Williams & Wilkins.

Glassman, A. H., Helzer, J. E., Covey, L. S., Cottler, L. B., Stetner, F., Tipp, J. E., & Johnson, J. (1990). Smoking, smoking cessation, and major depression. *Journal of the American Medical Association, 264*(12), 1546-1549.

Greenberg, P. E., Stiglin, L. E., Finkelstein, S. N., & Berndt, E. R. (1993). The economic burden of depression in 1990. *Journal of Clinical Psychiatry, 54*(11), 405-418.

Hough, R. L., Landsverk, J. A., Karno, M., Burnam, M. A., Timbers, D. M., Escobar, J. I., & Regier, D. A. (1987). Utilization of health and mental health services by Los Angeles Mexican-Americans and Non-Hispanic Whites. *Archives of General Psychiatry, 44*(8), 702-709.

Kelly, G. A. (1955). *The psychology of personal constructs*. New York: Norton.

Kessler, R. C., McGonagle, K. A., Shanyang, Z., Nelson, C. B., Hughes, M., Eshleman, S., Wittchen, H. U., & Kendler, K. S. (1994). Lifetime and 12-month prevalence of DSM-III-R psychiatric disorders in the United States: Results from the National Comorbidity Survey. *Archives of General Psychiatry, 51*(1), 8-19.

Lewinsohn, P. M. (1975). The behavioral study and treatment of depression. In M. Hersen, R. M. Eisler, & P. M. Miller (Eds.), *Progress in behavior modification* (Vol. 1, pp. 19-64). New York: Academic Press.

Lewinsohn, P. M., Muñoz, R. F., Youngren, M. A., & Zeiss, A. M. (1978). *Control your depression*, New York: Prentice Hall.

Lewinsohn, P. M., Muñoz, R. F., Youngren, M. A., & Zeiss, A. M. (1986). *Control your depression* (Rev. ed.). New York: Prentice Hall.

Magnuson, E. (1989, July 17). Suicides: The gun factor. *Time, 134,* 61.

Mahoney, M. J., & Thoresen, C. E. (1974). *Self-control: Power to the person.* Monterey, CA: Brooks/Cole.

McGinnis, J. M., & Foege, W. H. (1993). Actual causes of death in the United States. *Journal of the American Medical Association, 270*(18), 2207-2212.

Miranda, J., Muñoz, R., & Shumway, M. (1990). Depression prevention research: The need for scales that truly predict. In C. Attkisson & J. Zich (Eds.), *Depression in primary care: Screening and detection* (pp. 232-250). New York: Routledge, Chapman & Hall.

Mrazek, P., & Haggerty, R. (1994). *Reducing risks for mental disorders: Frontiers for preventive intervention research,* Washington, DC: National Academy Press.

Muñoz, R. F. (1995). Toward combined prevention and treatment services for major depression. In C. Telles & M. Karno (Eds.), *Latino mental health: Current research and policy perspectives* (pp. 183-200). Los Angeles: University of California, Los Angeles, Neuropsychiatric Institute.

Muñoz, R. F., González, G. M., & Starkweather, J. (1995). Automated screening for depression: Toward culturally and linguistically appropriate uses of computerized speech recognition. *Hispanic Journal of Behavioral Sciences, 17*(2), 194-208.

Muñoz, R. F., Hollon, S. D., McGrath, E., Rehm, L. P., & VandenBos, G. R. (1994). On the AHCPR Depression in Primary Care guidelines: Further considerations for practitioners. *American Psychologist, 49*(1), 42-61.

Muñoz, R. F., & Ying, Y. (1993). *The prevention of depression: Research and practice.* Baltimore, MD: Johns Hopkins University Press.

Muñoz, R. F., Ying, Y. W., Armas, R., Chan, F., & Gurza, R. (1987). The San Francisco Depression Prevention Research Project: A randomized trial with medical outpatients. In R. F. Muñoz (Ed.), *Depression prevention: Research directions* (pp. 199-215). Washington, DC: Hemisphere.

Muñoz, R. F., Ying, Y. W., Bernal, G., Pérez-Stable, E. J., Sorensen, J. L., Hargreaves, W. A., Miranda, J., & Miller, L. S. (1995). Prevention of depression with primary care patients: A randomized controlled trial. *American Journal of Community Psychology, 23*(2), 199-222.

Murphy, G. E., Simons, A. D., Wetzel, R. D., & Lustman, P. J. (1984). Cognitive therapy and pharmacotherapy, singly and together in the treatment of depression. *Archives of General Psychiatry, 41*(1), 33-41.

Osmond, H., Mullaly, R., & Bisbee, C. (1984). The pain of depression compared with physical pain. *Practitioner, 228*(1395), 849-853.

Pérez-Stable, E. J., Miranda, J., Muñoz, R. F., & Ying, Y. W. (1990). Depression in medical outpatients: Underrecognition and misdiagnosis. *Archives of Internal Medicine, 150*(5), 1083-1088.

Post, R. M., Rubinow, D. R., & Ballenger, J. C. (1984). Conditioning, sensitization, and kindling: Implications for the course of affective illness. In R. M. Post & J. C. Ballenger (Eds.), *Neurobiology of mood disorders* (pp. 432-466). Baltimore, MD: Williams & Wilkins.

Regier, D. A., Narrow, W. E., Rae, D. S., Manderscheid, R. W., Locke, B. Z., & Goodwin, F. K. (1993). The de facto US mental and addictive disorders service system: Epidemiologic Catchment Area prospective 1-year prevalence rates of disorders and services. *Archives of General Psychiatry, 50*(2), 85-94.

Roberts, R. E. (1987). Epidemiological issues in measuring preventive effects. In R. F. Muñoz (Ed.), *Depression prevention: Research directions* (pp. 45-75). Washington, DC: Hemisphere.

Schoenborn, C. A., & Horm, J. (1993). *Negative moods as correlates of smoking and heavier drinking: Implications for health promotion* (Advance data from vital and health statistics, No. 236). Hyattsville, MD: National Center for Health Statistics.

Scogin, F., Jamison, C., & Davis, N. (1990). Two-year follow-up of bibliotherapy for depression in older adults. *Journal of Consulting and Clinical Psychology, 58*(5), 665-667.

Scogin, F., Jamison, C., & Gochneaur, K. (1989). Comparative efficacy of cognitive and behavioral bibliotherapy for mildly and moderately depressed older adults. *Journal of Consulting and Clinical Psychology, 57*(3), 403-407.

Sime, W. E., & Sanstead, M. (1987). Running therapy in the treatment of depression: Implications for prevention. In R. F. Muñoz (Ed.), *Depression prevention: Research directions* (pp. 217-231). Washington, DC: Hemisphere.

Simons, A. D., Levine, J. L., Lustman, P. J., & Murphy, G. E. (1984). Patient attrition in a comparative outcome study of depression: A follow-up report. *Journal of Affective Disorders, 6*(2), 163-173.

Simons, A. D., Murphy, G. E., Levine, J. L., & Wetzel, R. D. (1986). Cognitive therapy and pharmacotherapy for depression: Sustained improvement over one year. *Archives of General Psychiatry, 43*(1), 43-48.

U.S. Bureau of Census. (1994). *Statistical abstracts of the United States* (114th ed.). Washington, DC: Government Printing Office.

Wells, K. B., Stewart, A., Hays, R. D., Burnam, M. A., Rogers, W., Daniels, M., Berry, S., Greenfield, S., & Ware, J. (1989). The functioning and well-being of depressed patients: Results from the medical outcomes study. *Journal of the American Medical Association, 262*(7), 914-919.

Zeiss, A. M., Lewinsohn, P. M., & Muñoz, R. F. (1979). Nonspecific improvement effects in depression using interpersonal skills training, pleasant activity schedules, or cognitive training. *Journal of Consulting and Clinical Psychology, 47*(3), 427-439.

Zuravin, S. J. (1989). Severity of maternal depression and three types of mother-to-child aggression. *American Journal of Orthopsychiatry, 59*(3), 377-389.

CHAPTER 17

Epilogue: Reframing Prevention Advocacy and Looking Ahead

MICHAEL M. FAENZA
SANDRA J. MCELHANEY

Primary prevention advocates and their allies in the "prevention movement" have had a very sobering and difficult experience over the last three decades of working within the context of America's community mental health movement. As students of the fledging prevention movement in mental health in the 1970s, the authors were among the mental health professionals in the United States who agreed that prevention was "an idea whose time had come" (Klein & Goldston, 1977). But as our country continued to struggle with the vastly complex issues of mental health, mental illness, and social class, we witnessed the failure to make good on the promise of primary prevention. This unfortunate reality becomes clear when one reads the daily headlines in the newspapers of every major city in our nation. Violence, substance abuse, school dropout, unemployment, and ultimately, despair are everywhere. Given the current political trend toward "federal downsizing" and "smaller government," the odds appear poor for a significant federal response to these major societal problems. Thus, if we are to take a preventive approach to tackling major social problems, we will need to mount local efforts and mobilize in neighborhoods, communities, and states across our nation to put our growing knowledge base in prevention to work to make a difference in the lives of children and families. Furthermore, if we intend to make any ground in this effort, "preventionists" and other groups that have traditionally not invested in prevention must work collaboratively.

National Mental Health Association (NMHA) and Prevention: A Brief Background

In some very important ways, NMHA has been a primary and rather singular voice for prevention in mental health from a citizens' advocacy perspective (McElhaney & Barton, 1995). During the last 15 years, growing mental health consumer and family organizing and related advocacy for people with psychiatric histories or mental illnesses have been extremely important in directing political, economic, and moral attention to the plight of people with severe mental illnesses. The National Alliance for the Mentally Ill, the National Depressive and Manic Depressive Association, the National Mental Health Consumers Self-Help Clearinghouse (part of the MHA in Southeastern Pennsylvania) and a number of other very effective consumer-led organizations have worked with dedication to change the tragically inadequate and fragmented services system for people with severe and persistent mental illnesses in the United States. The NMHA has worked diligently for the needs and rights of people with serious mental illness and all children and adults needing mental health services. But quite uniquely as a national advocacy organization, we have steadfastly spoken on behalf of the wisdom and humanity of supporting prevention research and the dissemination of programs that reduce the prevalence of emotional disorders and other poor outcomes for vulnerable children and adults.

NMHA has its roots in a prevention-focused organization founded in the early years of the 20th century by mental health consumer Clifford Beers, author of *A Mind that Found Itself* (1908). Beers is viewed nearly ninety years later by NMHA volunteer advocates and professionals as NMHA's practical and moral founder. In 1909, Clifford Beers joined forces with public health and with the psychiatry faculty at John Hopkins University and its School of Public Hygiene to form the NMHA predecessor organization, the National Committee for Mental Hygiene.

The authors share this history to give context to NMHA's long legacy of leading and supporting intensive, consumer-focused advocacy for people with mental illnesses and a consistent and concrete investment in promoting primary prevention. For NMHA, the challenges inherent in working, on one hand, for enlightened public policy and humane systems of services for people with severe disorders, and simultaneously for prevention research and interventions, are great. We believe the future opportunities and the very significant challenges to NMHA's advocacy for prevention mirror the challenges to the larger prevention field as it must forge ahead in an economic and political environment that is changing rapidly.

The Challenges

Missed Opportunities at Every Policy-Making Level

As the descriptions of the Lela Rowland Award winning programs in this volume so clearly evidence, we have learned a great deal as scientists and practitioners about the prevention of emotional disorders and the promotion of mental health in at-risk populations. The overarching problem of having prevention programs and concepts disseminated in any significant way is that we have learned so much more than we as a society have chosen to implement. It is not that we don't know what works—we do! Rather, it is our reluctance to put the knowledge found in this and other volumes into practice (see Price, Cowen, Lorion, & Ramos-McKay, 1988; Bloom, 1996). The 1994 Tenth Annual Rosalynn Carter Symposium on Mental Health Policy, which focused on children and families at risk, documented this last point vividly (Carter, Gates, Fitzgerald, & Hullum, 1995).

At the Federal Level

Although our failure to adopt prevention as a national mental health priority is well documented (General Accounting Office, 1989), discrete prevention efforts do exist within numerous federal agencies. In a recent landmark study, the Institute of Medicine identified prevention research enterprises being conducted within 23 federal agencies across 8 federal departments (Mrazek & Haggerty, 1994). Funding afforded to most of these enterprises, however, was minimal at best; and almost no coordination of programs was found across agencies or departments.

Although every federal effort has enriched our knowledge base, the research funded by the National Institute of Mental Health (NIMH) has been particularly fruitful. In fact, the research behind several of the Lela Rowland Award winning programs was funded by NIMH. Unfortunately, however, because NIMH is a "research" institute, its leadership has failed to prioritize implementation and dissemination of prevention programs. In essence, this means that programs that could literally save lives are not making their way to families and communities that desperately need them.

At State and Local Levels

At state and local levels, Community Mental Health Centers and other social service agencies of states and counties lack the clear mandate and often the resources to seriously plan or organize preventive services. Overwhelmed state and county public or quasi-public agencies that cannot meet the needs of people with the most severe disorders who need care are set up to fail at investing intelligently in prevention.

State mental health agencies that have traditionally operated state hospitals and funded an often large portion of community-based treatment services through contracts with county or metropolitan-based Community Mental Health Centers have created priority populations for service that have targeted adults and children with the most severe and long-term treatment needs. These state departments of mental health or cabinet-level commissions within state health and human services bureaucracies operate on general appropriations from the state legislatures and federal investments, including block grants and Medicaid entitlements.

Focusing on the legacy of treatment and supports for these populations illustrates some factors in the failure of primary prevention to find political and financial support in any significant way over the last three decades. The tragic reality is that these groups of people with severe and persistent mental illnesses and children with severe emotional disturbances have been poorly served by fragmented and underfunded systems ever since deinstitutionalization was initiated in the middle of this century. Despite the hard work and dedication of many thousands of mental health professionals, researchers and planners, and mental health advocates, the chilling winds of the 1990s find large numbers of people with mental illnesses and addictive disorders on our city streets and in homeless shelters, county jails, and state penitentiaries.

We know so much about how integrated systems of care and wrap-around services that treat and support children and their families with very serious problems can produce better outcomes for children and adolescents with emotional disturbances. We have also learned how to significantly reduce the incidence of out-of-home placements of these children and the related costs of institutionalization and other residential placements. But at this writing, tens of thousands of children with intensive mental health needs go untreated, and large numbers of children are caught in the webs of the juvenile justice and child protective services systems for lack of accessible, affordable community care.

It is not surprising that the social institutions that are directed by public policy to serve the most disabled citizens needing mental health services, and that have often been underfunded—at times to the point of parceling out strained core services to the most acutely ill—have not been able to rationally plan and implement primary prevention services. The case can obviously be made that these public systems have also failed to systematically provide treatment services for people whose disorders would have been less disabling if those services were available. The economic and political issues historically surrounding the funding and operation of state hospitals has caused an appalling sapping of scarce resources that would be better spent in community-based programs targeting intervention and primary prevention strategies. The politics of state hospitals has exacerbated a very complex and expensive social and health care dilemma in many states and communities, and it is one more reason for prevention's failure to show up on the community mental health services' radar screen.

At the community level, although the Community Mental Health Centers Act (1963) called on each of the Community Mental Health Centers to implement programs to prevent mental disorders, funding and the inability of the federal Center for Mental Health Services to adequately provide services for large numbers of

children and adults with the most intensive and long-term treatment needs has been and continues to be a factor in prevention's
falling significantly by the wayside. Many substantial contributions
to community mental health and to people at risk of emotional
disorders and other serious difficulties have been made by private,
not-for-profit community organizations who have implemented
prevention programs (including many local Mental Health Associations) in thousands of communities over many years. But efforts
have been sporadically funded and delivered piecemeal with little
consistent support or coordination.

Futility and Waste: Arguing About
Treatment Versus Prevention

NMHA has to struggle with our responsibility to provide clear
and responsible advocacy for adults and young people with the
most intensive, long-term mental health treatment needs, and to
simultaneously work for enlightened public policy, research, and
implementation of prevention programs that alleviate suffering and
save health care and social services dollars. The authors wish that
NMHA's determination to work from a conceptual base that values
primary prevention and also demands humane and effective medical and social services for people who are homeless and suffering
from schizophrenia could be shared by all stakeholders in community mental health. We believe much of the conflict between
prevention advocates and advocates for people with severe and
persistent mental illnesses has been a tragic waste of energy and
political capital.

Prevention advocates need to exercise caution in theorizing that
some mental illnesses, like schizophrenia and manic-depressive
disorder, can be prevented by environmental interventions alone.
It is clearly possible to be a prevention advocate, value the wisdom
of pioneers like Gerald Caplan writing in the *Principles of Preventive Psychiatry* (1964), and George Albee and the truth of his
formula (1980), and still share the suffering of parents of children
with major mental illnesses that helped fuel the "Family Movement" in the United States. There are parents who have felt per-
secuted and humiliated by how professionals have discussed the
"causal" factors related to the devastating illnesses that victimized
their healthy and loved children in young adulthood. Many of those

parents and other family members are on the volunteer boards and staffs of NMHA and MHAs across the country.

Likewise, it is ill-advised for proponents of biochemical and genetic explanations for dysfunctional behavior to ignore the importance of environment. Clearly, there is a dynamic and fluid exchange between the two. Unfortunately, many lives are wasted, children and adults die and are disabled, and communities fall apart for our failure to invest in a public health approach to many of the mental health and social problems that face Americans and their communities today.

Although it sounds clichéd, what is needed is a coming together of mental health advocates—including consumers, family members, and other citizen advocates—that works from a baseline of caring about the needs of all vulnerable citizens who are at risk for wasted potential and disability, including especially people with serious mental illnesses. Great social policy is not created through the neglect of other hurting populations that are deemed less worthy at a given point in history. The phenomenon of demeaning the mental health needs of people without a certain diagnosis, or dismissing prevention strategies in mental health and social services as irrelevant, is cut from the same cloth as America's unforgivable neglect of people with severe mental illnesses.

A more compassionate and rational advocacy environment within and extending beyond the mental health community will likely result in better community outcomes through the range of interventions that are important for all children and adults.

The Current Health and Human Services Environment: Managed Care and the "Sea of Change" in American Government and Politics

Even though prevention has never been a particular federal priority, in our current political and social environment, it seems that at best, this will continue to be the case. At worst, our relatively few existing federal prevention programs could also succumb to the carving knife that is being brandished wantonly by the crafters of "small government."

We are indeed entering a time of unprecedented change in mental health service delivery and policy. Managed mental health care, privatizing public systems, and restructuring state mental health programs with fast and broad strokes reflect a grand-scale, cost-driven experiment within one of the most frail and beleaguered social institutions in the United States. The public mental health system that exists today was built on the sweat and tears of people who have worked to find more effective and humane services and supports for people with mental illnesses compared to the huge state hospitals of the past. We admit that we have made important but incomplete progress toward building the systems we need. As discussed, prevention has not gained significant ground in this environment.

Now the role or even existence of public mental health services is brought into question. State health care reform, based on privatizing public mental health systems, is driven by a severe financial crisis that surrounds community mental health. This crisis is part of the larger dilemma that states and the federal government have with escalating health care costs and a political climate that directs reductions in public expenditures and in the size of government. Unfortunately, current reform efforts in states appear to be driven at times by cost containment at the expense of rational public policy that protects consumer interests. The major risk here is that market forces will direct reform without strong policy protecting vulnerable populations (Faenza & Rubenstein, 1996).

But theoretically, this is a time when prevention could take hold. If health promotion and prevention prove effective, then mental health costs for mental health services users could be saved through the use of sound prevention strategies like the San Francisco Depression Prevention Research Project, the Prenatal/Early Infancy Project, and Parents as Teachers, among others. But then again, do we really care? Is Head Start really that important? Is EPSDT really that necessary? Should we be concerned about the availability of alcohol and its relationship to so many other disorders? Your answer to these questions will help determine whether prevention does, in fact, take hold in the coming years.

Conclusion

A number of the themes discussed here can direct our search for solutions in bringing what we know about primary prevention in mental health to a much more substantial level of implementation in American communities and within America's social institutions. Given the circumstances described herein—the unprecedented need for prevention, coupled with the current realities of managed care and public vs. private service provision, "smaller government," and our growing knowledge base in the field of prevention—we have arrived at a place and time when it seems that the onus to really make a difference is on each one of us, in each of our homes and communities. We must reach out to local stakeholders (businesses, foundations, civic organizations, media, parents, youth, and local and state agencies) and help them understand the benefits of local investment in quality prevention efforts. Within the mental health community, the barriers that have grown between "preventionists" and people who care about services and treatment for people with persistent mental illnesses must come down.

In lieu of a "top down" national prevention policy, the time is right for a "bottom up" grassroots prevention groundswell. One person, one family, one neighborhood, one community, one city, one state at a time, we can help people to value prevention. The NMHA is committed to this ideal. Working hand-in-hand with the recipients of the Lela Rowland Award, our MHAs, mental health consumers and their family members, and other invested community stakeholders across the nation, we can make it a reality.

References

Albee, G. W. (1980). A competency model must replace the defect model. In L. A. Bond & J. C. Rosen (Eds.), *Competence and coping during adulthood*. Hanover, NH: University Press of New England.

Beers, C. (1908). *A mind that found itself*. New York: Country Life Press.

Bloom, M. (1996). *Primary prevention practices*. Thousand Oaks, CA: Sage.

Caplan, G. (1964). *Principles of preventive psychiatry*. New York: Basic Books.

Carter, R., Gates, J., Fitzgerald, J., & Hullum, E. (Eds.). (1995). *Children and families at risk: Collaborating with our schools*. Atlanta, GA: Carter Center.

Faenza, M. M., & Rubenstein, L. S. (1996). Public mental health systems, Medicaid restructuring and managed behavioral healthcare. *Behavioral Healthcare Tomorrow, 5*(2), 24-29.

General Accounting Office. (1989). *Mental health: Prevention of mental disorders and research on stress-related disorders* (GAO/HRD-89-97). Washington, DC: Author.

Klein, D. C., & Goldston, S. E. (Eds.). (1977). *Primary prevention: An idea whose time has come* (DHHS Publication No. ADM 80-447). Washington, DC: Government Printing Office.

McElhaney, S., & Barton, H. (1995). Advocacy and services: The National Mental Health Association and prevention. *Journal of Primary Prevention, 15*(3), 313-322.

Mrazek, P. J., & Haggerty, R. J. (1994). *Reducing risk for mental disorders: Frontiers for preventive intervention research.* Institute of Medicine, Washington, DC: National Academy Press.

Price, R., Cowen, E., Lorion, R., & Ramos-McKay, J. (Eds.). (1988). *Fourteen ounces of prevention: A casebook for practitioners.* Washington, DC: American Psychological Association.

Index

About the Authors

George W. Albee is Professor Emeritus at the University of Vermont (Burlington) and Courtesy Professor at the Florida Mental Health Institute. After 16 years at Case Western Reserve University, he spent 25 years at the University of Vermont, where in 1975 he established the Vermont Conference on the Primary Prevention of Psychopathology. He is past President of the American Psychological Association and 1993 recipient of an American Psychological Foundation Gold Medal Award for Public Service. He directed the Task Force on Manpower for President Eisenhower's Joint Commission on Mental Illness and Health and the Task Panel on Prevention for President Carter's Commission on Mental Health. He and his colleagues have edited 17 volumes on primary prevention, based on annual conferences at the University of Vermont. He is a longtime advocate of a sociocultural model of mental disorders and finds causation in class exploitation, sexism, and racism.

Heather A. Barton is a graduate student at the University of Illinois at Chicago (UIC), where she is working on several projects in collaboration with Roger Weissberg. She is also a predoctoral trainee in the National Institute of Mental Health Prevention Research Training Program in Urban Children's Mental Health and AIDS Prevention at UIC. Before coming to Chicago, she worked for the National Mental Health Association, where she was the Director of the Prevention Clearinghouse. In addition to prevention advocacy activities, she facilitated the administration of the NMHA Lela Rowland Prevention Award each year.

Laurie J. Bauman, Ph.D., is Professor of Pediatrics at the Albert Einstein College of Medicine and Co-Director of the Preventive

Intervention Research Center for Child Health. Her research focuses on social support, on childhood chronic illness as a risk factor for poor mental health, and on children orphaned by the AIDS epidemic.

Elsie R. Broussard is Professor of Public Health Psychiatry, Department of Health Services Administration, Graduate School of Public Health; Associate Professor of Child Psychiatry, Department of Psychiatry, School of Medicine, University of Pittsburgh. She is a psychoanalyst of adults and children and is a faculty member of the Pittsburgh Psychoanalytic Institute. She is certified by the American Board of Preventive Medicine in Public Health and the American Board of Psychiatry and Neurology in Psychiatry and Child and Adolescent Psychiatry. The American Psychiatric Association awarded the 1973 Hofheimer Award for Outstanding Research in Mental Hygiene in conjunction with her longitudinal studies of firstborns. She pioneered in developing programs for preventive intervention of psychosocial disorder in infancy. For this work she received the National Mental Health Association's Lela Rowland Prevention Award in 1983 and the Pennsylvania Public Health Association's Presidential Award for services and contributions to public health. She was the Principal Investigator of the Child Abuse and Neglect Interdisciplinary Training Program at the University of Pittsburgh from 1987 to 1991. Currently she is the Co-Principal Investigator of the Child Welfare Interdisciplinary Training Grant.

Linda Bruene-Butler, M.Ed., has been a Mental Health Clinician at the University of Medicine and Dentistry of New Jersey—University Behavioral Health Care since 1985 and has held a research faculty position working primarily out of the program's Department of Psychology, Rutgers University office from 1982 to 1985. She has published in the area, lectured extensively in the field, and provided training and on-site consultation to educators, consultants, and trainers across the United States.

Robert D. Caplan is Professor of Psychology and a member of the Center for Family Research at George Washington University. He is also Director of the Doctoral Program Area in Organizational Psychology. He was previously at the University of Michigan and is a past Fulbright Scholar and National Science Foundation Indo-

American Science Fellow. His primary research interests relate to stress and coping processes in organizations and their relationship to family coping and well-being, person-environment fit theory, and prevention-oriented field experiments. His articles have appeared in the *Journal of Applied Psychology, Academy of Management Journal, Journal of Personality and Social Psychology,* and *Social Science and Medicine.* He has provided consultation to federal agencies, foundations, and other nonprofit organizations.

John F. Clabby, Ph.D., is Director of the Social Problem Solving Program at the University of Medicine and Dentistry of New Jersey's University Behavioral Health Care at Piscataway, where he also serves as Chief Psychologist. In addition to the 1988 Lela Rowland Prevention Award, he received the National Psychological Consultants to Management Award for Excellence in Consulting Psychology in 1990, awarded by the American Psychological Association. A licensed psychologist and a certified school psychologist in New Jersey, he also holds an appointment as a Clinical Associate Professor with the Department of Psychiatry of the University of Medicine and Dentistry of New Jersey—Robert Wood Johnson Medical School.

Susan M. Coupey, M.D., is Professor of Pediatrics at the Albert Einstein College of Medicine, where she specializes in Adolescent Medicine. Her research interests include chronic illness, sexual behavior, and risk-taking behaviors in adolescents.

Steven J. Danish, Ph.D., is Director of the Life Skills Center and Professor of Psychology and Preventive Medicine at Virginia Commonwealth University. He previously served as Chair of the Department of Psychology and has held academic positions at Penn State University and Southern Illinois University following the receipt of his doctorate in Counseling Psychology from Michigan State University. He is a licensed psychologist and a Diplomate in Counseling Psychology of the American Board of Professional Psychology as well as a registered sport psychologist of the Sports Medicine Division of the United States Olympic Committee. He is a Fellow of the American Psychological Association, the American Psychological Society, and the Association for the Advancement of Applied Sport Psychology (AAASP) and is past President of the

Society of Community Research and Action (a Division of APA) and served on the Executive Committee of AAASP He has written over 80 articles and 8 books in the areas of counseling, community, and life span developmental psychology; health and nutrition; substance abuse prevention; and sport psychology. He is the developer of the Going for the Goal Program, was involved in the development and implementation of the Career Assistance Program for Athletes (CAPA) for the United States Olympic Committee, and the Youth Education through Sports (YES) program for the NCAA.

Maurice J. Elias, Ph.D., is Professor of Psychology and Coordinator of the Internship Program in Applied, School, & Community Psychology at Rutgers University, and cofounder of the Consortium on School-Based Promotion of Social Competence. His school-based life skills development and problem behavior prevention programs have been recognized as national models.

Michael M. Faenza, M.S.S.W., President and CEO, National Mental Health Association, has worked in community mental health for over 20 years as an administrator, planner, clinician, and community educator. For 5 years, he was CEO of the MHA in Dallas. He has seen firsthand the human suffering that results from the neglect of people with mental illnesses. He is committed to improving mental health in America and promoting prevention, including developing a coherent response to violence. He believes we should never put the needs of people with severe and persistent mental illnesses on the back burner. As President and CEO of the National Mental Health Association, a broad-based national mental health advocacy organization that includes community volunteers, consumers, and family members, he oversees program services, public policy, as well as technical assistance and coordination of services to 325 NMHA affiliates across the United States.

Thomas P. Gullotta, M.A., M.S.W., is CEO of the Child and Family Agency. He currently is the editor of the *Journal of Primary Prevention*. For Sage, he serves as a general series book editor for *Advances in Adolescent Development,* and is the senior book series editor for *Issues in Children's and Families' Lives.* He serves as the series editor for *Prevention in Practice.* In addition, he holds editorial appointments on the *Journal of Early Aolescence, Adolescence,* and the *Journal of Educational and Psychological Consultation.* Tom serves on the Board of the National Mental Health Association and is an adjunct faculty member in the psychology department of Eastern Connecticut State University. He has published extensively on adolescents and primary prevention.

June Hampson, Ph.D., is Mental Health Clinician at the University of Medicine and Dentistry of New Jersey—University Behavioral Health Care since 1993, is responsible for SPS evaluation, including the 1995 revalidation of the program by the U.S. Department of Education's Program Effectiveness Panel. She received her Ph.D. (1989) in Developmental Psychology from the City University of New York's Graduate School and University Center and held a faculty position at Vassar College prior to joining the University of Medicine and Dentistry of New Jersey.

A. Dirk Hightower, Ph.D., is Director of the Primary Mental Health Project (PMHP), Associate Director of the Center for Community Study, and Senior Research Associate and Associate Professor of Psychology at the University of Rochester. He was Research Director of PMHP for nine years. He is on the editorial board of numerous journals. He has been active with NASP and APA committees and is Past President of the New York Association of School Psychologists. He is serving his second term on the Board of Education of the Rush-Henrietta Central School District.

Cheryl Koeber, M.S.W., is a social worker who coordinated the TEEN Program and co-led training sessions. She specializes in mental health problems of adolescents with chronic health conditions and in bereavement counseling with children and adolescents.

Jennifer L. Lauby, Ph.D., is Senior Research Associate at the Philadelphia Health Management Corporation and Principal Investigator, CDC Prevention of HIV in Women and Infants Demonstration Projects. Previously, she was Assistant Professor at the Preventive Intervention Research Center at Albert Einstein College of Medicine. Her Ph.D. is in Sociology from Harvard University.

Danica S. McDonald is Communications Specialist at the Parents as Teachers National Center, Inc. She earned degrees in English and

Peace Studies at the University of Missouri and completed graduate work at Radcliffe College. Her child advocacy commitments include work as a Court Appointed Special Advocate in St. Louis County and as a volunteer labor assistant at Washington University Medical Center/Barnes Hospital.

Sandra J. McElhaney, M.A., Director of Prevention, National Mental Health Association, has been a member of the National Mental Health Association (NMHA) staff since 1989. In 1991 she was named NMHA Director of Prevention. Trained as a community counselor, she provides national leadership for all NMHA activities related to the prevention of mental and emotional disorders and the promotion of mental health, including collaboration with other national organizations and provision of information and technical assistance to the Mental Health Association network of 325 affiliates in implementing validated prevention programs. She is Staff Director to the National Prevention Coalition, a coalition of national organizations that works with Congress and federal agencies to advance prevention concerns. She implements the NMHA Prevention Advocacy Network, a national membership program for advocates, practitioners, and researchers in prevention. In 1994, she was appointed as NMHA Staff to the Association's Committee on Violence. That committee developed NMHA's 1995 Position Statement on Violence, which was published in a compendium that she edited, *Voices Vs. Violence.* She serves as Managing Editor for NMHA's quarterly prevention newsletter, *NMHA Prevention Update,* and recently authored the NMHA Getting Started in Prevention series.

Ricardo F. Muñoz, Ph.D., is Professor of Psychology in the Department of Psychiatry at the University of California, San Francisco (UCSF) where he serves as Director of the Clinical Psychology Training Program and Chief Psychologist at UCSF's San Francisco General Hospital (SFGH) campus. He earned his A.B. from Stanford University and his Ph.D. from the University of Oregon. His research program is focused on the development and evaluation of linguistically and culturally appropriate screening, prevention, and treatment approaches to major depression, using a social learning orientation and cognitive-behavioral self-control approaches. He was the founding Director of the SFGH Depression Clinic and the Depression Prevention Research Project, which received the 1994 Lela Rowland Prevention Award. He is also the recipient of the Health Promotion Award from the National Coalition of Hispanic Mental Health and Human Services Organization, and the Martin Luther King, Jr. Award from UCSF. He is a member of the American Association of Applied and Preventive Psychology, the American Association for the Advancement of Science, and a Fellow of the American Psychological Association and the American Psychological Society. He serves on the editorial boards of the *Journal of Consulting and Clinical Psychology,* the *Community Mental Health Journal,* and the *Revista Interamericana de Psicología.* He is a member of the Institute of Medicine's Board on Health Promotion and Disease Prevention. He has published many articles, chapters, and five books, including *Depression Prevention: Research Directions,* and *The Prevention of Depression: Research and Practice* (with Y. W. Ying).

David Olds, Ph.D., is Professor of Pediatrics, Psychiatry, and Preventive Medicine and Director of the Prevention Research Center for Family and Child Health at the University of Colorado Health Sciences Center in Denver, Colorado. In addition to the Lela Rowland Prevention Award, he has received the Charles A. Dana Award for Pioneering Achievements in Health and a Research Scientist Award from the National Institute of Mental Health for the research described in this chapter.

JoAnne Pedro-Carroll, Ph.D., is Senior Research Associate with the Primary Mental Health Project and an Associate Professor of Psychology and Psychiatry at the University of Rochester. She is the founder and Director of the Children of Divorce Intervention Program (CODIP), a prevention program for kindergarten through eighth-grade children that was the 1991 recipient of the Lola Rowland Award. Her areas of research include the effects of marital disruption on children and the development and evaluation of preventive interventions for children and families dealing with divorce. She provides consultation and training locally and nationally on prevention and family issues. She is a Fellow of the American Psychological Association, is on a number of Advisory Panels, and has been a member of the National Consortium of Researchers on Children and Divorce.

Richard H. Price is Professor and Chair of the Organizational Psychology Program at the University of Michigan. He is also Research Scientist and Program Director in the Social Environment and Health Program at the Institute for Social Research, where he serves as Director of the Michigan Prevention Research Center, funded by the National Institute of Mental Health. He is a fellow of the American Psychological Association, the American Psychological Society, and the Society for the Psychological Study of Social Problems. His articles have appeared in *Academy of Management Journal, Journal of Applied Psychology, Human Resources Management, Journal of Health Behavior* and *Psychological Bulletin.* He has served as a consultant to a variety of corporations, foundations, government agencies, and foreign governments.

Tom Schuyler, M.A., is a consultant with the University of Medicine and Dentistry of New Jersey's Social Problem Solving Program. He has had 24 years of experience as a school principal in the elementary and middle schools. He has classroom teaching experience at the elementary, middle, and high school levels and shares authorship in a number of publications concerning social problem solving skills.

Lawrence J. Schweinhart, Ph.D., is Chair of the research division of High/Scope Educational Research Foundation. He is a graduate of Indiana University. His major research focus has been on longitudinal projects such as the High/Scope Perry Preschool study, High/Scope Preschool Curriculum Comparison study, and others that reveal the lasting human and financial value of good early childhood programs. He has taught early childhood courses at High/Scope, the University of Missouri at Columbia, and Indiana University at Bloomington. He serves on the governing board of the National Association for the Education of Young Children.

Timothy P. Shriver is a research affiliate at the Yale Child Study Center. He chairs the Collaborative for the Advancement of Social and Emotional Learning (CASEL) and is an educational consultant on issues of urban education and primary prevention. From 1992 to 1996, he was President of the Special Olympics World Games, the largest sporting event in the world during 1995. A former teacher in the New Haven Public Schools, he led New Haven's innovative Social Development Project.

Myrna B. Shure, a developmental psychologist, is Professor in the Department of Clinical and Health Psychology at Allegheny University of the Health Sciences in Philadelphia (formerly Hahnemann). Her Interpersonal Cognitive Problem Solving (ICPS) programs, now called I Can Problem Solve (also ICPS), with George Spivack, have won four national awards. One of these, the Lela Rowland Prevention Award (1982), also with Kathryn Healey and Marshall Swift, was from the National Mental Health Association. Three were from the American Psychological Association: the Division of Community Psychology's Distinguished Contribution Award (1984), the Task Force on Promotion, Prevention, and Intervention Alternatives in Psychology (1986), and the Division of Clinical Psychology, Child Clinical Section (1993). Each task force chose ICPS as one of their nationwide model prevention programs. Shure's *Raising A Thinking Child* (1996) was recognized as a model juvenile delinquency program by the Strengthening America's Families Project, sponsored by the University of Utah and funded by the Office of Juvenile Justice and Delinquency Prevention (1996). In addition to her writing and research, she also consults with the media on issues relating to social adjustment and interpersonal competence in our nation's youth.

Ellen J. Silver, Ph.D., is a developmental psychologist who has worked at the Preventive Intervention Research Center for Child Health for over 10 years. As Assistant Professor of Pediatrics at the Albert Einstein College of Medicine, she specializes in the effects of children's chronic illnesses on child and maternal mental health.

Ruth E. K. Stein, M.D., is Professor and Vice Chairman of the Department of Pediatrics and Director of General Pediatrics at the Albert Einstein College of Medicine. Her research focuses on the mental health correlates of chronic physical disorders in childhood. She was Principal Investigator of the Preventive Intervention Research Center for Child Health from 1983 to 1995.

Amiram D. Vinokur is Research Scientist at the Institute for Social Research at the University of Michigan and Associate Director of the Michigan Prevention Research Center at the Institute. His research focuses on stress and coping processes and has involved a range of populations including U.S. Navy personnel facing retirement, breast cancer patients, and women who served in the Gulf War as members of the U.S. Air Force. His prevention-oriented research includes a focus on the design and evaluation of randomized field experiments that target psychosocial as well as economic outcomes. He has been a consultant to several federal agencies and private research organizations. He has published numerous scientific and professional articles. He is on the editorial board of Brunner/Mazel's book series, *Psychosocial Stress*.

David P. Weikart, Ph.D., is President of High/Scope Educational Research Foundation in Ypsilanti, Michigan, a nonprofit research, development, and training organization. He graduated from Oberlin College and the University of Michigan. He initiated the High/Scope Perry Preschool Project in 1962, and in 1963 he developed the High/Scope Institute for IDEAS for adolescents, which helps adolescent youth focus on education and community leadership. For use in these programs he and his colleagues developed the High/Scope curriculum now used throughout the United States and in many other countries. Working internationally, he serves as coordinator of the International Association for the Evaluation of Educational Achievement (IEA) Preprimary Project. This 15-nation study looks at 4-year-olds both in and out of home care settings, and the relationship of these experiences to achievement in formal schooling.

Roger P. Weissberg is Professor of Psychology at the University of Illinois at Chicago (UIC). He is the Director of Graduate Studies in Psychology at UIC and is a member of the Division of Community and Prevention Research and the Division of Clinical Psychology. He also directs an NIMH-funded Predoctoral and Postdoctoral Prevention Research Training Program in Urban Children's Mental Health and AIDS Prevention at UIC. He was a Professor at Yale University between 1982 and 1992. He collaborated with the New Haven Public School System to establish the New Haven's Social Development Project. He has been the President of the American

Psychological Association's Society for Community Research and Action. He is a recipient of the William T. Grant Foundation's 5-year Faculty Scholars Award in Children's Mental Health, the Connecticut Psychological Association's 1992 Award for Distinguished Psychological Contribution in the Public Interest, and the National Mental Health Association's 1992 Lela Rowland Prevention Award.

Grace-Ann Caruso Whitney has served on the faculties of Saint Joseph College, Florida Atlantic University, Eastern Connecticut State University, and the University of Connecticut teaching undergraduate and graduate courses in child development, child welfare, and public policy and management. Prior to teaching, she held a variety of positions in human services, including Director of Service Programs and Director of Children's Services at the South County Mental Health Center in Delray Beach, Florida, where she administered the Optimum Growth Project. Her research has focused primarily on prevention and intervention in early childhood and supportive relationships of young parents and caregivers.

Mildred M. Winter is Executive Director of the Parents as Teachers National Center, Inc., which provides training, curriculum development, and technical assistance to all Parents as Teachers programs internationally and promotes public policies and services that foster the well-being of young families. As Missouri's first Director of Early Childhood Education, she was the guiding force in the development of the Parents as Teachers program, initiated in 1981 to help parents effectively nurture their children's development and learning from before birth. She was a key player in the enactment of Missouri's landmark Early Childhood Development Act of 1984, and she has written numerous publications for professionals and parents on parent-child early education. She has received national and state recognition for her leadership in education. Most recently she was the recipient of the 1995 Charles A. Dana Award for Pioneering Achievement in Education. She serves as consultant to state and national decision makers on early childhood education and family support.